The Church as
a Political Factor
in Latin America

David E. Mutchler
foreword by
Irving Louis Horowitz

The Praeger Special Studies program—utilizing the most modern and efficient book production techniques and a selective worldwide distribution network—makes available to the academic, government, and business communities significant, timely research in U.S. and international economic, social, and political development.

The Church as
a Political Factor
in Latin America

With Particular Reference
to Colombia and Chile

PRAEGER SPECIAL STUDIES IN INTERNATIONAL POLITICS AND PUBLIC AFFAIRS

Praeger Publishers New York Washington London

PRAEGER PUBLISHERS
111 Fourth Avenue, New York, N.Y. 10003, U.S.A.
5, Cromwell Place, London S.W.7, England

Published in the United States of America in 1971
by Praeger Publishers, Inc.

© 1971 by David Edward Mutchler

Library of Congress Catalog Card Number: 74-153836

Printed in the United States of America

For my brother Dick

and his son, Johnny

The Church as a Political Factor in Latin
America is a major event in at least three separate fields of study: organization theory, political sociology, and church history. David Mutchler
has demonstrated one of the few inalienable truths
of sociological method: that the size of a study
does not uniquely determine its importance. Moreover, one can investigate intimate--and, by world
criteria, small-scale--structures and yet make a
contribution to macrosociology.

Lest the reader of this modest work feel that
the enthusiasm of the writer of the foreword is
the immodest result of his role as principal advisor on Mutchler's doctoral dissertation on the
same topic, I shall take the remaining space to explain my enthusiastic commendation of this work and
show why, in fact, it is appropriate.

First, in relation to organization theory,
this is one of the few studies that has been made
of intimate organizational life in Latin American
communities. And of major significance is the use
of documentary materials that reflect the everyday
functioning of organizational leadership--and its
search for self-maintenance, and even growth, in a
hostile and increasingly polarized situation.

This sort of documentation is both the hardest
in methodological terms--since it is incontrovert-
ible--and the hardest to come by, for the reason
that the documents are not abstract opinions on
sundry subjects but rather vital communications
that have binding legal and organizational meaning.

Mutchler shows that in each and every case
studied (DESAL, FERES, CIAS, ICODES) the prime im-
pulse of Church organization in Latin America is
not toward reform, revolution, or reaction, but

vii

toward something far more prosaic--survival. And given the fact that the Roman Catholic Church, whatever else it may be, is a bureaucratic organization having two thousand years of recorded history, it should be clear by now that survival no less than theological consistency has been a _primum_ _mobile_. From the outset, we have been presented with a Church of Christ sustained by the Organization of St. Paul.

Mutchler's work is a contribution to political sociology, both in theory and by example. He shows, by the use of a theory of international linkages, how the national aspirations of the Roman Catholic Church are directly linked to political considerations at a worldly level no less than on intimate parish levels. In fact, one would have to say that for Mutchler, the Church turns out to be primarily an instrument of political policy. If the politics are ambiguous and seemingly compatible with a wide range of concrete possibilities, it is by politics that always and everywhere the Church, as an institution with its own vested interests, manages its policy-formulating and policy-making. This work, then, is a study in the interrelation and interpenetration of interest-group politics and social class--more specifically, the social sub-classes that penetrate and permeate the Church hierarchy and the Church membership. Thus, in effect, it focuses not so much on Latin American paraorganizations in Chile and Colombia as on the general purposes and strategies of Roman Catholicism.

The work is a contribution to Church history. In the wake of the large-scale effort at "revisionist" theories about Church modernization, Mutchler in his sociological way parallels the direct warnings offered by Helder de Camara and Ivan Illich that the rather bland assumptions of Church adaptation to change are mired by Church affiliations to long-standing international commitments, both clerical and secular. These limit reform and even curb internal organizational innovation. In the face of the ongoing barrage of discourse about ideological rapprochement between Christianity and Communism, Mutchler reminds us that the seepage, organizationally at least, is considerably limited, that, in fact, the intricate network of relationships between the cross and the stars and stripes makes the connection between the cross and the hammer and sickle something less than a full blown romance, despite the optative mood of some Western European intellectuals.

In this respect Mutchler's book is of supreme value, because he compels us to examine the institutional sources of Church policy before taking too seriously the ideological efforts of a few clerics who argue the case of theological reformation. And this is a lesson for all social scientists. Too often the word has been substituted for the deed, particularly in the area of Roman Catholicism in Latin America, where it has been far too simple to substitute theology for policy, the words of a bishop for the sufferings of the silent parishioners.

Perhaps the worth of Mutchler's book can be better appreciated in the light of an unusual fact: the subjects of the study were, at the upper echelons at least, social scientists in their own right. Men like Roger Vekemans and Renato Poblete perceive themselves as prime examples of the fusion of sociology and religiosity. Mutchler has shown that this self-image is perhaps overly self-indulgent and that the role of ideological distortion is scarcely less for social scientists who are theologians than for ordinary mortals. In this sense, Mutchler has made a substantial contribution to the sociology of knowledge, by demonstrating that the role of social interests is even more telling and ultimate in the determination of social ideas than the professed humanist values of the people directing organizational life. It is not that Mutchler is ever unkind or tempted by an ad hominem line of reasoning. Rather, the force of institutional affiliations itself serves to make liberalism the style, while conservatism continues as the substance of the newly tooled organizational efforts

to gain the passions of the Catholic masses and prevent any further erosion of the Catholic base toward either secularism or communism (or both, where
they happen to coincide).

The <u>Church as a Political Factor in Latin
America</u> demonstrates a piercing intimacy at every
level. The author, steeped in the Catholic faith
as a result of his years as a Jesuit scholastic,
combines this intimacy with his knowledge of sociology. And it is not an arm-chair sociology.
Rather, his work was done in the field, in accord
with the strictest canons of overseas research.
But through it all there emerges in this book a
passionate concern for reform--a deep commitment
to the needs of ordinary people, both parishioners
and priests, that is in the highest tradition of
social justice, no less than social science. And
in this sense, I am left with the profoundly joyous
feeling that perhaps it is indeed possible to combine the wisdom of Catholicism with the wiles of
sociology--and that Mutchler is a bearer of this
new tradition of critical humanism.

Irving Louis Horowitz

This study examines the critical impact of the Catholic Church system in Latin America with specific regard to concerted attempts in Colombia and Chile to develop organizational capacity for influence and power. The discussion is concerned with three related issues: first, the interests that link Church policies and activities throughout the Americas; second, the internal state of Church resources; and third, the over-all impact of the Church on the developmental processes of Latin American nations.

The data assembled led to the following conclusions. *First, the Latin American Church is, in effect, an instrument of United States and Western European policy interests: since Church policy-makers deem Marxist Communism the one political system that precludes the survival of Catholicism as "church" over and above "sect," the Church system has willingly served as a channel for United States and West European forces of counter-insurgency in Latin America. *Second, Church resources are scarce and dwindling: rather than develop greater adaptability, increased structural complexity, heightened system autonomy, and new levels of internal cohesion, the Church system is fragmenting into irreconcilable competing factions in those countries in which the immediate danger of "communist subversion" has subsided. *Third, the Church system in Latin America is not only divided but also divisive, not only itself highly dependent on foreign policy interests but also an agent for the spread and legitimation of dependence: its chief effect in the 1960's was to weaken populist movements in Latin America through the creation and sponsoring of grass-roots organizations parallel to and competitive with sectors of the national left.

In terms of concept, the study clearly belongs
in the realm of theory that deals with "instrumental
capacity." This concept, after Nicholas Demerath's
definition, involves "the ability of a social actor
. . . to carry out and complete tasks associated
with transforming or mastering the external situation or environment."*

The conclusions reached lead to the rejection
of a prominent thesis of "Church development" in
Latin America that posits Catholicism as a requisite for societal improvement.** Ivan Vallier's
contention has been that the Catholic Church in
Latin America is indeed developing greater adaptability, heightened system autonomy, and new levels
of internal cohesion--all of which will be functional for the larger society.

But whereas Vallier's frame of reference is
derived from Weberian emphases on the primacy of
normative orientations, of the cultural system and
its incarnation in societal "roles," my own approach owes more to a reading of Marx and his
stress on the incompatibility of interests that
compete for scarce resources.

This study is an investigation focused not on
individuals but on linkages among organizational
elites--"elite" in a double sense, in that control
within an organization confers leverage "outside,"
in the society as a whole. It is an investigation
into the processes by which elites gain and maintain their dominance. A guiding insight has been
that of Stinchcombe:

---

*Nicholas J. Demerath, "Rationalization and
Instrumental Capacity: A Theory of Economic Growth
and Social Differentiation," a paper presented to
the Midwest Sociological Society Meeting, St. Louis,
Missouri, April 17, 1970.

**Ivan Vallier, Catholicism, Social Control,
and Modernization in Latin America (Englewood Cliffs,
N.J.: Prentice Hall, 1970).

> The political activity of different
> sections of the elite of modern so-
> cieties is oriented primarily toward
> the system of stratification <u>among</u>
> <u>organizations</u>, rather than the class
> system of individuals and families.*

I finished the final draft of this study in
June, 1970. Since then, monumental changes have
occurred in Chile. Salvador Allende, after failing to win the presidency of that country in 1958
and again in 1964, finally succeeded in September,
1970. What anti-Marxists had feared for a decade
finally came to pass.

In Part III, the apprehensions of certain
Church authorities are traced back to the election
of 1958, an election that Allende very nearly won.
It was then, on the morrow of that election, that
the priest-expert Sierens warned that the Christian
Democratic Party was dividing the "anti-Marxist"
vote by siphoning votes away from Jorge Allessandri.
Sierens' counsel was clear: Either back the Christian Democrats wholeheartedly or withdraw from them
all Church support. Church officials, under the
strong urging of Belgian Jesuit Roger Vekemans,
chose to go all out for Frei in 1964. Vekemans
designed a grass-roots political movement, Promocion Popular, which drew upon millions of dollars
annually from sources as disparate as the West German Government and the United States Central Intelligence Agency. Frei won in 1964. But it was at
that critical moment of Christian Democratic electoral victory that the fragmentation of Catholic
forces in Chile began. Fragmentation proceeded
with a vengeance throughout the late 1960's until
the final confrontation in 1970. Then, Catholic
forces were no longer simply divided between two
anti-Marxist candidates--one, Christian Democratic,
and the other, Jorge Alessandri. Then, for the

---

*Arthur L. Stinchcombe, "Social Structure and
Organizations," in James G. March (ed.), <u>Handbook of
Organizations</u> (Chicago: Rand McNally, 1965), p. 144.

first time, priests, such as the Jesuit Gonzalo
Arroyo, and Catholic lay leaders, such as Jacques
Chonchol, openly and fervently supported a Marxist
candidate, Allende.

With Allende's presidential victory, the
Chilean Catholic system was thrown into turmoil.
Vekemans fled with his DESAL organization and its
millions of dollars and Deutschmarks to Venezuela--
where he was denied entry by a Christian Democratic
government wary of repeating the Chilean experience. He and DESAL are at this writing in Bogota,
Colombia. And the Chilean bishops, long accustomed to quarrel with Vekemans while inevitably
following his prescriptions, now find themselves
without friends in the presidential palace--unless
one would count Gonzalo Arroyo, S.J., whom the
Chilean Cardinal once denounced in Rome. Unavoid-
ably, Church planning is now directed to 1976.

ACKNOWLEDGMENTS

This book originated as a doctoral dissertation in sociology at Washington University, St. Louis. Emerging as it does from the work of my teachers, this is an "individual" product only in the conventional sense. The most substantial contribution has been that of my mentor, Irving Louis Horowitz, whose unfailing support and exacting critiques over the past five years have affected every facet of the work.

The sociological training that I have been fortunate to receive from such men as Joseph A. Kahl, Alvin W. Gouldner, Robert L. Hamblin, and Nicholas J. Demerath will be, I hope, as evident to my readers as it is to me.

I want to thank William Barnes, Gary Glenn, and Bill Cloherty of Latin American Teaching Fellowships for the financial assistance that made possible the last phase of research.

This study could never have been undertaken without the unstinting cooperation of the Church officials whose organizations were studied. In Chile, I was overwhelmed by the immense warmth, candor, and insightfulness of Father Renato Poblete, S.J., who provided me with work space and secretarial assistance at a time when both were in short supply. At key junctures in the research process, the brilliant Jesuit executive-sociologist Roger Vekemans provided the type of rigorous dialectic which proved indispensable to the unravelling of the questions under consideration. On several occasions, Father Hernan Larrain shared with me his incisive analytical skills. If the latter chapters of the study achieve anything in conceptual clarity, it is due in large part to him.

In Colombia, I am richly indebted to Fathers Vicente Andrade and Gustavo Perez--each of whom has allowed me to tax his patience with incessant questioning about sensitive matters. Their great openness and selflessness suffered the boldest probings not merely with equanimity but with humor and affection.

There were many others whose assistance was invaluable. My gratitude to them is very great.

As profound as all these influences have been, they are as nothing when compared to the constant cheerfulness and bright delightfulness of fun-loving Sheila McPhelin.

CONTENTS

PART III.   FRAGMENTATION OF
CATHOLIC FORCES: CHILE

LIST OF TABLES

LIST OF CHARTS

LIST OF ABBREVIATIONS AND ACRONYMS

ADVENIAT (West German Bishops) Fund for Mission Churches

AID Agency for International Development, United States Department of State

ANOC (Chile) Asociacion Nacional de Campesinos: National Association of Farm Laborers (Church-oriented)

ASICH (Chile) Accion Sindical Chilena: Chilean Syndical Action (affiliated with CNC)

BISH (West German Government) Bureau for International Social Aid, West German Ministry for Economic Cooperation

CAL (Vatican) Comision Pontificia pro America Latina: Papal Commission for Latin America

CARITAS (Church) International Catholic Assistance Program with local national units under local episcopal control

CEDEP (Chile) Centro de Desarrollo Popular: Center for Popular Development (Chilean branch of DESAL)

CELADE (Chile) Centro Latinoamericano de Demografia, sponsored by the United Nations

CELAM Consejo Episcopal Latinoamericano: Latin American Bishops' Conference

CELAP (Chile) Centro Latinoamericano de Poblacion: Latin American Population Center (branch of DESAL)

CENAPO (Chile) Centro Nacional de Pobladores: National Association of Slumdwellers (organized by DESAL)

CERIS   (Brazil) Centro de Estadistica Religiosa
           e Investigaciones Sociales: Center for
           Religious Statistics and Social Research
           (FERES)

CIA   Central Intelligence Agency, United
           States Government

CIAS   Centro de Investigacion y Accion Social:
           Center for Research and Social Action
           (Jesuit)

CICOP   Catholic Inter-American Cooperation Pro-
           gram, United States Catholic Conference
           of Bishops

CIDOC   (Mexico) Centro Intercultural de Documen-
           tation: Intercultural Center of Documen-
           tation

CIF   (Mexico) Centro de Formacion Intercul-
           tural: Center for Intercultural Formation
           (now CIDOC)

CILA   Centro Interamericano de Libros Academicos:
           Interamerican Center for Academic Books

CIMS   Centro de Investigacion Motivational y
           Social: Center for Motivational and
           Social Research

CISEPA   (Peru) Centro de Investigaciones Socio-
           logicas, Economicas y Politicas: The
           Center for Sociological, Economic, and
           Political Research

CISOR   (Venezuela) Centro de Investigaciones
           Socio-Religiosas: Center for Socio-
           Religious Research

CLACIAS   Coordinacion Latinoamericana de CIAS:
           Coordination of Latin American CIAS
           (Jesuit)

CLAR   Confederacion Latinoamericana de Religiosos:
           Latin American Confederation of Religious

CLASC   Confederacion Latinoamericana de Sindical-
           istas Cristianos: Latin American Confed-
           eration of Christian Trade Unions
           (Christian Democratic)

CNC   (Chile) Confederacion Nacional de Campe-
           sinos: National Peasant Confederation
           (DESAL)

COGECAL   (Vatican) Consejo General de la CAL:
           General Council of the CAL

COLTEJER   (Colombia) Compania Colombiana de Tejidos,
           S.A.: Colombian Textile Company, Inc.

CONCORDE   (Chile) Coordinacion de Desarrollo
           Popular: Coordinating Commission for
           Popular Development (DESAL)

CTC   (Colombia) Confederacion de Trabajadores
           Colombianos: Confederation of Colombian
           Workers (Marxist)

CUT   (Chile) Central Unica de Trabajadores:
           Sole Headquarters for Workers (Marxist)

DESAL   (Headquarters in Chile until 1970) Centro
           para el Desarrollo Economico y Social de
           America Latina: Center for the Economic
           and Social Development of Latin America
           (Jesuit)

FANAL   (Colombia) Federacion Nacional de Agri-
           cultores: National Federation of Farmers
           (Jesuit)

FAO   (United Nations) Organization for Food
           and Agriculture

FEBRECH   (Chile) Federacion de Obreros Chilenos:
           Federation of Chilean Workers (Church)

FERES Federacion Internacional de los Insti-
       tutos de Investigaciones Socio-Religiosos
       y Sociales: International Federation of
       Institutes for Socio-Religious and Social
       Research (Church-sponsored)

FRAP   (Chile) Frente de Accion Popular: Popular
       Action Front (Marxist)

IBEAS (Bolivia) Instituto Boliviano de Estudios
       y Accion Social: Bolivian Institute for
       Study and Social Action

ICETEX (Colombia) Instituto Colombiano para Es-
       tudios Tecnicos al Extranjero: Colombian
       Institute for Technical Training Abroad

ICODES (Colombia) Instituto Colombiano de
       Desarrollo Social: Colombian Institute
       of Social Development

ICS   (Chile) Instituto de Comunicacion Social:
       Institute for Social Communication
       (Jesuit)

IDES   (Colombia) Instituto de Doctrina y
       Estudios Sociales: Institute of Doctrine
       and Social Studies (Jesuit)

IER   (Chile) Instituto de Educacion Rural:
       Institute for Rural Education (Church)

IHC   (Chile) Instituto de Humanismo Cristiano:
       Institute for Christian Humanism (Jesuit)

ILADES (Chile) Instituto Latinoamericano de Doc-
       trina y Estudios Sociales: Latin American
       Institute of Doctrine and Social Studies
       (Jesuit)

ILALD Instituto Latinoamericano de Cooperacion
       y Desarrollo: Latin American Institute
       for Cooperation and Development (CLASC)

ILAP	(Chile) Instituto Latinoamericano de Planificacion: Latin American Planning Institute (DESAL)
INDAP	(Chile) Instituto de Desarrollo Agro-Pecuario: Institute for Agricultural and Livestock Development (Chilean Government)
INDEP	(Chile) Instituto de Desarrollo Popular: Institute for Popular Development (later CEDEP) (DESAL)
INPROA	(Chile) Instituto de Promocion Agraria: Institute for Agrarian Promotion (Church)
INPRODE	(Colombia) Instituto de Desarrollo Profesional: Institute for Professional Development (ICODES)
IPLA	Instituto de Pastoral Latinoamericano: Institute for Pastoral Studies in Latin America (Church)
IPT	(Chile) Instituto para el Promocion de Trabajo: Institute for Work Promotion (Centro Bellarmino)
ISI	(West German) Institute of International Solidarity, Konrad Adenauer Foundation of the Christian Democratic Union
JEC	Juventud Estudiantil Cristiana: Young Christian Student Movement
JOC	Juventud Obrera Catolica: Young Catholic Workers Movement
MCI	(Chile) Movimiento de Campesinos Independiente: Independent Peasant Movement
MISEREOR	(West German Bishops) Fund for Socio-Economic Development (administered in Latin America by DESAL)

MUTCH	(Chile) Movimiento Unido de Trabajadores Chilenos: United Movement of Chilean Workers (DESAL)
NAM	(U.S.) National Association of Manufacturers
OCSHA	Obra de Cooperacion Sacerdotal Hispanoamericana: Hispano-American Work of Priestly Cooperation
ORIT	Organisacion Regional Interamericana de Trabajadores: Inter-American Regional Organization of Workers (sponsored by AFL-CIO)
ORMEU	(Chile) Organisacion de Movimientos Estudiantiles: Organization of Student Movements (sponsored by Christian Democratic Party, advised by DESAL, funded by CIA)
PAVLA	Voluntarios del Papa de America Latina: Papal Volunteers for Latin America
SETRAC	(Colombia) Seleccion de Trabajadores Colombianos: Selection of Colombian Workers (Jesuit)
SIDEAT	Servicio de Informacion, Documentacion, Estadistica y Asistencia Tecnica del CELAM: Informational, Documentary, Statistical and Technical Assistance Service of CELAM
UCC	(Chile) Union de Campesinos Cristianos: Christian Peasant Union
UCONAL	(Colombia) Union Nacional de Cooperativos: National Cooperatives Union (Jesuit)

USEC   (Chile) Union Social de Empresarios
            Cristianos: Social Union of Christian
            Businessmen (DESAL)

UTC   (Colombia) Union de Trabajadores Colom-
            bianos: Colombian Workers Union (Jesuit)

PART

I

**AN APPROACH
TO
LATIN AMERICAN
CATHOLIC BUREAUCRACY**

1

INTRODUCTION

Recent studies of the Roman Catholic Church in
Latin America may be classified in three overlapping
groups. The first are those statistical and/or
attitudinal surveys designed and carried out by
churchmen seeking "profiles" of their mass base.[1]
These are patterned after the "market research" or
voter-poll models of economic and political systems.

The second type of study is the analysis of
ideological "evolution" or doctrinal trends within
the Catholic normative system, the explanation of
theological developments according to functionalist
or other criteria.[2] This type of analysis owes much
to the classical sociologists of religion, especially
to Weber, Comte, and Troeltsch.

The third group consists of attempts to assess
the "instrumental capacity" of the Church system,
either in terms of evaluating the ability of Church
elites to compete politically with other interests,
or by gauging the capability of the same elites to
organize mass support for social change.[3] In this
perspective, Church developments are broken down
into organizational inputs and outputs that link the
Church system together internally as well as to
external actors and environments.

Each of these approaches carries with it a
distinct emphasis upon a different aspect of the
Church: the Church as mass market or political
base, the Church as body of doctrine or religious
ethos, the Church as bureaucratized political pressure group.

The present study is an attempt to unravel the
implications of the third type of perspective, without ignoring the indoctrination and manipulation of
masses. The aim is to identify some of the variables relating to the "instrumental capacity" of
the Catholic system, systematically if hypothetical-
ly accounting for its growth or contraction.*

----

*"Instrumental capacity" is used as defined by
Nicholas I. Demerath: the "ability of a social
actor (person, group, organization, or society) to
carry out and complete tasks associated with transforming or mastering the external situation or environment." According to Demerath, "when the instrumental capacity of a group, organization, or
society increases--and the total activity profile
changes correspondingly--there has been rationalization." ("Rationalization and Instrumental Capacity:
A Theory of Economic Growth and Social Differentiation." Paper presented to the Midwest Sociological
Society Meeting, April 17, 1970. Emphasis added.)
The concept of "rationalization," after Demerath, is akin to that formulated by Samuel Huntington to represent "political development." Vallier,
in his article, "Church 'Development' in Latin
America" (see note 3), adapts Huntington's concept
of "political development" to analysis of religious
systems. "Development," as Huntington uses the
term, "refers to major institutional changes brought
about by change-oriented elites to increase the
over-all capacities of a system to meet and deal
with its salient environments." The process involves four increments, which are the same involved,
according to Demerath, in the process of "rationalization": greater adaptability, an increase in

In examining the Catholic system in Colombia
and in Chile, the hope is to provide comparative
controls for what purports to be a thesis of "system fragmentation" and breakdown of instrumental
capacity. The point of departure for the present
analysis is the Vallier thesis that posits Colombia
as the first and Chile as the last phase of an
integrated developmental process within the Catholic
Church.[4] I hope to show that organizational conflict within the Colombian and Chilean Churches precludes the possibility of internal cohesion and increased instrumental capacity and therefore invali-
dates the Vallier thesis.

But in focusing upon the instrumental capacity
of the Church system, it will be necessary to pass
beyond the analysis of national systems to an examination of the ties that bind Catholic sectors to
international sources of support. No national
boundaries provide adequate framework for an assessment of Catholic forces in Latin America. The
linkages that bind the Catholic system together,
whether integratively or disintegratively, cannot
be contemplated in isolation from one another. It
is axiomatic to the present analysis that Church
policies in Colombia and Chile, for example, are
inextricably linked to the cold war environment and
to North American and Western European policy interests.

The most promising framework within which to
sift the organizational processes and events with

_____

structural complexity, heightened system autonomy,
and new levels of internal cohesion. In other
words, "instrumental capacity" is a "state," an
"outcome." "Rationalization" is the process that
leads to it.
    See Nicholas J. Demerath, op. cit., and Samuel
Huntington, "Political Development and Political
Decay," World Politics, XVII (April, 1965), 393.

which I will be working is that developed by James
Rosenau.[5] His research "agenda," or "linkage framework," will be presented in essentials below.

My own intent is to consider the Church as a
linkage system with ties to all strata in Latin
American society: to the military, the peasants,
the landowners, the new industrialists, United
States business interests and embassies, workers,
students, intellectuals, bureaucrats, and politicians.

At the same time, I intend to emphasize that
the basic incompatibility of many of the above interests, or their open antagonism to one another,
precludes the operation of the Church as a "reconciliation system." If the Church functions as a
linkage system it is because its elites act as
"brokers" among conflicting interests and therefore
profit from the hostilities inherent in the unequal distributions of wealth and power as well as
from the polemics of the cold war. The concept of
"linkage," as will be evident in the discussion of
Rosenau's framework, does not necessarily imply
integration, compatibility, or cohesion. Bitter
competitors, each seeking the destruction of the
other, are <u>linked</u> together no less than are symbiotic systems.

The basic hypothesis behind this study is that
the Church system in Latin America is a divided as
well as a divisive one, that it is fragmenting on
a massive scale, that the hierarchical organization is breaking down along both vertical and
horizontal axes into a welter of zero-sum conflicts,
that the very efforts that were intended to increase
the instrumental capacity of Catholicism in the
1960's have served instead to undermine it.

Critical to this analysis is the examination of
staff sectors within the Church, newly created to
"rationalize" or modernize Church operations so as
to render them acceptable to North American and
Western European sources of logistic and technical

support. The staff unit, as linkage to a richer environment, is especially susceptible to the types
of disruption that the introduction of wealth into
a system of scarcity so frequently guarantees.

Staff-line conflicts may be largely accounted
for, I suspect, by the Dalton model,[6] in other
words, by: (a) functional differences between line
and staff officials; (b) differentials in the ages,
formal education, potential occupational ceilings,
and status group affiliations of members of the
two groups (the staff officers being younger, having
more education but lower occupational potential, and
forming a prestige-oriented group with distinctive
consumption patterns and recreational tastes); (c)
need of the staff groups to justify their existence,
to defend the exclusivity of their expertise; (d)
fear in the line that staff bodies, by their expansion and well-financed research activities, will
undermine line authority; and (e) the fact that
aspirants to higher staff offices can gain promotion
only through approval of influential line executives.

But the conflicts between staff and line are, I
suggest, less disruptive and disintegrative than
are the conflicts among staff units themselves. Insofar as the latter are deeply committed to constructing bases of support autonomous of the Church
organizational hierarchy, they must forge symbiotic
linkages with outside sources ("fused linkages," in
Rosenau's terminology) and render these linkages
impervious to the tampering of other Catholic
groups. Differential access to relatively scarce
external resources soon becomes a divisive factor.
Those Catholic staff sectors that enjoy privileged
access to United States AID funds, for example, can
be expected to alienate the Catholic forces that
failed to win approval for their proposals.

The case studies of Chile and Colombia will attempt to demonstrate how the monopolization of a
lucrative source of supply entails definite risks
as well as gains. The monopolization of the source
leads to identification with the source, and in the

shifting political campaigns of the period studied each source is a potential loser. Sources external to the national political system that seek the legitimacy to penetrate national boundaries frequently link up to staff organizations composed of cosmopolitan technicians native to the target population. The Church system, and especially its staff sectors, is disposed to provide easy and ready access for external groups eager to gain entry into traditionally hostile environments.

The reciprocity that binds together local staff organization and foreign interest redounds to the mutual advantage of the units in question only in the short run. As successful operations become more conspicuous, the envy of competing staff sectors is aroused, and the hostility of nationalist groups is guaranteed.

The inherent instability of the Catholic staff system in Latin America (of those Catholic agencies and institutes that were originally created to "advise" the bishops and other line officials) will be documented in the following pages. This is a point that previous writers have virtually ignored.

Ivan Vallier, in his generally provocative discussion of "Catholic elites" in Latin America, formulates three categories of "new" Catholic elite forces, posits hypothetical causes for their emergence, and predicts interdependent cooperation among them based on mutual need and compatible values. Vallier's thesis warrants considerable attention because he maintains that "Catholic developments are not merely correlative with social developments, but are requisites; they play a causal role."[7]

His policy recommendations are no less incisive:

> Instead of simply more capital or shiny tools, support is needed to help the new Catholic elites transform their system in order that the "Catholic"

> factor and its cultural power can be
> applied to the whole task of social
> development. In short, religious
> reform is a requisite of social re-
> form.[8]

To Vallier's Weberian emphasis upon normative
considerations and the power of theology, I would
propose a counterthesis: that despite the prodi-
gious efforts of its theologians, the Catholic
Church in Latin America is not developing sources
of internal strength. It is being sapped of its
internal resources. In fact, it is difficult to
speak any more of "the Church" as a unified entity.
Where there was once a hierarchical and autocepha-
lous Church there is now an array of shifting alliances and antagonisms, linkages of the most
heterogeneous and disparate inputs and outputs, a
priesthood no longer under the control of bishops,
an increasingly rapid depletion of priestly ranks,
an ephemeral mass base that does not participate in
ritual observance much less in normative affiliation, and an utter absence of interaction between
Church functionaries and growing numbers of secu-
larist intellectuals and middle-class bureaucrats.
There are still churchmen who have political influence, but power has shifted away from the bishops
and higher line officials who rely upon their
ascriptive status to those who have built service
organizations to satisfy instrumental needs.

The most salient characteristic of the Latin
American Church system is not its abundance of progressive theologians, pastoral plans, and "commitment to change," but rather the abysmal state of
its internal manpower and financial resources,
coupled with the apathy of the "Catholic" masses.
The conflicts with which the Church is now riven do
not derive from scholarly quarrels over biblical
exegesis nor from the psychic needs of the faithful.
The conflicts are based, instead, upon opposing and
incompatible institutional interests that compete
for the same scarce resources with "winner-take-
all" intensity.

see Brunett

The weakness in Vallier's approach is that he differentiates emerging Catholic elites on the basis of their formal, stated ideologies. He gives equal weight to what a given group "calls for" in its program rhetoric and to what the group actually does, as well as to the nature of its interests, its linkages to funding and manpower sources, its function as "broker" between other antagonists. Constructed in this fashion, his typology of progressive, mutually necessary elites is based not on three conflicting sets of interests but only on three divergent conceptions of roles.

For Vallier, only the traditional elites, the "politicians," are interest based, "oriented to the power structure of secular society, . . . (looking) to outside groups for support, protection and legitimation." The three new elites are innocent of such gross preoccupations. Instead, they either stand for "re-Christianizing the world" (in the case of the "papists"), making "coalitions with 'the good' wherever and whenever possible" (the "pluralists"), or "building up strong, worship-centered congregations" (the "pastors").

As formally stated, the ideologies of the three progressive elites seem compatible. In fact, they appear to be logically dependent upon one another, so much so that Vallier concludes that the "pastors" and "pluralists" must wait until the "papists" have emerged before they can go about their own spiritual business:

> The papists appear to be a key transition elite for the effective development of the other two elites: pastors and pluralists. With their emphasis upon political detachment, improving Church organization, involving laymen, and on defining an articulated set of theologically based conceptions of "mission in society," the papists form a bridge between the traditional politicians and the new pastors and pluralists.[9]

My initial intention is to match each of Vallier's conceptual types with empirical referents.
In Colombia, I will try to show that there is little
reason for the pluralists to trust those groups that
come closest to Vallier's conception of "papist":
those who espouse "roles that have to do with the
'penetration' of the social milieu . . . (and) . . .
roles that give the Church internal strength, organizational power, and a new tie with rising status
groups, especially the urban proletariat." The
papist type is well exemplified in Colombia by certain members of the Society of Jesus who form the
directorship of the National Coordination of Catholic Action and the Center for Research and Social
Action (CIAS) and who act as "moral advisors" to
the labor and peasant unions that they founded.

This Colombian papist group, far from mediating
in any meaningful way between the traditional sectors of the Church and the new pluralist elites,
has been constantly battling the pluralists for influence both within and outside the Church system.
One very important phase of this struggle has been
the effort of several of the most powerful Jesuits
to discredit the Colombian Institute of Social Development (ICODES), which represents, if any organization does, what Vallier calls "pluralism" in
Colombia.

In Chile, Vallier thinks that the pluralist
elites are well integrated. Although this was the
case in 1964, it is no longer true, as I will try
to show in my case study of the disintegration of
the Jesuit Centro Bellarmino, by far the most successful pluralist organization in Latin America in
the early 1960's. The development of "pastoral"
tendencies in Chile, of grass-roots religious and
parish organization, which Vallier sees as complementary to pluralist organization, I see as anti-
thetical and even antagonistic. Evidence for this
will be presented along with the Centro Bellarmino
case study.

Although the national leveling of analysis is
important, it is vital to go beyond it to show how

the various national Church groups link up with each
other both within Latin America and internationally.
In this connection, the work of James Rosenau on
linkage politics offers a most useful set of hypotheses for the organization of data.

Rosenau identifies three basic types of linkage
processes: the penetrative, the reactive, and the
emulative.

> A penetrative process occurs when
> members of one polity serve as partici-
> pants in the political processes of
> another. That is they share with those
> in the penetrated polity the authority
> to allocate its values. . . . Virtually
> by definition, penetrative processes
> link direct outputs and inputs.[10]

"Penetrative process" [i.e., intended] is an
especially apt concept for dealing with Church
activity in Latin America, since there is abundant
evidence of Catholic organizations providing access
to Latin American polities for outside forces. As
Rosenau observes,

> the activities of an occupying army are
> perhaps the most clear-cut example of a
> penetrative process, but the postwar
> world has also seen foreign aid missions,
> subversive cadres, the staffs of inter-
> national organizations, the representa-
> tives of private corporations, the
> workers of certain transnational polit-
> ical parties, and a variety of other
> actors establish linkages through such
> a process.

The Catholic Church in Latin America, I suggest,
is fragmented into nearly as many factions as there
are external groups desirous of access to the Latin
American polities. Since it also seeks to service
internal groups, the Church can be seen as a linkage system par excellence that is breaking down

because of an "overload" of inputs not all of which
are compatible with one another.

A reactive process is the contrary of a penetrative one.

> It is brought into being by recur-
> rent and similar boundary-crossing
> reactions rather than by the sharing
> of authority. The actors who initiate
> the output do not participate in the
> allocative activities of those who
> experience the input, but the behavior
> of the latter is nevertheless a re-
> sponse to behavior undertaken by the
> former. Such reactive processes are
> probably the most frequent form of
> linkage, since they arise out of the
> joining of both direct and indirect
> outputs to their corresponding in-
> puts.[11]

The reaction of the Catholic line authorities
to Communist and other Marxist organizing in Latin
America after World War II and to the Cuban revolution is of fundamental importance in explaining
present Church policies, organization, and linkage
patterns. The response to Protestant organizing
activities is also of great importance, especially
in Chile and Brazil.[12]

The Catholic staff system in Latin America, I
suggest, was created especially to counter these
threats. So long as they were perceived as immediate and intense, staff sectors remained loyal to
and appreciated by higher- and lower-line officers.
In the minds of many churchmen, the Marxist danger
receded in the days following the Cuban blockade
and then after the election of Eduardo Frei in
Chile. Staff sectors were given less attention by
Church line officials, and the former began to
quarrel among themselves over the allocation of the
remaining resources. Some eventually abandoned
their anti-Communist posture entirely and began to

court leftist and populist sectors within their
countries.

Protestantism continues on the rise in Latin
America, but has to some extent been absorbed by
"progressive" bishops of "ecumenical mentality,"
who rely upon the legitimation provided by the Second Vatican Council to support their cooperation
with "the separated brethren."

The third type of linkage process is a special
form of the reactive type.

> An emulative process is estab-
> lished when the input is not only
> a response to the output but takes
> essentially the same form as the
> output. It corresponds to the so-
> called "diffusion" or "demonstra-
> tion" effect whereby political ac-
> tivities in one country are per-
> ceived and emulated in another.[13]

In the case of the Catholic Church in Latin
America, it is clear that not only are North American political activities perceived and emulated but
also bureaucratic ones. As will be shown in a discussion of Latin American and North American joint
conferences at the episcopal level, the bureaucratization of the Latin American Church proceeded apace
with North American inputs in the form of money,
manpower, and demands. My contention is that deep
splits along classic line-staff divisions have occurred in the past ten years in many Latin American
"national Churches," as clearly unanticipated consequences of bureaucratization imposed from outside.[14]

A critical nuance of the Rosenau linkage concept is the awareness that the interdependence of
linked systems does not necessarily involve their
greater integration: "Some linkages may in fact be
founded on enmity and be highly disintegrative for
(the systems involved)." This notion of the "disintegrative linkage" is quite helpful in explaining

the interaction of Catholic sectors that are hostile
to one another. A formal organization chart of the
Latin American Church would include many linkages
on paper which are in no way indicative of internal
cohesion, but are just the opposite--disintegrative
linkages.

Greater integration does result from linkages
that Rosenau terms "fused." A fused linkage "arises
out of the possibility that certain outputs and inputs continuously reinforce each other and are thus
best viewed as forming a reciprocal relationship."

In other words, a fused linkage is
one in which the patterned sequence of
behavior does not terminate with the
input. Stated in positive terms, a
fused linkage is conceived to be a sequence in which an output fosters an
input that in turn fosters an output
in such a way that they cannot meaningfully be analyzed separately.[15]

It is my contention that fused linkages are
much more likely to occur at the present time between Church sub-systems and systems external to
the Church than among Church sub-systems, or between them and the formal Church hierarchy. The
internal resources of the Church are much too
limited to be able to generate a significant number
of fused linkages among system parts. For this
reason, Church internal cohesion and integration
are weak, while linkages to powerful outside interests, such as the United States government and the
West European Christian Democratic Parties, are
strong and mutually reinforcing. Paraphrasing
Rosenau, the fused linkages between Church policy
and decision-making and the policies and decisions
of the above groups are so strong that they cannot
meaningfully be analyzed separately.*

---

*In this respect, see Miles Wolpin, "Chile's
Left: Structural Factors Inhibiting an Electoral

The chapters that follow will attempt to substantiate the above assertions. The variables involved in the increase or decrease in Church instrumental capacity have yet to be fleshed out.
The prediction here is that they will include the
processes of linkage formation both as regarding
internal relations along line-staff vectors as well
as ties to the variety of external environments.
The pivotal theoretical question is, When does linkage formation lead to increased long-run instrumental capacity, and when does it not? To answer this
question we must first turn to an analysis of the
background factors that conditioned Church development in the Latin America of the 1960's. Once
these have been established, we can proceed to the
case studies of Church fragmentation in Colombia
and Chile.

Victory in 1970," Journal of Developing Areas, III
(January, 1969), 207-30. Wolpin accurately pin-
points the Church in Chile as a channel for anti-
Communist funding and manpower. He is unaware,
however, that the Church is breaking apart from internal conflicts and will not be able to continue
to play this role very far into the future. The
left did achieve electoral victory in Chile in 1970,
and the fragmentation of anti-Marxist Catholic
forces was critical to this outcome.

NOTES

1. The studies by the International Federation of Institutes for Socio-Religious and Social Research (FERES) were the first comprehensive attempt to survey Church resources in Latin America. They were published beginning in the early 1960's. Studies by the Jesuit Center for Research and Social Action (CIAS) dealt mainly with popular religiosity, attitudes toward birth control, and attitudes of priests toward their religious superiors and toward the roles they were required to play.

2. See documents published throughout the 1960's by the Center for Intercultural Formation (CIF), Cuernavaca, Morelos, Mexico, later to become the Intercultural Center of Documentation (CIDOC). Of special importance are the analyses published in CIF Reports and CIDOC Informe. See also Herder Correspondence (Dublin), Mensaje (Santiago de Chile), passim.

3. Ivan Vallier's work here is especially important, although his conclusions are fundamentally unsound. See his "Roman Catholicism and Social Change in Latin America: From Church to 'Sect'," CIF Reports, III (May 3, 1964); also "Religious Elites: Differentiations and Developments in Roman Catholicism," in Seymour Martin Lipset and Aldo Solari (eds.), Elites in Latin America (New York: Oxford University Press, 1967), pp. 190-232. See also Vallier's "Church 'Development' in Latin America: A Five Country Comparison," The Journal of Developing Areas, I, 4 (July, 1967). A recapitulation of these articles is found in his Catholicism, Social Control, and Modernization in Latin America (Englewood Cliffs, N. J.: Prentice-Hall, 1970).

4. Ivan Vallier, Catholicism, Social Control, and Modernization in Latin America (Englewood Cliffs, N. J.: Prentice-Hall, 1970).

5.   James Rosenau (ed.), Linkage Politics; Essays on the Convergence of National and International Political Systems (New York: Free Press, 1969), especially chap. iii, "Toward the Study of National-International Linkages." See also "Of Boundaries and Bridges: A Report on a Conference on the Interdependencies of National and International Political Systems," ed. James Rosenau (Princeton, N. J.: Center of International Studies, Woodrow Wilson School of Public and International Affairs, Princeton University, 1967); and James Rosenau, "Pre-Theories and Theories of Foreign Policy," in R. Barry Farrell (ed.), Approaches to Comparative and International Politics (Evanston, Ill.: Northwestern University Press, 1968).

6.   Melville Dalton, "Conflict Between Staff and Line Managerial Officers," American Sociological Review, XV (1950), 342-45.

7.   Vallier, "Religious Elites," p. 221.

8.   Ibid., pp. 225-26.

9.   Ibid., pp. 207-08.

10.   Rosenau, Linkage Politics, p. 46.

11.   Ibid.

12.   See, for example, Emilio Willems, "Protestantism and Culture Change in Brazil and Chile," in William V. D'Antonio and Frederick B. Pike (eds.), Religion, Revolution, and Reform (New York: Frederick A. Praeger, 1964), pp. 93-108. See also, Prudencio Damboriena, "The Pentacostals in Chile," Catholic Mind, LX (1962), 27-32.

13.   Rosenau, Linkage Politics, p. 46.

14.   For the unique style of North American Catholic bureaucracy, see Edward Wakin and Joseph Scheuer, The deRomanization of the American Catholic Church (New York: Macmillan, 1966).

15.   Rosenau, Linkage Politics, p. 49.

2

**THE
RISE OF
STAFF
STRUCTURES
(1960-64)**

The bonds between Church and state in post-
independence Latin America have been examined almost exclusively in national terms.[1] But even if
the Church is inseparably wedded to national society, an age of Church "independence" is visible
only when one scants the constricting ties of market relationships and internal colonialism--the dependence of the national state upon the "imperium"
of an outside force. Chile's dependence upon U.S.
and European markets, technical skills, and capital finds a correlative dependence in the relationship of the Chilean Church to North American and
European ecclesiastical bankers and technicians.

The Church system in Chile (as well as in
Colombia) will therefore be treated as a dependent
entity, and a "subversive one." It is not only
"dependent," it spreads dependence. It is a kind
of Trojan horse that introduces the "giver" inside
the "gift" and makes of each a contributing influence to continued dependence upon gifts. This approach leads me to view the present role of the
Church as very similar to that which it played during the Spanish conquest. It continues to legitimate the presence of the colonizer in return for
substantial material favors. Of course, not all
churchmen in Colombia and Chile, either directly
or indirectly, legitimate North American and

European interests or advance their pretensions.
But certain key sectors do--and they have the power
to make a difference.

Ivan Vallier, in emphasizing the differences
between traditional elites within the Church and
the new "progressive" forces, charts the rise of
the latter to coincide with what he calls the "bank-
ruptcy" of the former: "The credits of the Church,
built up over the years through political coalitions, a permissive morality, property involvements
and other worldly promises, are largely depleted."[2]
Vallier shrewdly locates the points of dissolution
of influence in sectors of structural rather than
ideological change.

> This crisis is partly due to the
> anticlerical attacks of the nineteenth
> century that forced the Church out of
> key areas of public life, but more im-
> portantly to a series of subtle socio-
> logical trends that have more recently
> cut across the whole social order:
> the growth of an urban-based working
> class, population shifts, a strengthen-
> ing of technical and scientific cen-
> ters in secular universities, and the
> emergence of aggressive interest
> groups making clamorous and immediate
> demands on the resources of these
> societies. Old and familiar lines of
> power, influence, and status are weak-
> ened and confused, if not totally
> broken.[3]

This is a masterful summary of the breakdown
of the older investment system, expressed in terms
of new opportunities for investment. The picture
painted is by no means black with respect to continued Church influence. The urban-based working
class and the newly strengthened technical and
scientific centers would seem to offer abundant
promise for renewed Catholic effort. And Vallier,
in positing his three progressive types of new

elites, emphasizes the contribution the Church can
make within the changing society.

But Vallier, as we have seen, conceives the
new Church elites as "interest-free" and "value-
plentiful"; they are "in the world" but demand
no material returns. The traditional elites bar-
tered spiritual legitimation and normative influence for political power and a voice in the allocation process. His new elites provide normative influence gratis.

My own view is that the credits of the traditional elites are indeed depleted. The old investments have finally gone bad, and they have had to
be changed. But in changing them, the more recent
ecclesiastical entrepreneurs have not only not
"donated" their dwindling moral influence free of
charge, they have striven mightily to shift their
own efforts from the normative to the instrumental
sphere--that is, to create commodities that are far
more scarce than values and much more in demand.
The Church has been "retooling" its system to compete more effectively in the marketplace. It has
not abandoned the marketplace but has developed a
whole new range of "services" that can be profit-
ably merchandised.

As Church manpower reserves dwindled in comparison with rising population, and as societal demands switched from calls for normative support to
those for technical services, the bishops eventually
shifted their emphases from normative to instrumental strategies.[4] No longer could they simply rely
upon parish priests to preach Catholic values and
dogma to rural masses since, as Vallier rightly
points out, the needs of the growing class of urban
workers were perceived as being equally important.
No longer could the bishops rely entirely upon personal influence with a small group of societal
decision-makers since the landed oligarchies were
giving way to more heterogeneous elite forces, many
of which were based upon technical and professional
skills instead of landownership.

The increasing difficulty of recruiting middle-
and upper-class boys to the priesthood, combined
with the demographic growth of the masses, made it
all the more difficult for the bishops to use the
resident parish priest as the principal agent of
Church contact with the lower classes--the key to
mobilizing mass support and sustaining it whenever
the bishop felt it necessary to impress societal
elites with his power.

The rise of Protestantism and the concomitant
strengthening of Marxist movements further complicated the bishops' problem. Faced with an extremely complex situation, in which the one thing clear
was loss of influence, the bishops looked for one
simple solution. The solution first fixed upon was
the recruitment of more priests--a solution they
thought would entail no great change in the internal
power arrangements of the Church but would greatly
increase flexibility and influence. With more
priests, the bishops could maintain strength in
areas of traditional influence--the upper-class
parishes and rural villages--while making inroads
into the new working-class sectors and the secular
universities.

In other words, the bishops originally conceived their problem to be that of beefing up the
"line" sectors of the Church, of increasing the number of parish priests so that new parishes could be
added and existing ones strengthened. New churches
were to be built where the traditional activities
of proselytization and socialization by line officials (parish priests) could take place.[5] The parish church building is the locus of traditional
line activity--it stands as a symbol of formal authority and provides a controlled setting for the
rituals that are indispensable to traditional Catholic indoctrination.

But in attempting to solve the problem of line
expansion the bishops were soon faced with the necessity of diverting much of their time and resources
to the creation and maintenance of staff sectors.

And this has had profound repercussions at all levels of the Church system.*

Advised that if more priests were to be had,
they would have to be imported, the Latin American
bishops turned to Europe and the United States. The
initial response, in the 1950's, was not very encouraging. But when Pope John XXIII formally requested that during the 1960's religious orders in
the United States send 10 per cent of their priests
to Latin America, the flow of foreign priests began.

Staff sectors had been present to a considerable degree in Latin American Catholicism since the
1930's. The Guia Apostolica, published by the Latin
American Bishops' Conference (CELAM), lists hundreds
of associations, confederations, centers, committees,
institutes, movements, offices, organizations, and
secretariats, most of which were founded prior to
1960 and which still function as they were originally designed to: exclusively within the ecclesiastical system and strictly subordinated to the hierarchy. Insofar as they seek to incorporate youth,

————————————

*Although staff sectors were formally created
and occupy part of the formal structure, they continue to operate within the "total institution" both
at the formal level prescribed by canon law and at
the informal level, working out their own solutions
to recurrent problems unforeseen by moral theologians. In this way, Goffman's concept of "secondary arrangements" has come to life not only among
the lower participants of the Roman Catholic Church
but even among some of its higher functionaries.
Some of these "secondary arrangements" are among
the most important activities of Catholic staff sectors today: the contracts with U.S. government
agencies, for example, which were never formally
approved by any bishop. (Erving Goffman, Asylums:
Essays on the Social Situation of Mental Patients
and Other Inmates [Garden City, N.Y.: Anchor Books,
1961].)

labor, and other sectors, they do so within traditional Catholic Action units. They do not attempt
to influence directly secular groups or institutions.
In this sense, these staff sectors are for the most
part "papist" in Vallier's terms, stressing "collaboration" with the hierarchy and sacramentally centered, overtly "religious" socialization.

It can be argued that staff sectors of a "papist" orientation are structurally more similar to
"line" than to "staff." They exercise many of the
line functions of religious indoctrinizing and socialization. In many cases they substitute the community center or chapel for the parish church, but
their activities are much the same. The national
congress of the organization, the monthly bulletin,
etc., become vehicles for the dissemination of doctrine.

A good example of this type of organization is
the Young Catholic Workers Movement (JOC), which in
1958 had 1,320 centers in 272 cities of Latin America, with 23,125 "militants."[6] According to the
official report, the main activity of the JOC in
Latin America in 1959 was a Fourth South American
Congress, held in Lima on October 21-29. The principal themes of the conference were "the situation
of working-class youth," "the development of Communism in Latin America," and the "formation of
leaders." The priest-advisors to JOC held their
own reunion immediately after the congress.

This type of organization is part of the "line"
insofar as the priests involved are acting under the
orders of the bishops. It can be considered staff,
however, insofar as these same priests meet together
to compare notes and to formulate policy alternatives and recommendations for the bishop. The formal ecclesiastical jargon can be confusing here.
The priests involved in movements such as the JOC
are called "advisors" (asesores) because they are
considered to be "advising" lay movements. Their
role in informing and influencing the bishop is
overlooked.

The important factor, however, is that these priests are in positions that give them access to <u>information</u> needed by Church decision-makers. Insofar as this information is of a specialized nature, either because it concerns specific groups with special problems or because it has been specially analyzed, the groups that possess it are considered here as "staff" sectors within the Church organization as a whole.

Although staff sectors had long been present in the Latin American Church, their "functional autonomy" had always been low and their allegiance had been unremittingly pledged to the bishops. With the realization by the Latin American bishops that they were losing influence both with the masses and with the elites, and their subsequent decision to expand line sectors to regain their broad mass base, it also became evident that:

1. New priests to fill line positions (the parishes) would have to be imported from the United States and Europe.

2. This would entail bargaining with the more rationalized bureaucracies of the developed countries, presenting them with a statistical picture of the existing Latin resources, long-range planning, development of specialized communications, training institutes, etc.

3. This, in turn, would entail the expansion of staff sectors within the Latin American Church; men were needed to act as liaison with the Americans and Europeans, to collect statistics, to organize planning, and to draw up the aid proposals.

In other words, the decision to expand line sectors led to the necessity of expanding the staff.

THE SECOND VATICAN COUNCIL

Unfortunately for the bishops, the decision to expand staff sectors came at precisely the time when

these positions were being given international attention. It was the Second Vatican Council that,
in spectacular fashion, elevated the status of
staff theologians, sociologists, and other periti
("experts") to a level of preeminence. Priests of
international reputation were present at the Council: Congar and Danielieu of France, Rahner and
Haering of Germany, McKenzie and Murray of the
United States. But the ranks of the periti were
swelled by men who had yet to make a reputation outside their dioceses, and it was this group that
took advantage of the special conditions of the
Council to enhance its status outside the Church
and thereby to increase its functional autonomy
within it.

On the eve of the Council, John XXIII had
named 200 experts, or rather, had approved 200 of
the names proposed by individual bishops. The list
grew to 300 by the end of the first session of the
Council. The official program distributed to the
bishops at the end of the session (dated November
4, 1963) contains a list of 382 names. The list of
Annuario Pontificio of 1964 counts six more. La
Civilta Catolica of March 21, 1964, adds eight more
names to the total. The point is that many of the
men who had been advising bishops all during the
Council were given recognition only at the end, when
it was agreed by the bishops that their contributions
had been useful and discreet.

Efforts by line officials to keep staff sectors
under control were made as early as December 28,
1962, when the Cardinal Secretary of State of the
Vatican Coordinating Commission sent the following
guidelines to the experts:

        1. With respect to the work that
        is demanded of them, the experts
        should respond with all their knowl-
        edge, prudence, and objectivity to
        the questions the Commissions entrust
        to their examination.

2. It is forbidden them to ex-
cite currents of opinion, to give
interviews, or to take public positions concerning their personal
opinions during the Council.

3. They must refrain from criticism of the Council, from divulging
news concerning the activities of the
Commissions, observing the norms established by the Holy Father regarding secrecy.

The emphasis upon secrecy is interesting in
the light of the organizational model we are using.
The relation of power to control of information is
conceived of here as correlative and mutually reinforcing. Within any organization, secrecy functions as a mechanism of control. Especially within
hierarchical organizations, the flow of information
is structured so as to enhance autonomy. To an important extent, the greater the striving for functional autonomy of any part of a system, the greater the attempt to control the information others
receive and the greater the attempt to regulate
feedback.

The text of the guidelines, which was also secret, was published without episcopal approval in
the diocesan newspaper of the Canadian bishop and
vicar apostolic of Grouard, Monsignor Routhier,
O.M.I. That it was promptly and universally disregarded by staff sectors is evidenced by the raft of
press "leaks," briefings, and "background" sessions
that supplanted the official press commission meetings as sources for the many "insider" reports published during the Council. Le Monde reporter Henri
Fesquet was perhaps the most successful in exploit-
ing the confidences of the periti, but John Cogley
of Commonweal, Robert Kaiser of Time, and Michael
Novak of Harpers and The New Republic were also
able to gain access to secret episcopal proceedings.

The effect was revelation of the fact that at
all levels of policy-making, council experts were
formulating proposals that were dependent upon episcopal sponsorship yet indispensable for episcopal
action. The staff theologian could not speak his
views on celibacy except through the mouth of a
bishop, but a bishop was usually at a loss in Council debate to express his own ideas. The vast majority of bishops are not theologians, sociologists,
or even "intellectuals" in the broad sense of the
term. They are administrators, fund raisers, and
ritual leaders whose interests and concerns are seldom broader than the pressing resource needs of
their own dioceses.

The bishops were quite aware, however, of their
own degree of functional autonomy vis-à-vis the Vatican Curia, and much of the Council debate of the
second session, for example, centered on the "decentralization" of power, transferring juridical decisions from Rome to national episcopal conferences.
But even here, where issues of administration were
paramount, proposed changes and rebuttals had to be
phrased in ideological or doctrinal terms, justified not, as Cardinal McIntyre remarked, by "human
wisdom" but by "supernatural" considerations. The
role of the theologian is to provide these justifi-
cations. But at the Vatican Council it soon became
evident that the traditional theologians were being
challenged by younger men who were either steeped
in nonscholastic, and especially nonthomistic theol-
ogies, or were atheological in their complete es-
pousal of secular disciplines.

The traditional staff theologian, quite possibly
a seminary professor or rector, finds his own interests quite tightly bound up with "doctrinal purity"
or centralization of ideological decision-making in
Rome. His resources are the "doctors of the Church"
and the Scriptures interpreted traditionally. His
function is to repeat infallible teachings--to disseminate, not to innovate.

The newer staff member, if a theologian, is
needed precisely insofar as modern developments in

philosophy (especially the philosophy of science)
are deemed important and salutary. His resources
are more disparate and most costly; they include
access to secular universities and congresses. His
function is to synthesize, to criticize. His interests are bound up with "adaptation" and decentralization of power so that his bishop may have room to
maneuver in a changing, secular environment.

It is small wonder that scholastic theologians
were chosen as advisors by traditional bishops, who
were most likely to come from Spain, Italy, and
other traditional strongholds of Catholicism. The
bishops of France, Germany, and the Netherlands
chose men to advise them according to their needs--
men who could justify the pluralism of their countries in doctrinal theological terms.

The bishops of the third world, however, and
especially of Latin America, were more intent upon
sociological realities than upon theological discussions. They were not as wealthy as the North
Americans, nor as intellectually respectable as
the Europeans. Nor were they known as outstanding
administrators. They were not in a position to
lead a fight for "decentralized" power when they
were dependent upon European and North American
money, manpower, and techniques. Yet they were intent upon making their "case" for concrete aid.
Their chief advisors were sociologists and economists: men such as Francois Houtart of Belgium,
Emile Pin of France, Afonso Gregory of Brazil, and
the Belgian Jesuit Roger Vekemans.

THE CREATION OF FERES

As early as 1958, the Vatican was petitioned
by Latin American bishops to undertake policies,
or at least to issue encyclicals, favoring the participation of the Church in the distribution of aid
monies. Msgr. Ligutti, the Vatican observer to the
Food and Agriculture Organization (FAO), decided that
the first need was a census of the Latin American
Church to determine its resources and capabilities.

To this end, a Belgian priest, Francois Houtart,
was authorized to form a federation of some of the
more prominent clerical staff agencies. He con-
tacted two priests who had been former students of
his at Louvain, Gustavo Perez of the Colombian Institute of Social Development (ICODES) in Bogota,
and Afonso Gregory, the director of the Center for
Religious Statistics and Social Research (CERIS) in
Rio. Through the Belgian Jesuit Roger Vekemans,
contacts were established with the Centro Bellarmino, the Jesuit research team in Santiago, Chile.
These principals agreed to form the International
Federation of Institutes for Socio-Religious and
Social Research (FERES). The Latin American coordinating secretary was to be Gustavo Perez.

It was originally intended that FERES would
concentrate on the internal Church system and on
cataloguing its manpower reserves. But when the
Vatican Council revealed strong pressure for an
official Church position on the concrete problems
of development, this role was expanded, and FERES
was commissioned to develop a policy proposal on
"the tasks of the Church in Latin America." Theologians were added to the sociological staff, and
FERES set out to interview priests, bishops, and
laymen in order to arrive at some kind of consensus
concerning the role of the Church in Latin American
development.

Even before the Council met in 1962, several
FERES studies, or censuses, had been completed.
Houtart was able to extract from these a quantitative representation of a problem of great interest
to the bishops: the scarcity of priests. Other
census data had been collected from secular sources.
From these, the dimensions of a Protestant "threat"
were carefully drawn. With statistical precision,
the implications were made clear: as the number of
priests per country fell, the number of Protestants
grew. The parishes were only census units. There
was little chance for effective priestly contact or
creation of community in parishes of the size of
those in Latin America.

The number of priests per parish rarely reaches three. The urban parishes of Latin America are huge, as the following figures presented by Francois Houtart show:[7]

	Inhabitants per Parish
Bogota.	15,000
Lima.	16,000
Sao Paulo	22,000
Rio de Janeiro. . .	25,000
Montevideo.	25,000
Buenos Aires. . . .	27,000
Santiago.	30,000
Mexico City	40,000
Havana.	60,000

The rural areas are, of course, even more unfavorable for proselytization, since the distance between dwellings adds to the difficulties of the few priests who work there. Houtart concludes from his data that the "pastoral methods" of the Church must change to take into account the fact that while the parish unit is very large, in many cases reaching 100,000 persons, the churches are empty or half-filled at weekday mass and not overcrowded on Sunday. The grass-roots strength of the Church has been sapped.

Meanwhile, the strength of Protestantism is on the rise. Not only are the numbers of faithful increasing, but the percentage of native ministers is also climbing, at the very time when Catholic clergy have to be imported from the United States and Europe.

The figures for Protestants:

	Members	Ministers	Native Ministers
1948	3,171,900	10,340	65
1951	3,380,300	16,223	65
1956	4,230,400	20,660	70
1961	7,710,400	41,088	84

The growth of Protestantism is matched by the growth of other value movements. Marxism is not explicitly mentioned, but its presence is acknowledged along with that of other value movements that are alien to Christian values. The working class's tendendency toward Marxism is matched by the middle classes' emphasis upon conspicuous consumption and materialism.

Houtart proposes as the solution to the loss of clerical influence the introduction of the laity into the pastoral "mission" of the Church. This involves a process of decentralization that may well terminate in the institution of lay deacons in the Church. For the present, laymen should assist the hierarchy in spreading Catholic values through catechesis and through utilization of mass media. The hierarchy should rationalize its own planning to incorporate the kinds of data presented by Houtart. The over-all thrust of Houtart's thesis is toward increasing participation by staff sectors in the policy-making and implementation of the Church.

The reaction of Latin American bishops to the Houtart report was not uniformly positive. By 1962, many had expressed their alarm at the encroachment of the staff sectors. The FERES document The Tasks of the Church in Latin America was sponsored by a few Brazilian and Chilean bishops long used to dealing with staff members. Over-all support of other Latin Americans was not rounded up until later. Even then, the official Conference of Latin American Bishops (CELAM) did not endorse the proposal. In return, early in the 1960's, the staff sectors of FERES began to talk and write of the necessity of working with those bishops who are "more open," as if "openness" were a characteristic of personality more than a functional strategy.

FERES eventually incorporated into its publications the writings and compilations of laymen writing on secular themes such as population, urbanization, education, and labor unions. These "studies" tended to be statistical abstracts, carefully

edited, but lacking analysis. The same method was
applied to the statistical censuses of the Latin
American national Churches. One effect of this
strategy was to establish FERES as a nonideological
entity whose data were "objective" because quantitative. The assumption that statistics are nonparti-
san is of course open to question, and the very
fact that certain structures were catalogued and
quantified to the exclusion of others would be reason enough to search for underlying motives.

It is clear that one of the main preoccupations
of the editors of FERES publications has been the
"scarcity" of native priests and native resources in
Latin America and the necessity of foreign aid. At
first, during the years of the Vatican Council, this
aid was sought mainly from foreign bishops, conferences of bishops, and the Vatican. The initial results were encouraging. Pope John XXIII asked bishops and generals of religious orders to earmark a
full 10 per cent of their manpower in the 1960's for
Latin America. Although this goal proved unrealis-
tic, large numbers of North American and European
priests were sent to Latin America; in most cases,
their financing also came from abroad. As the next
two chapters will demonstrate, this foreign aid soon
led to even greater problems.

NOTES

1. The definitive work is, of course, J.
Lloyd Mecham's trail-blazing classic, Church and
State in Latin America (Chapel Hill: University of
North Carolina Press, 1934).

2. Ivan Vallier, "Religious Elites: Differentiations and Developments in Roman Catholicism," in
Seymour Martin Lipset and Aldo Solari (eds.), Elites
in Latin America (New York: Oxford University Press,
1967).

3. Ibid.

4. Much of the analysis in the following pages of this chapter is borrowed from that of Father Francois Houtart, whose book La Iglesia latinoamericana en la hora del concilio (Fribourg: FERES, 1961) is a compendium of ideas that came to prevail among the Latin Americans in Rome. My conversations with Father Houtart, and with many other staff experts who were present at the Vatican Council, provide the source for my analyses here.

5. I am again indebted to Father Francois Houtart.

6. Carlos Alfaro, Guia apostolica latinoamericana (Guide to Apostolic Organizations and Movements in Latin America) (Barcelona: Editorial Herder, 1965).

7. Houtart, op. cit., p. 42.

3

CONFLICT WITHIN THE LINE:
UNITED STATES
AND LATIN AMERICAN BISHOPS
IN MIAMI, 1967

The relationships between North American bishops and Latin American bishops gradually became institutionalized as the flood of requests for manpower began to generate tensions between the two
Churches. Concomitant with this institutionaliza-
tion, and a determining factor in it, was the rise
of staff sectors in the Latin American Church.
Staff sociologists were called upon to submit budgets and proposed operations for episcopal, in this
case joint episcopal, approval. Presumably their
expertise would enable both donor and recipient to
reach agreement on the amount and the allocation of
funds and manpower.

The tensions that were to be resolved by the
operation of staff sectors are not usually visible
in the public business of the Church. The Vatican
Council itself, while revealing differences of opinion and of ideology, usually concealed the underlying strains caused by dependence of one sector upon
another and by the unreciprocated demands and expectations that were latent yet abundant.

To analyze these tensions it is necessary to
turn to the minutes of meetings that were held in
private, in executive session as it were, between
Latin American and North American bishops, and to
the correspondence between superiors of religious
orders.

The following material is taken from the official, although confidential, minutes of the Reunion of the U.S. Bishops' Committee for Latin America with Representatives of CELAM and of the Latin American hierarchy which took place in May, 1967, in Miami, Florida. The meeting was presided over by Bishop Coleman F. Carroll of Miami, the vice chairman of the U.S. Bishops' Committee for Latin America. Other members of the committee present were Bishop Joseph M. Marling, Bishop Joseph H. Hodges (president of a subcommittee on lay personnel), Bishop Joseph M. Breitenbeck (president of a subcommission on inter-American understanding), Bishop Joseph L. Bernardin (president of a subcommission on allocations), and Bishop Joseph Green.

The Latin American bishops present were the Cardinal of Santiago de Chile, Paul Cardinal Silva; the Cardinal of Sao Paulo, Angelo Cardinal Rossi; the president of CELAM, Brazilian Archbishop Avelar Brandao Vilela; the Colombian Archbishop of Bogota and president of the Colombian Bishops' Conference, Anibal Munoz Duque; and the president of the Latin American Conference of Religious Orders, Manuel Edwards, who although not a bishop acts with the powers of a provincial of religious order. His American counterpart, James M. Darby, was also present. Present as secretaries were Father John J. Considine of Maryknoll, the director of the Latin American Bureau of the U.S. Bishops, and Father Eugenio del Busto, a Cuban, who is secretary to Bishop Carroll.

The Miami meeting lasted two days and was concerned for the most part with attempts by the North Americans to obtain information from the Latin bishops concerning their alternate sources of support. The Americans asked how they could help the Latins recruit priests _from_ Latin America. The Cardinal of Santiago replied that recruitment was very difficult because of a "lack of good Catholic families"; priests were needed to socialize family units, which would then provide recruits for the priesthood. The Bishop of Miami noted that 367 Latin American seminarians were studying in the United States; he asked

if this were a good idea. The Cardinal of Santiago
replied that it presented problems, since the U.S.
standard of living was so high that many seminarians
were discontented when they returned to their native
countries. He suggested, instead, that Latin American priests of mature age be sent to the United
States for graduate work (to be financed by the
North Americans).

The Latin Americans were questioned about the
extent of Church lands in Latin American countries.
For their reply it is best to quote directly from
the minutes (as translated from the original
Spanish).

> The Latin American bishops ex-
> plained the tremendous complexities
> that prevent giving a satisfactory
> over-all answer to the question.
> They said that the Church was the
> only institution that held land in
> every Latin American country and,
> although the amount held in each
> country was small, the aggregate
> made the Church the largest single
> landholder. . . .
> Although in Mexico, Colombia,
> and a few other countries (Cuba)
> anticlerical governments have con-
> fiscated property from the Church,
> the Church still has extensive hold-
> ings; but these are not productive
> to the same degree as are stock hold-
> ings and other industrial investments.

The Latin American bishops expressed the desire
to be rid of their landholdings, since these were so
highly visible that they gave the impression that
the Church was wealthy whereas in reality the low
productivity of the land precluded wealth. Cardinal
Silva said that the agrarian reform of the Chilean
Church (which donated five farms to sharecroppers)
was known worldwide, but that the Church canon law
had made such a reform very difficult. The Roman

Curia had forbidden the Cardinal to give away the land, and it was permitted only through the direct intervention of John XXIII.

The Cardinal said that it was the religious orders, not the bishops, who had the greatest amount of land. In Chile, the bishops had repeatedly sought to have the land distributed, but the religious orders had refused, ignoring the joint pressure of the Chilean bishops and the Papal Commission for Latin America (CAL). Cardinal Silva said that when the Christian Democratic government later confiscated land from the religious orders, the latter complained to the bishops and to the Vatican and urged reprisals. Other bishops confirmed Silva's point that many of the national hierarchies in Latin America had tried to divest themselves of land,

> due to the odious public characterization of being big property-holders in farmland. . . . Although the claims of the Church's holdings are exaggerated, in some countries the Church has considerable land and possesses substantial acreage in all Latin American countries. It would not be easy to prove that any other organization possesses a greater quantity of land on the Latin American continent.
> Monsignor (Bishop) McGrath informed the meeting that a new department of CELAM (The Latin American Bishops' Conference) had been instituted to dissipate the misunderstandings that had arisen concerning the alleged wealth of the Church. The department is named SIDEAT (Servicio de Informacion Estadisticas y Consejo Tecnico).

Cardinal Silva and Bishop McGrath briefly reviewed the sources of financial aid given to Latin America by European and North American groups for religious purposes.

1. The ADVENIAT fund, collected in Europe in Catholic churches each December, amounts to $8 million per year. This money is used for overtly religious projects, such as proselytization.

2. The MISEREOR fund, collected annually in Europe for distribution throughout the world, amounts to $12 million a year, of which "several million" is given to the Latin American Church. (The MISEREOR money is channeled to Latin America through the staff organization, DESAL, and not through the Cardinal or bishops. This was a sore point for Cardinal Silva.)

3. The Central Organization of the German Church and State, Protestant and Catholic funds matched by the West German government and applied to Latin America, total $25 million per year. The funds are used to subsidize technical projects. The Church in Chile received $1.5 million for a Catholic hospital just prior to the Miami meeting. (This is also administered by DESAL.)

4. The IUVATE fund, which is worldwide and is derived from 4 per cent of the priestly salaries of clerics in developed countries and 2 per cent of the income of the dioceses.

5. The North American Fund for Seminary Scholarships provides $150 per year per Latin American seminarian.

Holland and Belgium also provide money for the Church through separate annual collections. The Fund for the Church Persecuted and in Peril, which is administered by Belgian Bishop Van Straaten, collects an average of $8 or $9 million a year, some of which is sent to Latin America.

The Bishops' Conference reaffirmed the norms recommended by the Vatican General Council of the Papal Commission for Latin America (COGECAL) in Rome in 1965. These guidelines were intended to keep policy and allocative decision-making within line sectors. They have not been as effective as

the bishops would wish, since most of the funds
listed above are administered largely by staff sectors of the Church.

The 1965 guidelines, reaffirmed at Miami, are
these:

1. All requests for funds should be presented
or at least recommended by the respective episcopal
authority within the area represented by the project
concerned.

2. A project within a particular diocese must
be recommended by the local ordinary (bishop or
religious-order superior).

3. A project of national or sectional scope
within a nation must be recommended by the National
Conference of Bishops.

4. A project of continental or regional scope
within the continent must be recommended by CELAM.

5. A project presented by a religious order
that touches sectional, national, or continental interests of the order or orders must be recommended
by authorities of corresponding competence in the
area concerned.

6. In those countries whose National Conference of Bishops, as recommended by COGECAL, estab-
lishes episcopal committees for promoting financial
aid, the U.S. bishops propose in each case to submit all requests received from these countries to
this committee for review.

Although the tensions between staff and line
sectors occupied the primary subject of concern at
the Miami meeting, there was also evidence of tension between the North American and Latin American
hierarchies. The North Americans were anxious to
verify the extent of Latin need and to investigate
alternative sources of income. The Latin Americans
emphasized the need for foreign personnel who would

nevertheless be under the control of local bishops.
This concern for autonomy is evident at all levels
of the Church internationally, with much of the
change in contemporary Catholic theology explicable
in these terms. New formulations of, or appeals to,
traditional values frequently adorn emerging interests which are struggling to be free. Dysfunctional
consequences for a traditionally autonomous unit
frequently result from its acceptance of "aid" even
when this is offered without conditions.

Archbishop Avelar Brandao Vilela, the Brazilian
president of CELAM, gave evidence of this when he
said that the North American bishops could depend
upon CELAM or the National Conferences of Bishops
for information concerning the places to send North
American priests.

Cardinal Silva added that the Conference of
Chilean Bishops had formed a new committee to coordinate the distribution of native and foreign
priests in Chile. He also revealed another aspect
of the problem:

> His Eminence informed the group
> that some foreign priests refuse sti-
> pends (payment for religious services
> given by the recipients) and offerings
> because they receive good salaries
> from their home countries. This causes
> problems for native priests who have no
> salaries and also dissuades the local
> faithful from supporting the Church.

The priest who is maintained from abroad has an
autonomy that complicates episcopal control. As
will be evident later on, native priests in the
staff sectors also seek alternate financing, which
at once frees them from the total control of the
local bishop.

Despite the problems involved in controlling
foreign priests, there has been tremendous competition among Latin American bishops to obtain them.

The growing bureaucratization of the international
Church system, in the form of guidelines and rules
for the interaction of bishops from different countries, is in large part an attempt to mitigate tensions deriving from the struggle for scarce resources by allocating these resources according to
rules rather than personal influence.

Bishop Carroll of Miami alluded to this situation when he mentioned, early in the meeting, that
it was impossible for the North American bishops to
relate to 500 Latin American bishops; he advocated
greater reliance upon the bureaucratic machinery of
CELAM.

> Bishop Carroll said that the allo-
> cation of personnel and the establish-
> ment of priorities were very delicate
> matters. Nevertheless he thought it
> was necessary to maintain some norms.
> He suggested that the Bishops of
> Latin America and the United States
> meet every six months (to review the
> norms).

It is significant that a frequent spokesman
for the Latin American bishops was the Bishop of
Panama, Mark McGrath, whose parents were American
citizens and who would seem by appearances to be
an American himself. The vice president of CELAM,
Bishop McGrath acted as liaison between the Latins
and the North Americans. He headed SIDEAT, the department of CELAM concerned with presenting a better image of the Church through the use of mass
media.

THE FUNCTIONS OF CELAM

CELAM is an attempt, supported fully by the
Vatican, to alleviate tensions arising from problems of control and of allocation within the Latin
American Church. The control problems are many,
but include principally those of: (1) staff sectors
in general, (2) foreign clergy, (3) religious orders.

1. Controlling staff sectors of the Church.
Thirteen special departments of CELAM seek to "coordinate" staff activity by screening and evaluating
the information that is to come to the bishops acting in committee. Staff recommendations are sifted
and weighed by department heads and then either approved, rejected, or changed for submission to consideration by the board of directors of CELAM. The
bishops draft "working documents" from these recommendations, which are then subject to approval by
meetings of Latin American bishops' representatives
who presumably speak for the entire Latin American
episcopate. The final documents are submitted to
Rome for papal approval. In Chapter 6, I will analyze this process as it was operative in the meeting of Latin American bishops at Medellin in 1968.
For the present, it is sufficient to point out that
CELAM, through its department system, tries to pull
staff sectors into the hierarchical decision-making
process, depriving any single staff group of "too
much" autonomy and approving new initiatives only
after they have been reconciled with competing interests.

The CELAM departments cover all areas of staff
proficiency, which can be effectively "pigeonholed"
into thirteen boxes: (1) pastoral planning; (2) liturgy, or ritual; (3) religious education, or proselytization; (4) ecumenism; (5) mission territories;
(6) recruitment; (7) seminaries; (8) clergy; (9) university youth; (10) education; (11) social action;
(12) lay apostolate; (13) public opinion. Since the
Church does not formally recognize that it operates
in the political realm, there is no category for
political questions. Staff recommendations or considerations concerning political questions are generally subsumed under "social action."

The Vatican finances the CELAM departments
directly, but the money is raised in the United
States. According to the minutes of the meeting
in Miami, each department of CELAM receives $5,000
per year, or $1 million annually for the total or-
ganization. The latter sum represents 5 per cent

of the total of all collections made each year in
North American Catholic schools and churches for
"foreign missions." This sum is sent to the Vatican, which then allocates or invests it.

2. The coordinating, or control, function of
CELAM extends beyond local staff sectors to embrace
foreign clergy working in Latin America. That this
clergy is considered indispensable is evident from
the uncontested remarks of Cardinal Silva, who
placed the weakness of the Church's present position
upon the forced exodus of Spanish clergy after the
wars of Latin American independence and the subsequent severance of ties between Church and state.

> Cardinal Silva . . . praised the
> missionary labor realized by the Span-
> ish missionaries who came to America
> with its discovery. Nevertheless, he
> noted that the political independence
> of the colonies took the Church by
> surprise and interrupted the mission-
> ary task of the Church due to the
> exodus of the Spanish priests. . . .
> Many communities that were only half-
> Christianized were left without
> priests. The Latin American Church
> was left decapitated for thirty years
> while new bishops were named. The
> governments of the new nations ob-
> structed the naming of bishops and a
> lack of adequate communications with
> Spain prevented the approval of the
> Spaniards to the process. . . .

The Cardinal said that of the 600 dioceses in
Latin America, 400 had been created in the last
twenty years, indicating that the Church had only
begun to catch up with the organizational tasks
left unfinished by the Spanish conquest. It is
clear that the Cardinal conceived the state of the
Latin Church to be one of weakness and dependence
upon foreign resources, which were to be welcomed
but to be administered locally. The fact that 400

dioceses (and an equal number of bishops) were created suddenly and with little precedent must be considered in any assessment of the sources of strain
within the Church system. Four hundred new bishops,
each in need of a personal staff, created administrative problems at the national level hitherto un-
seen.

The bishops found their own authority threatened by the sudden influx of foreign clergy. CELAM
sought to place control of these sectors in the
hands of the local bishops. Cardinal Silva was explicit in emphasizing the importance of this problem:

> Cardinal Silva said that, in his
> opinion, the control of Latin Ameri-
> can parishes by foreign clergy was
> acceptable; but that it was not ad-
> visable to create multiparish zones
> of any kind that were directed by
> foreign priests.

This type of organization is not uncommon in Latin
America. The Cardinal noted that there were "large
areas of Latin America in which not only zones but
also dioceses are controlled by foreign priests."
His solution was to have foreign priests assigned
to parishes by local bishops rather than by their
foreign superiors. The United States bishops were
unwilling to accept this proposal since they finance
their priests completely, paying for language training, transportation, and subsistence in the field.
European priests are usually sent to Latin America
by an international Catholic organization, the
Hispano-American Work of Priestly Cooperation
(OCSHA), which pays for training and transportation
but leaves the day-to-day financing to the local
Latin American bishop, or conference of bishops.
The European is thus forced to live at the financial level of the native clergy. (The North American priests were frequently criticized at this
meeting for maintaining too high a standard of living in comparison with native priests.)

3. The third sphere of control that CELAM was
created to exercise involved the religious orders,
which are by Church canon law exempt from the direct
authority of bishops. CELAM embraces the Latin
American Confederation of Religious (CLAR) by including CLAR's president, Fr. Manuel Edwards, on
its board of directors. At the Miami meeting, the
tensions between religious orders and secular or
diocesan clergy was manifest during discussions of
such topics as landholdings (see above) and foreign
religious-order priests. The latter were clearly
perceived as threatening episcopal power. Fr. Edwards tried to reassure the bishops by citing the
statistic that between 70 and 80 per cent of
religious-order priests are located in the line
structures of parishes and schools, directly under
the control of the local bishop. He traced the
problem of the autonomy of these priests to faulty
socialization and suggested that training institutes for North American priests be sponsored by
the Latin and North American bishops to provide the
necessary internal controls and to make explicit
what would be expected of foreign priests in Latin
America. As we will see, the problem of the training center has had profound repercussions on the
relations between North American and South American
hierarchies.

The Miami meeting ended with episcopal consensus concerning a state of crisis in the Latin
American Church. The bishops accepted the dictum
of Cardinal Silva that "in Latin America, every
day, the Church loses to its enemies as many souls
as are won in the rest of the world combined." The
CELAM apparatus was proposed as the solution to
these problems. The North Americans refused to
allocate any money for church construction in Latin
America. They agreed to send priests and some financial assistance, but only after CELAM had submitted carefully budgeted proposals. The Latin
Americans agreed to this, but as Bishop Larrain of
Chile noted, they feared an "excessive bureaucratization, because of which the Church might appear
too technical, purely commercial."

NORMATIVE VS. INSTRUMENTAL STRATEGIES

The Latin Americans were still emphasizing the
normative bases of the Church--the line offices of
preaching, teaching, and indoctrination, which they
deemed most effective in an atmosphere of personal-
ismo and institutional charisma. The North American
bishops were constant in their emphasis upon instrumental strategies--new techniques in community organization, manipulation of mass media, better investments. They too realized the dangers inherent
in creating new staff sectors within the clergy and
proposed instead to send lay technical specialists
through the Papal Volunteers for Latin America
(PAVLA) program. The Latin Americans, especially
Cardinal Rossi of Brazil and Cardinal Silva of
Chile, agreed to this in principle, but expressed
doubts as to the technical proficiency of volunteers
who would work for low financial rewards. (These
volunteers were not highly esteemed for their contribution to the Latin American dioceses by the
Latin American bishops.)

4

CONFLICT WITHIN THE LINE:
UNITED STATES
AND LATIN AMERICAN BISHOPS
IN SANTIAGO, 1967

From November 18 to December 1, 1967, the reunion of the U.S. Bishops' Committee for Latin
America with the president of CELAM and the presidents of the Episcopal Conferences of Latin America
shifted from Miami to Santiago de Chile.

The principals were for the most part the
same, with a few notable exceptions: Cardinal Rossi
of Brazil was not present, nor was Archbishop Munoz
Duque of Colombia. The Archbishop of Quito, Monsignor Pablo Munoz Vega, sat in as a vice president
of CELAM. Archbishop (now Cardinal) Dearden of
Detroit, the president of the U.S. Episcopal Conference, presided. In addition to the North American
bishops who had attended the Miami meeting in May,
there were also present the bishops of Paterson,
New Jersey, and of Reno, Nevada, and the Auxiliary
Bishop of Madison, Wisconsin. Bishop Humberto
Medeiros, then Bishop of Brownsville, Texas and now
Archbishop of Boston, was also there.

Present by special invitation were the Bishop
of Temuco, Chile, and the Auxiliary Bishop of Santiago. The latter, Monsignor Gabriel Larrain, one
of the principal formulators of Church policy in
Chile, had initiated the donation of Church lands
to sharecroppers in that country. Also present was
Fr. Renato Poblete, S.J., the director of the Centro
Bellarmino.

At this meeting a clearer picture emerged of
the dilemma the Latin American bishop faces when he
seeks to increase the Church's labor force. He is
confronted with the need to recruit more parish
priests and priests to teach in seminaries, high
schools, and universities. But these priests tend
to become disoriented:

> The parish priest asks himself
> what his role should be. . . . The
> people among whom he tries to work
> are increasingly less interested in
> him. . . .

The parish priest seems to have no function that is
in demand. Old women, for the most part, are his
chief admirers. Except on the great feast days,
his church is always empty. The priest-teacher
faces a similar problem:

> It is only when he stresses sec-
> ular concerns, the utility of knowl-
> edge for status and power-striving,
> that he finds an attentive audience.
> Religious dogmas do not appeal to the
> young people with whom he tries to
> work.

The bishops blamed these problems on the "materialism and secularism of the age," but implicit-
ly they were concerned with the effect on the priest
in the line. The priest's role ambiguity and confusion about what he should do led the bishops to
turn to "specialists" for help in "redefining" the
role of the priest.

The specialists are a likely resource because
they have solved their own role ambiguities by committing themselves to specific disciplines, acquir-
ing skills that are in demand. They possess information that is readily marketable, either because
it deals with so-called crucial sectors, such as
the working class or university youth, or because
it is quantifiable and therefore "objective" in the
estimate of policy-makers.

The linkages between policy-makers and their
specialized staff are not without strain, however.
The Miami meeting of Catholic bishops stressed the
latter's preoccupation with limiting the functional
autonomy of priest-specialists, especially when
this autonomy was augmented by staff linkages to
foreign sources. The linkages that bind Latin
American to North American bishops depend in large
measure upon the support of staff priests, who also
find their ties with foreign chanceries to be
fruitful.

In Santiago, the bishops recognized formally
what they had long accepted implicitly--that staff
sectors of priest-specialists were indispensable to
their conception of an expanding Latin American
Church, which by necessity would rationalize its
bureaucracy to conform to the expectations of its
foreign creditors and to meet the strong competition of Marxism and Protestantism at home.

> Bishop Brandao, the president of
> CELAM, said that Latin America needed
> every type of missionary (foreign
> priest) but, above all, specialists
> and theologians. It needed mission-
> aries who would multiply their own
> efficacy: a clergy capable of form-
> ing others, of inspiring those who
> are committed to pastoral tasks.

Cardinal Silva of Chile, still concerned with
the danger of North American "saturation" of line
positions in the Chilean Church, urged the American
prelates to send staff specialists instead.

> He explained that there were zones
> in Latin America already saturated by
> foreign priests. He said that a great
> number of foreign priests gave the
> Latin American Church a foreign image
> and impeded local recruitment. He
> asked the North American bishops to
> train Latin American priests in the

United States as specialists in religious, technical, and academic disciplines.

Brazilian Bishop Brandao complained that American bishops frequently sent men to serve as
priests in Latin America who were unfit for one
reason or another to serve in the United States.
He asked that "quality" instead of "quantity" be
the guideline for the future.

Archbishop Dearden of Detroit questioned this
analysis of the situation. He asked that the "saturation" of which Silva had spoken be documented,
and that CELAM obtain statistics concerning the location of foreign clergy and set priority areas for
the future.

At this critical juncture, a staff specialist,
Jesuit Renato Poblete, the director of the Chilean
Centro Bellarmino, took advantage of Dearden's call
for objective criteria to support Silva's plea for
specialized experts. Poblete's statement is evidence of the kind of linkage that can be forged
among episcopal decision-makers by the clerical
staff expert: he reconciles divergent definitions
of a situation by proffering what purports to be
impartially applied expertise.

Father Poblete said that SIDEAT
and FERES could cooperate in the task
requested by Archbishop Dearden. Then
Father Poblete proposed that CELAM and
the Episcopal Conferences of each nation create a group of technicians to
establish the priorities of each country and of the continent.

Poblete, who was one of the founders of FERES,
although, of course, not himself a bishop, stood to
gain prestige and financial support for his research
center as well as continued access to episcopal
decision-makers. As will be made evident in the
chapters on Chile, the staff priest is able to act

as liaison between groups within the national and
international Church, but he is in demand only insofar as these groups are in conflict with one another or with their environment. He is a key linkage, but one that depends for its existence upon
disintegrative forces. It is in his interest to
emphasize the perils at hand, the tensions within
the Church, the need for unity. His function as
mediator, or broker, is called into question only
in times of calm. In times of instability, when
sudden basic changes in resources and relationships
are likely, the staff priest can be relied upon to
reconcile warring factions by appealing to what he
is able to substantiate are their common interests.
When Latin American and North American bishops
squabbled over the quality of manpower being sent
south, Poblete could point to his research center
as the source of "objective" (statistical) information that would "scientifically" resolve the question of how many priests were needed from the United
States, and in which areas.

     At the Miami meeting, staff specialists Poblete
and Edwards had presented a proposal for improving
the "image" of Catholic education in Latin America.
The conundrum posed by an emphasis on forming "societal elites" in an age of "mass awakening" was a
source of tension that would later prompt CELAM to
call a meeting of all Latin American bishops in
Medellin, in August, 1968. The decision-making
process that emerged at that meeting will be examined in Chapter 6. But in November, 1967, the issue of religious "institutions" (especially schools)
was already being raised in a crisis context.

     The linkages between the official Church hier-
archy and political and social elites were seen as
prejudicial to the formation of strong ties to mass
movements. Father Edwards cited the Cuban case.

          Father Edwards related to the
     bishops that at a prior reunion of
     CELAM, the auxiliary bishop of Havana,
     Fernando Azcarate, had detailed

confidentially some of the errors the
Church had committed in Cuba. He emphasized the dysfunctional consequences of the concentration of religious education among the most privileged classes. Azcarate told the
bishops participating in the Santiago
meeting that the Castro government in
Cuba had erased with one decree all
the work in education that the Church
had done.

The Cuban experience was clearly foremost in
the focus of the ensuing debate on Church schools.
Poblete and Edwards were called upon to list the
policy alternatives to the present system of Catholic linkages to elite sectors. The debate was, for
the most part, removed from the immediate participation of the bishops, because it involved one
highly divisive issue--the fact that the bulk of
North American assistance to the Latin Church was
in the form of North American priests and nuns who
taught middle- and upper-class Latin American children. The "elitist" or class image of the Latin
American Church was perceived by many Latin churchmen to derive from linkages forged by foreign "missionaries" who had penetrated the Latin system with
practices and styles of operation unsuited to the
new environment.

Since a discussion of Catholic educational systems in Latin America would quickly call into question the critical linkages that North Americans had
constructed without Latin episcopal direction, the
matter was left to the priest-experts, Poblete and
Edwards, who threshed out the issue in theoretical
terms while the bishops looked on. By the time the
two priests had finished, the issue had lost much
of its emotional freight and was safe for discussion by the policy-makers.

Poblete carefully refrained from placing any
blame upon the bishops for the "state of anxiety"
that he said prevailed over discussions of Catholic

schools in Latin America. He placed the burden of
blame, instead, upon secular governments. The latter's insistence on setting standards and reserving
to themselves the granting of degrees hampered
Church operations and limited Church freedom. The
alternative to Catholic education was state education. But since state education was not susceptible
to Church influence, it was not an acceptable alternative. However, Catholic schools were not feasible unless the students paid tuition. Thus only
those with money could take advantage of Catholic
education. Therefore, said Poblete, the Latin
American Church "appears to be identified with the
rich classes."

This set of syllogisms conveniently relieved
the bishops, whether North American or Latin American, of any blame for the current crisis over
dwindling mass support. However, as Edwards was to
insist, the crisis in Church credibility and the
precarious position of Church structures vis-à-vis
leftist governments and movements remained. The
obvious answer, he said, was to begin a shift in
Church operations away from the heavy investments
in money and manpower concentrated in upper-class
sectors to lighter investments in money and use of
the same manpower to service the under classes.

The main difficulty with this strategy was
that the crucial variable--manpower--was in the
hands of the North American bishops. The latter
had always insisted on the advisability of elite-
oriented Church operations, following the North
American model of plugging into an upwardly mobile
middle class by means of parochial schools run by
nuns and religious-order priests, while maintaining
parishes and some schools among the lower classes.
The bishops and the prestige orders (Jesuits, Do-
minicans) courted the upper classes and political
elites. This North American model of the nineteenth
and twentieth centuries, with its more or less
clearly defined division of labor, was applicable
in a context of manpower reserves and steady recruitment. In the Latin American context, from the

point of view of many Latin bishops, it clearly
could not be maintained.

The North American nuns and religious-order
priests, who made up the bulk of manpower assistance to Latin America, had carried over their
North American styles of life and operation. They
had concentrated their energies on building bridges
to the emergent middle classes, to the neglect of
the masses. The bishops were clearly opting for a
linkage network extensive enough to spread the
risks of Church commitment. In this vision, all
possible interest groups within the national society would be serviced, and exclusive ties to particular international spheres could be scanted.
There was a clear attempt to draw in Canadian,
British, French, West German, and Italian manpower
in order to balance the demands already made upon
the United States.

For the present, however, the Latin American
bishops were dependent upon the United States for
the bulk of manpower assistance. Poblete was given
the task of negotiating more direct control by Latin
American bishops over North American priests and
nuns in Latin countries. Edwards would try to convince the North American bishops that they must
exert pressure upon the North American religious
orders of priests and nuns, which are, technically,
at least, independent of direct episcopal control.
It should be remembered that the North American
bishops were not sending many of their own "diocesan" parish priests to Latin America. Instead,
they had permitted or persuaded the provincials of
religious orders to send their personnel to Latin
America. The control linkage that the Latin American bishops sought to forge between their chanceries
and the local American missionary must extend to the
North American bishop, who would then apply pressure upon the North American religious orders. The
alternative was to forge links between Latin bishops
and the international headquarters of some of the
religious orders. The Generals Superior of Jesuits,
for example, are headquartered in Rome; a Latin

American bishop seeking control over the manpower
resources of the Jesuits would seek to strengthen
his own links to the Roman base of operations, if
attempts to persuade local Jesuit provincials
failed.

But the process of forging linkages to remote
control centers is difficult, time-consuming, and
costly. One of the aims of the U.S.-Latin American
bishops' meetings was to facilitate the formulation
of policy directives that would link both North
American and Latin American hierarchies collective-
ly; this would eliminate competition among the
Latins for scarce manpower resources and ease the
burden on the North Americans, who had their own
national needs to attend to.

But this issue also was a touchy one. The
Latin American bishops were convinced that they
needed a strategy for developing mass support in
their countries. Some of them were equally convinced that North American "missionaries" were
alienating the under classes by their North American style of life and by their concentration on the
middle sectors. The solution was thought to lie in
a massive overhaul not only of the life style but
also of the bases of autonomy the missionary had
hitherto enjoyed.

The suggestion that North American bishops
seize the initiative in limiting the autonomy of
the North American religious functionary was
broached by Poblete in piecemeal fashion.

He first observed that North American priests
and nuns who came to Latin America should feel free
to work at "all levels" of education and not be
confined to primary and secondary schools. Since
Catholic universities in Latin America are in the
hands of Latin American churchmen, this proposal
would entail the incorporation of North Americans
into existing Latin institutions, where they could
be coordinated by local decision-makers, and the
surrender of much of their autonomy.

Following a discussion by several bishops, it was agreed to limit the proposition to the statement that "something had to be done," without committing the hierarchy to specific policies. It was agreed that the North American religious functionaries had not been used to fullest benefit and should be redistributed. The manner of their redistribution was to be studied by a CELAM committee.

Poblete then suggested a sociological study of the worth of Catholic education in Latin America in order to inform the CELAM study group. He wisely left the concept of "worth" ambiguous--to be defined later by sociologists rather than to be debated by bishops. He proposed as a partial solution to the dilemma of Church education the setting up of Church-sponsored normal schools to train secondary-school teachers, who would then teach in non-Church institutions.

The main issue had not yet been joined: What degree of autonomy was to be granted to the foreign missionaries? Were they to retain their own organizational base (fund-raising initiatives, schools), or were they to be "integrated" into the local Church system?

Cardinal Silva and Archbishop Brandao reaffirmed the need for Catholic universities, couching their arguments in the following terms. In those Latin American countries where the government is in exclusive control of universities, the universities do not meet the needs of the countries. The state-run universities give courses in arts and letters, when what is needed is technical and scientific training. (At the Santiago meeting, the bishops agreed that the end of Catholic education was "to prepare Christians as men ready to work for the bettering of society.")

Poblete then clarified the intent of his statement concerning normal schools for training secondary schoolteachers. The Latin bishops, especially Silva and Brandao, were eager to concentrate

Church manpower resources in Catholic universities
and to deemphasize Catholic secondary schools. Resistance to this was bound to be great among the
religious orders, especially those that had beefed
up their high-school staffs with foreign members of
the order.

Father Manuel Edwards, a member of a religious
order but also a technician in charge of a staff
organization, the Latin American Confederation of
Religious (CLAR), placed himself squarely on the
side of the bishops in assigning the blame for the
crisis in Catholic image-making. He noted that
the bulk of Catholic secondary education was in
the hands of religious orders of women, who were
responsible for the "bad image" with which the
Church was burdened. Since women were not represented at the Miami or Santiago meetings, these
criticisms went uncontested.

Edwards went on to cite a series of directives
to superiors of religious orders which Latin American bishops had drawn up in Lima several months
earlier:

> We suggest that the following steps
> be taken:
>   1. A revision of the formation
> of social conscience made in the
> novitiates and in the schools of for-
> mation of the order.
>   2. Efforts to make Catholic
> educational institutions accessible
> to the poor and an instrument of
> service for the common good.
>   3. An end to the construction
> of luxurious high-school buildings,
> which constitute an insult to the
> poor.
>   4. A study of Catholic schools
> to be carried out by the department
> of education of CELAM and by FERES
> and CLAR.

5.   The creation of a social conscience among other classes concerning
the needs of the less privileged.
6.   The petitioning of the national conference of Bishops for a
pastoral plan for the care of youth.

None of these proposals called for the dis-
mantling of the Catholic school system in Latin
America or for direct accessibility to the under
classes.   The social base would continue to be the
monied classes, whose financial support was needed.
The main preoccupation of the bishops was with the
"image" of the Church in the eyes of the masses.
The concept of elite-led social change based on
Catholic altruism remained.   The identification of
the Church with monied elites was to be kept, but
made less visible.   Expensive buildings were to be
maintained, but no new ones were to be built.
"Planning" and consultation would be concerned not
with policy goals but with the most effective allocation of personnel and resources to achieve them.

The discussion on religious education found
the bishops unwilling either to force the religious
orders to change their base of operations or to
submit to episcopal control.   They did agree on the
following point.

The bishops agreed that the
religious-order teachers who come to
Latin America do not necessarily have
to teach in academic institutions;
they should keep an open mind toward
a greater diversification of education; they should be disposed to make
economic sacrifices to make education
accessible to the popular classes and
to the poor; finally, they should receive local orientation to ensure
their efficient cooperation in parish
tasks and in the education of adults.

This set of principles was to be spelled out in
"concrete recommendations" by Father Edwards when
he returned to advise the members of CLAR, the superiors of the major religious orders.

It is important to remember that, while the
North American bishops have no direct authority
over the internal policy-making of the religious orders of men, and only a slightly more powerful position with regard to nuns, they do hold veto power
over the operation of the orders within a given
diocese. At the same time, the bishops are dependent in large measure upon the religious orders for
the maintenance of the parochial school system.
The North Americans were therefore not willing to
apply direct pressures upon the North American religious orders to ensure their compliance with the
Latin American directives. Although the Latin American bishops were clearly concerned about changing
the "image" of their schools, and therefore in
changing the policies of the North American nuns
and priests who operated many of them, they were at
the same time aware of their relatively weak position and bargained accordingly. They would have
liked the North Americans to have put more money
and manpower into projects for reaching the lower
classes. But they realized that this would entail
the sacrificing of the interests of the religious
orders, making it necessary to retrain and expose
to hardship religious functionaries who had spent
their lives living among and servicing the middle
and upper classes in the United States. At the
same time, the Latin American bishops could hardly
expect the North Americans to forego the sources of
financial support within Latin America that stem
from upper-class sectors and from North American
government and business personnel living abroad,
especially when these resources had gone relatively
untapped in the past.

It is clear, then, that it is unwise to consider the "image" problems of a Latin American
bishop as entirely of his own making. He finds himself linked in the popular mind with the Pope, with

other bishops, with nearly any Catholic spokesman,
when any of these issue pronouncements on such controversial topics as violent revolution, birth control, imperialism, and celibacy. He must react to
these specific linkages that are in large measure
not of his own choosing.

The Latin bishop also finds himself dependent
upon foreign (Spanish, American, French) manpower
for the maintenance of his own organizational base.
If he is dependent upon one source of supply (the
United States, for example), he has little room for
maneuver, scant credit to veto very often the decisions reached by his foreign "partners," even when
the latter alienate native clerics or laity.

The formal prescribed linkages that bind all
the bishops of the world to one another and to other
members of the Church are precisely described and
weighted in Church canon law. The popular conception of such linkages, however, is not troubled by
such subtleties. When the Pope speaks, the press
seldom bothers to ascertain whether he is speaking
"ex cathedra" ("infallibly," and binding on all), or
expressing a personal opinion he expects to be considered and debated. From the bishop's perspective,
any publicized papal or episcopal utterance is a
challenge: a problem to be resolved either by public agreement or disagreement, partial or complete.

There is thus a distinction to be made between
the formally prescribed linkage and the popularly
conceived linkage. A third type of linkage further
complicates decision-making: informal linkages
made to resolve ad hoc contingencies, or even deep
structural problems. (Foreign assistance is a case
in point.)

But the linkages between Latin and U.S. bishops
originated and have been maintained through a kind
of exchange process. In return for the money and
men they send South, North American bishops can enjoy the status of men important in the worldwide
fight against Communism, hunger, disease. They have

access to officials in the U.S. government who are
concerned with these issues and who are useful contacts in the domestic lobbying U.S. bishops do. It
is common to see vice presidential and other administrative assistants at meetings of the Catholic
Inter-American Cooperation Program (CICOP).

The North American bishop who sends assistance
to Latin dioceses finds himself in a larger arena
than the one to which organizational mobility has
relegated him. A bishop whose domain is Reno or
Madison may come to prize the opportunity to attend
conferences in Rio de Janeiro or Santiago de Chile,
especially when his attendance is garnished with
the authority to make decisions affecting the lives
of thousands of people.

As Bishop Brandao asserted, another attractive
feature of inter-American cooperation, from the
point of view of some North American bishops, is
that it provides them with disposal facilities for
unwanted personnel. Priests who cause trouble can
be sent to try out their disruptive techniques in a
remote "mission" diocese. The Latin American bishops may complain about the "quality" of manpower
they receive, but they cannot complain too strenu-
ously, since they are not "paying" for such resources in any currency that can be counted.

The Latin American bishops did have one powerful argument that appealed to both the self-interest
and the ideals of the North Americans, and they used
it frequently during the meeting in Santiago: the
threat of "another Cuba," which, with its expropriation of Church schools and other properties, would
benefit neither Latin nor North American churchmen.
The self-interest of North American religious orders
would seem to dictate that they carefully consider
the danger they were courting in concentrating their
attentions and services on the monied classes in
Latin America. Cuban Bishop Azcarate's testimony at
the Santiago meeting was directed at North American
bishops who could convey his warnings to their associates in the religious orders.

The link between Castro and Latin American
Catholic episcopates could be considered in Rosenau's
terms a "disintegrative linkage," since it is founded
on enmity and keeps the two groups apart. But, of
course, from the Catholic organizational perspective,
so long as Castro is considered an external threat
to the Catholic system, Catholics have common interest. It will be my contention that Latin American-
North American cooperation was strongest, and that
Latin Catholics were most supportive of one another,
when the "threat" of a Castro-style revolution
seemed imminent. (This was certainly the case in
Chile.) The internal state of the national Church
derives from many international linkages, and not
only the formal ties with Rome and with sister
Churches. Unforeseen contingencies that threaten
the chain of Catholic influence can remake a national Church system practically overnight. The
massive influx of North American, French, Belgian,
and West German priests into Latin America in the
1960's cannot be explained apart from the traumatic
effect of Castro's revolution. In fact, the Cuban
revolution may be seen as the decisive event in the
development of Latin Catholicism in the 1960's. An
examination of the remedies taken against "Protestant competition" would reveal that Church policy-
makers never really felt compelled to compete with
Protestants. Protestantism was instead often viewed
in the light of "ecumenism" and "brotherly cooperation." It was seen as a kindred value movement that
would provide support for religious sentiments and
offset the gains made by leftists bent upon the radi-
calization of a secularized mass base.

It is thus important not merely to identify as
many salient linkages as pervade the international
Catholic system, tying it to other actors and polities. It is crucial to weight the respective influence of salient links--to measure not only the direction but also the strength of different linkages.
The North American bishops seemed to propose a model
of Church organization that was pluralistic in its
emphasis on checks and balances, on providing a net
of corrective linkages to ensure that no one link
became too tight or too commanding.

At the Santiago meeting, the North Americans were quick to point out that if their "missionaries" abandoned their organizational bases among the middle and upper classes in Latin America, as the Latin American bishops were urging them to do, they would be at the mercy of the Latin American bishops. The latter, they implied, had in the past disregarded pleas for reciprocity when they had been in position to do so.

Bishop Joseph Breitenbeck, the auxiliary to Archbishop Dearden of Detroit, and the head of the bishops' complaint department underlined the necessity of local Latin American pastoral plans to incorporate foreigners, spelling out their specific roles. In the past, he said, this has not been done, and there have been cases of North American nuns who were persuaded not to establish traditional high schools only to find that there was a lack of local direction for their work as parish auxiliaries.

This type of problem is characteristic of a system that is threatened and yet low on resources. The North Americans had been at pains in Miami to pinpoint the causes for the loss of religious influence in Latin America and had probed the resources of the Church there, notably the landed properties from which, they suspected, their Latin brother bishops derived the bulk of their income.

The Latin bishops, bristling under charges from secular sources that the Latin American Church was wealthy and aligned with the rich, denied their own culpability for the loss of Church influence. The issue was debated again at the Santiago meeting, because the North Americans again raised it and forced its consideration. But this time the Latins were able to choose the ground and to shift discussion to their own perspective.

In Miami, the Latin bishops had blamed the
Latin American religious orders for holding on to
their land.   In Santiago, the Latin bishops insinu-
ated that the bad image of the Church stemmed from
the concentration of North American religious education in the upper-economic strata.   The North
American bishops were not attacked.   The North
American male heads of religious orders were not
blamed.   The blame was placed, instead, upon the
religious orders for <u>women</u>, whose superiors lack
status and power within the Church system.

Blame was effectively placed upon those sectors
of the Church that could not lobby effectively.   The
potentially explosive issues of "saturation" of foreign priests and of the functional autonomy of sub-
units were effectively defused and forgotten.   Episcopal "unity" was regarded as more important than
functional effectiveness.

The North American bishops did continue to
probe sources of strain with the Latin American
dioceses.   Before the conference had terminated,
Archbishop Dearden of Detroit gave this interesting
piece of advice to the Latin Americans:

> It is dangerous to establish formal
> communities of persons of the same so-
> cial status, race, interests, or eco-
> nomic resources.   In the United States,
> we are trying to remedy this situation,
> which has created serious problems.

Dearden had mentioned earlier in the meeting that
the preoccupation of the Chilean bishops with concentrating on the Chilean middle classes would result in the alienation of both the upper and lower
classes from Church interests.   Better to spread
one's resources to cover all.

The Archbishop of Detroit was speaking just a
few months after racial violence had devastated
massive sections of his home diocese.   The link

between the "serious problems" encountered in his
North American context and potential violence in
Latin American cities was underscored by other American bishops. Policy-making in the international
Church is not divisible strictly along national
lines. Latin American bishops are not autonomous
within national boundaries. They are dependent
upon inputs from wealthier systems. These inputs
include not only manpower and money but also policy
recommendations. Dearden feared that what happened
in Detroit--massive concentration of Church resources
among white ethnic groups, to the neglect of Negroes--
might find parallels in Latin America. This fear was
based not on the history of the Church in Latin America but on the demands of present-day churchmen who
advocated identifying the Church with leftist social
movements representing "the poor."

Events in Detroit can influence events in Santiago de Chile, although perhaps not in predictable
patterns. The lesson that the Archbishop of Detroit
drew from his city's riots and applied to Latin
America was that the Church could not afford to
"overcommit itself" to any one interest group--
neither the exploiters nor the exploited, neither
rich nor poor. Church bets were to be hedged. Communications were to be kept open with all parties to
a conflict. The Church, and especially the bishop,
was to act as broker.

The problem with this policy is that only one
actor, the bishop, can play the role of broker among
all contending factions. Other Church officials,
especially the staff priests, are soon deeply committed to the special sectors they serve. It is
true that the line priest, the parish priest, has
often been considered "a bishop within his parish,"
just as the bishop has been termed "a Pope within
his diocese." But few parish priests can remain
for long, even conceptually, within the confines of
their own parishes. Few parish units are self-
sufficient. Usually linkages must be forged to
sources of legitimation, financing, and approbation
that lie outside parish boundaries.

In parish units that have sharp economic or
ethnic divisions, it is nearly impossible for the
priest to suit his own life style to all of those
around him. One solution is priestly isolation;
the parish house becomes a sort of monastery, a for-
tress within which the priest is protected from the
incessant and conflicting demands of "the world."
The alternative is to go out into "the world" and
commit oneself to action. Even here there is a pro-
tective cliché which cautions the priest to "be in
the world but not of it," an admonition which could
be interpreted as "do not become attached to any
one part of the whole." The kind of detachment
Dearden was proposing to the Latin bishops seemed
designed to change existing policies of "overcommit-
ment" to the upper or middle classes without fall-
ing into the equally hazardous enterprise of concentrating all of one's resources upon the poor, the
students, or some other interest group.

The reaction of the Latin Americans to this
suggestion, and to the probing of other "weaknesses,"
was not positive. When Bishop Green asked if there
was much tension in Latin America between the younger clergy and their elders, he was met with plati-
tudes:

> Cardinal Silva said that in Chile
> the older clergy had made the transi-
> tion in policy required by the Vati-
> can Council easy, because they had al-
> ways been progressive. Bishop Munoz
> Vega said that there were some small
> problems in Ecuador. Bishop McGrath
> said that there was some tension in
> the Antilles and in Central America,
> but that these problems were caused
> by small groups of young priests.

This type of response came from bishops who
were actively courting North American manpower and
monies. Brazilian Bishop Brandao, however, operated in a Church sub-system that was striving to emphasize self-sufficiency and nationalist aspirations.

When Green asked Brandao about the generation gap
among clergy,

>Bishop Brandao said that he did
>not like the question, nor the dis-
>tinction between young and older
>priests with respect to the renova-
>tion of theology and pastoral plan-
>ning. He said that the real problem
>was the secularization of society.

But the question of the functional autonomy of
younger priests remained. When the North Americans
warned of the tendency of young clerics to find
employment part time to support themselves, instead
of relying upon Church support, the Latin Americans
minimized the dangers:

>Bishop McGrath emphasized the good
>will and acceptable motivation of this
>tendency. He said that the desire to
>support oneself on the part of many
>seminarians is inspired by their de-
>sire to contribute and not be a burden
>for the Church during their period of
>formation more than by an attempt to
>escape priestly poverty and dependence.

Bishop Larrain of Chile agreed, expressing the
opinion that the young men wished to be self-
sufficient so that they might:

>1. Work with other young people
>in the evangelization of society;
>2. learn to share the life of
>others; take part in the common lot
>of men and not be isolated by privi-
>leges or like a caste apart;
>3. reach adult status and form
>their personalities in an adult
>manner.

The only dissident voice was that of Cardinal Silva,
who took issue with his fellow Chilean to label the

tendency toward self-sufficiency the effect of "excessive secularization." He sided with the North
Americans who were concerned with the "latent functions" of outside employment.

The final probe of Latin Catholic "weaknesses"
was directed at class consciousness and conflicts
within the Latin American clergy. This question,
too, was parried by the Latin bishops, who used it
as an occasion to gently admonish their North American benefactors.

> When Bishop Carroll of Miami at-
> tempted to ascertain the problems
> that might obtain in Latin America
> between priests supported by wealthy
> parishes and priests living in pover-
> ty, he was told by Bishop Larrain
> that the North American bishops
> should send financial assistance
> directly to Latin American dioceses
> and quit supporting their own men at
> a higher level.

Once again a North American probe was turned into a
North American problem by the Latin American bishops.
Class differences in the Latin Church were ascribed
to North American inputs. The North American bishop
became defensive, forgetting his original sally.

> Bishop Dearden of Detroit said
> that it was not always possible to
> control the aid sent from North Amer-
> ica to South American dioceses, and
> that in many cases the missionaries
> received financial aid from their
> families and friends. He said that
> the answer lay in forming a social
> conscience among the missionaries.
> The local Latin American bishop
> should keep watch to make sure that
> the foreign missionaries did not
> live in better conditions than did
> the native clergy.

Strains in the linkages between North American and Latin American bishops seem to have been somewhat alleviated at the conclusion of the Santiago meeting by a protracted discussion of common grievances against the Vatican commission for Latin America (COGECAL).

The commission had sought to ensure, through a set of guidelines, that the influx of foreign Church aid into the Latin American Catholic system be channeled through formally constituted agencies and not be handled "personalistically." The guidelines (outlined in Chapter 3) had met with little opposition prior to the Santiago meeting. But in Santiago, the attempts by the North Americans to exert pressure over their Latin confreres resulted in alienation. The North American bishops were eager that requests for aid be kept to a minimum, be specific, and be submitted with the approval of all Latin American bishops. The requests would then be considered by the North Americans, who would reserve the right to reject or approve, and who, in the case of approval, would initiate measures to ensure proper implementation. In other words, the North Americans had wished to avoid alienating interests that they could not satisfy and, at the same time, wished to ensure their own control over the funds and manpower that they did allocate.

The Latin American bishops wanted to make sure that whatever monies were sent to Latin American Catholics were subject to "the needs of the Latin American Church" and dispensed by local bishops. At the same time, they sought to avoid becoming enmeshed in complicated "bureaucratic" reporting procedures, seeking instead a wide measure of discretion in allocating North American monies and men. They demanded not only aid but autonomy.

The issue of autonomy was never settled. The debate it provoked at the Santiago meeting is interesting because in its course concrete programs and specific personalities were offered as examples of the vexations that plagued the respective episcopates.

The problematic staff sectors of the Church were consistently linked to loss of episcopal power by the
Latin American bishops and to resolution of difficulties by the North American bishops. The Latin bishop felt threatened, the North American bishop felt
reassured, by staff strength.

In the eyes of the North American bishop, the
staff expert could present "objective" appraisals
of competing programs and assist in the administration of controversial projects. To the Latin American bishop, however, the staff expert signaled a
threat to episcopal power and autonomy. His participation in decision-making frequently outweighed
his formal status. He was not always subject to
episcopal control. He did not derive substantial
legitimation nor funding from sources dependent
upon the bishop. His achieved secular status was
in clear opposition to the sacred status of the
episcopacy.

While the North American donors were anxious
that aid be administered according to "objective"
impersonal criteria, the Latin American recipients
were just as adamant that aid be subject to their
own personal control. The debate, as presented in
the minutes of the Santiago meeting, follows:

> Bishop Bernardin (of Atlanta)
> suggested that the norms outlined by
> the Papal Commission (COGECAL) be fol-
> lowed in the allocation of North Amer-
> ican monies to Latin America. Never-
> theless, he said that he was not sure
> that these norms reflected the think-
> ing of the Latin American bishops
> present.
> Bernardin suggested the possibil-
> ity of establishing a coordinating
> committee in each episcopal confer-
> ence of each Latin country and another
> body that would coordinate all of the
> episcopal conferences. This body
> would be directed by CELAM, which

would study and make recommendations
concerning the various petitions of
the episcopal committees before these
petitions were submitted to the bishops of the United States. In this
way, he said, it would be possible to
avoid a situation in which projects
were submitted without much consideration.

Furthermore, according to Bishop
Bernardin, a scientific study by the
CELAM committees would guarantee that
aid was directed to common problems
and not just to the stopgap needs of
specific individuals.

Bishop Bernardin concluded that
not all of the North American bishops
were convinced of the necessity of
channeling all their monies through
the Latin American Bishops' Committee (CELAM). He said that many good
projects would never have been initiated if they had had to depend upon
the approval of the local bishop.

The Latin Americans took umbrage at this last
remark. In a huff, the Cardinal of Santiago advised
his fellow Latin bishops to forget the North Americans:

Cardinal Raul Silva replied that
the great projects of the Latin American bishops that received aid from
abroad should in the future be made
self-supporting, so that they could
be continued if foreign assistance
were terminated. He cited the example of some programs of the Church
in Chile which had been affected when
the American Ambassador had withdrawn
U.S. monies.

The Cardinal also referred to the
bureaucratic element that had been
imposed upon certain Chilean projects

by foreign donors. He cited the example of Chilean CARITAS (the Chilean
branch of the Church's welfare and
food distribution complex: DEM)
which had to send reports to the
United States and admit supervision
of projects, and which therefore
must employ 300 people when it could
have gotten along with twenty or
thirty.

Silva went on to say that the most delicate question before the bishops was to determine who was to
evaluate petitions for aid: the local bishops or
the North American donors.

He cited as possible guides for decision-making
the examples of the German Catholic foundations,
MISEREOR and ADVENIAT. (See page 39.) Cardinal
Silva maintained that the ADVENIAT funds posed no
problem, since they were under the control of Latin
American bishops and merely "supervised" by the German foundations. The MISEREOR monies, however,
were another story.

Cardinal Silva said that, concretely, in Chile, DESAL had been
put in charge of making aid proposals and of allocating MISEREOR funds.
The Cardinal regretted the fact that
DESAL depends entirely upon one person (the Jesuit Roger Vekemans: DEM)
to whom MISEREOR has given all
decision-making power. In this situation the Church in Chile feels controlled by outside forces and this
creates conflicts and lessens autonomy.

The Jesuit staff expert, as we shall see,
forms linkages with international sources of support and with the international organization of
the Jesuits that give him a unique influence in
the national Churches. In fact, national Churches

are finding it more and more difficult to retain
their own identities. Situations increasingly come
to be defined by those who fuse the linkages between "donor" and "recipient," between North American or European and South American. In the case of
Chile, as will be made evident, the DESAL organization was itself a linkage, embodying both Latin
American and North American (European) elements of
personalism and bureaucratic planning As the
Chilean Cardinal complained, not only did DESAL
forge linkages to sources of support, it itself was
the linkage. To challenge DESAL would be to threat-
en one's lifeline.

The Cardinal's example is the classic citation
of a line-staff conflict at the level of formal organization. At another level, the level of international linkages, the conflict acquires a new di-
mension. For it is becoming increasingly evident
that the Catholic hierarchical system is linked
horizontally much more through the "informal" linkages of staff organizations and cosmopolitan priest-
experts than by the prescribed formal linkages of
the episcopal college. Cardinals gather in Rome at
the death of a Pope or, with bishops, to attend a
Vatican Council. But Popes die infrequently, and
there have been only two Vatican Councils in the
last century.

Staff experts, on the other hand, meet frequently at international symposia, planning councils, and conferences. They have access to secular sources of support, to funding for travel and
meetings as well as for research. They are often
supported by research and development organizations
which they themselves founded (DESAL, ICODES, CIAS),
and which guarantee mobility and professional rather than solely ecclesiastical legitimation.

It is the contention of the present study that
the staff expert is the "cement" of the Church system and that this critical bonding is breaking down.
Staff priests are formally obligated to bishops who
can offer them few rewards. Reciprocity is breaking

down within the Church because the one reinforcer
the bishop is equipped to employ, sacral legitimation, no longer reinforces. Secular society no
longer esteems a man simply because that man was ordained by a bishop. The ascribed status of the
priest is on the wane. The status disparity expe-
rienced by the priest-Ph.D. in economics, or the
priest-executive of an international agency, ex-
plodes the traditional linkages of priests to bishops and to the hierarchical system. The Church, especially the Latin American Church, is fragmenting
massively because it has been forced to develop linkages with secular groups which then compete with
Church authorities, the bishops, for the allegiance
of the linkage, which is an organizational staff
unit. The linkage is not merely conceptual. It is
a process embodied and shaped by an organization or,
in some cases, by a single individual. This is probably an effect of the tendency of the Latin American
to "personalize" relationships, to send couriers instead of letters, to concretize a linkage by incar-
nating it. Or perhaps it would not be too farfetched
to suggest that this is a distinctively Catholic approach to relation. The Catholic concept of God
posits a Father and a Son who are related precisely
by Spirit, and this Spirit is another Person whose
sole reality consists in being the relationship of
Father to Son. Likewise God's relation to man is
the Son.

At any rate, the linkages that bind the Latin
American Catholic system to Northern American and
European sources of supply are not viewed as abstract contractual arrangements. The linkages are
not merely the combination of "outputs" and "inputs"
impersonally joined. There are mediating agencies
that handle outputs and inputs. And it is the mediating agency that actually "links" the national
Churches. It is not the fact that the North Americans have sent men and money to the Latin Americans
that explains the ties between these two groups.
It is, more saliently, the fact that the transfer
has been institutionalized through such highly personalistic agencies as DESAL, CELAM, CIDOC. These

agencies, or staff organizations, are the crucial
linkages. And they are increasingly coming into
conflict with the terminals they were intended to
join.

The Santiago meeting of bishops gives evidence
that at least some of the Latin American bishops understood this problem and attempted to remake the
linkages that bound them to the North Americans in
the form of episcopal rather than impersonal bureaucratic ties. Instead of embodying the linkage in a
staff bureau, which would then employ "objective"
measures to determine who received how much aid,
Silva was eager to eliminate the staff function at
that level entirely, reducing it to a purely advisory role.

> Speaking hypothetically, the Car-
> dinal said that if it were Chile which
> were giving aid to other countries he
> would create a governing body with one
> delegate for the bishops, one for the
> religious orders, and one for the dio-
> cesan priests to establish the norms
> for approving aid requests.

In this way, all the formally recognized interest
groups would be represented: the bishops, their
priests, the religious orders. The staff organizations and staff advisors, who had never been formally intended to constitute autonomous interests,
would not exercise discretion over decision-making.
They would have no allocative power, no vote, no
organizational base from which to "govern."

The North Americans, especially Bishop Bernardin, were eager to emphasize staff contributions
because they perceived them as more objective and
as providing rationale for refusals to send men and
money to questionable areas. CELAM (the staff organization of the Committee of the Latin American
Bishops) makes decisions that are subject to the
approval of a majority of Latin American bishops,
each of whom theoretically has access to the pool

of staff resources; this arrangement provides little
encouragement for the maneuverings of individual
decision-makers such as Raul Silva, even though they
carry the high rank of cardinal. CELAM, as a formal
bureaucracy bolstered by an international hierarchical framework and advised by a group of technicians,
constitutes a sizeable threat to more personalistic
local dynasties such as the Archdiocese of Santiago.

The only staff person to speak at length at the
Santiago meeting was the personal advisor of Cardinal Silva, the Jesuit Father Renato Poblete. He
tried to smooth the rift between Silva and Bernardin
by accepting the latter's emphasis on the need for
objective project evaluations and the former's insistence on informality. Poblete was himself a kind
of bridge between two worlds. Educated at Fordham
University in sociology, he spoke excellent English
and knew North American foundation heads, State Department officials, and administrative assistants.
Yet he was a Chilean with close ties to the Cardinal
and to officials of the Christian Democratic Party.
He was a personal friend of Eduardo Frei, Radimiro
Tomic, and other prominent Chileans. Poblete was
therefore accepted by North American and Latin
American bishops alike.

At both the Miami and Santiago meetings,
Poblete sought to smooth over the conflicts between
line officials (the bishops) by emphasizing the
"impartial" contribution to be made by staff
priests such as himself, and he sought to alleviate
the competition for scarce resources by arguing for
increased supply. He called for the North American
bishops to lobby more effectively for an "end to
the arms race" and the promotion of "world peace"
so that the American defense budget might be tapped
for aid to developing countries. He called for an
informal group of staff priests who would advise
the national episcopal conferences (thereby bypass-
ing CELAM) and help to set aid priorities. As
director of a staff agency, the Centro Bellarmino
in Chile, Poblete would be in a position to enhance
the prestige of his own enterprises, secure Jesuit

influence at a time when fellow Jesuit Roger Vekemans
of DESAL was under attack, and obligate to himself
Chilean Cardinal Silva. At the same time, the North
Americans would be reassured that their money was
being protected and their manpower allocated by "experts" with technical training.

The Santiago meeting closed with projected
plans for a meeting in Detroit in June, 1968, when
Archbishop Dearden would attempt to ensure North
American episcopal attendance at the Eucharistic
Congress of August, 1968, in Bogota.

5

JESUIT CIAS:
A DIVIDED
AND DIVISIVE
STAFF FORCE

Conflicts between line officials (the bishops) have been sketched in their main outlines above. The rise of staff sectors as linkage phenomena has been described as a response to these line conflicts. (It is true, of course, that conflict also binds parties together, that some linkages are "integrative.")

Conflicts between line and staff, between the bishops and the "experts," will form much of the content and substance of what follows. Staff sectors within the Church were intended in large measure to dampen, or "rationally" resolve, tensions between line officials. But the staff sectors themsleves had their own autonomy to nurture and protect. In some cases, staff organizations were able (as did DESAL) to preempt traditional line prerogatives.

Before discussing line-staff conflict, it may be helpful to examine a critical linkage between line and staff and between different staff groups. The Jesuit Center for Research and Social Action (CIAS) functions in most Latin American countries, as it does throughout the world. The assembled

members of the individual (read "national") CIAS
groups (CLACIAS) do not form a single interest
group. They are themselves divided, rent by dissen-
sions and involved in "winner-take-all" competition.

This chapter will set the stage for the case
studies of Colombian and Chilean Catholic bureaucracy that follow. In both cases, the North American
and West German funding agencies are important. In
both cases, the bishops are faced with severe
threats to their traditional power, albeit from different sources. In both cases, the Jesuit CIAS
organization (while internally divided) is a divisive force, competing with non-Jesuit staff sectors
and attempting to play a major role in secular as
well as ecclesiastical politics.

The evidence here again is constituted primarily by confidential internal documents, in this
case the private correspondence of CIAS members and
the minutes of their closed meetings. It has been
supplemented by informal conversational interviews
with several of the principals over the course of
five years.

THE ACTIVITIES OF CLACIAS

The joint activities of CLACIAS have been
limited for the most part to periodic meetings of
the heads of the national CIAS centers. These
meetings, which will be discussed below, have been
marked by internal dissension and rivalry. However, in early 1968, on orders from the Jesuit
General in Rome, Father Pedro Arrupe, the first
steps were taken toward joint-action projects and
coordinated research. This decision, made from
above, has had the effect of suppressing overt differences within the order, commanding collaboration between Jesuits of diverse ideologies and
interests.

In a document entitled "CIAS Activities in
1968 and Plans for 1969," the Jesuit members of the

organization were informed of the new organizational
structure of the staff group within the framework of
the international church. What follows is an analysis of this document.

The report opened with a significant announcement:

> On February 13, 1968, Very
> Reverend Father General accepted
> the resignation as Secretary Gen-
> eral of CLACIAS of Chilean Jesuit
> Hernan Larrain, the editor of
> Mensaje (Chilean Jesuit review).

In conversation, Larrain told me that he had
resigned under duress. He was personally convinced
of the necessity of working exclusively in research
and withdrawing Jesuit support from anti-Marxist
Catholic labor unions, cooperatives, neighborhood
organizations, businessmen's groups, etc. Larrain
was vigorously opposed to the massive U.S. government aid channeled through the Church (specifically,
through the Jesuit order and through CARITAS) into
Latin America. He was convinced of the need for a
united Catholic and non-Catholic left to oppose
entrenched rightist interests in the hemisphere.

Larrain was replaced as secretary general by
French Jesuit Pierre Bigo. Jesuit General Arrupe
affirmed in the same letter that the post of secretary general should be dissociated from that of
general coordinator, following a suggestion made by
CLACIAS members in December, 1966. Arrupe named as
General Coordinator for the South (Argentina,
Uruguay, Paraguay, Bolivia, Peru, Chile) Father
Alberto Sily. The other regional coordinators, each
retaining a distinct sphere of influence, were as
follows:

> The Regional Coordinator for
> North I (Mexico, Central America,
> Antilles): Father Luis Aleman, Di-
> rector of CIAS, Santo Domingo.

The Regional Coordinator for
North II (Colombia, Ecuador, Vene-
zuela): Father Jaime Martinez,
Director of CESDE, Medellin.

The Regional Coordinator for
Brazil: Father Nelson Queiroz.

Father Bigo was named acting coordinator for
Bolivia, Peru, and Chile while Alberto Sily finished
work on prior commitments. This fact was to play an
important role in the dissolution of the Jesuit
research and development center, the Centro Bellarmino. It placed Bigo in a position of formal
authority over Roger Vekemans, the Belgian Jesuit
who headed DESAL.

The formal activities of CLACIAS in 1969 were
set out as follows:

1. The coordination of the national CIAS groups with financial
aid to be proffered to each indi-
vidually.

2. Consultation to Jesuit
provincial (line) superiors and
to the Jesuit General in Rome.

3. Formation of a secretariat
for the mutual information of the
CIAS group.

The document analyzed the progress made in
ensuring the autonomy of CIAS staff groups vis-à-vis
traditional line sectors. Within the four regions
of Latin America, various activities were inaugurated in 1968. In Santo Domingo, a magazine, Commission Social, was founded. In Panama, conversations between the Jesuit provincial superior and
the CIAS coordinator Aleman were held to set policy.
In Venezuela and in Colombia, CIAS groups moved
into buildings of their own.

In Colombia, the Jesuits of CIAS were permitted to focus their own educational activity upon a select group of thirty-six students drawn from all over Latin America and incorporated into a special institute, IDES, instead of having to spend all of their time teaching at the Universidad Javeriana in Bogota.

In Ecuador, also, the Jesuits of CIAS were granted added autonomy. They moved into private residences and set up a special institute, the Institute for Pastoral Studies in Latin America (IPLA), to educate selected students.

In Brazil, attempts were made to devise a structure to replace the CIAS institute that had been suppressed by the government in 1966. An educational institute instead of a research organization was formally constituted, the Brazilian Development Institute (IBRADES).

In 1968, Jesuit General Arrupe asked Bigo to plan the creation of a special institute dedicated to the study of "the Indian problem" in Latin America. Bolivia, Ecuador, and Peru were each chosen as sites for study, and a meeting was held in Cuzco in December, 1968, to discuss implementation. The meeting was held in Cuzco because the Jesuit Archbishop of Cuzco, Bishop Durand, had already founded a similar organization there, and the CIAS staff experts did not want to go out of their way to alienate local line officers.

All CLACIAS members met with the top Jesuit line officials (the provincial superiors) and the General in Rio de Janeiro in May, 1968. They were responsible for policy decisions that anticipated those made by the Latin American Bishops' Conference meeting in Medellin three months later.

The CLACIAS document to which we have been referring ended with a quotation from the internal discussions of the provincial superiors in Rio: the _informe_ which they sent to CLACIAS head, Pierre

Bigo. The report is interesting because it envi-
sions the CIAS structure as functioning to <u>control</u>
rather than to stimulate staff initiatives. It
seeks to incorporate into an official, malleable
organization the diverse and potentially disruptive
tendencies of independence-minded specialists. The
conclusion of the <u>informe</u> reads as follows:

> The principal difficulty with
> CIAS is the following: Jesuits have
> been trained as specialists in uni-
> versities of the United States and
> Europe. When they return to their
> countries, no coherent common proj-
> ect awaits them. They disperse
> into diverse activities, which are
> not always of much value. They be-
> come disheartened. According to
> their temperaments, they yield to
> the attractions of the universities
> or to some social action, seeking
> opportunities which CIAS does not
> offer. Therefore, many times CIAS
> exists only in name. This is a
> history that could be illustrated
> by many examples.

This observation reveals the problems of line
authority in controlling staff autonomy. The typical solution, as we saw in the discussion of CELAM
(Chapter 3), is the attempt to construct an umbrella
organization to coordinate and control staff initia-
tive--to bureaucratize in order to limit functional
autonomy. Although this is the manifest function
of bureaucratization, with respect to the Latin
Catholic line organization the latent consequences
have frequently been unexpected and undesirable.

Staff organizations, once constituted, have a
way of escaping line control. They first seek to
free themselves from the jurisdiction of local
lower-line officials. Staff officers move into
residences not governed by the ordinary line
"rector" or "superior." They form teaching

institutes whose norms are not set or students
chosen by Catholic university deans. Staff officials may eventually come to carry more clout in
internal Church decision-making and in external
political matters than do even the top-ranked line
superiors (as we will see in the chapters on Colombia and Chile).

The horizontal linkages between staff officials
are much more flexible and durable than those among
line officers. Interstaff linkages are based upon
mutual interests of the most specific type imagin-
able--concrete fundable projects of intercontinental
import. Whereas the staff priest of CIAS is accustomed to living and traveling in other countries,
speaks fluent English and other languages, and depends for his career success on his ability to "make
contacts" with secular sources, the line official
is absorbed with the problems of his province or
diocese. The Jesuit "provincial" superior is by
definition not a cosmopolitan actor. As will be
evidenced later, these officials are not accustomed
to international cooperation and depend upon vertical linkages, notably the linkage of command from
Rome, to furnish whatever mutuality they enjoy.

FERES, CIAS, CELAM, AND DESAL

The rise of staff organizations within the
Church, however, created common problems for most
local line officials, whether Jesuit provincials or
Catholic bishops. The 1960's witnessed the growing
alarm among line officers who were discovering that
newly autonomous staff units might conceive of such
"problems" as Communism, Protestantism, and dictatorship in quite novel terms.

It was then that attempts were made from above,
that is, from the line, to control, or "coordinate,"
autonomous staff units. Either an international
board of Cardinals and bishops (in the case of
CELAM) or the General (in the case of the Jesuits)
attempted to impose broad controls and a hand-
picked coordinator upon the disparate staff groups.

This action has sometimes been taken to eliminate
competition among staff centers that threatened to
wreak irreparable damage upon the church system as
a whole by alienating sources of financial and other
aid.

The document "Coordination of Social Action and
Investigation in Latin America" illustrates this type
of attempted "coordination." Written for the internal
use of the organizations involved, the document derives from conversations held in Buenos Aires in
1962 between Father Sily, Father Poblete, Father
Houtart, and Father Velazquez. It attempts to
specify the areas of control to be granted the following competing staff units:

1. FERES (Houtart's International Federation
of Institutes for Socio-Religious and Social Investigation), advised by Poblete.

2. CIAS (Jesuit Center for Research and Social
Action), headed by Sily, Poblete, and others.

3. CELAM (the staff committees of the Latin
American Bishops' Conference), advised by Poblete,
headed by Velasquez.

4. DESAL (the Jesuit Center for the Economic
and Social Development of Latin America), headed by
Belgian Jesuit Roger Vekemans, based in Santiago.

In terms of the present analysis, it is of the
utmost interest that Jesuit Father Renato Poblete
occupied positions of official control on three of
these staff boards. He also worked closely with
Vekemans and was therefore in a position to represent the interests of the fourth staff unit, DESAL.
Poblete was thus a crucial linkage connecting all
four of the competing staff units.

In the early 1960's, the competition between
these staff units was potentially destructive of
the entire Latin American Catholic hierarchical
system, since the latter was heavily dependent upon

infusion of resources from North America and Western
Europe that would pass through some sort of staff-
screening mechanism.

(The chapters on Chile will outline points of
contention between DESAL and the other groups. We
have already seen how DESAL is regarded by the
Cardinal of Santiago as an interloper, and how CELAM
was created to cope with the until then unregulated
scramble for resources. The chapters on Colombia
will describe the bitter conflict between the
Colombian CIAS and the local FERES affiliate.)

In 1962, the representatives of the four groups
met in Buenos Aires and attempted to agree upon a
delimitation of their respective spheres of influence and their degrees of autonomy and interdependence. In the document "Coordination of Social
Action and Investigation in Latin America," each
of the staff units was given rights over a specific
area, not of geography but of "thought and action":

> One has to distinguish four
> fields of thought and action: so-
> ciological investigation, doctrinal
> thought and investigation, the es-
> tablishment of concrete models of
> social action, and social action.

Although these "four fields" might not seem
conceptually discrete, they did describe the different styles of operation that pertained to the
four staff units. "Sociological investigation"
referred to the types of statistical surveys for
which FERES was equipped. "Social doctrine" appealed to the CIAS Jesuits, who possessed neither
the equipment nor the training for FERES-type projects. DESAL, which was functioning as a clearing-
house for MISEREOR projects, was to elaborate
models for development projects.

CELAM was left with what amounted to a re-
sidual category: "social action." CELAM benefited
from the ambiguous character of the concept yet

was given no direct control over the other three
staff units. CELAM, it must be remembered, is the
official staff organization of the Latin American
bishops. The other three organizations were
created independently of CELAM; they were not opposed by CELAM, it is true, but they were outside
its direct control.

Formally, the three staff organizations--CIAS,
FERES, and DESAL--are only indirectly subject to
the bishops (who have theoretical veto power over
operations within their dioceses). FERES is an
international federation of independent research
groups, itself independently financed by Belgian,
Spanish, French, and other monies. CIAS is a
Jesuit institution, responsible to a secretariat
in Rome. DESAL is technically a private corporation with far-reaching influence and dispersed
sources of support. Its founder and chief is a
Jesuit, but his autonomy from the Church hierarchies is evident from the outcome of the contro-
versies in which he has often been embroiled.

It is clear from the 1962 document that at
the time at which it was written all four staff organizations were conceived by their principals as
complementary yet autonomous. In seeking financial
support, in undertaking investigations, in publishing reports and studies, in advising decision-
makers, and in creating action projects, each entity was conceived to be specialized enough to escape
interference from the others.

Unfortunately, the arbitrary differentiation
of "investigation," "ideology," "planning," and
"implementation" is not isomorphic with the cleavages of interests and demands that obtained in the
Latin America of the 1960's. It soon became evident that CELAM would not leave the development of
ideology exclusively to CIAS, that CELAM and CIAS
would not permit FERES to monopolize research
monies for sociological investigation, and that all
three would become uneasy in the face of the incredible growth and power of DESAL.

DESAL took the initiative in outlining priorities; from the outset, it conceived itself as a
planning agency that would set the rules and the
objectives for sociological investigator, ideologist,
and social engineer. It supplied the Buenos Aires
assembly with a list of "some examples of models
that are needed with urgency," which included any
possible project to be undertaken by CIAS, CELAM,
and FERES. With its millions of dollars from
MISEREOR and from the Belgian and West German governments, DESAL was able to research its own projects, develop its own brand of "social doctrine of
the Church," and implement its ideas--all without
either the cooperation, much less the specific
authorization, of any staff or line group within the
Latin American Church. FERES and CIAS affiliates
were left to fight for the crumbs of subsidiary
sources of support. CELAM contented itself with
issuing directives for action and organizing the
Eucharistic Congress of Bishops and Pope in Bogota.
These contentions will be spelled out at length
below. For the present, it is necessary to turn to
an analysis of the changes within CLACIAS, the coordinating agency for the various Jesuit CIAS groups.

THE BIGO PLAN

The meeting of Jesuit CLACIAS coordinators in
Rio in May, 1968, reversed the optimistic policies
of CIAS, FERES, CELAM, and DESAL representatives in
Buenos Aires in 1962. The six intervening years
had seen reason enough for pooling manpower and
money and for setting firmer controls over Jesuits
involved in research and social action.

Before the 1968 meeting, attempts had been
made to redefine the objectives of the CIAS organizations, prior to "coordinating" them. As the
general coordinator appointed by the Jesuit Father
General, the French Jesuit Pierre Bigo called a
meeting of CIAS heads in 1967 to set policy and to
specify objectives. A paper delivered by Bigo, entitled "Objectives of CIAS," comprised the point of
departure for a prolonged discussion.

Bigo emphasized the necessity of integrating
all CIAS units into a single ideological "line,"
suppressing differences, emphasizing "coordination"
and a "united front." He proposed the formulation
and dissemination of a "global conception of development," the formation, orientation, and coordination of lay Catholics, and the parallel orientation
of Jesuits, clergy, and Catholic social movements.
The following is a translation from Bigo's paper:

> Two types of criticism (to these
> proposals of mine) seem inevitable.
> Some people are going to say that
> they are not scientific--that scien-
> tists should not get mixed up in con-
> flicts of interest. They should keep
> themselves free of any commitment to
> concrete movements.

Bigo disposed of this criticism by saying that
the needs of Catholic movements were too great to
ignore. He cited Camilo Torres in Colombia as an
example of radical elements moving into the vacuum
created when moderate churchmen refused to commit
themselves to specific groups. (The threat that
Camilo Torres posed to CIAS leadership of labor
unions will be examined in Chapter 6.)

Bigo went on to say:

> We must not forget the value of
> these action movements. The leaders
> themselves need and ask for orienta-
> tion during the tremendous crises
> their countries experience, during
> such countermovements as that of
> Camilo Torres, for example. . . .
> What we lack are not principles
> but formulations: in the fields of
> planning, of economic policy, of the
> structure of industry, of political
> reform, of birth control, etc. What
> we need is what Marxism has: a glob-
> al conception of change.

Only then, Bigo explained, could the Jesuit
CIAS groups be effective. He reminded his colleagues that they had as yet been unable to publish
a common reader on development, a failure he attributed to a lack of consensus within the CIAS "family." Bigo underlined the importance of the task:

> In Chile now there is a book by
> Father Emilio Silva [a diocesan
> priest not a Jesuit] which is, from
> the doctrinal point of view, very
> questionable. But it exists. And
> because it exists, everyone refers
> to it. Why can't we Jesuits, not
> all the Jesuits, but the competent
> ones--those with ILADES [a Chilean
> CIAS subsidiary], those with social
> movements, etc., why can't we do
> something like this?

There followed a long discussion on the legitimate demands a CIAS unit might make on the scarce
resources of the Jesuit order and, reciprocally,
the demands that might be made on the autonomy of
the unit and its members by the order.

A Peruvian Jesuit (unidentified) warned of
competition from other groups within the Jesuits
that would seek the same privileges and resources
accorded CIAS. He cited especially the instance of
Jesuits operative in the mass media. If the CIAS
groups were to be given special facilities and ex-
emption from line control, the Jesuit editors and
writers, for example, would demand the same.

The Chilean Centro Bellarmino was proffered as
a possible solution to this problem--the rewriters
and other free-lancers who would otherwise have
been left to compete had been absorbed into the
CIAS team. (As we shall see later, the Centro
Bellarmino was eventually torn apart by the tensions inherent in their type of "solution"; even at
the time of the CLACIAS meeting, the harmony of the
Chilean Center was more apparent than real).

Linkages between staff decision-makers and
media technicians, writers, editors, and such were
deemed crucial. To survive, CIAS depended upon the
approbation of higher line superiors. This would
be forthcoming as long as the latter were convinced
that CIAS experts were getting good results in whatever activity had been defined as of crucial concern. The cooperation of Jesuit journalists and
magazine editors would be of critical importance,
since adverse publicity in Jesuit organs would
jeopardize any Jesuit project. The CIAS unit, if
separated from the means of communication with a
larger public, not only lacks the opportunity to extend its influence and to manifest its "global conception" of social change but also finds itself
competing for legitimation of its basic purpose.
For a Jesuit, membership in the order need not necessarily include legitimation of all of his activities, nor even of those activities carried out within an officially approved sub-unit of the order.
In any system, sub-units often take on goals and
purposes of their own that are at variance with the
official goals of the organization.

The problem of competing or conflicting loyalties was brought into the open by Father Roger
Vekemans, the head of DESAL and member of Chilean
CIAS. Vekemans cited the instance of role conflict
when one is a member of many different groups within
the Jesuit order. (Vekemans' special difficulties
in this regard will be examined below.) The proliferation of staff structures within the Jesuit order
was severely hampering the efforts of Bigo and of
higher line officials to "coordinate" or to impose
a common set of interests and a common "global
conception" of reality.

It is interesting that binding together and
coordinating--but not linking--disperse strata
was viewed primarily as a problem of ideology by
Bigo and other officials. Ideologically "global"
or all-encompassing concepts were seen as the nets
by which diverse interest groups might not so much
be "linked" as "corralled." The objective was to

preclude special relationships, nontransferable al-
legiances, and other linkages that might disrupt the
process of achieving consensus.

The CIAS participants sought to guarantee consensus among CIAS members scattered among the many
nations of Latin America by demanding that CIAS membership require full-time participation on the part
of a core of specialized personnel involved in the
elaboration of "doctrine." Mass-media people were
to be channels for disseminating the newly shaped
ideologies; they were to lend form, not content, to
publishing CIAS studies and positions without comment.

The main difficulty with this solution is that
appropriate sanctions could not easily be applied.
In a system fast losing its internal resources--
consensus as well as legitimacy in the wider soci-
ety--it would be difficult to control the behavior
of members who achieved status in secular activities.
The problem was compounded by the fact that it was
individual achievement and not communal effort that
found rewards outside Catholic circles.

Father Hernan Larrain, the Chilean Jesuit editor of Mensaje, placed the blame for individualism
and rivalry between Jesuits upon the system of
socialization employed by the order.

> I have noticed allusions here,
> and I think they are correct, to the
> individualistic nature of our forma-
> tion. . . . We are all of us here
> the victims of this individualism.
> We have become accustomed to work
> alone and to converse together only
> in banalities, never in depth. So
> it has easily come about that there
> are definite rivalries and competi-
> tion established between us.

Nevertheless, Larrain made it clear that he
could not accept any "line" or "global conception"
imposed from above.

> A work group is not an instrument
> for suppressing dissent. It cannot
> pretend to arrive at a consensus with-
> out dialogue, which presupposes dif-
> ferent points of view expressed with
> spontaneity.

Larrain went on to discuss the competing loyalties to the Church and to the Jesuit order.

> Evidently we must be open to the
> Church and to our fundamental duty.
> We cannot become hermits living only
> within the Jesuit order, but neither
> can we depreciate the importance of
> the order. We must be open to the
> Church, but it is as Jesuits that we
> are open to it. . . . Therefore, we
> are a group of individualists, a
> group of priests, a group of Jesuits,
> and finally a group of specialists.

This outline of the multiple roles filled by
each CIAS member--linked as he is to different
groups, himself a linkage to all of them--identifies
the staff specialist as a source of strain within
the Catholic system. Insofar as the individual not
only orients his own behavior to different reference
groups but also formally links these different
groups, he becomes the focal point of conflict within the system.

(The 1968 CLACIAS meeting in Rio did not discuss specific conflicts of interest reflected in
the activity of Jesuit experts. These cases were
discussed at a meeting held several months earlier
and attended by, among others, members of Chilean
CIAS, headed by Larrain, and members of Colombian
CIAS, headed by Father Vicente Andrade. The meeting
was a confrontation between two nationalistic teams
of priests. Although the Jesuits were expected to
orient their activities and beliefs to the international needs of the Catholic Church, they belonged
to national units of that Church and clearly

identified with the national Church and order. The
confrontation was the culmination of a long-standing
conflict that had seen one Chilean Jesuit expelled
from Colombia at the insistence of Father Andrade.
The history of this affair will be discussed in
Chapter 8.)

The CLACIAS meeting terminated with the major
issues unresolved: What degree of autonomy should
the CIAS unit possess? What degree of autonomy
should its individual members have? Both problems
were urgent. As Father Sily, the new regional
coordinator for Argentina, asked,

> What do I, as a member of CIAS,
> do in the middle of an interview when
> I am asked to discuss a controversial
> issue such as land reform, reform of
> big business, etc.? Do I express my-
> self as an individual, or as a member
> of CIAS?

The answer, Sily suggested, depended upon
whether there was a willingness of the whole CIAS
group to take responsibility for backing the positions of their members. But the difficulty noted
by Roger Vekemans was not confronted: that the
individual staff expert might be a member of many
different groups, each with a different social base
and different, perhaps even conflicting, norms.

In the meantime, the General and his advisors
in Rome had decided that the achieving of consensus
could best be effected through a "scientific survey"
of the "works of the Society of Jesus." CIAS groups
throughout the world were given the task of describing national economic, political, and educational
needs and of assessing the resources of the Jesuit
order for helping to meet those needs. Priorities
would then be set up "scientifically" and policies
fitted to the priorities. Presumably this joint
effort, focused upon national units, would shore up
sagging morale and provide comprehensive policies
around which disparate Jesuit forces might reach a

consensus. (As we shall see, the Chilean phase of
this program eventually fragmented the Chilean Centro Bellarmino.)

At the same time, some of the same actors were
engaged in research under the auspices of the International Federation of Institutes for Socio-
Religious and Social Research (FERES), the Brussels-
based research federation headed by Father Francois
Houtart. FERES did not seek to develop a "global
conception" of change but, in keeping with the decision made in Buenos Aires in 1962, accepted its
role as that of sociological investigator. Nevertheless, its Colombian affiliate ran afoul of Colombian CIAS during the Camilo Torres affair. FERES
director for Latin America Gustavo Perez also collided with Roger Vekemans of DESAL over issues that
will be spelled out below. Finally, at the CELAM
meeting of Latin American bishops in Medellin in
August, 1968, FERES directors Perez and Houtart
were excluded from the deliberations. This maneuver
was engineered by Colombian CIAS director Vicente
Andrade, S. J., through the Archbishop of Bogota.

By the end of 1968, FERES had conducted more
than twenty statistical censuses of the Latin American Church, as well as attitude surveys in four
Latin American countries on the subject of birth
control. Its contacts with North American foundations and with the Agency for International Development were continuing strong. Two CIAS members
were also affiliates of FERES during this period:
Father Renato Poblete of CIAS in Santiago, and
Father Albert Sily of Argentine CIAS. The Jesuit
concept of full-time CIAS specialists could not
compete with FERES organization and contacts with
sources of research funds.

CELAM, the fourth member of the 1962 staff
conference in Buenos Aires, prepared for a meeting
of all Latin American bishops and their advisors
set for August, 1968, in Medellin, Colombia. The
bishops were expected to discuss not only matters

of internal ecclesiastical concern, such as the
training and autonomy of priests, but also matters
of economic development and violent revolution.
Pope Paul VI was to be present to open the conference; he would be the first Pope ever to visit
Latin America.

6

FRAGMENTATION
OF LINE AND STAFF:
MEDELLIN
1968

THE WORKING DOCUMENT FOR
THE BISHOPS' CONFERENCE

Two months prior to the Medellin meeting, a
"working document" for the conference was released
to the press. This document, officially commissioned by CELAM, had been drawn up by the Brazilian
bishops and their advisors. (It will be remembered
that the president of CELAM is Brazilian Bishop
Avelar Brandao.) The document was published throughout Latin America by the secular press on the morn-
ing of July 16, 1968. The immediate reaction of
many of the Latin American bishops who had not previously read it--chief among these, the Colombians--
was tumultuous.

The working document was the first official
Latin American Church document ever to call for an
explicit condemnation of U.S. "imperialism," under-
lining the economic "dependence" of developing countries upon the more developed.

Violence as an instrument of social change was
given a new theological legitimation. The existing
social structures of many Latin countries were
judged to be already "violent" in terms of permanent patterns of exploitation. The traditional
Catholic condemnation of force was to be shifted

from condemning the rebel to a condemnation of the
"overlord."

The following are quotations from the working
document as it appeared in the Bogota daily El Espectador, on July 16, 1968 (translated from the
Spanish):

> In Latin America per capita in-
> come barely reaches $300. This
> equals one-third of what obtains in
> Europe and one-seventh of the North
> American per capita income. In re-
> cent years the majority of Latin
> American countries have had a rate
> of economic growth very much lower
> than that programmed by the so-called
> Alliance for Progress.

After listing the pressures of demographic
growth and the failures of Latin American agriculture, the document proceeded to a condemnation of
the Latin American class system. In describing the
political systems of Latin American countries, the
document maintained that:

> There is a lack of correspondence
> between the political systems and the
> growing needs of integration. Our
> political systems have been copied
> from the Europeans and imposed upon a
> very different reality. Latin Ameri-
> can politics continues to be depen-
> dent upon the great world powers.

The political system was held to lack representation and legitimacy.

> We live in a democracy more for-
> mal that actual. . . . The politi-
> cal systems in Latin America are
> characterized by distinct forms of
> oligarchy. The lack of intermediary
> groups to facilitate participation

in national life, the lack of unions,
university, and <u>campesino</u> organizations enable small groups to govern
without check.

In summary, the document outlines a "revolutionary situation" in which the "temptation to violence" was "very real."

> It is undeniable that the Contin-
> ent, in many areas, finds itself in a
> revolutionary situation. . . . We
> need not be surprised that changes
> are proposed in terms of violence,
> because the situations above de-
> scribed are already violence since
> they contradict the dignity of man
> and oppress freedom. One must in-
> stead be surprised at the patience
> of a people which has supported for
> years a condition scarcely acceptable
> by those who have had a full awareness
> of human rights.

In Catholic theological terms, the document
concludes, a state of tyranny exists. If changes
cannot be brought about by legal means, violence
is permissible.

> The lack of technical development,
> the oligarchical classes, the great
> foreign capitalist systems: all are
> obstacles to the necessary changes
> and offer an active resistance to
> whatever threatens their interests
> and create, therefore, a situation
> of violence. . . .
> But the alternative is not be-
> tween the "status quo" and change:
> it is instead between the peaceful
> way and the violent way.

This section on the Latin American "reality"
is supplemented by an analysis of the religious

situation, the difficulties of prosyletization, and
the low level of religious practice. This is followed by a criticism of the Church, which has not
shown itself "sufficiently concerned" with social
development. It has not been "prophetic" enough,
in Old Testament terminology; it has failed to denounce injustice with the frequency and vigor required. It has not adequately served the marginal
urban populations. Its priests do not speak the
language of the young, in a continent where 40 per
cent of the population is under fifteen years of
age. Finally, the Church is identified in the eyes
of many with political power and power holders.
The special privileges enjoyed by the clergy have
contributed to this image.

The second section of the working document
consisted of an extended theological treatise linking the salvation of man to economic and social development. The document maintained that the spiritual and temporal were inextricably bound, that the
Christian's duty was to work in the world for worldly development. The final section of the document
urged the Church as a whole to identify via concrete "pastoral projects" with the poor and the
young.

Except for the Brazilian and Chilean hierarchies, the reaction of the bishops to the working
document prepared by the CELAM staff was highly
critical. But although many bishops, as well as
the Vatican itself, sent private critiques, only
the Colombians publicly repudiated the document,
offering one of their own in substitution.

On July 25, the Colombian Jesuit Miguel Angel
Gonzalez, the chief advisor of the Colombian CIAS,
published a critique of the working document in El
Espectador. Father Gonzalez reserved his most bitter blasts for the "experts of CELAM," especially
the "French and the Dutch," who, he insisted, had
written the document. His words afford a glimpse
of inter-staff tensions within the Church, which
will be expanded in subsequent chapters.

> The document of the "experts of
> CELAM" complains that the crumbs of
> bread on the table of the Latin Amer-
> ican people are too small, but says
> nothing about how more bread is to
> be provided. . . . The experts of
> CELAM, especially the Dutch and the
> French, well know that in their own
> countries the recovery made after
> World War II was made because of the
> work, organization, and capital in-
> vestment of private industry, in
> large part with foreign help.
>
> The document is distressed by
> political and economic colonialism
> in Latin America, but it doesn't
> speak of a certain religious colonial-
> ism that supports certain foreign ex-
> perts who do not understand even the
> epidermis of the continent. The myth
> of revolution, which they reject for
> their own countries--as in the recent
> events in France--serves as a refuge
> for their utopic thought, and becomes
> the mysterious unforeseen instrument
> for realizing the ideal. . . .

Father Gonzalez stated that "if the Latin
American bishops accept the contention that the
Latin American situation is already one of _insti-
tutionalized_ violence, then revolution in the form
of _guerrillas_ or whatever is justified." In Colombia, especially, such justification would belie the
condemnation of Camilo Torres made by Colombian
bishops in 1965. (See Chapter 9.)

As will be evident later on, the Colombians
are isolates within the Latin American Church, enjoying unique linkages with the national state that
sensitize them even to theoretical discussions of
action against established powers. Linkages between the Colombian episcopate and other churchmen
who are also closely implicated with Western governments are strong. The public reaction of the

Colombian Jesuit, Gonzalez, was supported privately
by Archbishop Munoz Duque of Bogota and most of the
other Colombian prelates.

There were many confidential criticisms of the
CELAM working document. The major episcopal conferences and the Vatican congregations all sent private
appraisals to CELAM. A private CELAM document, issued to its preparatory commission for the Medellin
conference, lists all of the private appraisals in
summary form:

> The Roman Congregations (of the
> Vatican) found the section of the
> working document on "Latin American
> Reality" too long. They observed
> that the section was "fairly close
> to reality," but that it tended to
> "reduce the explanation of every-
> thing, religion included, to socio-
> economic causes." They pointed out
> that the document lacked mention of
> Marxist activity on the continent,
> and they provided a summary of such
> activity, replete with statistics,
> which might be included in the re-
> vised document. They considered the
> entire first section to be "too
> pessimistic." They also objected to
> the criticisms of the Church made at
> the end of the chapter.

It is a measure of the relatively high autonomy of the CELAM organization vis-à-vis the Vatican
that none of the above criticisms was acted upon.
The criticisms were received before the preparatory
commission of CELAM met on June 2-8, 1968; they were
read and then filed. The working document was released to the press on July 16, substantially unchanged. No section on Marxism was added, the
pessimistic tone was not eliminated, the emphasis
upon the socio-economic was maintained.

(The tremendous weakness of linkages between
Rome and the Latin American Catholic line system is
evidenced by the impunity with which Latin Catholic
bishops may disregard Vatican decrees. The sanctions that the Vatican can safely employ are few in
practice. The inputs into the Latin Catholic system that the Vatican can withdraw are almost non-
existent: a papal visit is one of the few valuable
inputs the Vatican has at its disposal. As has
been clear in the case of the Dutch bishops, the
Vatican will not resort to excommunication or inter-
dict, the withdrawal of sacral legitimacy, even
when its policies are directly and explicitly attacked. In fact, it is powerless to stop the activity.)

In more detail, here are some of the further
criticisms of the Roman Congregations (translated
from the Spanish original):

> The Congregation for Bishops
> found the first part simply "too
> long." . . . The Congregation for
> the Clergy found the first part too
> "reductionist" and "lacking a treat-
> ment of the Marxist presence and its
> danger." The Congregation for the
> Doctrine of the Faith found nothing
> heretical but also criticized the
> document for excessive concern with
> the temporal and not enough for the
> "eschatalogical." The Congregation
> for the Clergy also insisted in its
> commentary on the second and third
> parts of the working document that
> "the mission of the Church would be
> more pure and authentic insofar as
> it made social action a necessary
> condition for the spread of the Gos-
> pel" (rather than an end in itself).
> It mentioned especially the need for
> a "competition with Marxism for the
> attention of the people, especially
> for the attention of workers and uni-
> versity students."

The Congregation for Catholic
Teaching faulted the working document in all of its sections for failing to refer to the "social doctrine
of the Church, except for references
to the Second Vatican Council and to
Progress of Peoples (Pope Paul's encyclical which incorporated progressive concepts of the French Dominican
liberal Lebret)." The congregation
also criticized what it called "an
underestimation of the supernatural,
a tone of discontent and a lack of
confidence in the Church." It warned
that "structural changes in the Church
that would follow from this posture
could well deprive the Church of its
means of influence."

The Pontifical Commission for
Social Communication called for "an
explicit reference to means of communication, insisting on the right
of the Church to use them and advo-
cating more effort towards penetrating existing means of communication than in creating ecclesiastical organs which were generally in-
adequate." The Commission urged the
inclusion of the presidents of OICC
(The International Catholic Office
of Motion Pictures) and of UNDA (The
International Catholic Association
of Radio and Television) in the
Medellin Conference of Bishops.

It would be a mistake, however, to assume that
the Vatican was the only source of negative feedback. Various national episcopal conferences also
found fault with the CELAM working document. Their
criticisms, also compiled by the CELAM preparatory
committee, reveal that the working document was
"pushed through" unaltered by Bishop Brandao, supported by Bishop Marc McGrath of Panama and Chilean
Cardinal Silva. Although Silva was later to withdraw

active support from this troika, he did nothing actively to impede its operations. The other Brazilian
bishops, especially Dom Helder de Camara, Candido
Padin, and Eugenio Araujo Sales, supported Brandao
and ensured that the working document, written in
large part by priest experts close to the Brazilians
(who were indeed French and Dutch, as affirmed by
Gonzales) would remain intact.

Quoting again from the confidential CELAM document summarizing the reactions of the bishops who
headed the national episcopal conferences:

> The Argentine conference accepted
> the working document as a base of dis-
> cussion, although pointing out the
> need for more "balance."
> The Cuban bishops emphasized the
> importance of the race problem in
> Latin America. They suggested criti-
> cism of the racial discrimination they
> said exists in the Church. They also
> criticized what they called the "mer-
> cantilist" orientation, which they
> said characterized the educational
> mission of the Church, the lack of
> planning in the allocation of Church
> resources, the ideological dependency
> of the Latin American Church upon for-
> eign countries, and the absence of a
> message that would commit the Church
> concretely to development.
> The Ecuadorian conference of bish-
> ops said that the working document de-
> scribed economic and social conditions
> of the past and not of the present.
> It criticized the document for treat-
> ing mainly socio-economic problems,
> ignoring the religious problems of
> recruitment to the priesthood, train-
> ing of priests and lay apostles,
> problems of schooling, etc. "It
> undervalues the natural religiosity
> of our peoples." It warned of

confusing "the serious economic, social and ethical questions of the
demographic situation with the mate-
rialistic oversimplifications of the
advocates of birth control." Finally, said the Ecuadorian conference,
"the prophetic function is not to
simply 'denounce injustice' but to
educate in the Faith." They said
that "to respect the autonomy of the
layman" the Church must denounce only
"absolute evil," keeping silent about
situations that contained both good
and bad factors.

The Peruvian conference of bishops advised "deepening the study of
the family to understand better the
influence of the economic factor upon
the demographic problem."

The bishops of Santo Domingo emphasized the need of economic planning, of the economic situation of
business enterprises, of the need to
establish base organizations of workers, associations of businessmen,
neighborhood groups, campesino leagues.

In making these remarks, the Santo Domingo conference echoed many of the fundamental preoccupations
of DESAL planners. DESAL, as will be shown in the
chapters on Chile, has had an important role in
planning Church activity in Santo Domingo, especially after the American intervention of 1965.

The bishops of Santo Domingo
also emphasized the need for cor-
recting the document's "lamentable
lack of vision of the importance of
means of communication."

The Venezuelan conference labeled
the document's description of "Latin
American Reality" as "too negative"
and "at times, unjust." The Church,
they said, "should recognize the

efforts of certain governments and
international agencies and encourage
them." It also objected to the document's statement that in Latin America the military budget exceeds the
educational budget in most countries.
"It is not true," said the Venezuelan
bishops, "that the Church has not condemned injustice nor inspired necessary changes in the society." There
have been "many Church documents in
the past thirty years" fulfilling
this function. The bishops also
criticized "ideas imported from European magazines" which "do not sufficiently appreciate the values of our
popular Christianity." The bishops
denied that secularization was as
great a problem in Latin America as
in Europe and the United States.
They also objected to the treatment
of the Catholic Church in respect to
Protestantism and maintained that it
was "unjust to place all the blame
on the Catholics." Besides, they
said, "the real problems of ecumenism
are not found in Latin America."

The Colombian bishops restricted
their comments to the simple statement that the working document was
"pessimistic and negative."

The main efforts of the Colombians were saved for
the Medellin discussions. When the Colombians
failed to shape events at Medellin, they published
their own conclusions separately in the secular
press, voicing disapproval of the conclusions
reached by the majority of bishops at Medellin.

In addition to the appraisals of the national
episcopal conferences--the Brazilian and Chilean
bishops did not submit critiques, since they had
exercised considerable influence upon the original
document--various Latin American bishops who were

not in agreement with the appraisals of the national
conferences wrote their own separate reports. A
group of Argentine bishops and priest-advisors
called for support of national popular movements
which pressured for change.

The CELAM summary includes the following critiques:

> Bishop Proano of Ecuador suggested
> that positive factors be accentuated
> in discussions of Latin American de-
> velopment. He also urged more thorough
> discussion of the problems of religious
> pluralism and especially of the "pros-
> elytizing presence" of Protestantism
> and Marxism. His third recommendation
> was for a clearer demonstration that
> Latin American living conditions were
> so terrible that they "impede the de-
> velopment of the human person." Fi-
> nally, he called for a fuller treat-
> ment of the "marginality" of rural
> and urban masses.
> Bishop McGrath of Panama re-
> stricted his suggestions to a call
> for greater clarity in the use of
> the term "Church," differentiating
> the hierarchy from the action of the
> Church as a community of believers.
> He also insisted upon a treatment of
> the "crisis" of the priest in Latin
> America, since priests were leaving
> their ministry in significant numbers
> and no ready replacements could be
> found.

The Vatican had been concerned from the outset
that the Medellin meeting might result in an un-
precedented measure of autonomy for the Latin American bishops involved. For this reason, Cardinal
Antonio Zamore, the Italian in charge of the Papal
Commission for Latin America, was to co-preside
over the formal meetings in Medellin. He would

share the dais with a stanch conservative, Cardinal
Juan Landazuri Henriquez of Lima, and with Brazilian
Bishop Brandao who, as president of CELAM, would
share ex officio in the presidency.

Brandao had presided over the preparatory meeting prior to Medellin without the accompaniment of
the above two Cardinals, who outranked him. With
him at the preparatory meeting in June, 1968, were
Marcos McGrath and Pablo Munoz Vega, both strong
supporters of CELAM and both identified, since the
Vatican Council, with efforts to "decentralize" the
Church. It was at this preparatory meeting that
the working document was presented by the Brazilians
with the support of the Chilean Cardinal Silva.

As we have seen, the Vatican's initial reaction
to the working document was highly critical. A special annex to the official report of the Vatican
Roman Congregations referred to the working document
as the "Document Elaborated by a Group of Secretaries." This pejorative allusion to the staff of
CELAM, without mention of episcopal sponsorship, enabled the Vatican to attack the working document
directly without explicitly slighting the dignity
of the Latin American presiding bishops.

Vatican Cardinal Zamore called for a "fundamental reformulation" of the working document. In
a memo containing twenty-three directives, each
couched in the imperative, Zamore outlined his revi-
sions. He demanded that the document "clearly express that the Medellin conference of bishops was
called by the Latin American bishops themselves,
and not at the request of the Holy See." He ordered that quotations from the speeches of Pope Paul
be inserted into the document "to enrich it." He
insisted that specific secular governments be "com-
mended for their social accomplishments and plans"
and that "ideological as well as physical violence
be condemned so that charity may be maintained in
word as well as in action." He emphasized that
"in all situations, the main problem is the crisis
of the youth in all areas who can be characterized

as having lost confidence in the ruling generation."
He reminded the Latin American bishops that there
was "an enormous world that escaped their ken"--a
world which, presumably, only the Vatican could examine whole. Finally, he directed that references
to "indigenous" peoples, a potentially inflammatory
designation, be replaced by the more neutral "plurality of cultures," or "ethnic pluralism."

Zamore's demands were to be considered at the
full meeting of bishops at Medellin in August. However, the history of the working document shows that
Zamore's twenty-three points were never implemented.
The working document was not fundamentally changed,
and not even the final pronouncements of the Latin
bishops bore the mark of Zamore's memorandum.

The chain of events leading up to the August
meeting of Latin American Bishops in Medellin, Colombia, was, then, the following: The Brazilians, who
controlled the CELAM apparatus, wrote a proposed
"working document" that explicitly defined the
"Latin American reality" as one of institutionalized
violence, a state of "tyranny" maintained from within by national oligarchies and from without by "imperialism." In such circumstances the Thomistic
doctrine of justifiable revolution could be invoked.
The working document did not mention Marxism. It
did affirm that if peaceful change was not forthcoming, violent change was necessary. It identified
Christian commitment in theological terms with commitment to socio-economic change instead of merely
to personal spiritual conversion.

As the preparatory conference met to discuss
the working document, the Brazilians found tacit
support from the Chilean hierarchy and from Bishop
McGrath of Panama, each of whom may have thought
his own country to be exempt from the threat of
revolution.

The other episcopal hierarchies, especially
that of Venezuela and that of Colombia, differed
sharply with the working document and expressed

their official decisions in private critiques sent
to CELAM.

Within the episcopal conferences, however,
there were many bishops who (like the Argentines)
were not truly represented by the official position
of the national conference because the latter tended
to reflect the views of the Archbishop or Cardinal
of the capital city. These "underrepresented" bishops would later support the working document during
the egalitarian meetings at Medellin.

The Vatican reacted very strongly to the proposed working document, but was not represented at
the preparatory meeting and so could not suppress
it. Nevertheless, the Roman Congregations (which
form the bulk of the Vatican bureaucracy) sent negative appraisals to the CELAM presidency before the
preparatory meeting of June, 1968. These appraisals
were not acted upon. The preparatory committee issued the working document, substantially unchanged,
for publication. Contrary to the wishes of the Vatican, the working document was published in the secular press on July 25, 1968.

Cardinal Zamore, the Vatican head of its Commission for Latin America, then sent his list of
twenty-three "observations" to the "secretaries" or
staff members of CELAM to whom he attributed the
"errors" of the working document. His demands were
to be considered by the full meeting of bishops at
Medellin in August.

THE VISIT OF POPE PAUL VI

On July 30, 1968, Pope Paul proclaimed his encyclical Humanae Vitae (Of Human Life), in which he
condemned as immoral all forms of artificial birth
control.

The reaction to this encyclical on the part of
Latin American bishops was mild, to say the least.
No ringing appeals for "enforcement" were heard

from the national episcopal conferences, not even
from the Colombian bishops. On the other hand, no
"examinations" of the encyclical were demanded by
critical bishops (as occurred in Europe). The
Colombians and Venezuelans did not overconform, nor
did the Brazilians become publicly upset. The latter had long condemned birth-control programs sponsored by the North American foundations as "imperial-
istic" and were never prepared to stake progressive
reform of Church doctrine or policies on the issue
of birth control. Several of the more eminent Brazilian progressives, such as Dom Helder de Camara,
have repeatedly stated that Brazil is an underpopu-
lated country--a position that may explain some of
the personal rapport that exists between Dom Helder
and Pope Paul.

The Pope was scheduled to open the meeting of
Latin American Bishops in Medellin on August 24,
1968. Before this, he was to make a triumphal entry into Bogota for the opening of the Eucharistic
Congress.

Amid all the fanfare and confusion of the
Pope's visit to Colombia, one thing was clear: he
had come to Latin America to speak against violent
revolution. The day before he left Italy for his
trip to Bogota, the Pope spoke with reporters at
Castelgondolfo, his summer residence. He here set
the tone of his speeches in South America. Violence was not the answer. Change would come about
through spiritual transformation. (The Pope's remarks have been translated from Spanish-language
newspaper reports.)

It has been said that we will
find (in Latin America) currents of
impatience and rebellion, even among
the clergy and the faithful. We believe that the solution in these sad
situations--very sad, in some places--
does not lie in revolutionary action
nor in the use of force. For us, the
solution is love. . . . This is the

fit moment for Christian love among
men.

In Colombia, the Pope's rejection of violent
revolution was reiterated on three important occasions: in an address to a symbolic representation
of peasants, on the "day celebrating development"
in Bogota, and in his allocution to the Latin American bishops opening their formal meetings scheduled
for Medellin.

To the peasants, the Pope expressed his awareness of their situation in the following terms:

> We are aware of the conditions
> of your existence, conditions of
> misery for many of you, conditions
> which are sometimes below the level
> required for human life. . . . We
> want to be united with your good
> cause, the cause of the lowly, of
> the poor.

But the Pope was unyielding in his insistence upon
peaceful methods:

> Finally, let us exhort you not to
> place your confidence in violence nor
> in revolution; such an attitude is
> contrary to the Christian spirit and
> can also retard the social betterment
> to which you legitimately aspire.

The ironic element in this speech is that it
was delivered not before radical or even desperate
campesinos, but before the leaders of groups affiliated with and assembled by the Jesuit-run rural
unions--the National Agrarian Federation (FANAL).
If there were groups in Colombia prone to the use
of violence or to the creation of revolution, there
is no evidence that they are found within the FANAL,
which was founded precisely to counteract revolutionary tendencies.   (This assertion will be supported by data in Chapter 8.)

In Bogota, during the mass on the "day celebrating development," the Pope addressed himself to
the youth of Latin America, to the workers, and to
the ruling classes, attempting to dramatize the
linkages that Catholic churchmen on the continent
had been trying to forge throughout the 1960's to
replace, or at least to complement, the fused linkages that had long bound the Church to the landown-
ing classes. The Pope urged workers and the young
to protest peacefully, and he asked for greater re-
sponsiveness on the part of the powerful.

> Many, especially among the young,
> insist upon the necessity of urgently
> changing the social structures which,
> according to them, will not permit
> the creation of effective conditions
> of justice for individuals and com-
> munities. Some conclude that the
> essential problem in Latin America
> cannot be resolved except through
> violence. With the same fidelity in
> which we recognize that such theories
> and practices frequently are moti-
> vated by noble impulses for justice
> and solidarity, we must reaffirm that
> violence is not evangelical nor Chris-
> tian; and that sudden or violent
> changes of structures would be false,
> inefficient, and would not correspond
> to the dignity of the people, which
> dignity requires that necessary trans-
> formations be realized from within,
> that is to say, by means of an awaken-
> ing of conscience, an adequate prepa-
> ration and an effective participation
> by all in the realization that ignor-
> ance and conditions of life which are
> sometimes nonhuman impede the attain-
> ment of that dignity.

To the workers, the Pope said:

> Your love should have force--the
> force of numbers, the force of social

dynamism. But not the subversive
force of revolution nor of violence.
Rather the constructive force (which
will build) . . . a new, more human
social order.

To the bishops assembled to discuss the CELAM
working document attacking the established "order"
as one of "institutionalized violence," the Pope said:

It is we ourselves who reaffirm
once again this proposition: not
hate, not violence, but the force of
our love. Among the diverse paths
toward a just social rebirth, we cannot choose atheistic Marxism nor systematic rebellion, nor even less,
anarchy and the shedding of blood.
Let us distinguish our responsibilities from those who make of violence
a noble ideal, a glorious heroism, a
theology. To repair the mistakes of
the past and to cure present infirmi-
ties we do not have to commit new mistakes which would be against the Gos-
pel, against the spirit of the Church,
against the very interests of the
people, against the happy sign of the
present occasion, which is a sign of
justice on the road to brotherhood
and peace.

In place of violence or revolution, the Pope
proposed gradual reform initiated by legitimate governments and financed by the upper classes and by
foreign aid. Speaking to the peasants, the Pope
promised:

We will continue to encourage
the initiatives and programs of the
responsible authorities, of the international organizations, and of
the prosperous countries, in favor
of the developing peoples. We will

exhort all of the Latin American governments and the governments of the
other continents. We will exhort
all of the ruling and upper classes
to continue to initiate with broad
and courageous vision the necessary
reforms that guarantee a more just
and efficient social order, with progressive advantages for the classes
that are today less favored, and with
a more equitable allocation of taxes
to the monied classes. We will also
continue to support financially the
cause of the countries that require
fraternal assistance, so that other
peoples, blessed with greater riches
which are not always well employed,
may be generous in their contributions.

All of these speeches were clearly nonsupport-
ive of the Medellin working document. Whereas the
latter neglected any mention of Marxism, the Pope
was unequivocal in his condemnation of what he considered a dangerous and seductive enemy. Whereas
the working document focused upon institutionalized
violence, the Pope equated violence with revolution.
Whereas the bishops were appealing to the Church
hierarchy and priests to forge linkages with the
aspirations of the workers, peasants, and students,
the Pope appealed to these groups to forge linkages
with the aspirations of the Church. In the mind of
the bishops who would defend the CELAM working document, change of structures could come about only if
the under classes demanded it. In the words of the
Pope, a change of heart, a conversion of the ruling
classes, was the necessary and sufficient condition
of social change. The Pope relied upon altruism
and good faith. The CELAM bishops were beginning
to rely upon political coalition.

Pope Paul departed Bogota after opening the
first session of the CELAM conference, but Vatican
Cardinal Zamore remained at the CELAM and kept in

close contact with Rome. Cardinal Zamore told reporters (see El Tiempo, August 28, 1968) that any
documents issued by the bishops at the conclusion
of their meeting in Medellin would be sent to the
Pope, who would then decide what authority and attention was to be granted them.

MEDELLIN: THE MEETING OF
LATIN AMERICAN BISHOPS

The bishops' conference began with a series of
closed meetings and open press briefings which, from
the outset, centered on the themes of revolution and
class conflict. The Brazilians comprised the largest delegation at the conference, accounting for 38
of the 197 participants. Colombia was next highest,
with 20 representatives. Representation was made on
the basis of number of "baptized" in each respective
national unit.

Bishop Brandao did not attempt to dominate the
conference directly, even though he was president
of CELAM. Instead, he selected Brazilian Bishop
Eugenio de Araujo Sales of Salvador (Bahia) as president of the important Committee on Justice and Peace,
which chose to treat the issues of violent revolution, institutionalized violence, and colonialism.
The Subcommittee on Peace was directed by Bishop
Carlos Parteli, the Archbishop of Montevideo and
president of the Uruguayan Conference of Bishops.
Brandao himself headed a committee to prepare a
"message" to the Latin American peoples. This was
the only committee permitted to publish a document
immediately, without papal approval.

The press conferences were dominated almost
daily by the interventions of Brazilian Bishop Helder
de Camara and Brazilian staff expert Father Afonso
Gregory. Dom Helder early called for an "active nonviolence" with explicit references to Gandhi and to
Martin Luther King. He advocated the Church's obli-
gation to assist the "awakening of the masses" to
their own conditions and, while he admitted that

the Church had no blueprint for development, it had
the duty, he maintained, to denounce injustice wherever it occurred. Dom Helder said that "the masses
are not prepared" for revolution; that they were
only "prepared to be the victims of violence." Further, he warned that a revolution on the continent
would only occasion foreign (United States) intervention (translated from El Tiempo, September 2,
1968):

> Our objective is the integration
> of Latin America, without external
> or internal imperialism. We have no
> desire to simply exchange masters
> (patrones). The United States, Rus-
> sia, China. They are all patrones.

These remarks were made immediately after the
Soviet intervention in Czechoslovakia. Dom Helder
repeated references to the similarity of the Rus-
sian and North American styles of domination. In
this way it was possible to echo the Pope's condemnation of (Soviet) Marxism and still not alienate
the Latin American "left."

Dom Helder has always had an acute sense of
balance and an ability to maintain his linkages to
competing interests. At Medellin he showed himself
quite capable of retaining respectability with the
Catholic left, legitimacy and friendship with Pope
Paul, influence with other Latin American bishops,
and even economic ties with the North Americans
(who support many of his projects in the Northeast
of Brazil and who have financed, through U.S. AID
grants, for example, his staff expert, Father
Afonso Gregory).

Dom Helder's concern at Medellin reflected
that of Dom Eugenio Sales' Committee on Justice and
Peace: it was to create a visible alternative to
violent revolution, defense of the status quo, or
elite-led social reform. In championing a movement
geared toward "active nonviolence," he was able to
take advantage of the respectability of concrete

precedents (linking himself symbolically to the
movements of Gandhi and King) without sacrificing
the blessings of ambiguity. Linkages could be maintained with conflicting groups if the conflicting
groups were not aware of the precise nature of all
the linkages. Presumably, no one could legitimate-
ly object to the growing awareness or "consciousness" of the masses, if this were not explicitly defined as "class consciousness." Dom Helder never
made such an explicit definition, and neither has
he explicitly disavowed one.

An interesting sidelight is the fact that neither Dom Helder, CELAM, nor any other Latin American
Catholic agency had ever publicly denounced the "imperialism" of the U.S. government until meetings of
Latin American and North American Catholic bishops
had broken down over the problem of control of
shared resources. This would seem to lend support
to the theory that economic linkages are dominant;
that when they break down, ideological linkages
atrophy.

In any case, with his new emphasis on U.S. imperialism, Dom Helder was able to reject violent
revolution and still salvage a progressive image,
not only for himself but also for the assembled
bishops at Medellin. Violent revolution would not
"work" against the power of the Yankee colossus to
the North. The Brazilian strategy for forging new
ties with the Latin American young while remaining
in the good graces of Rome was exercised with bril-
liance in Medellin.

One example is a "dialogue" conducted on September 1 between Dom Helder and two hundred young
Colombians. As reported by El Tiempo (September 2,
1968), the prelate made the following assertions:

> I respect all those who, follow-
> ing their conscience, choose vio-
> lence, but I do not respect anybody
> who obliges another to think the
> same as he does. . . . I think that

> at this bishops' conference we are
> going to arrive at valid conclusions
> and will go beyond the mere use of
> words. You understand that we are
> not going to topple governments, but
> that, yes, we must have the courage
> to make demands of the powerful. . . .
>   I know that you do not expect us
> to prepare a war, but you do expect
> courageous positions of nonalignment
> vis-à-vis oligarchies and govern-
> ments. . . . I am not so naive as to
> think that the established powers
> will be moved by the pressure of our
> statements. We need a more effective
> moral pressure.

The "confrontation" ended in a community mass.
Those attending had been reconciled to the position
outlined by Dom Helder for the Latin American bishops. The hands of the laity were to be untied.
The bishops would "back up" radical students and
workers, legitimizing their ideological positions
if not their tactics. To a great extent, the Brazilian experience in the 1960's, with bishops granting asylum to students and workers from the military, had served to provide an episcopal strategy
for retaining the allegiance of the young without
consenting to civil war. The Church-as-refuge theology of the traditional theologians was resurrected,
although this time refuge was provided not to individual "souls" against the incursions of "the world"
but rather to groups of the "hunted" against the repressive powers of the state. Both conceptions are
predicated, however, upon the notion of an impregnable Church. To be impregnable in the face of
seduction always required detachment from secular
rewards. But to be impregnable in the face of ag-
gression requires the closest of linkages to secular sources of power. The Brazilian Church, in
cultivating revolutionaries, has been at pains to
construct a new power base.

The formal meetings of the conference saw the
early rejection of Vatican Cardinal Zamore's

directives and hegemony in favor of the Brazilian
model. The bishops elected their own heads of committees and determined to open full debate on the
working document rather than merely endorsing the
papal positions on violence, reforms, and cooperative development outlined in papal encyclicals and
in Bogota.

During proceedings of the Committee on Justice
and the Subcommittee on Peace, both Eugenio Sales
and Carlos Parteli described their respective sees
as characterized by revolutionary ferment, unrest
among young workers and students. Both were anxious
to meet the expectations of these groups, which
meant clear denunciations of capitalism and imperialism. The documents that issued from the Committee
on Justice and Peace reflect this preoccupation.

The final document on "justice" concentrated on
what is called "neocolonialism."

> The small artisans and industrial-
> ists are pressured by larger inter-
> ests, and the larger industrialists
> of Latin America are, little by little,
> coming to depend upon international
> corporations which control almost ex-
> clusively resources such as applied
> science, patents, marketing studies,
> etc. . . .

The remainder of the document consists of an appeal
to the enlightened self-interest of businessmen and
government officials in the hope that they would
initiate a more equitable system.

The "justice" document does not go beyond calling for elite-initiated change. The only possible
reference to the masses is in the form of an exhor-
tation to churchmen to encourage the "formation of
a political consciousness in our people" so that
"Christians will consider it their duty to participate in political life."

The document on "peace" is much more explicit
concerning the nature of "dependency" in Latin
America, and shows a sympathy for radical reform
and a sensitivity to the types of change being advocated by specific groups. For example, after discussing the "relative depreciation of the terms of
trade," quoting the Prebisch thesis practically word
for word, the document condemned the flight of domestic capital and technical manpower, the preva-
lence of tax evasion and deception by foreign in-
vestors.

> Diverse foreign companies which
> are active in our midst (also some
> national companies) are accustomed
> to evade with subtle subterfuge the
> established tax systems. At times
> they send their profits and dividends
> abroad without contributing to the
> progressive development of our coun-
> tries with adequate reinvestment.

Without being specific, the report condemns
the "international imperialism of financiers" and
political imperialism "under whatever ideological
standard." It also decries "internal colonialism"
and the "tensions between classes." "The growing
frustration of the Latin American masses" is derived from the perception of actual injustices, and
not merely the result of Marxist demagogues. Discontent among the masses is warranted by the situation.

> The universal phenomenon of ris-
> ing expectations assumes in Latin
> America a particularly aggressive
> dimension. Inequalities systemati-
> cally impede satisfaction of legiti-
> mate aspirations of the deprived
> sectors. . . . A similar state ex-
> ists in those middle classes that
> . . . are in a process of disinte-
> gration and are being reduced to
> the proletariat.

The document condemns "repressive force" by the dominant groups in society.

> They . . . label as subversive
> any attempt to change a social sys-
> tem that guarantees their privi-
> leges. . . . They resort to the use
> of force to drastically repress any
> opposition. It is very easy for
> them to find apparent justifications
> based on ideological (e.g., anti-
> Communist) or practical (maintenance
> of order) considerations.

The bishops assert that an "awakening of consciousness" is occurring among oppressed groups and
that the latter will not permit the present structures to endure. The document on "peace" characterized the current state of Latin America as a state
of oppression, a state of established violence.

> The oppression exerted by the
> groups in power under the pretext of
> maintaining peace and order is in
> reality nothing else than the seed,
> continuously and inevitably growing,
> of rebellions and wars.

This statement is followed by perhaps the most
significant paragraph in the document. It asserts
that, according to Catholic theology, revolutionary
insurrection "can be legitimate" in the case of
"evident and prolonged tyranny that seriously attacks the fundamental rights of the person and dangerously injures the common good of the country."
For the first time in any official Church document,
the Latin American bishops assert that the term
"tyranny" need not be restricted to cases of personalistic dictatorship but is applicable to "structures that are evidently unjust."

The report ends with a plea to societal elites
to heed the "signs of the times" and the frustra-
tions breeding revolutionary sentiment, and to
change the social system.

The other committee charged with analyzing social structures was the Committee for the Study of
Pastoral Planning for Elites and Masses. The committee was headed by Bishop Marc McGrath of Panama,
who took care of the Subcommittee on Elites, dele-
gating the Subcommittee on the Masses to Bishop
Luis Eduardo Henriquez, the Auxiliary Bishop of
Caracas. The mass-elitist distinction had never before been so conspicuous in Church policy-making.
Here it was explicitly built into the formal structure.

The document on elites constructs a typology
of elite forces in Latin America. It is remarkable
for its clear attempt to appeal to "revolutionary
elites," whom it treats with sympathy and respect.
The other elite types, treated with less sympathy,
are termed "traditionalists" and "reformists."

> The traditionalists, or conserva-
> tives, manifest little or no social
> conscience and have a bourgeois men-
> tality. For this reason they do not
> question social structures. In gen-
> eral, they busy themselves with the
> maintenance of their privileges which
> they identify with "established order."
> Their action in the community pos-
> sesses a paternalistic character with
> no preoccupation for the modification
> of the status quo.

The conservatives are said to share an attitude frequently found in some professional groups, in business sectors, and in those with established power.
Government sectors are often "corrupted" by these
groups, and "the military in many places supports
them . . . and intervenes to reestablish them."

The reformists are quite different:

> The reformists concern themselves
> mainly with the means of production,
> which, according to them, should be
> improved in quality and quantity.

They place great value upon technology and planning. They insist that
marginal groups be integrated into
society as producers and consumers.
They place more emphasis upon economic progress than upon social welfare, seeking the participation of
all in decisions which pertain to
the economic and political orders.

Reformists are frequently found among "technicians
and in the various development agencies." The document contrasts them with the "revolutionaries."

The revolutionaries question the
socio-economic structure. They want
radical change for itself, as an end
and as a means. For them, it is the
people who should be the subject of
this change. . . . This attitude is
found with most frequency among intellectuals, scientific investigators,
and university students.

The document on elites then proceeds to evaluate these groups, with special regard for their
orientation to the Catholic religious system. It
finds that the "revolutionaries" are potentially a
prime target group--that strong linkages can and
should be forged between them and Church policy-
makers. The "reformists" are indifferent to the
Church, linked neither positively nor negatively to
the Catholic system since they consider the Church
unimportant. The "conservatives" are wont to treat
the Church as their private preserve and to take
for granted the ties of long standing that have
linked their interests with traditional Church
policies.

1. In the group of conservatives,
or traditionalists, one finds with
most frequency the separation of personal belief and social responsibility. Faith appears to be more an

adhesion to a set of formalized beliefs than to a set of moral principles. . . .
      2. Among the reformists one can
find the gamut of belief, from indifference to personal conviction.
There is a tendency to consider the
Church as an instrument more or less
favorable to development. In some
of these groups, especially among
university students and young professionals, there is an evident tendency to depreciate religion . . .
due above all to a preoccupation
with problems of a social nature.
      3. The revolutionaries tend to
identify unilaterally faith with social responsibility. They possess a
very active sense of duty to one's
neighbor. At the same time, they experience difficulties in relating
personally to a transcendent God in
any liturgical expression of faith.
In reference to the Church, they
criticize certain historical forms
and some of the behavior of Church
officials . . . in the present time.

The document of the Subcommittee on the Masses
reflects the concern of the Venezuelan bishops that
the popular religiosity of the masses be respected,
lest linkages to the masses be further weakened.
The short document deals mainly with religious rather than political considerations. It says little
that has not been seen before in the pastoral letters of bishops and in manuals of catechesis.

The Medellin Conference consisted of 248 participants, but only the bishops and heads of religious orders could vote. By September 6, 1968, all
of the documents had been approved, but only after
extensive modifications. (The documents cited
above were quoted in their final approved form.)
The document on "peace" was originally approved by

fifty-four bishops, while sixty-one suggested modifications and five rejected it outright. Eighty-
seven bishops approved the original document on
elites, while thirty-seven asked reformulations and
three voted against it without reservation.

The number of voting members of the conference
usually did not exceed 120. An equal number of
staff experts did most of the work of writing documents and preparing for their presentation before
the assembled bishops. Therefore, the staff-line
ratio was about one to one. At the beginning of
the conference, a large number of staff experts
startled most of the bishops by requesting the
right to vote. Had they been given voting rights,
the documents on justice, peace, masses, and elites
would doubtless have been very different, and the
conflicts over their resolution much more bitter;
this is not because staff advisors are necessarily
more prone to conflict but because they are more
likely to represent specific interests while the
bishops are more intent upon reconciling the diverse
interests that fall within their respective domains.

The vagueness of episcopal documents betrays
this preoccupation. It would be difficult to find
any document by a conference of bishops that has
ever singled out a specific interest group by name
(other than the Communist Party) and condemned or
even reprimanded it. The specific condemnations of
the Medellin Conference were leveled for the most
part at the prosperous countries and at foreign
business interests, without mentioning any by name.
Even so, the grade of specificity of the Medellin
assembly was greater than that of any previous conference. In this case, specificity seems to have
been the product of urgency as well as of autonomy.

In many ways, the ability of the Latin American
bishops to satisfy the demands of the young for a
specific delineation of their positions depends upon
the level of autonomy vis-à-vis linkages to established interests other than the young. With the increased difficulty in extracting money and manpower

from the North American Church came the concomitant realization that the weakening of this linkage brought benefits as well as costs. Nothing was to be lost by attacking North American imperialism and intervention in Latin American affairs, once the ties to North American aid had been sufficiently weakened or supplanted.

In the early 1960's, while there was still a great deal of Latin American enthusiasm for North American clerical aid missions, no attacks were ever leveled by formal conferences of bishops at the economic policies of the North American government or at the Alliance for Progress. With the rapid diminution of this aid, however, the Latin Americans found themselves bereft of foreign assistance, but free to recoup their own lost influence with the nationalistic student movements, which could be reached without massive numbers of parish priests and without great expense. Linkages to the left could only be forged by a Church that had surrendered its economic resources and its dependence upon foreign functionaries. All the Church needed to do was specifically to denounce the enemies of the left.

The Medellin Conference of Latin American Bishops was a signal to North American decision-makers that the nationalistic barriers to Latin Catholic integration had been challenged. There were clear signs that the Brazilian progressives who controlled CELAM might be able to forge strong ties at both the ideological and the structural levels throughout the Latin American Catholic system.

At the end of the 1960's there were clear signs that Latin American bishops were operating across national boundaries, linked by common concerns, affected each in his own diocese by what was being said and done by other bishops in other nations. The impact throughout Latin America of Dutch, North American, Cuban, and Brazilian episcopal decision-making was immediate and profound. But what could be termed the "integration" of the Catholic system

at the formal episcopal level, that is, at the top,
contrasted starkly with the sharp divisions that
had begun to fragment all of the lower levels of the
Church.

The Medellin Conference witnessed the defection
of the Colombian bishops from the CELAM consensus,
but this public demonstration of division served to
bring the other bishops closer together. The votes
on conference documents treating the delicate issues of "imperialism," "violent revolution," "tyranny," and "class conflict" were always overwhelm-
ingly in favor of acceptance of the "Brazilian"
position as evidenced in the working document.

But the Medellin Conference not only witnessed
a growing episcopal solidarity, it also demonstrated
the fragmentation of staff sectors within the Church:
their keen competition with each other, their alienation from the higher-line officers (the bishops)
whom they had been recruited to advise, and their
basic conflict of interest with lower-line officers
(the parish priests) whose status they so clearly
threatened.

The following chapters will document these
assertions.

FRAGMENTATION OF
CATHOLIC FORCES:
COLOMBIA

The majority of the Colombian bishops rejected
the final documents of the Medellin Conference and
published their own report on September 5, the day
before the Medellin documents were formally voted
upon. (The text of the statement appeared in El
Espectador of September 5, 1968.) The rationalization made was that the deliberations at Medellin
had been meant for Latin America as a whole, and
that the sweeping generalizations they had produced
were to be qualified by local interpretation and
revision.

In line with their earlier private criticism
of the CELAM working document, the Colombian bishops rejected the "negative picture" of a frustrated
continent embroiled in prerevolutionary turmoil.
They also rejected any criticism of the Church.
Instead, they argued that the "religious situation
in Latin America places in the hands of the Church
the most powerful instrument of social action and
promises her the directive role in the evolution
that is now taking place." The Church was to "increase her influence in the present moment" by
"offering a Christian solution to every problem"
facing planners of the new social order.

The Colombian document did not recognize a
state of conflict, nor even one of opposed social

classes; development lagged not because of structured social inequality but because of "the dilato-
ry and irregular" process of industrialization. To
speed up industrialization, the bishops called for
increased private investment and "solidarity" among
nations, the latter to be evidenced by foreign aid.

The Colombian bishops deplored the results of
land-reform efforts, which had "destroyed the large
land units" without taking into account the "decreasing value of land." They insisted that "concentration of the means of production" was vital if
costs were to be reduced. The mass emigration of
campesinos to the cities was to be "accepted as a
given fact."

> The Church must accompany the
> campesino on his sad but inevitable
> exodus. The spiritual fragility of
> the indigenous peoples (for whom it
> is impossible to subsist in the coun-
> tryside) requires Christian solidar-
> ity and apostolate.

In the countryside, concentration of the means
of production was advocated. In the city, jobs
were the problem.

> The creation of employment is
> today, and will be in the immediate
> future, the most important objective
> of the social transformation process.
> This is taught by the science of eco-
> nomics and is demanded by the dignity
> of the humanity that forms the urban
> substrata.

The slumdwellers, said the Colombian bishops,
should be given "at least a minimum" of productivity, however inefficient that might be, to "integrate them into the new social order." They
stressed the role of (Christian) labor unions in
helping workers "maintain their dignity."

In contrast to the Medellin statement, the
Colombian bishops refused to blame anyone for underdevelopment.

> One must be very cautious in
> analyzing Latin American underdevel-
> opment and in isolating the factors
> that determine it. A rigid criterion
> can lead us to exaggerate our own
> culpability and to exonerate others
> who are more responsible.

The "others" more responsible were never named
by the Colombian bishops, who did stress, however,
that the responsibility did not lie primarily with
the wealthy. They deplored the attempts to explain
underdevelopment in terms of the unequal distribution of income as a "facile tendency that distorts
investigation, disfigures the problem, and can impede the possible development of the continent."
This shaft, aimed at the Medellin documents on
"justice" and "peace," stemmed from a conviction of
the "subversive" nature of class preoccupations.

> To propose (unequal distribution
> of wealth) as the sole cause . . . of
> underdevelopment . . . stimulates dis-
> cord, focuses all energies upon an
> internal struggle and sterilizes the
> opportunities for fraternal action.
> It encloses us in a circle of hate,
> without positive projections.

The "circle of hate" that the Colombians professed to dread was a linkage pattern applicable
not only to the larger secular society but also to
the Church system itself. The class differences
and antagonisms endemic to a system low in internal
resources and high in expectations are mutually reinforcing. Class differences breed antagonisms
that deepen the existing class differences. Instead of a "circulating elite," in Pareto's terms,
there is produced a "circulating antipathy." Within
the Church, the circle of hate overtly recognized

by the Colombian bishops linked rebellious priests,
staff advisors, and bishops. What the Colombian
bishops would come to comprehend was that, in attempting to "break" the circle of hate, of mutual
antipathy, it would be necessary to abandon common
ventures and specific regulations. When this was
done, the antipathy borne of constant friction and
close contact was eliminated, but so were most of
the informal linkages and communication webs that
bound together the warring elements. Fragmentation
resulted: a situation in which hitherto opposing
forces were released from their centripetal conflicts to be flung out in pursuit of secular rewards, statuses, and contracts.

The circle of hate that bound staff priest to
bishop was eliminated by turning the staffer loose
to find his fortune in the world. Instead of being
bound unto a bishop who felt free to disregard his
advice, he was unleashed upon the market of foundations, governments, and corporations that were all
too eager to profit from "local" expertise and legitimation in their quest for acceptance into
strange new cultures.

The loathsome linkages that bound all priests,
regardless of their own class background or present
class base, to one another were dissolved by the
expedient of letting priests "choose" their ministries, respecting personal preferences, and no
longer requiring that close communication be maintained between priests and bishops, or between
pastors and assistants. The norm became discretion.
"I don't care what you do as long as you don't, or
somebody else doesn't, tell me about it," became
the stock response of bishops and religious superiors. It was tacitly understood that liturgical experimentation, radical political activity, and
theological speculation could be practiced as one
wished so long as they did not provoke open comment
and so long as the practitioner did not claim official sanction for his actions. One could travel
abroad on North American stipends, organize slumdwellers, celebrate mass in a suburban living room,

deny the corporal resurrection of Christ--so long
as these actions were performed "on one's own,"
without involving the bishop or religious superior
in explicit decision-making, without outraging
("disedifying") sectors of the Church unsympathetic
to such "innovations."

The linkages that were fast forming within
what might be termed, in Rosenau's words, the Latin
American "regional environment" were consistently
undermined during the days at Medellin by Colombian
insistence upon the primacy of the "cold war environment," and specifically, upon the crucial importance of United States aid.

In their dissenting statements, the Colombian
bishops proposed a "raising of the level of production and an increased emphasis upon education" as
the key to Latin American development. This policy
was to supplant initiatives aimed at increasing
class consciousness within national boundaries, or
national consciousness across them. (Instead of
emphasizing the communality of Latin American interests, the exploited state of Latin American colo-
nies, the "internal colonialism" of the "third
world," the Colombian bishops insisted upon international linkages to the developed countries.]

The Church itself was conceived as a suprana-
tional institution, linking developed and developing
peoples alike, irrevocably opposed to "atheistic
Communism," fundamentally committed to strengthening the bonds between "all citizens, rich and poor."

> In Latin America the Church was
> first a missionary and then the pro-
> moter of all the arts and forms of
> knowledge. . . . The education of
> the masses has always been her in-
> tent. Toward this end she has dedi-
> cated her best efforts.

Linkages between elite and mass were to be
initiated by the former, who would be trained for
this task in Catholic universities.

> The Catholic universities that
> form the intellectual elite of the
> countries cannot be content in turn-
> ing out men who are, from a profes-
> sional point of view, highly qualified
> and capable, but must prepare them to
> commit themselves to collective action.

The Colombian bishops replied to the charge
that Catholic schools ignored the masses and were
closed to them by reminding critics that funding
for expansion and accessibility would have to come
from local governments, toward whom the Colombians
professed to have reservations.

Intranational linkages were viewed with far
more distrust by the Colombians than were international ones with Western countries. The activity
of the national state was viewed in the Colombian
document as a source of concern. They saw its
"aggressive power" increasing daily. Its "bureaucratic inefficiency" threatened to hamper the more
effective and productive efforts of private enterprise. The bishops warned:

> The Church as always fought
> against totalitarian states of all
> tendencies and all compositions and
> cannot now fall into the trap of an
> autocratic state that absorbs private
> initiative for the dictatorship of
> the technocracy.

The Colombian document ended with a call for
solidarity among classes and among peoples. It
condemned those tendencies that impeded such bonds:
the tendencies of "negativism, of comparing one's
own condition to that of others who are better off,"
the underestimation of spiritual values, the ex-
citement of hatred toward those who are prospering
and the fomenting of class struggles.

> Against the cries of the apostles
> of conflict we raise our anguished

> voices in favor of the most intimate
> solidarity among Latin Americans . . .
> and (deplore) . . . the systematic
> destruction of all of the traditional
> values, without replacing them with
> others devoid of hate, violence, or
> loathing.

The Colombian bishops appealed, in closing, to
the Latin American peoples to begin a worldwide
drive toward international solidarity. Latin Americans were to unite, not against other interests
but with all others in "fraternal solidarity."

The Colombian document was presented to the
Latin American Bishops' Conference (CELAM) during
the Medellin Conference. The CELAM leadership refused even to consider it, "for reasons still unex-
plained" as commented the conservative Bogotano
daily El Espectador. No concessions were made to
the Colombians, even though they were the official
hosts of the conference, and even though the conference had been officially inaugurated by a Pope
who shared the principal assumptions of the Colombian bishops. Since the Colombian bishops had directly attacked the staff arm of CELAM, they were
answered with the most direct rebuff available:
silence. (The CELAM technical staff was jubilant,
considering itself "vindicated" from the attacks
made by the Colombian Jesuit expert, Miguel Angel
Gonzalez.)

The significance of this development upon the
evolution of Church organization is not to be under-
estimated. Bishops in the Catholic Church do not
normally offer official public rebuffs to other
bishops. In this case, a conference of bishops,
acting as a group, pointedly rejected the official
views of a national episcopate. This breach in the
wall of episcopal solidarity had repercussions
elsewhere, and its traces in more fundamental conflicts of interest were soon evident.

Any analysis of the roots of the conflict reveals a fundamental disintegrative tendency in

Latin American Catholicism. The highest formal
decision-makers of the organization cannot present
to their subordinates, or to the world at large, an
undivided united front because decision-making has
ceased to be, within the Church, a matter of administrative fiat predictably followed by compliance.

Latin American Catholic bishops are dependent
for their most routine manpower and resource supplies upon extranational and extraregional sources
who will supply needs only upon a technical, "objective" basis since they, too, have limited resources. Technical proposals for aid that must be
submitted to the funding sources require a staff of
Church technicians whose skills and loyalties alone
can guarantee the continued survival of the Latin
American episcopal bureaucracies.

The Colombian Catholic system might be taken
as an "extreme case" in Latin American Catholicism.
Bitter rivalries between privileged Catholic staff
sectors (those with the ear of the bishops) and
their competitors might be expected here because
the Colombians are notorious for the conservatism
of their Cardinal and their educational institutions. May contention, however, is that "conservative" or "liberal" ideologies do not explain much
of the variance within the Latin American Catholic
system. The fragmentation process that is tearing
at the Colombian Church is also wreaking havoc in
Chile, where "progressive" cardinals and bishops
have long been celebrated.

The next two chapters will present the internal conflicts that run rife through each of these
national churches. My thesis is that the fragmentation that is occurring in Colombia and Chile
(and, by extension, in the rest of the Latin Church)
is the latent consequence of externally imposed
bureaucratization. The rise of new types of staff
sectors within the Latin Catholic system is a direct result of North American clerical intentions.

The rise of staff structures that depend for
their identity and support upon linkages to groups

external to the national Church is the linchpin to
my analysis of the breakdown of Latin American
Catholic organization. As we shall see, in Colombia, the Jesuit Center for Research and Social Action has been unsuccessful in its attempts to raise
money and manpower abroad. It has therefore forged
strong links to the traditional internal powers of
the Colombian Church--the bishops--and waged war
upon those other, non-Jesuit, staff groups that are
competitive both for the favor of the bishops and
for the support of North American and West European
foundations.

In Chile, the Jesuit CIAS has succeeded in ac-
cumulating vast resources (upwards of $40 million
per year) and is bitterly divided over control of
these resources. Jesuit sectors excluded from policy decisions over the allocation of North American
and Western European monies are increasingly willing to "break ranks" publicly with those Jesuit
sectors that make the decisions and with the Chilean
Cardinal whose relief program, CARITAS, is funded
from the United States. In Chile, staff sectors
that were initially quite willing to oppose Marxism
internally and externally as long as they were
brought into the inner circle of decision-making
have become increasingly sympathetic to leftist
movements as their counsel goes unheeded and their
budgets are outstripped by those of others. The
precise moment of this transition from staff cohesion to staff conflict in Chile can be readily identified: it was the election of Eduardo Frei as
President, in 1964, an event that signalled the
triumph of Christian Democracy over Marxism, at
least electorally, and that culminated a six-year
effort by all Catholic staff and line sectors to
defeat Salvador Allende, the leftist candidate.

The event that marked the point of intensification of intra-Church conflict in Colombia was the
proclamation by Camilo Torres of his United Front.
Clerics in Colombia were forced to make a choice:
open support or disaffiliation, tacit or explicit.
Paradoxically, those who defended Torres were able

to command more United States AID funding, albeit
indirectly, than those who attacked him, even
though the United States government and military
was one of the United Front's chief targets. This
is another indication that conflicts within Catholicism and linkages from Catholic to external sectors are contingent more upon instrumental than
upon expressive criteria.

8

CIAS:
THE
TRUSTED
ADVISORS

The burden of this chapter will be an intimate examination of the conflictual relationships between two groups within the Colombian religious system: the Jesuit Center for Research and Social Action (CIAS), which includes key advisors to the Archbishop of Bogota, and the rival staff group, composed of the diocesan priests who direct the Colombian Institute of Social Development (ICODES). The Jesuits of CIAS had a chief role in the writing of the Colombian bishops' statement that challenged the Latin American Bishops' Conference at Medellin. ICODES has, since its inception, been closely linked to CELAM, but its directors were excluded from the Medellin meetings of CELAM by the Colombian hosts, at the express urging of the CIAS Jesuits.

What follows is an analysis of the competing ideologies, operations, and support bases of these two staff groups. Since each is a key linkage center with other sectors in the international Catholic system, the patterns of action that surround them are indicative of the special strains that are now fragmenting Latin American Catholicism. Staff-line and staff-staff conflicts are not restricted to Colombia, nor do they necessarily take the same form here as elsewhere. But the Colombian case illustrates certain basic dilemmas for Roman Catholic bureaucratization--dilemmas which may be resolved differently in different settings but which in any case must be faced.

CHART 1

Colombian Church: Internal Linkage
System: Jesuit CIAS as Linchpin

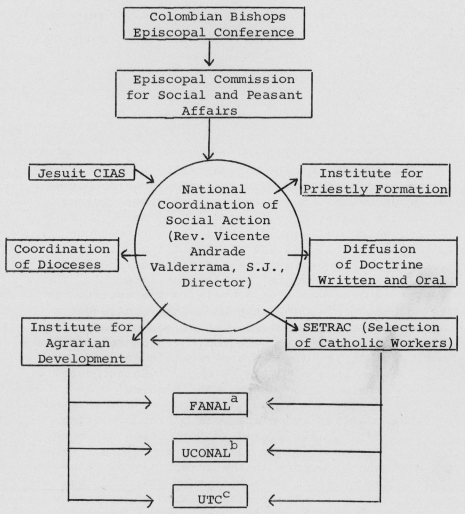

a
 National Federation of Farmers: Jesuit-directed

b
National Cooperatives Union: Jesuit-directed

c
Colombian Workers Union: Jesuit-directed

The Colombian Jesuit Center for Research and
Social Action (CIAS) represents the traditional
clerical staff unit in a country that has long
granted ecclesiastics a major voice in decision-
making. Chart 1 affords an outline of the formal
relationships between Colombian Jesuit CIAS and the
key decision-making and operational sectors of Colombian Catholicism. (The diagram is based on a document meant for internal Jesuit use.)

CIAS acts, together with the Colombian bishops
and their advisory staff (the Episcopal Conference
and the Episcopal Commission for Social and Peasant
Affairs), to set policies for the National Coordination of Social Action, which is itself headed by a
Jesuit CIAS member, Father Vicente Andrade Valderrama.

Andrade controls the Institute for Priestly
Formation, which provides orientation for Colombia's
2,000 diocesan priests. These priest would normally
be subject directly to the bishops, since they are
not members of religious orders. In Colombia, however, the Jesuits are intermediaries who look after
all "priestly formation" through the National Coordination of Social Action. Colombia's 1,500
religious-order priests are also linked to outputs
from the Institute for Priestly Formation, which
attempts to define "the social needs" of Colombia.

The mass media at the disposal of the Colombian Church are also coordinated by Jesuit Father
Andrade, under the rubric of the Center for Diffusion of Doctrine, Written and Oral. All Church
publications, press releases, radio and television
programs, and any participation by priests in secular media are formally subject to his approval.

The Selection of Colombian Workers (SETRAC)
is composed of the local leaders of the Jesuit-
founded and -directed labor unions: the National
Federation of Farmers (FANAL), the Colombian Workers Union (UTC), and the National Cooperatives
Union (UCONAL). SETRAC and the National Coordinator (Andrade) set policies for the workers' training

centers, which are run by the Jesuits' Institute
for Agrarian Development.

The Coordination of Dioceses, the principal
jurisdictional units of the bishops (one bishop,
one diocese), involves one of the most delicate organizational problems, since the individual bishop
is, by canon law, subject only to the Pope and not
to any other bishop, cardinal, or conference of
bishops. But in the Colombian system, even diocesan coordination is responsive to staff initiative. The National Coordination of Social Action
must approve any proposals concerning national diocesan coordination although, of course, it does not
have the final say on any decision.

In actual practice, the National Coordinator
of Social Action, Father Andrade, has lost considerable control in recent years over all these sectors. The Jesuit-founded UTC is quite independent
of Jesuit directives so long as the latter are specific. The UTC does remain under the "protection"
of the Church. Decisions when and if to strike are
made with Jesuit advisors present, but these tend
to support whatever the lay leaders decide.*

The FANAL is much weaker organizationally and
enjoys a much closer and more harmonious relationship with the Jesuits. One index of Jesuit influence in the unions is the attendance of the top
leaders of UTC or FANAL at SETRAC meetings. The
FANAL head is always present, the top UTC men very
seldom. If the latter do show up, it is only to
give speeches, after which they hurry off again.[1]
This is significant because SETRAC is labeled by

---

*Conversational interviews were held with
SETRAC members immediately preceding and following
closed SETRAC meetings of July, August, and September, 1968. I attended the meetings as the guest of
a North American Jesuit who was acting as a SETRAC
advisor.

the Jesuits as the "heart" of the Catholic labor
movement. Its chief function is expressive and theological rather than instrumentally ideological. It
is more overtly religious and devotional than any
other union enterprise. SETRAC meetings emphasize
Catholic "altruistic" values, brotherhood, and solidarity with the social doctrine of the Church rather than concrete union actions undertaken "out of
self-interest."[2] UTC officials, in charge of an organization that is politically viable (whereas FANAL
is not), are clearly not interested in the expressive rituals that the Jesuits (particularly Father
Andrade) associate with "social justice" and trade
unionism.

There are also tensions between the Jesuit
staff members of CIAS and the Jesuit line officials
at the Jesuit Universidad Javeriana in Bogota.
These stem from the refusal of CIAS Jesuits to
teach at the University. There are other conflicts
of a more muted nature with Jesuits working in
lower-class neighborhoods in Medellin (there are no
Jesuits doing this in Bogota). There are perennial
problems between Andrade and the diocesan coordinator and some of the staff of the Colombian Bishops'
Conference.

But over the years, the Jesuits at CIAS have
been able to maintain their influence with key members of the hierarchy and have derived prestige
from their labor unions. The unions are the most
successful on the continent in terms of membership
and access to governmental decision-makers. They
were founded by the Jesuits immediately after World
War II, when a fear of Communist labor activity
prompted many to entrust to the Jesuits the intensification of anti-Communist organizing.

The UTC is the largest trade-union federation
in Colombia. It consists of twenty-nine federations, 1,400 unions, and 600,000 affiliated members.
These statistics are from official CIAS sources and
probably inflated, but not even the rival Confederation of Colombian Workers (CTC) claims to be larger.

FANAL is much smaller, consisting of 300 sections of organized rural community-action groups (the government-sponsored Community Action) and has 350 affiliated "unions," which are in many cases simply the monthly meetings of the parish burial society organized by the parish priest.

The National Cooperatives Union (UCONAL) is composed of 530 savings-and-loan associations, with deposits of upwards of 34 million pesos, and with 122 million pesos on active loan.

In recent years, the monopoly that CIAS has long held over Catholic Action coordination and access to the episcopacy has been challenged by other groups within the Church. The diocesan councils of priests have occasionally disagreed with the running of the trade unions, and the theological and doctrinal counsel once demanded of the Jesuits has been supplanted to some extent by the call for sociological and economic expertise. The main impact of these new initiatives has been to force the original founders of CIAS to open their ranks to younger Jesuits, many of whom hold advanced degrees in sociology and economics from abroad. These men have accepted their assigned places within the CIAS system but have also pressed for more autonomy than has been traditional vis-à-vis higher-line officers (rectors, university presidents, provincial superiors). Eager to devote themselves to their own research and teaching, in facilities separate from the traditional Jesuit university, they have constantly been faced with the necessity of securing financing from outside the Jesuit and Church systems. Jesuit provincial superiors in Colombia have permitted these new staff experts to plan their own schedules and to select, for the most part, their own research priorities, but they have not been lavish with financial support.

It has become imperative, therefore, for the younger, technically trained Jesuit staff experts to appeal either to foreign Catholic foundations, such as ADVENIAT or MISEREOR, or to North American private groups and U.S. AID. One such proposal to AID, a

critical one from the standpoint of CIAS staff members in Colombia, is indicative of the image CIAS
tries to project in order to secure funding.   Although CIAS is Jesuit-directed and integrated into
the Jesuit network of national centers (CLACIAS),
the proposal to AID describes Jesuit activities in
Colombia as "nonconfessional."   To the extent that
there are some nonclerics collaborating with the
Colombian Jesuits, this is perhaps warranted, but
the over-all direction and orientation of the Colombian Jesuit CIAS group is toward the internal needs
of the Catholic system.

The proposal to AID first states some basic
propositions concerning Colombian development.

> A minority, who possess an almost
> total monopoly of education and wealth,
> control the country in its economic
> and political spheres.
> A majority of Colombian citizens,
> who make up the rural and urban masses,
> are marginal to, or totally absent
> from, the political and economic life
> of the country.   Every day, however,
> they become more aware of their rights
> as citizens and, as their discontent
> grows, the social situation becomes
> more tense.

The CIAS Jesuits warn that this "new awareness" of
the masses will result either in violent revolution
or in "total, rapid, yet pacific and well-ordered
change of socio-economic and political structures."
There is hope for peaceful change because there exists in Colombia an elite that is eager to initiate
it.   The only missing factor is "guidance," which
the Jesuits will supply.

> Many social leaders who desire
> this latter (peaceful) type of change
> are aware of the critical situation
> and, though they consider change
> necessary, they lack clearly defined
> goals and programs.

> One basic necessity is an organi-
> zation of serious investigators
> which can become aware of the social
> tragedy that exists in Colombia, ob-
> jectively analyze this situation, de-
> velop a plan of action to remedy this
> situation, and promote and make known
> some models of development which can
> be applied. . . .

The viability of elite-led social change was taken
for granted.

> The CIAS hopes to aid in the solu-
> tion of this pressing need by: in-
> creasing the number of its trained
> investigators, increasing its library
> resources, extending the publication
> of its investigations, creating an
> awareness of the need for change
> among the nation's upper classes,
> and forming an increased number of
> socially conscious leaders who will
> be the agents of the basic social
> change that the country desperately
> needs.

AID rejected the proposal, refusing to allocate $45,000 for the securing of a residence to
house CIAS activities. Earlier CIAS proposals for
a study of Roman Catholic attitudes toward birth
control were also turned down.

Jesuit activities in the labor field were also
running into difficulties at this time. The Jesuit-
founded Union of Colombian Workers, which had been
instituted in the 1940's to fight Communism, began
to take a more militant stance vis-à-vis the national government than the Jesuit founders desired.
Led by the mercurial Tulio Cuevas, the UTC broke
with the Carlos Lleras Restrepo government in July,
1968, threatening a general strike unless their demands were met for higher wages and an end to "repressive legislation."

July was a frenzied time in Bogota as the entire city groomed itself for the visit of Pope Paul
VI. At SETRAC meetings in late July, the UTC lay
leadership threatened to present the Pope with a
list of complaints against the Colombian government
to provoke his intervention. The Jesuits who directed CIAS-sponsored UTC, as well as the Archbishop
of Bogota, were horrified. The papal nuncio privately expressed alarm. At closed SETRAC meetings,
Jesuit advisor Hector Bollanos expressed Jesuit support for whatever decisions UTC leaders would make.
But Father Andrade was on the phone daily with the
Colombian Minister of Labor, and finally was able
to persuade both government and union leadership to
compromise so as not to "mar" the Pope's visit.

On July 12, the Colombian daily El Espectador
had printed the original UTC ultimatum in an open
letter to President Lleras Restrepo. On July 13,
Archbishop Munoz Duque of Bogota held a press conference (reported in El Mercurio on July 14) to
call for "an atmosphere of social peace" during the
Eucharistic Congress that the Pope would officially
inaugurate. The Archbishop addressed himself particularly to the labor unions.

On the night of July 13, the Colombian Labor
Minister went on television to discuss the labor
situation. He did not mention the UTC, but instead
focused his attention on the leftist CTC labor federation, which had just announced its support of
UTC demands. For the first time since the 1940's,
a united labor front seemed a distinct possibility.[3]

By July 23, it was evident that the UTC would
back down. UTC leaders had maintained a public
silence for ten days, and when President Lleras
Restrepo met with labor to discuss grievances, he
met only with CTC leaders. The UTC had never formally acknowledged the offers of CTC support. It
was clear that the UTC, although the largest union
in Colombia and the initiators of the current
crisis, had reached an agreement in private with
the government.

At a SETRAC meeting on July 25, Tulio Cuevas
explained why it was not necessary to strike or dis-
turb public order. Other speakers explained the
preparations for a "day of repentance" at the Eucharistic Congress when the Colombian Minister of Labor
and the leaders of Catholic labor unions would all
make "public confession" of their joint failure to
work for social justice. UTC members were assured
that they "would be taken care of" and that the
long-standing "state of siege" in Colombia, with
its accompanying strictures against strikes and
labor activity, would be lifted soon after the
Eucharistic Congress.[4]

During the same period, UTC activity was mainly confined to the defense of workers who had "taken
over" the operation of factories in the Bogota vicin-
ity whose owners had defaulted their obligations.
These "takeovers" were curious affairs, engineered
while the government maintained a reserved silence.
The UTC organizers, backed by Father Andrade, carefully respected private property and even banked
the profits in the account of the locked-out owner.
On a visit to one of these factories, Andrade remarked that the owner's profits had actually increased during the period of the takeover, due to
increased production.[5]

The CTC and the small Latin American Confederation of Christian Trade Unions (CLASC) in Bogota
were furious over such instances of "bourgeois" co-
optation of the working class, but they seemed powerless to check UTC growth. The CLASC is also "nonconfessional," but it is prone to rely upon papal
encyclicals and Church theology when these seem appropriate to current needs. However, CLASC has a
reputation among Jesuits in Colombia of being "leftist." At any rate, it is regarded by the UTC as a
competitor. CLASC attempts to organize Colombian
labor had been resisted violently by Colombian bishops, who termed it "Marxist," and by Colombian Jesuits, who warned that it would "divide" the
Christian-inspired labor movement.

In July, 1965, the Chilean Jesuit Mario Zanartu (whose role in the Christian Democratic rise to power in Chile will be detailed below) was "expelled" from Colombia by the local Jesuit superior on order from the Archbishop of Medellin, Tulio Botero Salazar. Zanartu was ordered to leave Colombia because he was helping to form a CLASC-affiliated union in Medellin, the Antioquenan Syndical Association (ASA). On July 27, 1965, the Medellin daily El Espacio published the Archbishop's order, together with the mandate issued by Jesuit provincial superior, Alberto Campillo.

The Archbishop's decree follows (as translated from the Spanish):

> With respect to ASA:
> 1. It uses violent language that incites class hatred.
> 2. It directly advocates social revolution in terms inadmissibly violent.
> 3. It does not take into account the orientations of the Colombian Bishops' Conference which, according to the norms of the Holy See, already is aware of the necessary changes in society but considers only those that must be realized in a constructive manner, in accord with rapid evolution, with normal cautions.
> 4. By television and radio programs it has slandered the social apostolate of our clergy, which, as the people well know, is in general distinguished by its self-denial and generosity.
> 5. It has tried to deceive the people by describing the clergy as if it were divided: some acting in favor of the people while others are alleged to act against them.
> 6. On repeated occasions and under tactical pretexts it has not

hesitated to act in conjunction with
Marxist movements.

7. The attitudes of its present
representatives are not in accord
with the norms of the hierarchy in
this diocese.

8. Although it pretends to ex-
alt the efforts of some priests whom
it calls revolutionaries, it foments
an anticlerical spirit among workers
and peasants.

WE COMMAND

1. That priests abstain from
supporting the ASA in the city as
well as in the countryside.

2. That priests abstain from
giving conferences or talks during
ASA reunions without previous permission from the bishop for each meeting, and in general, not to give any
kind of help to any activity sponsored by ASA.

3. The present document should
be read in all of the churches and
chapels of our Archdiocese this Sunday and at all masses.

July 13, 1965   (signed)
          FDO: TULIO BOTERO SALAZAR
          Archbishop of Medellin

The Archbishop's letter was sent to the Jesuit
provincial superior of the Western Colombian Province, Father Alberto Campillo, S.J., who on July 13
sent a private letter to Father Zanartu. (The following is translated from the Spanish.)

Reverend Father Zanartu:
     From other sources (not from you
or from your Jesuit superiors), I
have learned that you will arrive
today in this city to give a talk
in the auditorium of the ASA.

> Yesterday a representative of
> Archbishop Tulio Botero Salazar
> called me to ask about you and to
> tell me that the Archbishop would
> not permit you to give talks in that
> auditorium. I for my part forbid
> you to give talks in Medellin or in
> any other place under the jurisdic-
> tion of this the Western Colombian
> Province of the Society of Jesus.
> The situation of the country and of
> the Colombian Church is not conducive
> to this type of talk which may be of
> some use in other places.
> I command you: either place your-
> self this very day in my presence or
> leave the jurisdiction of this prov-
> ince. I advise you that as long as
> you do not see me personally, you
> have no ministerial faculties.

The reaction to Father Zanartu's projected
talks with Catholic labor leaders was quite comparable in Bogota, where Jesuit Father Andrade was
kept fully informed of the proceedings in Medellin.
UTC leaders were told that a Chilean Jesuit was trying to divide the Colombian Catholic labor movement,
and that if not a Marxist, he was at least "very
friendly with the 'comrades.'"

Andrade was thus successful in repelling this
threat to his control of the UTC movement. As we
shall see in the next chapter, the Chilean Jesuits,
fresh from the victory of Christian Democracy in
their own country, were eager to form linkages with
fledgling movements throughout the continent. CLASC
and its local affiliates were Christian Democratic
in leadership and orientation and afforded a potential linkage system throughout Latin America at the
urban and rural grass roots. Old-style clerical
polemicists such as Andrade could not be accommodated or absorbed into this new type of Catholic
"leftist" movement, which avoided head-on collisions
with the Marxist left whenever possible, and sought
to establish a clear reputation for "militance."

Andrade's attempts to maintain control of the UTC labor movement ran into other obstacles from internal sources. Although he was able to persuade UTC lay leaders not to strike or create "a public disturbance" during the Pope's visit, he had had to guarantee government acceptance of their demands beforehand and was faced soon afterwards with a sullen Tulio Cuevas. As the president of the UTC, Cuevas had acquired a reputation, among SETRAC members, at least, of being "hard-headed and independent." His personal life style was reputed to be at variance with the strict Catholic regimen preached by the Jesuits. His stormy relationship with Andrade was spoken about openly at informal breaks in the SETRAC meetings. When the UTC, under Cuevas' leadership, moved into a spacious new building built with contributions from the AFL-CIO-sponsored ORIT, Andrade was left behind in the old house that had been the original meeting place for the combined rural and urban labor movements.

With the departure of the urban union, the UTC, Andrade turned his energies to his languishing rural union, the FANAL, in hopes of building it into a potent political force. No longer, however, could he employ the strategy of linking FANAL activities to UTC strength. He would instead try--successfully--to link FANAL to the highest ecclesiastical authority: the Pope.

Andrade responded to questions concerning the early organization of FANAL by referring to a copy of Harold Seeberger's unpublished report, dated 1964. He vouched for all of the data in the report. The following account is based on Seeberger's description.

The UTC and FANAL started off together in 1945, after earlier attempts by Eugenio Colorado and other "Young Catholic Workers" to "infiltrate" the leftist CTC were unsuccessful. The Jesuits were convinced that the CTC was "dangerous." (An article published in the Jesuit Revista Javeriana in 1943 had reported that the CTC executive committee was

made up of "nineteen liberals and twelve Communists--
all of a Marxist mentality.")[6]

Vicente Andrade represented the Colombian bishops at a conference of the Confederation of Latin
American Workers (CTAL) in 1944 in Cali. The conference president was a leftist, Vicente Lombardo
Toledano of Mexico, and Andrade was not able to
gain the floor to debate. This incident marked the
beginning of a feud between Andrade and CTAL leaders that has lasted more than two decades.[7] At the
end of 1944, Andrade formed the National Coordination of Catholic Action (described above), with himself at the head. He still occupies this position,
linking all sectors of Catholic episcopal control
in Colombia.

In 1945 the UTC and FANAL were formed. At
this time, FANAL was merely the "office of rural
affairs" of the UTC. Marxist "penetration" of the
urban classes was considered more advanced and dangerous than their influence in the countryside.
The Jesuits were quite willing to neglect the peasants in the hope of forging strong alliances with
the urban workers.

By 1950, FANAL claimed 330 affiliated local
unions with a total enrollment of 100,000. These
figures are highly inflated, however. Seeberger
suggests that they refer to the population of rural
Catholic parish units within which a FANAL action
group was operating. Andrade did not dispute this
interpretation.

FANAL's main activities in the 1940's and
1950's consisted in "adult education" and indoctrination into Catholic "social doctrine," as well as
the creation of "food supply centers," or cooperatives, that sought to establish transportation
links between farm and urban market and to handle
distribution. These were first established in
1946. Shares were sold in values of five pesos or
multiples thereof, and the venture was soon reported
to be economically unfeasible.

In 1959, the First Campesino Congress was held
in Bogota by FANAL. President Alberto Lleras addressed the 3,000 persons who attended. The congress issued declarations on agrarian reform, community development, education, problems of indigenous groups, and credit. It also condemned "la
violencia," the internecine political strife that
raged through Colombia during the 1950's.[8] The
French Jesuit Pierre Bigo, the head of the international Jesuit CLACIAS, wrote an article in the Colombian Jesuit <u>Revista Javeriana</u> in which he termed
FANAL "an essential factor in the evolution of Colombia, and one which has been instrumental in containing Communism and in cooling rural violence."[9]
The counterrevolutionary nature of FANAL, and by extension, of the UTC, has never been more clearly expressed. FANAL grew quickly. The third national
congress was attended by 10,000 delegates, each
elected by the local FANAL chapters. President
Lleras Camargo again addressed the assembly.

The core of the FANAL decision-making group is
the executive secretariat, which includes a president, secretary general, comptroller, treasurer, secretary for legal affairs, secretary for education
and propaganda, and a priest-advisor. All except
the priest-advisor are appointed by a national directorate. The priest is appointed by Father Andrade.

The executive secretariat, which meets twice
monthly, is theoretically responsible to periodic
national congresses and to the national directorate.
But it holds six of twenty-five seats on the latter
and usually gets its way in the national congresses.

The linkages between the Jesuit-directed FANAL
and the National Front Colombian government remained
strong through the 1950's and 1960's. The FANAL consistently supported government measures against "la
violencia" and confined its own militant activities
to a few "land invasions" that were carefully and
peacefully led by priest-directors. In this way,
as Bigo noted, FANAL operated as a safety valve
upon the restless and violence-prone rural system.

In interviews with U.S. and Colombian government officials, Seeberger attempted to gauge the
orientation and response of some of FANAL's chief
reference groups.

Saul Moskowitz, the labor attache to the U.S.
Embassy in Bogota, characterized FANAL as "land-
grabbing" because it had authorized several land
takeovers by frustrated peasants. (Andrade later
justified this type of activity as a "lesser evil"
than a Communist takeover of the peasant movements.)

Charles Seckinger, the rural development officer of the U.S. Embassy, said facetiously that
FANAL was "not completely bolshevist," but that it
was the only group "organizing the little guy" and
was dangerous because it used "collective farming."
He added that the Embassy was "interested in FANAL
but didn't know how to use it."

Javier Bray, former labor attache to the U.S.
Embassy in Bogota, in conversations with me, said
that he was confident that FANAL could be an effective deterrent to Communist penetration in Colombia,
although his previous experience with Father Andrade
had led him to suspect that "Andrade takes all of
our money and says the hell with our business methods." Bray had left his U.S. Embassy post to take
a position as field representative for the Center
for Rural Development, a Boston-based private foundation. Bray tried to channel money and technical
expertise into FANAL's leadership-training program,
with the assistance of Harvard Business School
graduates.

Lynn Bramkam, the director of cooperative programs for the Peace Corps in Colombia, said that
the UTC, FANAL, and the Jesuit-directed National
Confederation of Cooperatives (UCONAL) formed an
"interlocking directorate." He said that UCONAL
was constantly in conflict with the Colombian Association of Cooperatives. This "embarrassed" the
United States, which was supporting both groups

financially through a grant to the National Association of Credit Unions.

Al Chable, a U.S. advisor to the Colombian government's land-reform agency, INCORA, said that
FANAL's "land invasions" irritated INCORA, which
favored legal transfers. He felt that such illegal
activities could open the way "for more radical
groups, as happened in the Dominican Republic."

Vicente Pisano, chief of Colombian ACCION
COMUNAL (AC), which seeks to "organize community
development programs in the countryside," said that
the government cooperatives the AC sponsored benefited from FANAL activities, since "FANAL can act
as mediator between peasants and government in matters where ACCION COMUNAL could not operate effectively." (As we shall see, the fused linkage between
ACCION COMUNAL and the Jesuit FANAL was threatened
by Camilo Torres' attempt to radicalize the former
organization at the grass roots. Camilo had a long-
standing personal acquaintance with the AC movement,
of which he was one of the founders. Jaime Trujillo,
the credit department chief of the Colombian government's Ministry of Agriculture, said that Trujillo
had very friendly relations with FANAL and was a
personal friend of FANAL leaders Eugenio Colorado
and Mario Yolanda.)

The reactions of a private citizen are also of
interest and are indicative of the sources of FANAL
support. Hernan Tobar is the executive secretary
of the Center for Study and Social Action of the
"Mano Negra," or "Black Hand," a group comprised of
business and other interests and dedicated to the
suppression of "Communist activity" in Colombia.
The Mano Negra has frequently been labeled a terror-
ist organization and would not seem proper company
for a "Christian-inspired labor movement." However,
Mr. Tobar said, "we agree with FANAL's objectives"--
stopping Communism--"and so we aren't concerned
about the means which they use"--taking over private property in land invasions.

Seeberger has estimated FANAL's annual income
from dues-paying members at 50,000 pesos--which
probably couldn't pay the rent on FANAL's offices.
The source of the remainder of the money for FANAL's
budget is undisclosed.

The above data suggest that FANAL's linkages
to North American sources of financial support were
weak in the 1960's, since the American Embassy in
Colombia regarded it as a halfway house to radicalism. But, within the Colombian political system,
FANAL commanded some respect, since it represented
the only attempt to organize the peasants, who had
been engaged in twenty years of fierce and costly
rural violence. FANAL did not need to look to
either the United States or the National Front government for legitimacy. Instead, it was able to
offer legitimacy in return for other favors.

This reciprocal relationship, this fused linkage, was to be threatened by Camilo Torres. The
threat to the rural labor movement was all the more
frightening to the CIAS Jesuits insomuch as they
had already lost much of their control over the
urban-based UTC.

One index of the deterioration of Jesuit influence is the diminishing stature of the Selection
of Colombian Workers (SETRAC) throughout the 1960's.
SETRAC had been promoted by the Jesuits as the
"core" of their "Christian-inspired" labor movement.
Insofar as the Jesuits were not experts in cooperatives, unionism, or group dynamics but specialists
in Thomistic ethics and theology, the "social doctrine of the Church" became their reason for being
central to the movement. SETRAC members were to be
recruited from the top, middle, and lower levels of
union leadership--in this way melding the local
grass-roots units to the national leadership and
its clerical direction.

Two problems arose. The top leaders began to
communicate that they were too busy for the

"devotional" and religious exercises of the monthly
SETRAC meetings, and it was difficult to require
attendance of local leaders who would have to travel
across the city after work. Since SETRAC was meant
to function as a coordinating body--one that would
develop strong internal ties of religious solidar-
ity--its failures to develop meant the loss of coordination between FANAL and the UTC, as well as
diminishing Jesuit influence in the latter.

Precisely because the UTC had been successful
in winning the respect of the Colombian government,
in building up membership so that it was the largest union in South America, and in attracting financial aid from the U.S. labor movement, its leaders possessed enough functional autonomy to disregard Jesuit directives.

FANAL, insofar as it was considered dangerous
by the North Americans, and insofar as it lagged in
leadership, needed the continued support and protection of a legitimate body. The Jesuits were determined that they, and not ACCION COMUNAL, Camilo
Torres, or some other group, were to provide the
needed legitimacy.

In February, 1965, the 11th National Assembly
of SETRAC met in Bogota to discuss these realities.
The confidential report issued by the assembly mentioned several difficulties: UTC and FANAL leaders
chosen for SETRAC posts felt that their duties were
a waste of time, since they involved "spiritual development" and not concrete labor organizing. Finances were a problem, since local unions did not
wish to see their own funds siphoned off to support
SETRAC "training courses" that emphasized the "social doctrine of the Church."

The assembly reflected the fact that although
the Jesuit directors were losing real decision-
making power within the urban labor movement, they

still retained a good deal of say in the official
formulation of "policy." This is manifest in a
series of "complaints" that the assembly issued in

lieu of binding decisions. The following excerpts
are translated from the body of the assembly's report.

> One of the faults that we think
> is fundamental is the lack of con-
> tinuity in the Directorate of SETRAC,
> obliging a continual improvisation
> in the recruitment of officials.
> The brothers have collaborated with
> all good will, but only in a tempo-
> rary manner. Together with the dif-
> ficult exercise of office in SETRAC,
> it may be added that the external
> front organizations (UTC, UCONAL,
> FANAL) offer greater rewards in pres-
> tige, money, and concrete tasks.

The report goes on to deplore the consequences
for the development of SETRAC.

> From the preceding, one uncovers
> a serious problem: while the exter-
> nal movements grow prodigiously,
> SETRAC maintains its incredible tiny-
> ness. . . . We can state that for
> every 100 leaders of the UTC or of
> UCONAL, there is only one SETRAC
> participant.

The national directorate of SETRAC is a paper
organization comprised of the top leadership of the
front organizations. In 1965, Luis Alfonso Perdomo
was president; Jose T. Nino, secretary general;
Pablo Jaime Garzon, secretary of education; Gregorio
Duran Naranjo, secretary of agrarian affairs; Hernando Baquero, secretary of union affairs and secretary of cooperatives. On paper, these names correspond nicely to those of the top leadership of
the UTC. An informal poll of sources intimately
acquainted with the functioning of the UTC yielded
the following as top decision-makers (whether formally prescribed as such or not): Tulio Cuevas,
Antonio Diaz, Jose T. Nino, Luis Alfonso Perdomo,

and Alvaro Ramirez, in that order; following, as im-
portant consultants if not decision-makers, were
Hernando Rodriguez, Eugenio Colorado, and Manuel
Velez Castilla.[10]

Diaz, Nino, and Perdomo, today top leaders in
the UTC, were SETRAC functionaries in 1965. But
further interviews with these men and a close reading of the SETRAC 11th Assembly report made it
clear that while SETRAC membership was an important
prerequisite to top leadership in the UTC, once top
leadership had been achieved, SETRAC could be quiet-
ly ignored. For a man to be elected president or
executive secretary of the UTC in the early 1960's,
he had to have Father Andrade's backing, or, rather,
"spiritual clearance." But once elected, it was
not easy for Andrade to remove or discredit him
without severely compromising the movement.

A special section of the 11th Assembly's report makes it clear that the major part of SETRAC
funds came through Father Andrade as Coordinator of
Social Action for the Colombian bishops, and not
from the contributions of local UTC and FANAL unions.

> Let this be the opportunity to
> say what bothers us and to manifest
> the hope that, considering the impor-
> tance that SETRAC has not only for
> the front organizations but also for
> the Church and the nation, one day
> we will be able to say that we have
> guaranteed an amount of money to fi-
> nance the movement . . . financial
> support that derives not solely from
> the valuable assistance which the Co-
> ordination of Social Action has pro-
> vided, but which would come from the
> front organizations themselves.

The "front organizations"--UTC, FANAL, UCONAL--
for the Jesuit-directed and religious-oriented
SETRAC had become, by the early 1960's the dominant
centers of activity and power. The secularization

process was clearly a result and not a cause of organizational success. Before the UTC had won any
"victories" in terms of increased membership or
concessions wrung from confrontations with government, SETRAC had been the focal point of the organization. Ideological certitude had been a substitute for political success.

With the growth of the power of the UTC, the
Jesuit advisors became more and more alert to the
deterioration of their former influence and sought
to emphasize the hostility of the environment. Not
only were the Communists lurking within the CTC,
but within Catholicism itself there were dangerous
competitive forces that required clerical exorcism.

The UTC had been founded to combat Communism.*
But when it began to outstrip the membership of the
leftist CTC, UTC leaders began to act independently
of the Jesuit founders. In 1963, UTC president
Tulio Cuevas threatened the Colombian government
with a general strike and frightened President Leon
into calling a special session of Congress to meet
UTC demands. According to Andrade (in his conversations with the author), Cuevas ignored Jesuit
counsel, became obsessed with this accomplishment,
and squandered the subsequent bargaining opportunities. Within SETRAC this incident became a favor-
ite example of those who urged subordination of the
"front organizations" to the "prayerful planning"
of SETRAC members.

As the external threat of the CTC began to
diminish, an alert was declared against the "internal subversion" of the Catholic labor movement
in Colombia. The organizing activities of the
Latin American Confederation of Christian Trade
Unions (CLASC) became the target of intense hostility.

---

*This is clear from an examination of testi-
mony of the original founders as well as from the
early literature of the movement.

As described above, Chilean Jesuit Mario Zanartu
was expelled from Medellin in 1965 when he attempted
to bring his reputation as a CLASC organizer in
Chile and Venezuela to Colombia. The degree of hostility between CLASC and the UTC can be gauged from
the fact that Andrade and Zanartu are both Jesuits
and are therefore not accustomed to arguing publicly with one another.

The 11th Assembly report of SETRAC emphasizes
the danger of the CLASC threat:

> The action of the Latin American
> Confederation of Christian Trade
> Unions has been one of disorienta-
> tion for our union organizations.
> They have used the financial re-
> sources they possess and have suc-
> ceeded in seducing some of our lead-
> ers who have gone over to their
> ranks. Such men as Miguel Molano,
> Alfonso Sanabria, Manuel Lopez
> Giraldo have become not only func-
> tionaries of CLASC but also enemies
> of ours insofar as they use their
> knowledge of our organizations and
> its leaders to promote divisive cam-
> paigns against us, seeking on all
> sides to weaken our front organi-
> zations.

The UTC, UCONAL, and FANAL members of SETRAC
were, in turn, frequently condemned by CLASC leaders for their "dependence" upon United States "imperialist" organizations such as the AFL-CIO sponsored ORIT and the American Institute of Free Labor
Development (AIFLD).[11]

The SETRAC report hints at Communist subsidi-
zation of CLASC, in allusions to its "mysterious
and enormous resources," and states that the Colombian bishops have been alerted:

> The national directorate (of
> SETRAC) has produced indispensable
> documentation to inform the Vener-
> able Ecclesiastical Hierarchy of
> the danger CLASC represents for our
> country.

The fight against CLASC seems all the more important for the Jesuit-oriented SETRAC group in that
in recent years the traditional enemy, the Colombian
CTC, has sought to ally itself with UTC goals. As
Landsberger reports, "by the 1960's, both groups
belonged to the same Latin American regional trade
union organization, announced their intention to
merge, and cooperated in a number of educational
ventures."[12]

The Jesuits maintained tighter control on the
FANAL and stressed the importance of the parish
priest in the organizing of rural unions. According to FANAL lay organizers, the rural parish
priest faces religious passivity among his people,
yet maintains high prestige as an intercessor with
local officials and even national elites. The
labor organizer finds that the peasants are suspicious of any new organization but in many cases
will trust the initiatives of the parish priest.
A symbiotic relationship springs up between lay
union organizer and parish priest as long as the
"theological" emphasis of SETRAC is maintained and
union members are encouraged to participate regularly in Catholic rituals in order to fulfill their
obligations to the union. In this way, the priest
is heartened by "spiritual renewal" and increased
"reception of the sacraments," while the lay organizers gain legitimacy and protection.

Eugenio Colorado, one of the lay cofounders of
the UTC and FANAL, said that the priest was indispensable when organizers had decided to initiate a
land invasion. The priest, especially during the
years of "la violencia," was a guarantee against
jail and death. Another organizer told me that he
and a group of thirty peasants would surely have

been killed if they had not been accompanied by a
priest one rainy night in the early 1950's, when
local landowners routed their union meeting and sum-
moned a local army contingent to take them away.
The priest told everyone to sit in the road to
block the trucks; no army officer dared give an order that would harm the priest.

The Colombian Jesuits of CIAS try to take full
advantage of the power of the rural priest in Colombia. A training program for priest-coordinators of
FANAL recruits hundreds of Colombian clerics and
tries to hold them close to the policies set by
Father Andrade. The watchword of FANAL was well
stated by Luis Antonio Palacios, its chief lay
strategist. "There is a saying, 'If the priest is
involved, all is well; otherwise, no.'" Jesuit
CIAS member Father Gustavo Jimenez, in a doctoral
dissertation on "the role of the rural priest as an
agent of social change," found plenty of support
for what FANAL organizers had been saying all along,
that the rural priest was intimately connected with
all sectors of the community, enjoying access to
elites as well as masses.[13]

FANAL's organizing activities centered around
the priest, but also demanded full-time lay organizers, since part of the official FANAL-UTC ideology is that the Church proper (the clergy and hierarchy) is apolitical and that priests connected

with labor movements should be merely "moral advisors" and not decision-makers. The hierarchy
pays for the upkeep of priests, Andrade channels
funds from the Coordination of Social Action into
SETRAC, and there is very little left over for
FANAL. (The UTC is able to raise a lot of its
funds through dues, as well as getting money from
the U.S. Government and other sources.)

According to Luis Antonio Palacios, the FANAL
organizer quoted above, the FANAL derives its financing in large measure from Colombian government
funds. In 1967, Palacios told me, FANAL received
a contract from the government to propagandize on

behalf of the new Association of Creditors, a sub-
unit of the Department of Agriculture. It also received contracts from INCORA and from international
organizations of a private nature, such as the Center for Rural Development. Palacios stated that
FANAL's finances were always in a "state of catas-
trophe" due to its dependence upon ad hoc sources
of support.

In summary, the ability of UTC leaders to build
their own financial base independent of the Jesuits
is no doubt responsible in large measure for their
increasing ideological and operational independence
from the Jesuits. On their side, the Jesuits have
turned more attention to the development of the
FANAL and have only become outwardly concerned
about UTC leadership whenever the latter has appeared to be approaching merger with the more militant CTC. When this has happened, Father Andrade
and Father Jairo Gomez (who organized the UTC in
the Cauca Valley of Colombia) have been quick to
give strong public warnings of the Communist "threat"
they say hovers over the country.

NOTES

1. Observation of SETRAC meetings, 1968, and
interviews with SETRAC members, 1968.

2. Ibid.

3. Observation of SETRAC meetings, 1968.

4. Ibid.

5. Conversation with Andrade, September 12,
1968.

6. Juan Alvarez, "Tacticas del comunismo ruso
en Colombia," Revista Javeriana (Bogota), XXI (1944),
192.

7. Robert J. Alexander, <u>Labor Relations in Argentina, Brazil, and Chile</u> (New York: McGraw Hill, 1962), p. 65.

8. German Guzman Campos, Orlando Fals Borda, and Eduardo Umana Luna, <u>La Violencia en Colombia: Estudio de un proceso social</u> (Bogota: Ediciones Tercer Mundo, 1964).

9. Pierre Bigo, S.J., "Reflexiones sobre la situacion Colombiana," <u>Revista Javeriana</u>, LXI (1964), 223.

10. Poll conducted by the author of fifteen non-UTC and fifteen UTC members in August, 1968. The non-UTC respondents were, for the most part, U.S. "advisory" personnel. There was near unanimous agreement among the UTC members and high congruency among the non-UTC respondents concerning the composition of top leadership, even though the poll focused upon "informal" leadership patterns.

11. See Emilio Maspero, "Comments," in William V. D'Antonio and Frederick B. Pike (eds.), <u>Religion, Revolution and Reform</u> (New York: Frederick A. Praeger, 1964).

12. Henry A. Landsberger, "The Labor Elite: Is It Revolutionary?," in Seymour Martin Lipset and Aldo Solari (eds.), <u>Elites in Latin America</u> (New York: Oxford University Press, 1967), pp. 267-68.

13. The dissertation was published as: Gustavo Jimenez Cadena, <u>Sacerdote y Cambio Social</u> (Bogota: Ediciones Tercer Mundo, 1967).

9

THE

THREAT

TO

JESUIT PREEMINENCE

CAMILO TORRES AND THE UNITED FRONT

Although the Jesuits of CIAS, and particularly those closely connected with SETRAC and the labor movement, have long warned of danger from the non-Catholic CTC and from the small leftist CLASC, their greatest moment of apprehension in recent years was due to the "united front" formed by the young Colombian priest Camilo Torres Restrepo. The history of his movement, which terminated in his violent death in the mountains near Bucaramanga, is not to be recounted here.[1]

For present purposes, it is important to recall that the guerrilla phase of the movement came only after Father Torres had made an attempt to construct an urban base of operations. Why he ceased his efforts in the city is unclear. His former associates, many of whom talked with me at length, disagree about his reasons for taking up arms in the countryside. Some say that his assassination was imminent (in the mode of Gaitan's); others, that he wished to follow the Cuban model of revolution; still others, that he simply found little support among the urban sectors.

One fact is clear: he profoundly threatened the leaders of the Jesuit-advised UTC with his talk

of a united front embracing Catholic and non-
Catholic, leftist and moderate sectors. And he
frightened the Jesuits in particular, as well as
the majority of Colombian bishops. The united
front of Camilo Torres was soon met by another:
that of the Church hierarchy and the Jesuit order.

Father Cesar Jaramillo Velasquez, S.J., the
dean of the faculty of medicine of the Jesuit Universidad Javeriana, wrote in El Espectador on June
20, 1965:

> Father Camilo Torres, in some
> things may be right . . . when he
> talks about the Church. In other
> matters, he is expressing his own
> personal opinions. He should not
> talk except under the direction of
> the Church. If the Cardinal is not
> in agreement with his opinions,
> Father Torres should not disobey the
> hierarchy.[2]

The opinions to which Father Jaramillo alluded
had been set forth by Father Torres in his "Platform for a Movement of Popular Unity," which was
issued on March 17, 1965.

> To all Colombians, to the popu-
> lar class, to the middle class, to
> the organizations of ACCION COMUNAL,
> to the labor unions, cooperatives,
> mutual-assistance organizations,
> peasant-league and worker organiza-
> tions, to the indigenous peoples, to
> all the nonconformists, men and women,
> to all the young people, to all those
> who are not affiliated with the tra-
> ditional political parties, to the
> new parties, we present the follow-
> ing platform in order to unite to-
> ward concrete objectives ourselves
> with the Colombian popular class.[3]

Camilo Torres sought to forge linkages among nearly all of the groups with which the Jesuit CIAS had been working: the UTC, FANAL, UCONAL, university youth, high-school boys, ACCION COMUNAL, etc. But he set himself in opposition to the leaders of the Liberal and Conservative parties, who had been so successfully cultivated by the Jesuits in recent years, as well as to the government bureaucracy, INCORA, private enterprise, the Universidad Javeriana, and the Army.

The Jesuits had sought to organize peasants around a legal conception of land reform, with compensation to the owners of expropriated holdings. Camilo Torres presented the prospect of more violent action:

> Land will belong to those who work it directly. The government will designate rural inspectors to give titles to those peasants who are in these conditions, but will be able to demand that cultivation be by means of cooperative and communitarian systems in accordance with a national farm plan, with credit and technical assistance.
> Land will be bought from no one. What is deemed necessary for the common good will be expropriated without indemnification. . . .[4]

The Jesuits had sought to foster in their urban labor unions respect for free enterprise and solidarity between owner and worker. Torres presented a program for the "abolition of the free-enterprise system and its replacement by a system of cooperative and communitarian enterprise."

Privately owned and operated banks, hospitals, laboratories, and schools would be replaced by nationalized agencies. The Jesuit universities and high schools, which charged high tuition and were therefore open only to the monied classes, would be destroyed or absorbed. Public transportation would be run by cooperative and communitarian enterprises. The press, radio, and television were to be "autonomous but submitted to the control of the state in view of the common good." The university was to be autonomous and organized "as a community of directors, professors and students." It would be "exempt from any intervention by political parties, by the Army, or by the clergy."

Father Torres revived the dormant issue of ecclesiastical wealth in Colombia and demanded an accurate accounting of all Church holdings in land, businesses, and corporations. This was never rendered, of course, but the conservative daily El Siglo reported on June 22, 1965:

> Including residences and churches, the goods of the Church total 5 billion pesos at census value, according to official statistics. This figure is calculated on the basis of reports given periodically by the Agustin Codazzi Geographical Institute, the Census Office of Bogota and that of Medellin. . . . These figures do not include the urban properties of the different ecclesiastical orders nor the private property of bishops and priests.[5]

On June 24, 1965, Camilo Torres asked to be relieved of his priestly duties, and from that day broke off his "dialogue" with Cardinal Concha of Bogota concerning the theological definition of the Church and the role of the Church in Colombian development. Just prior to this action, he had leveled strong accusations against the Colombian Church, describing its efforts in the field of "social action" as "paternalistic" and lamenting the fact that the Church possessed great economic and political power.

Father Vicente Andrade, S.J., the head of the Coordination of Social Action for the Colombian

Bishops and founder of the UTC and FANAL labor federations, took public issue with the statements of Father Torres and with the platform of the United Front. On July 10, 1965, he published a lengthy attack on Torres and the United Front in the major government newspaper of Bogota, El Tiempo, and in the conservative daily El Espectador:

> To say that all of the activity of the Church in the field of social justice has been paternalistic is lamentable ignorance. The person who says this has the duty by the fact that he is a priest to know the truth and by the same fact the possibility of knowing the truth so that this attitude of his casts doubt upon his good faith.
>
> It is clear that Father Camilo Torres, neither in the affirmations he makes that slander the Church nor in the role he tries to assume in the politics of the country, has been faithful to his duties as a priest nor to the loyalty a Christian owes to his Mother the Church.
>
> The platform of the United Front does not once mention the labor unions and other associations as instruments of social reform. Everything must be done by the State, and everything must be under its control.
>
> In these circumstances, all guarantees of civil liberty would disappear before the State and all would end in Nazi or Communist totalitarianism.

The following day, another Jesuit, Father Manuel Foyaca de la Concha, director of the Latin American Secretariat of the Social Apostolate of the Society of Jesus (since absorbed into CLACIAS), wrote in Occidente that the platform of Camilo Torres gave too preponderant a position to the state and that "in some points there is certain Communist inspiration."

THE ICODES AND FATHER GUSTAVO PEREZ

The purpose in presenting the above discussions was not to determine who was right and who wrong, but simply to set the stage for an analysis of the subsequent conflicts that have fragmented the Colombian Church, with special reference to the bitter feud between Colombian Jesuits and the Colombian Institute of Social Development (ICODES), whose priest-director was an intimate friend of Camilo Torres.

Father Gustavo Perez Ramirez, the head of ICODES, is a diocesan priest who studied with Camilo Torres at Louvain in the 1950's. He was one of a group of Colombian students at Louvain who formed the Colombian Socio-Economic Research Team (ECISE), in 1954. Not all the members of the group shared the same political ideology, but all shared a faith in the efficacy of social science for promoting development. Camilo Torres founded European branches of ECISE wherever he found nuclei of Colombian students: in Rome, Paris, London, and Madrid.

The ECISE group soon merged with members of the Colombian Institute of Administrative Sciences (INCCA). At that time the executive committee of the ECISE included Fernando Gaviria, an economist with a Harvard degree who taught at the Jesuit Universidad Javeriana in Bogota and at the Universidad de los Andes, and who was then chief of the Department of Economic Investigations of the Bank of the Republic of Colombia; Cesar Garces Vernaza, an architect who was then head of the Inter-American Housing Center (CINVA); and Lucia Holguin Pardo, a secretary at the Center of Information of the United Nations in Bogota. Although this group was heterogeneous from an ideological standpoint, it provided both Torres and Perez with important linkages to elite planning and diplomatic sectors in the Colombia of the 1960's.

In 1958, the ECISE group became known as the Colombian Team for Study and Progress (ECEP). Gustavo Perez became the secretary general of ECEP

upon his return to Bogota as a newly ordained priest.
Perez took over the task of formulating the ideology
of the group. He chose to minimize the differences
among the members, emphasizing "humanism" and a common interest in scientific study.

In 1959, Abel Naranio Villegas, the Colombian
Minister of Education, designated Camilo Torres,
Gustavo Perez, Orlando Fals Borda, Leonor Martinez
de Rocha, Cesar Garces, Gerardo Tamayo, and three
others as the Committee for the Promotion of ACCION
COMUNAL. Torres, Fals Borda, Perez, and Jaime
Quijano Cabellero wrote the first platform for AC.
The document was circulated, without the names of
the authors, under the aegis of the Minister of Edu-
cation.[6]

The ECEP group continued its collaboration with
bureaucratic and other elites in Colombia until the
early 1960's, when Camilo Torres lost faith in the
process of "legal, evolutionary reform" and directed
his attention to the masses.

Although Camilo Torres and Gustavo Perez disagreed over many things, including the importance
of ideology and of political action by clerics,
Perez supported the Torres United Front when its
manifesto was issued in 1964. He was publicly committed to the Front and to Camilo. In private, however, he had his doubts, and frequently complained:
"Camilo, if they gave you the government tomorrow,
what would you do with it?"[7]

The fact that he was on record as supporting
the platform was remembered after Torres' death.
It reminded the Colombian bishops that the threat
of Camilo Torres continued in the person of Gustavo
Perez and, more dangerously, in the ICODES. As
Jesuit Father Andrade said to me, Gustavo Perez'
"public support of the platform of Camilo Torres
was his fatal mistake." It was fatal from the viewpoint of the Colombian bishops, to whom Gustavo
Perez had been a trusted advisor.

In 1959, when he returned newly ordained from
Louvain with a degree in sociology, Father Gustavo
Perez had been assigned by Bogota's Cardinal Concha
to the Center for Social Investigation (CIS), the
official staff research organization. CIS had had
constantly to fight for its autonomy vis-à-vis the
Jesuit CIAS operation, whose director, Father Vicente
Andrade, was in charge of "coordinating" all works of
the Church's "social apostolate" in Colombia.

Perez used his contacts and early experience
with ACCION COMUNAL to good advantage, working with
Colombian government agencies and eventually obtaining government grants to do case studies of Colombian
rural communities and municipalities. In 1959, CIS
completed a study of the "Conditions of Development
of the Municipio of Santo Domingo, Antioquia." This
was followed by a nearly identical study of the
Municipio of Venecia, also in Antioquia. In 1960,
Perez initiated two more studies: one of the barrio
Alfonso Lopez, in the city of Cucuta, and the other
of the conditions for development in the Region of
Tibu, Catatumbo.

The style of the CIS studies reveals much about
the peculiar bind felt by Perez and his researchers.
They needed money to organize and execute sophisticated surveys, or case studies, of underdevelopment.
But money could only be secured from powerful interest groups. Therefore, they had to make the findings palatable to these sponsors without denying all
of the facts.

The solution took the form of presenting alternate sections in the research report. The first
section would be entitled "negative factors." It
included graphic reports by economists, sociologists,
and medical doctors on disease, the lack of sanitation, unemployment, infant-mortality rates, alcoholism, prostitution, etc. Immediately following would
come a chapter on "positive factors," which praised
the patron of the study and some elite group or government agency for its efforts in helping to correct
some of the "negative" conditions.

The following paragraphs are taken from the
hexographed report on the Municipio of Santo Domingo,
the first study done by CIS under the supervision of
Gustavo Perez. It was commissioned by the Federation of Coffee Growers of Antioquia, a group of
large landowners who were eager to protect their investments. (The CIS research team lavishly praised
the Federation in the introduction to the study):

> Element #1. The Level of Health
> and Sanitation. This is a general
> impression of the situation as held
> by persons competent to the region:
> doctors, midwives, nurses, inspectors
> of hygiene.
>   A. Negative Factors . . .
>   The sanitary needs of Santo
> Domingo are multiple: among other
> problems for urgent solution are con-
> taminated drinking water, infant mor-
> tality, typhoid fever, intestinal
> parasites, sicknesses deriving from
> anemia. In general the population
> is undernourished.
>   B. Positive Factors . . .
>   Thanks to a well carried out
> and exemplary health campaign under-
> taken by professionals of great pres-
> tige and sponsored by the Foundation
> of Coffee Growers, there is a general
> and active preoccupation on the part
> of the population to solve its health
> and sanitation problems. Thanks to
> the Foundation, a basic problem has
> been solved: the consciousness of
> the population has been awakened to
> the possibilities of betterment.

The study report moves on to other problems:
alcoholism, "low level of social ethics," lack of
initiative, prostitution. The solutions to these
problems were not attributed to any rearrangement
of the social system that involved redistribution
of wealth or even community organization. Instead,

the investigators proposed that educational efforts
be continued to teach the people "the intrinsic
worth of individual human beings" and the necessity
to work "for the common good."

> The women promoters and their
> helpers will try to assemble as many
> poor people as possible in the home
> economics centers of ACCION COMUNAL
> . . . or in the churches to give
> them, at least once a month, simple
> instructions concerning how they may
> best struggle against injustices:
> that is, by understanding them. . . .

"Injustices" in this context referred to the patterns of exploitation the poor exercised over one
another, rather than to any acts involving different social classes.

Gustavo Perez hoped that the extremely low
levels of health, education, living conditions, and
economic life depicted in the studies would move the
large landowners or the government ACCION COMUNAL to
improve the situation. He was disappointed.[8]

The study of the Municipio of Venecia is also
instructive, because here, too, the money for the
study came from the Federation of Coffee Growers of
Antioquia. The report begins with recognition of
the efforts of the Federation and of the bank that
it sponsors, then passes on to a detailed analysis
of the problem of peasants who walk around without
shoes and pick up a type of tropical anemia called
ancylostoma. Infant mortality is 179 for every
1,000 births, and there is general undernutrition.
The study reports that 80 per cent of the population does not practice dental hygiene. All water
supplies are contaminated. (The juxtaposition of
infant mortality rates with the number of people
who do not brush their teeth does not constitute an
attempt at humor. It reflects the actual composition of the study report.)

Land tenure is discussed: 37.4 per cent of
the farms (396) have less than one hectare; 85 per
cent (904) have less than 10 hectares. Haciendas
with more than 200 hectares, which make up 2.3 per
cent of the farms and 53 per cent of the area of
the municipio, are not termed latifundias by the investigators. The term is explicitly rejected. However, this section of the report poses the question
it says is being asked by many small farmers: "Is
it possible with the produce from less than one hectare of coffee plants to sustain a peasant family?"
The investigators do not attempt to answer the question.

The recommendations made by the investigators
involve two proposals: first, introduce new tools
and farming methods; second, teach the use of the
new tools and methods to the small farmers. In
other words, diffusion of innovations, with the
large farms granting "visiting days" or holding
demonstrations of new equipment for the benefit of
the small (one hectare and under) farmers.

Land reform is not mentioned in the report, nor
are peasant unions. Instead, it is pointed out
that most small farmers know nothing about eugenics
and frequently, out of ignorance rather than necessity, plant bad seed.

Nevertheless, there are positive factors. One
is the very existence of "model farms" in the municipio, especially that of "Esteban Jaramillo," which
belongs to the Federation of Coffee Growers.

At the conclusion of the study, however, an observation is made that offsets even this most positive of factors.

> Perhaps the reason why small cof-
> fee growers are not applying the
> techniques of the experimental farm
> of "Esteban Jaramillo" is because of
> the poverty in which they live. . . .

> The typical small producer is a man
> with five to forty coffee bushes who
> is trying to support a wife and six
> children without any possibility of
> obtaining credit. Besides this, he
> is ignorant.

The pattern set by these first studies by CIS
was admirably maintained in the later ones written
after CIS had been incorporated into ICODES as the
latter's "department for the investigation of social
problems and social planning." From 1959 to 1969,
twenty studies were made by CIS/ICODES.

The studies undertaken by CIS/ICODES before
the death of Camilo Torres were never widely distributed. They were usually hexographed, with fewer than a dozen copies made. In three cases: a
study for the mayor of the city of Cucuta (1960), a
study of the textile firm COLTEJER (1961), and a
study of the textile firm FABRICATO (1965), the results were termed "confidential" and fewer than six
copies were made. (As a result, it is impossible
today even for ICODES to locate a copy of the study
done for the mayor of Cucuta, and several other
studies are to be found only in the private library
of ICODES.)

Until the death of Torres, all the studies were
done under contracts with either the Federation of
Coffee Growers, ACCION COMUNAL, or private business,
in other words, always with groups that had interests to defend in the area being studied. As a result, the CIS studies continued, until Torres' death,
to address themselves primarily to elites involved
in the area. There is only one instance of a CIS
report reprimanding a study's patron. This occurs
in a study of the FABRICATO textile firm in Medellin,
completed while Camilo Torres was publishing his
platform for the United Front.

The death of Camilo Torres in February, 1966,
brought to an end the careful, polite dissections
of misery that were done at the behest of powerful

private or governmental elites. Nevertheless, CIS/
ICODES did not become openly critical of these
elites. They merely shifted their focus of attention to problems of religious sociology, to studies
of Catholic youth centers and high-school students,
to attitudes toward birth control. In 1967 and
1968, ICODES again turned to a study of underdevel-
oped regions in Colombia, but Gustavo Perez did not
personally supervise these endeavors. He was, by
this time, very busy with the largest project of
his career: a study for U.S. AID.

ACCION COMUNAL: THE PRIZE
IN THE COUNTRYSIDE

Throughout the ten years of CIS/ICODES operation, Gustavo Perez had maintained excellent contacts with ACCION COMUNAL, the Colombian government's attempt to "incorporate peasant sectors into
national life" by encouraging them to solve their
problems through their own efforts. Gustavo Perez,
together with Camilo Torres, Orlando Fals Borda,
and Jaime Quijano, had written the first platform
of ACCION COMUNAL in 1959.

It is obvious from Camilo Torres' later platform for the United Front that he conceived the importance of ACCION COMUNAL to lie in its political
potential. He emphasized in the platform that
Colombia was ruled by "a minority that will never
decide against its own interests," and that ACCION
COMUNAL should be "a foundation for democratic planning . . . a base . . . toward achieving the free
election of municipal authorities by the residents."[9]

Camilo Torres was careful to include the ACCION
COMUNAL groups in his appeal for a united popular
front, but he was not happy with the way they had
been organized nor with their actual procedures.
Gustavo Perez was more willing to accept the actuality of ACCION COMUNAL. His studies of municipalities that contained AC groups always mentioned them
in glowing terms. Moreover, Perez was eager to

cement his close ties with the mayors and governors
who could help ICODES with recommendations for government funds and with collaboration on specific
projects. One such official was the Mayor of Circuito, Manuel G. Rossi Pacheco, who was a member of
the planning staff of ACCION COMUNAL in the department of Boyaca, in the Tenza Valley.

Perez' CIS/ICODES team had done a study of the
"Conditions of Development in Northwestern Boyaca"
in late 1964. It was highly laudatory of AC leadership and incorporated into its extensive treatment
of ACCION COMUNAL many of the points made by the
mayor of Circuito in his "Manual Prepared for the
Locals of ACCION COMUNAL in the Municipality of
Garagoa."

Rossi Pacheco's manual was written in the form
of a Catholic catechism, presenting questions and
the approved answers. It was used as a guide for
CIS/ICODES investigators in their treatment of
ACCION COMUNAL. Excerpts from the manual follow
(translated from the original Spanish):

> What is ACCION COMUNAL?
> It is the union of the peasants
> of a community organized so that they
> can with their own efforts solve
> their own problems. Some of these
> problems might be: the construc-
> tion of a school or its improvement,
> the paving of roads, the construc-
> tion of rural aqueducts, the improve-
> ment of agriculture. . . .
> Who are the people who have the
> most serious problems in the com-
> munity?
> The peasants. We have been the
> victims of politics at all times.
> We have been the victims of violence
> and hate between brothers. But the
> fault is ours, because we have not
> been organized. We have sought to
> live always isolated.

It is clear from the rest of the manual that the mayor conceived ACCION COMUNAL as a substitute for more radical organizations. It would be an organization that would strengthen rather than subvert existing government programs and policies.

Does ACCION COMUNAL have anything to do with Communism?

No. ACCION COMUNAL is a democratic organization formed by the peasants, for the help and bettering of problems in the community. Communism is a bad doctrine that tries to make peasants the slaves of the government. The only thing that Communism offers is hunger and misery. In Communism we cannot practice our Catholic religion, because Communism is atheistic, which means that they do not believe in God.

Besides building schools, aqueducts, and roads, what else may be done by ACCION COMUNAL?

We can seek help for organizing cooperatives, and by means of these assure that the agronomists and veterinarians of the government help us with our crops and cattle.

What is the moral character of a member of the junta of ACCION COMUNAL?

He is a man of moral value who guards it as a precious good. . . .

He practices his religion, because he is Catholic.

He loves his country and is willing to sacrifice himself for her. . . .

He does not get discouraged. . . .

He respects the laws and helps enforce them.

What is the greatest honor that a peasant can obtain in his community?

The greatest honor he can obtain is to belong to the Directive Committee of the Junta of ACCION COMUNAL, because this is serving God and his family.

The ACCION COMUNAL groups were counseled not to expect financial aid from the government, with the possible exception of credit, which was sometimes available to cooperatives. They were expected to supply their own labor, money, and working materials.

> What are the contributions that the members make to the organization of ACCION COMUNAL?
> 1. To give to the junta the greatest work effort possible.
> 2. Each of the members should contribute for the works which the junta initiates money, materials, work.
> 3. Etc. . . .

In many cases, the local priest was the president of the junta of ACCION COMUNAL. These priests were, of course, prime targets for the organizing activities of Jesuit FANAL, which sought to "collaborate with" ACCION COMUNAL to the extent of turning the juntas into locals for the FANAL union organization.[10] These efforts were strongly resisted in many places, such as the northwest of Boyaca, where ICODES was operating in close contact with ACCION COMUNAL, the mayor of Guateque, and the governor of the province.

Father Andrade encountered ICODES again and again during the 1960's in all parts of Colombia. ICODES director Gustavo Perez had been one of the early proponents of the AC movement, and his contacts were spread throughout Colombia: Catatumbo, Antioquia, Casanare, Valle de Cauca, Santander, Meta, Boyaca. As a fellow priest, Andrade had at first expected Perez to be receptive.[11] When the latter rejected any cooperation with the veteran Jesuit "labor specialist," Andrade was at first surprised. He later came to understand that the Jesuit network of "advisory" organizations was being fundamentally challenged by ICODES for the allegiance of the same clientele: the local community

organizations of ACCION COMUNAL, the Colombian Catholic Bishops' Conference, the Colombian private sector. Within a few years ICODES would name as its
own board of directors precisely those prominent
Colombians who had been earlier enlisted by the
Jesuits to form the advisory board of Colombian
Jesuit CIAS. The wealthy and powerful Colombian
Coffee Federation would support studies by ICODES
and not those by CIAS. ACCION COMUNAL would become
an elusive prize to the Jesuit FANAL organization
as ICODES counseled it to "remain out of politics."
Foreign Church monies would flow to ICODES, bypass-
ing for the most part CIAS and the Jesuits. U.S.
AID monies, flooding into Colombia in the early
1960's, would be denied the Jesuits in lieu of
ICODES' studies of attitudes toward birth control.
The Conference of Latin American Bishops (CELAM)
would adopt Gustavo Perez as one of its principal
advisors while ignoring the Colombian Jesuits.
Only the Colombian bishops, and in particular, the
archbishops of Bogota, would give preferential
treatment to Jesuit CIAS and heed Andrade's dire
warnings concerning the dangers courted by ICODES.

I have been trying to demonstrate in the preceding pages that the chief distinction between the
Jesuit CIAS group and the Perez CIS/ICODES group
did not lie in their ideologies. Both groups were
fundamentally conservative, anti-Communist, nonrevo-
lutionary. Both groups sought to function as agents
of social control, servicing powerful interests.
Both groups were in the process of bureaucratization, seeking to develop sophisticated specialist
responses to emergent market demands. The cutting
point between them was not ideology. It was the
carving out of an adequate organizational base.

The Jesuits had long sought to incorporate into
their operations the "leaders" or the "elite" of
problematic sectors. Through these leaders they
sought to absorb into the religious system the
masses of urban workers, campesinos, students, and
businessmen. The Church always formed the prime
point of reference. Father Andrade, as head of the

Coordination of Catholic Action, was the most prominent (some would say most powerful) Jesuit in Colombia, and had extended Jesuit and Catholic influence
markedly by founding the FANAL and the UTC. His
prime referent was the episcopal hierarchy to which
his own Jesuit superiors were irrevocably committed.
The first major threat in the 1960's to Colombia's
episcopal hierarchy also constituted a major threat
to Andrade's influence over the Catholic labor sector. Camilo Torres openly attacked the religious
system and ignored the commands of Colombian bishops to be silent. Jesuit Father Andrade, along
with a host of other Jesuits, vigorously attacked
Father Torres.

The Jesuit letters published in El Mercurio,
El Espectador, and other Bogota dailies differed
markedly from the letters of diocesan and other
priests of similar intent. The latter usually emphasized the analytical errors of Camilo Torres,
whom they called a "madman" or a "demagogue" for
entering politics. The Jesuits did not take this
tack, but were instead adamant on one point: that
Camilo Torres had disobeyed the Cardinal. His
error was not so much in what he had said as in the
fact that he had gone against the wishes of his religious superior. The Jesuits are a religious order that from its inception has emphasized obedience
to ecclesiastical authorities above all other vir-
tues, and in Colombia, as elsewhere, its identification with these powerful interests has often guaranteed its survival.

Gustavo Perez was not a Jesuit but a diocesan
priest. He was directly subject to the Cardinal of
Bogota, who had permitted him to study abroad upon
the recommendation of seminary officials. When
Father Perez returned to Colombia in 1959, he was
assigned to work with the Center of Social Investigation (CIS) which had been founded by other diocesan priests to carry out studies for the Colombian
Bishops' Conference. But Perez soon became aware
that the bishops were less interested in sociological studies than in directly affecting the course

of Colombian history through intervening in the
Rojas Pinilla government (via Jesuit law school dean
Giraldo)[12] and through gaining control of a sizeable
sector of organized labor (via Jesuit Father Andrade).
They also controlled most of Colombian primary and
secondary education, the Jesuit Universidad Javeriana,
and, through the Concordat, had veto powers over the
selection of professors and curricula at the National
University. The bishops offered CIS no money for
sociological research, although they did encourage
CIS specialists to write anti-Communist pamphlets
setting forth the "social doctrine of the Church."

In short, the Catholic episcopal hierarchy had
little to offer Gustavo Perez, who already possessed
wide-ranging international and cosmopolitan contacts
(through Camilo Torres' ECISE group and other sources),
with the heads of government agencies, ACCION COMUNAL,
the university communities, and even with the Colombian ministers of education and economics.

It might have been possible for Fathers Andrade
and Perez to have followed different paths, continuing to draw their support from and confining their
services to distinct sectors had it not been for the
following developments:

1. Father Andrade was forced to turn to FANAL
to offset his diminishing influence within the urban-
based UTC. This meant that Father Andrade looked to
the ACCION COMUNAL organizations as ready-made bases
for his organizationally weak FANAL, and thus collided with mayors, governors, and others who had
control of AC and to whom Gustavo Perez was oriented.

2. Father Perez secured through his former
mentor at Louvain, Francois Houtart, the position
of executive secretary of FERES for Latin America.
Father Perez thus became the coordinator of centers
that were publishing studies for the Catholic Bishops' Conference of the United States and Latin
America as well as for the Vatican. The first study
published was a census of the priests and other religious functionaries in Colombia. For the first

time, the Colombian bishops were given an accurate picture of their own manpower resources. For a short while Gustavo Perez became a sought-after advisor of the Colombian hierarchy. The status of Father Andrade was threatened.

3. Camilo Torres made his break with the Colombian power elite, calling upon all "the popular sectors" to unite for an assault upon the established political and economic system. Father Andrade felt that his entire labor movement, rural and urban, was being stolen from him by Camilo Torres. At the same time, Gustavo Perez was led by his long-standing friendship with Torres to commit himself publicly to a platform he would otherwise never have supported. The Colombian bishops, to whom Camilo Torres was a "renegade priest," were outraged. They began to treat Gustavo Perez as a co-conspirator with Torres and the United Front.

Father Andrade had strong allies in the Colombian chancery (the Colombian Cardinal's bureaucracy). This coalition was prompted to control ICODES directly, but discovered that this was impossible since Perez had constructed an organization that was not formally clerical but which displayed a lay board of directors consisting of the president of the Federation of Coffee Growers, the former Minister of Agriculture, two prominent Colombian businessmen, and the head of the Colombian Institute for Technical Training Abroad (ICETEX), which controls scholarships given to Colombian students by foreign foundations and governments.

The Cardinal tried to place an ecclesiastical representative on the board of directors, but he was told that the priest could not vote or take part in decision-making, since this would impair lay autonomy. The Jesuit CIAS team had originally attempted to form their own board of directors with some of the same people who later "adopted" ICODES. In fact, for a time, the president of the Federation of Coffee Growers, among others, was so listed. But no formal collaboration took place between him

and the Jesuits after he was invited to participate
in ICODES operations.[13]

THE GROWTH OF ICODES

By 1964, ICODES had become "a private development agency, non-profit, operationally oriented
with a multi-disciplinary focus, dedicated to investigation, planning, operation of programs and
formation of persons."[14]

It comprised four sections: the Center for
Social Investigations (CIS); the Institute for Professional Development (INPRODE), which gave talks
and training courses to priests, teachers, and
other "professionals"; the Operational Development
Center (CODESA), which was to function as a consulting firm for government, Church, and private industry; and the Institute of Audio Visual Systems
(ISAV), which soon became the second largest (to
Kodak) film-processing laboratory in Colombia and
which produced newsreels and offered screening
facilities for 35 mm. movies.

ICODES was housed in the former offices of ex-
dictator Rojas Pinilla, in downtown Bogota. The
building was purchased with the aid of a massive
loan from ADVENIAT, the German Bishops' Fund, and
with the help of the Dutch government. The financial assistance was negotiated by Francois Houtart
and by the Belgian Jesuit Roger Vekemans.

To pay off the newly acquired debts of ICODES,
Gustavo Perez sent his CIS team into the field of
industrial sociology, contracting them to do labor-
management studies for the Colombian textile complex, FABRICATO.* He had learned how profitable

---

*According to Frank Brandenburg's report The
Development of Latin American Private Enterprise
(Washington, D.C.: National Planning Association,

such studies could be from a study that his CIS team
had done in 1961 for COLTEJER, the largest of Colombia's textile and manufacturing plants. Perez
showed the FABRICATO people a copy of the COLTEJER
study report, and they were understandably enthusiastic. The entire report was a glowing tribute to
the "great family of COLTEJER," by which was meant
the corporation: owners, managers, workers. The
COLTEJER study is, once again, an example of the influence of a study's patron upon the sociological
analysis which he pays for.

In quoting from the study in the following
pages, I have taken pains to show how conciliatory
to management CIS/ICODES chose to be in a period
(1961) when their research operation was small and
financially insecure. The COLTEJER study contrasts
with the later (1965) study of FABRICATO, where
CIS/ICODES researchers found very similar labor conditions but chose to be far more critical of ownership and management. This change in the research
style of CIS/ICODES can be traced to the different
phases of organizational development that each
period represents.

In 1961, the CIS depended entirely upon the
contracts it could garner from government, industry,
and private groups such as the Federation of Coffee
Growers. In 1965, CIS became linked to a larger,
more diversified operation, ICODES, which was making
money with its film-processing and distribution
plant and which had forged strong ties to FERES, and
therefore to European Catholic foundations, as well
as to U.S. AID.

1964) (Planning Pamphlet No. 121), COLTEJER is the
eighth largest enterprise in Colombia (the third
largest private enterprise). FABRICATO is the nineteenth largest. BAVARIA breweries is the third
largest enterprise in the country, after the ACERIAS
PAZ DEL RIO steel complex and the National Railroads.
    ICODES not only contracted studies for COLTEJER
and FABRICATO, but also contracted to do a public
relations film for BAVARIA.

1965 marked the beginnings of the Camilo Torres revolt which appeared, for a time, as if it might be successful in projecting the young priest into a position of political power. Camilo Torres was well aware of the studies his close friend and fellow sociologist Gustavo Perez had been making for elite groups that Camilo considered part of the Colombian oligarchy. Some gesture of solidarity with Camilo was required of Gustavo Perez at this time. The FABRICATO report, with its strong criticism of paternal ownership, is consistent with the public allegiance which Gustavo Perez was offering Camilo's United Front.

Following are excerpts from both the COLTEJER (1961) and the FABRICATO (1965) studies. Both reports were marked by ICODES "confidential."

The COLTEJER study begins with a tribute to the "great family of COLTEJER" (excerpts translated from the Spanish):

> In the case of the Colombian Textile Company, COLTEJER, the term "great family" is not purely figurative. There is really an extraordinary love and identification on the part of most workers for their company and on the part of the director of the company for the workers.

There are problems, to be sure, but these do not diminish the family spirit.

> It is natural that there exist mutual deficiencies in isolated cases, but it is undeniable that there is the solid Christian structure of the relations between the workers and the patrones.

Moreover, this "solid Christian structure" has not been recently constructed, nor has it been built without much self-sacrifice on the part of the owners:

> The conditions of harmony already
> noted took root in the founding of
> COLTEJER, because its founders and
> their heirs radiated and continue to
> radiate . . . a fraternal and Chris-
> tian love which eliminates the possi-
> bility that the company will become,
> unintentionally or through neglect,
> the kind of inhuman machine that
> creates a proletariat.

Whatever problems there are can be eliminated by
Catholic altruism.

> Although one finds great defi-
> ciencies, the dynamism of the direc-
> tors of COLTEJER . . . is the creative
> force for the construction of condi-
> tions for a human civilization. They
> have begun by truly loving humanity,
> giving to it the full gift of them-
> selves.

The CIS report continues in this vein. However, buried in the pages of statistics documenting
worker satisfaction lie some interesting findings.

Fifty per cent of the workers' houses have contaminated water. Infant mortality is 54/1000 for
the first year of life, 70/1000 for the first five
years; this is only slightly less than the figures
for Medellin as a whole, even though the Medellin
figures include the families of the unemployed as
well as those of the employed. Bronchial pneumonia
among the workers of COLTEJER is documented at 874
cases out of 8,000 studied. There were present 168
cases of typhoid at the time the study was taken.

The statistics on the "economic level" of the
workers are also interesting. Eight thousand workers made less than 1,200 pesos ($60) per month. An
average worker income, including "family benefits,"
was 560 pesos per month. Average expenditures for
such a family (living in company housing and buying

from the company store) was calculated at about 590
pesos. As a result, most of the workers were in
debt to COLTEJER and had been for years. Thirty-
six per cent of the workers had worked for the company for more than eleven years; another 36 per cent
had worked there for less than eleven but more than
five years.

Not surprisingly, the CIS investigators found
that "most of the workers, with a few exceptions,
love the company very much." However, the report
warned that the "few exceptions" could cause problems:

> Negative factors:
> 1. Some few workers manifest def-
> inite aggressivity against the company,
> against the wealthy, and against the
> clergy.
> 2. The activity of agitators is
> undeniable. . . .

The CIS team also listed as a "negative factor"
the fact that 28 per cent of the workers at COLTEJER
had been with the company less than four years, suggesting that the troublemakers derived from the
ranks of these "newcomers." There was clearly a
correlation between degree of economic indebtedness
(or low degree of autonomy) and positive affect.
The older workers, almost all of whom had heavy
debts to the company, were the ones most positive
in their evaluation of the firm. The investigators
also found that the long-term workers rejected
unionization attempts with more intransigency than
did the workers who had been employed fewer than
four years at COLTEJER.

The study report listed as a negative factor
its finding that "many workers who are unionized
look upon the union as a means of being served and
not of serving . . . (the employer)." The study
complained of the COLTEJER unions: "They have no
great concern with increasing culture, work capacity,
responsibility, or better care of the machinery."

The investigators noted that "many of the unionized
workers think that the first thing is to ask, the
second thing is to ask, and the third thing is to
ask, and they don't even consider the reciprocal
act of giving." This section of the study closed
with advice for the union leaders at COLTEJER:

> True union leaders should not
> feel a temptation to aggressive re-
> vindication nor political pressure
> tactics, but they should take upon
> themselves the task of lifting up
> the working class and leading it to
> a higher spiritual and moral level.

It is interesting to note that in many ways
the ICODES' conception of unionization is very
close to that of the Jesuit founders of the UTC
labor unions in that the Jesuits also talk frequently of solidarity between owner and worker and emphasize (as in SETRAC) the moral and spiritual "formation" of the workers over and above any militant
pressuring for "demands."

The FABRICATO study, done in the closing
months of 1964 is, like the COLTEJER study, confidential. Few copies were ever made and those were
hexographed and never published for a wider audi-
ence. The Fabrica de Hilados y Tejidos del Hato,

S.A. (FABRICATO) is also situated in Medellin and is
built upon the COLTEJER system of labor-management
relations. In many ways, FABRICATO seems to have
improved upon COLTEJER's working conditions and aid
to workers.

Nevertheless, the study by CIS/ICODES of
FABRICATO is notably different from that of its
study of COLTEJER. Instead of merely describing
"positive and negative factors" related to the economic and social condition of the workers, the CIS
team introduced the typology of Alain Touraine,
which outlines three phases through which an industrial firm may pass as it becomes increasingly
bureaucratized.[15]

The first of these phases finds the worker an
"artisan" with a great deal of functional autonomy.
Problems of quality manufacture are more important
than problems of mass production. In this phase,
the owner is himself a craftsman and dominates his
employees as much by his superior craftsmanship as
by control of capital. The second phase is the
phase of standardization and mass production. The
worker loses his functional autonomy as he becomes
replaceable. Mechanization replaces hand labor,
and there is further task specification and division
of labor. Phase three is characterized by the replacement of the owner-operator by a professional
manager, an increase in impersonal controls, and increased bureaucratization.

The model of Touraine was employed by the CIS/
ICODES investigators in an ingenious way. They
placed FABRICATO "in transition" between phase one
and phase two. The workers were being prepared for
mass production and the owner-operator still exercised personal controls. As was the case of
COLTEJER, he continued to give ample evidence of
"Christian love and fraternal solidarity."

CIS/ICODES investigators found that, in marked
similarity to the findings of the COLTEJER study,
88 per cent of the FABRICATO workers looked upon
the company as "a great family," while 98 per cent
felt proud when they heard others speak well of
FABRICATO products. (The reliability of these responses must be called into question because of a
glaring contradiction in responses to another item
on the questionnaire: 85 per cent of the workers
declared that they had no debts to anyone, while a
check of company records revealed that almost all
were in fact in debt to FABRICATO.)

Although the salaries and living conditions of
FABRICATO workers were in every way comparable to
those of the COLTEJER employees, CIS/ICODES had
harsh words for FABRICATO owners. The company com-
pound was called "a true home for adolescents."
The study report upbraided the company owners for

"paternalism" and strongly condemned the pressuring
of workers to attend daily mass, to make monthly
"spiritual retreats," etc. The investigators advocated the raising of salaries and labeled the economic gains of the workers as "insufficient," although "high when compared to the majority of Colombian workers."

The CIS/ICODES team leaned heavily upon the
condemnation of "paternalism" contained in a study
of workers in Bogota.[16] This study was made in
1964-65 by Father Ireneo Rosier, the "spiritual advisor" and close friend of Father Camilo Torres.[17]
Conversations with former members of the CIS/ICODES
research team who had participated in the FABRICATO
study revealed that the introduction of Rosier's
orientation, together with the inclusion of the
theories of the French sociologist Touraine, was
the result of the influence of Father Camilo Torres,
who took a personal interest in the study.

The recommendations of the CIS/ICODES study report to FABRICATO were not acted upon. The managers evidently felt that their methods and incen-
tives were adequate.

CIS/ICODES undertook no further management-
consulting projects for some time. In 1968, when
the BAVARIA brewery in Bogota sought a study of its
own personnel problems, it turned not to CIS/ICODES
but to the "Office of Sociological Research" of the
Archdiocese of Bogota, a newly formed entity directly subject to Archbishop Munoz Duque.[18] After the
death of Camilo Torres, Gustavo Perez found himself
and his organization under attack from the right-
wing business interests who formed the "Mano Negra"
("Black Hand"), and also was snubbed by the North
American National Association of Manufacturers
(NAM), whose president, W. P. Gullander, he had
cultivated on previous visits to the United States.[19]

But these losses were more than offset by the
gains inherent in the investiture of Gustavo Perez
as executive secretary for Latin America for FERES.

In 1964, the former mentor of Gustavo Perez and Camilo Torres, Father Francois Houtart, used his position as head of FERES to arrange financing of the purchase of CIS/ICODES headquarters in Bogota. That year marked the date of the formal constitution of ICODES as a juridical civil entity registered with the Minister of Justice.

ICODES retroactively labeled all studies done by CIS as ICODES productions, and there was actual continuity back through the years as long as Gustavo Perez had been director. But now Perez was in charge of an organization that--

1. Had financing completely independent of the Colombian bishops; its chief ties were to ADVENIAT, the German Bishops' Fund "for religious research."

2. Coordinated FERES centers in Brazil, Chile, Argentina, Venezuela, and Mexico; two of these centers, those in Chile and Argentina, were intimately linked to Jesuit CIAS groups.

3. Advised the staff departments of the Conference of Latin American Bishops (CELAM), whom it had greatly impressed by publishing the first comprehensive censuses of the Church in Latin America.

4. Could lobby effectively for research grants from North American and Northern European foundations and governments.

In the mid-1960's, ICODES, acting as the regional secretariat for FERES in Latin America, may have appeared to many as a unifying agent for what appeared even then to be conflicting forces within the Latin American Catholic system.

On December 19, 1965, Francois Houtart and Gustavo Perez met in Bogota to draft a plan whereby the major centers of sociological investigation within the Latin American Church might be "coordinated" into the official staff structure of CELAM.

This, it was hoped, would eliminate rivalries and
help to redress unequal access to the funds of the
North American and European bishops.

According to the ACTA (Minutes) #5 of this
meeting, Archbishop Eugenio Sales, then president
of the Department of Social Action of CELAM, was to
make formal invitations to all FERES-affiliated centers in Latin America, to all Jesuit CIAS centers,
to DESAL (Jesuit Roger Vekemans' Center for Economic
and Social Development), and to Ivan Illich, head
of the Center for Intercultural Formation (CIF),
based in Cuernavaca, Mexico.

These principals were to agree upon specific
projects, which would then be submitted to the North
American bishops through CELAM. In this way, the
North Americans would not be besieged by aid requests
from many disparate sources, and the major organizational staff interests inside the Latin American
Church would be able to divide, amicably, the major
chunk of research allocations.

The minutes of this meeting are not yet available, but it is clear that it did not go as planned.
Instead of mutual agreement concerning specific
projects, there was the widest possible disagreement. No common purpose emerged from the meeting.
On the contrary, the participants left the parley
nursing bitter personal antipathies.

Within a year, Father Ivan Illich would publish an article in the North American Jesuit weekly, America, condemning any and all kinds of aid
sent by the North American bishops to Latin America.
The Colombian Jesuit CIAS would become irrevocably
committed to the suppression of ICODES and to the
"restructuring" of Chilean Jesuit CIAS. DESAL
would be quarreling with ICODES over population
studies for which each was seeking funds. This
welter of fragmenting staff forces will be dissected
and analyzed in the pages to follow.

NOTES

1. For a compilation of the speeches, procla-
mations, letters, and other documents of Camilo
Torres, see <u>Camilo Torres</u>, por el Padre Camilo
Torres Restrepo (1965-66), Sondeos No. 5, Centro
Intercultural de Documentacion (CIDOC), Cuernavaca,
Mexico.

Biographies and interpretations include
German Guzman Campos, <u>Camilo, El Cura Guerillero</u>
(Bogota: Servicios Especiales de Prensa, 1967);
and John Alvarez Garcia, <u>Camilo Torres, His Life
and His Message</u> (London: Templegate, 1969). See
also John Womack "Priest of Revolution," <u>The New
York Review of Books</u>, XIII, 7 (October 23, 1969).

2. Guzman, op. cit., pp. 77-79. Translation
here and below by DEM.

3. <u>Ibid</u>.

4. <u>Ibid</u>., p. 78.

5. <u>Ibid</u>.

6. <u>Ibid</u>., pp. 65-72.

7. Conversation with Father Gustavo Perez,
July 10, 1968.

8. <u>Ibid</u>.

9. Guzman, <u>op. cit</u>., p. 79.

10. Conversation with FANAL organizers, July
21, 1968.

11. Conversation with Vicente Andrade, September 8, 1968.

12. Conversations with the wife of a cabinet
minister so appointed, and with a former aide to
Rojas Pinilla.

202   THE CHURCH AS A POLITICAL FACTOR

13. Conversation with Gustavo Jimenez Cadena, S.J., September 7, 1968.

14. From an official ICODES brochure addressed to the public, 1967.

15. Typology of Alain Touraine as discussed in Friedman Navillo, Traite du socilogie du travail (Paris: Armand Colin, 1961), I, 387-429.

16. Ireneo Rosier, Problemas humanas en las zonas sub-urbanas de Bogota (Facultad de Psicologia, Universidad Nacional, 1965).

17. Ireneo Rosier, "Camilo Torres, La Contradiccion," Mundo Nuevo (Buenos Aires), No. 28 (October, 1968), pp. 4-12.

18. Conversation with Father Hubert Schuan, the head of the Office of Sociological Studies of the Archdiocese of Bogota, September 12, 1968. ICODES, as mentioned above, did obtain a contract with BAVARIA in 1968, after they ran into difficulties with ADVENIAT.

19. Conversation with Gustavo Perez, July 20, 1968.

10

THE

ICODES-FERES STUDY

OF

THE CHURCH

FERES, and especially its Colombian affiliate, ICODES, was not particularly concerned about these misunderstandings in mid-1966, because it had secured $140,000 from United States AID to study Church attitudes toward birth control in Latin America. The proposal to AID was made in September, 1965, and was itself the source of contention with the Colombian Jesuit CIAS and with Chilean DESAL. But by the time the proposal was accepted, months after the attempted reconciliation of staff sectors in Bogota, ICODES had abandoned any role of peacemaker among competing interest groups and was determined to get on with what would prove to be its most profitable and prestigious undertaking.

What FERES was proposing to United States AID was an inside look at the Catholic decision-making process, so that the interested parties who funded the study might develop strategies for changing official Church policies concerning birth control. The FERES proposal, which was never released to Church line sectors (the bishops and the Vatican), began with the following introduction:

> The social and cultural change taking place in Latin America and the religious transformation occurring in the organized religions cannot but

come to the attention of scholars, as
well as to international and national
development agencies and research institutions interested in the fate of
these countries.

The inner workings of the Catholic system would be
revealed.

A group of Social Scientists of
the Latin American Section of the International Federation of Institutes
for Socio-Religious and Social Research
(FERES) decided to approach this issue through a research that would explain the interlocking functioning of
the patterns of policy and administration procedures of Organized Religion in its relationship to the development of religious systems. . . .

Explicit attention would be directed to policy formation and implementation processes:

The problem to be clarified consists in the question of how religious systems go about finding the
broad lines for orientation (policy)
and for work-a-day administrative
conduct in a context of change, and
how the Churches actually implement
those policies and administrative
tasks in the fact of social development. . . .

According to the FERES proposal, the study
would not only describe policy formation and implementation but would be used to influence it.

The goal of this research is to
create an awareness among religious
leaders and members so that they
might be. more effective in areas related in so many ways to the solution
of the Latin American crisis.

The "crisis" with which FERES was concerned (as was AID, presumably) was the Church's ban of artificial means of birth control.

> In considering the factors that maximize potential and reduce obstacles for socio-economic development, we will give top priority to the study of the relationship between religion and the current demographic problems of Latin America.

The FERES group then inserted the notion of a "Catholic ethic" of rationally ordered change sanctioned and promoted through hierarchical organization.

> An organized religion has unrecognized potential to undertake the role of change agent with regard to institutions it is actually related to. . . . Therefore, if organized religion is allowed to become more flexible and to see where it can direct its influence, one can expect that:
> a. It will help to modernize other sectors of social life which in turn affect population characteristics.
> b. It will avoid lagging behind the society, while it provides an ethos for social development.
> c. It will influence the adoption of rational patterns of fertility practices, education of future parents, responsible parenthood, etc.
> This study can further open the first stage of the new role of religion with respect to social development in Latin America.

(The idea of a Catholic ethic as a requisite to Latin American development has since been presented by Dr. Ivan Vallier of the Institute for

International Studies of the University of California.[1] The coincidence of his views with those of
the FERES proposal to AID is not accidental. Dr.
Vallier was the principal consultant for the FERES
proposal and assisted with the study after the proposal was accepted. Meetings that took place between FERES directors and Dr. Vallier will be discussed below.)

The FERES-AID study was originally to have involved FERES centers in Argentina, Brazil, Colombia,
Chile, and Mexico. The Argentine group ran into
trouble when the U.S. Ambassador there vetoed the
project because he felt it was too controversial.*
The most traditional Argentine bishops, those most
likely to take offense at attempts to challenge
Church policy on birth control, were closely allied
to the military government of Ongania, which had
just taken power in a coup d'état. Argentina was
eventually dropped from the study; it was replaced
by Venezuela.

The chief consultant for the FERES-AID study
was Professor Ivan Vallier of the Institute for
International Studies of the University of California. Other consultants were: Father Rocco Caporale,
a North American Jesuit and colleague of Dr. Vallier's at the Institute for International Studies;
Father Francois Houtart, the secretary of FERES
International at Louvain University; Father Emile
Pin, French Jesuit sociologist at the Gregorian

---

*Their expectations would be rudely dashed two
years later, in 1967, as the North Americans began
to assert control over aid monies with stringent
regard for bureaucratic reforms, and then later
placed all decision-making power in the hands of
the North American ecclesiastical bureaucracy. By
1969, Father Louis Collonesi of the Latin American
bureau of the North American Bishops' Committee
would be dividing the collection monies himself and
keeping a list of approved recipients secret even
from CELAM.

University in Rome; Professor Schelzky of the University of Munster, Germany; and Professor Hanns-Albert Steger of Sozialforschungestelle an der Universitat, also of Munster.

These consultants were to advise the regular directors of the national FERES centers: Father Jose Enrique Miguens of the Center for Motivational Research, Buenos Aires; Father Afonso Gregory of the Center for Religious Statistics and Social Research, Rio de Janeiro; Father Gustavo Perez of ICODES, Bogota; Father Renato Poblete, S.J., of CIAS, Santiago; and Luis Lenero of the Mexican Institute of Social Studies, Mexico City.

From the outset, there were tensions between the consultants and the directors. But since all were mutually interested in the successful termination of the project, no open splits ever occurred. (There was some disagreement about the remuneration of consultants. Father Poblete of Chilean CIAS wrote to Father Perez that he and Father Houtart were both opposed to the consulting fee requested by Father Caporale.)

The preparatory work, the field work, and the write-up of the project were each originally scheduled to take eight months, with completion of the project planned for December, 1968. Originally, $120,000 had been requested for a study covering five countries; the actual costs of the study ran to $140,000.*

_____

*The initial proposal suggested the following budget: preparation, $19,290; field work, $64,800; codification and tabulation, $5,085; analysis of data, $13,095; presentation and publication, $4,990. Total: $120,000. Sub-itemed expenses included $5,000 for consultants; $23,525 for salaries and wages of directors and their personnel; $5,878 for travel and transportation (to meetings at Berkeley and at Bogota); $1,057 for per diem expenses; $800

The consultants were expected to act in all
stages of the study. The date of the AID approval
of the proposal was March 1, 1966. The dates of
disbursement ran from August 9, 1966, to February
15, 1969.

The content of the study, according to the
proposal, would contain

> . . . data gathered so that they will
> meet two conditions:
> a. Data rendering information
> on the subjacent (sic) dynamic prin-
> ciples governing decision-making on
> fertility and related factors.
> b. Information concerning fer-
> tility that will provide data of max-
> imum source for change and action
> programming. As a way of determining
> the influence of cultural and reli-
> gious factors on fertility and of re-
> lating the findings to the wider
> framework of socio-economic develop-
> ment and religion, we will observe:
> (a) the general orientations, formal
> policies, and changes of organized
> religion with regard to fertility be-
> havior; (b) the teaching and influence
> of the priest and of lay leaders with
> regard to this issue; (c) the actual
> behavior of the people with regard to
> fertility and the sources of incoher-
> ence and difficulty with the norm en-
> forced by the traditional setup.

---

for communications; $1,800 for computer time;
$3,000 for translation of the study and offset
printing. The ICODES center and the FERES affiliates were to receive $10,615 in total for overhead
expenses. Field work was estimated at $12,200 for
each country, not counting the coordination expenses of the local director.

Data collection was to consist in:

    1. Analysis of existing data.
    2. The survey of 1,000 women.
    3. Qualified interviews with
priests and other community leaders.
    4. Documents and public state-
ments made by religious leaders.

The objectives of the research were:

    1. To secure comparative data
on the fertility behavior and the use
of contraception in a selected sample
taken from the rural areas of five
Latin American countries.
    2. To examine the influence of
religion as one of the variables affecting fertility.
    3. To produce a set of bases of
which programs for responsible parent-
hood could be built up and make effective in the countries studied.

The FERES proposal to AID contained these
"hypotheses":

    1. The delay in integrating or-
ganized religion in social life and
its rationalization is one of the factors in the rejection of fertility
control.
    2. The formal religious leaders
in rural areas have an influence on
the acceptance, delay, or rejection
of family planning, because of their
moral teaching and their status in
the community.
    3. Depending on certain social
and cultural conditions, a number of
Catholics violate the norms of their
Church by using contraceptive methods,
abortion, etc. This introduces confusion, irrationality, and loss of

resources that could be avoided by
resorting to proper education, medical assistance, and counseling.
    4. Priests are in a situation
of anomie, some taking a strong position, others a lax one, some being
in contradiction between their public
preaching and their private counseling, and others not well acquainted
with developments in doctrine.

The FERES proposal also included a sketch of
what it termed the "etiology of deviant behavior"
to describe the hypothesized state of non-compli-
ance with Church directives on the part of Catholic
married couples. This analysis was to follow "the
theoretical approach of Professor Kingsley Davis,"
as outlined in "Scheme I." The FERES investigators
stated that they assumed that "changes at the psychological level develop with reference to sources
of discrepancy in the conformity to the norms."
Scheme I and a copy of the proposal as a whole are
to be found in the appendices to this study.

The actual operationalization of the FERES
study entailed major changes in the research design. FERES had secured a grant of several thousand dollars from the Ford Foundation to do "content analysis" of formal pronouncements by Church
leaders on birth control. Some of this material
was included in the proposal and study for AID.

As early as February, 1965 (six months before
the FERES proposal was submitted), Gustavo Perez
realized that he faced a possible conflict of interest with Jesuit Roger Vekemans, whose DESAL organization in Chile had just signed a contract for
$100,000 from AID to conduct seminars on family
planning and to do studies of fertility in Latin
America. The Latin American Population Center
(CELAP), the DESAL sub-unit, was also to focus on
the influence of Catholic doctrine upon the behavior of Catholic married couples. In attempting to
resolve this problem, Perez leaned heavily on the

advice and support of Jesuit Father Renato Poblete, who was (a) a FERES member as head of the center in Santiago, and (b) a close associate of Vekemans as director of the Chilean Centro Bellarmino and as a co-member, with Vekemans, of Chilean Jesuit CIAS. With Poblete acting as go-between, the dilemma was resolved, at least temporarily.

On February 26, 1965, a meeting took place at the Centro Bellarmino in Santiago. Present were Fathers Renato Poblete, Argentine Jesuit Antonio Donini, Gustavo Perez, and Ruben Talavera, the sub-director of CELAP.

Gustavo Perez related that he had been in Washington in January, where he met with Edgar Berman and Benjamin Duffy of AID. The latter offered him $2,000 to do a feasibility study for the proposal which FERES/ICODES would submit in September. However, Perez continued, since AID had made a grant to DESAL for the development of CELAP, and since CELAP was to function not only in Chile but throughout Latin America, AID insisted that the $2,000 for the feasibility study be given to FERES by CELAP.

Perez and Poblete prevailed upon Talavera to give FERES the money, promising FERES' sociological consultation in return. Vekemans was not present at this meeting, but he seems to have approved the outcome.

As a result, the FERES study eventually shifted away from an analysis of the use of contraceptives by married couples and concentrated entirely upon the attitudes of Catholic priests toward such behavior. Empirically speaking, the FERES study would consist of the attitudes of 500 priests, not part of a probability sample, in each of the five countries. Coupled with these were the views in each of the countries of about twenty bishops.

The CELAP study (which will be examined in Part III) focused entirely upon the behavior of

Chilean women. Thus, temporarily, the conflict of
interests was resolved. FERES was able to get
$140,000 from AID, and CELAP was able to keep the
AID grants that it had already contracted.

But in return for its cooperation with FERES,
DESAL was asking something that Gustavo Perez does
not seem to have understood. DESAL was assuming
that ICODES in Colombia would act, thenceforward,
as one of the DESAL affiliates: in effect, the local Colombian branch. This expectation (which
Perez apparently did not fully realize, and certainly did not fulfill) resulted in a break between
Perez and Vekemans.

The course of this "misunderstanding" can be
followed in a series of eight letters that passed
between Perez and Vekemans.[2] Poblete had not been
informed of the course of the controversy and so
was unable to intervene and effect a compromise between the interested parties. This was unfortunate
for Poblete, since his interests were tied to each
of them.

Gustavo Perez declined throughout the period
to commit ICODES to DESAL, neither agreeing nor
disagreeing with Vekeman's suggestion concerning
the representation of DESAL in Colombia. He did
consent to a future meeting, but left such a con-
tingency indefinite. There was little urgency any
longer for coming to terms with DESAL-CELAP. Perez
had already decided to forego the $2,000 from CELAP
for the feasibility study and to finance the latter
out of FERES funds. It was also clear that Vekemans
did not see it as in his interest to exclude ICODES
and Perez from participation in the "triangle" of
Catholic resource centers: Notre Dame University
in the United States, Louvain in Belgium, and the
Catholic University of Chile. These linkages would
remain unbroken, committing ICODES and DESAL staff
services to what would prove an abortive attempt to
fund Christian Democracy in Latin America.

At the conclusion of the episode, Gustavo
Perez sent the series of letters to Father Renato

Poblete, whom he had upbraided earlier for not
writing him to inform him of the progress of nego-
tiations with CELAP. Poblete, a close friend of
both Vekemans and Perez and affiliated institution-
ally with both of them, had been sick and unable to
intervene at an earlier date, even if he had been
told what was transpiring. As director of the
Chilean Centro Bellarmino, of which Vekemans was a
member, and as a director of the Chilean FERES affiliate, Poblete's interests clearly lay in effect-
ing a reconciliation between Vekemans and Perez.
But Vekemans had already given evidence in his letters to Perez that the differences between them
were not primarily due to "personality factors."
Remaining good friends and "fellow workers in the
Lord," their differences were interest- and
organization-based.

Poor communications retarded discussions of
their divergent interests and thus dampened the
conflict as much as it hindered its resolution.
The main problem was that Vekemans had secured
monies from AID to form a population study group
(CELAP) for all of Latin America. As he had been
able to do with MISEREOR, all of whose funds he
"administered" in Latin America, so he was attempting to do with the monies that AID had set aside
for the study of Catholic reaction to birth control. Gustavo Perez wished to contract with AID
directly, but he was forced to act through Vekemans.
This entailed great costs in terms of communications,
bureaucratic delays, and diminished organizational
autonomy.

NOTES

1. Ivan Vallier, Catholicism, Social Control,
and Modernization in Latin America (Englewood
Cliffs, N J : Prentice-Hall, 1970).

[2]Roger Vekemans/Gustavo Perez, correspondence,
April-May, 1965.

11

ICODES:
SECULAR APPROVAL
EPISCOPAL DISAPPROVAL

Meanwhile, the quest for the AID monies went on. The FERES proposal was being written during these months, and Perez had already decided to rely upon his own resources to finance the feasibility study. In a letter to Poblete on May 4, after he had renounced the representation of DESAL, Perez wrote that Argentine Jesuit O'Farrell would be in charge of the feasibility study and that $200 would be allocated by FERES to each of the five participating centers. Another $1,000 would pay for consultants, overhead, and so on.

During the summer of 1965, the proposal to AID was put into final shape by Perez and his consultants, chief among whom were Father Rocco Caporale, S.J., and Dr. Ivan Vallier of the Institute of International Studies of the University of California, Berkeley.

FIRST PROPOSAL TO AID

This was not the first proposal Perez had submitted to AID. Earlier in 1965, Perez, Roger Vekemans of DESAL, Afonso Gregory of the Center for Religious Statistics and Social Research (CERIS) in Rio, and Jaime Otero of the Bolivian Institute for Study and Social Action (IBEAS) in La Paz, had

worked up a proposal with North American business
interests interested in "the coordination of popular organizations in Latin America."

The proposal was entitled, "A Proposal to U.S.
AID to Provide Planning and Training Assistance for
Grass-Roots Organizations and Voluntary Agencies in
Latin America." The planners of the project were
especially interested in local institutions "which
are indigenous to the country and which are private
nonprofit voluntary associations." These would include the widest range of influence:

      1. Communications: newspaper
production, publications, radio
broadcasts, radio schools, transportation, etc.
      2. Community development: lead-
ership training for civic and social
responsibility, rural and urban
      3. Construction, housing, and
planning: work camps, training of
engineers and architects, etc.
      4. Cooperatives, credit unions,
and loans: production, purchasing,
and marketing
      5. Education:
        Fundamental: literacy classes,
          adult education
        Higher and professional: col-
          leges and universities, in-
          cluding teacher training,
          agricultural, engineering,
          medical, nurses training
          and social workers' schools
        Teacher training: normal
          schools
        Technical and vocational:
          business and trade schools,
          courses in languages,
          handicrafts, etc.
        Women: courses in home eco-
          nomics, domestic sciences,
          child care, etc.

6. Equipment, material aid, and relief: food, clothing, medicines, tool kits, books, etc.

7. Food production and agriculture: crop improvement: seeds, fertilizers, etc.

   Extension: agricultural schools, experimental plots and gardens, 4-H-type clubs, etc.

   Irrigation: water supply

   Land reclamation: resettlement, reforestation, soil conservation

   Livestock: poultry, animal husbandry, dairy projects

8. Industrial development:

   Small industries: cottage industries, handicraft production

   Trade unions: organization of trade unions, study of manpower

9. Medicine and public health:

   Disease control: anti-malaria and anti-TB campaigns, public health education, medical research

   Medical services: hospitals, clinics, dispensaries, mobile clinics, home visits, dental clinics.

   Mental health: mental hospitals, psychiatric clinics, child guidance clinics

   Nutrition: school-lunch projects, child feeding, use of protein-rich food, development of new types of food, etc.

   Sanitation: building of sewage systems, toilet facilities, water purification, etc.

Training of medical personnel:
doctors, nurses, and other
medical assistants
10. Public and business administration: training of civil servants,
economic development and planning,
"law and government"
11. Research: economic and
social
12. Social welfare:
Centers and hostels: recrea-
tion centers, youth hostels,
summer camps, counselling
services, etc.
Homes for aged: nursing homes
Orphanages: day-care centers,
baby folds
Rehabilitation: centers for
physically and mentally
handicapped
Training of social workers:
other social welfare
workers
13. Special projects and other:
family planning and other which do not
fall into the above categories.

In accordance with this proposal, pilot projects were to be selected from the above categories
and administered by ICODES, DESAL, IBEAS, and CERIS
in their respective countries. For example, Vekemans in Chile was to found an organization named
the Coordinating Commission for Popular Development (CONCORDE), which would control the resources
AID would allocate to the Union of Christian Workers (UCC), the National Association of Slumdwellers
(CENAPO), Chilean Union Action (ASICH), the Institute for Work Promotion (IPT), and the Institute
for Agrarian Promotion (INPROA), among others.

If the pilot projects proved successful, then
ICODES, DESAL, IBEAS, and CERIS were to be in charge
of administering U.S. AID funds allocated to the
thirteen types of "nonprofit local institutions"

listed above. ICODES, DESAL, IBEAS, and CERIS would
form a special corporation, the Institute for Human
Progress, with headquarters in Washington, D.C.
They would thus be able to "coordinate" not only
local grass-roots Latin American organizations but
would also assist all U.S. voluntary agencies (such
as Catholic Relief Service, YMCA, CARE, Rockefeller
Foundation, Ford Foundation) by screening requests
and proposals made by Latin American "grass-roots
organizations" to them. The Institute for Human
Progress would also "assist" the Alliance for Progress resource agencies (AID, the Inter-American Development Bank, etc.) in allocating their resources.

What the proposal suggested was the creation
of a Latin American "linchpin" to link all U.S. aid
initiatives to all Latin American organizational inputs, with the exception of political parties and
governments. Even trade-union development would be
subject to the approval of this proposed super-
agency.

The proposal, calling for the creation of a
screening agency for U.S. AID that would be managed
by Latin American Catholic churchmen, might have
sounded incredible to AID programmers, but it carried the enthusiastic endorsement of a broad cross
section of North American business interests. The
"board of directors" of the proposed Institute for
Human Progress was as follows:

> J. Peter Grace, President, W. R. Grace and
>   Company, Chairman
> John T. Barnett, retired executive, Sears,
>   Roebuck & Co.
> Joseph A. Beirne, President, Communications
>   Workers of America
> Daniel W. Bell, President and Chairman of
>   the Board (retired), American Security and
>   Trust Company
> John A. Coleman, Senior Partner, Adler,
>   Coleman & Co.
> David Danzig, Associate Director, American
>   Jewish Committee

Mark Evans, Vice President, Metro-Media, Inc.
John F. Gallagher, Vice President, Sears,
   Roebuck & Co.
Harold S. Geneen, President, International
   Telephone & Telegraph Corporation
Harry C. Hagerty, Vice Chairman (retired),
   Metropolitan Life Insurance Corporation
Charles M. Kellstadt, Chairman of the Board
   (retired), Sears, Roebuck & Co.
Thomas A. Lane, Maj. Gen., U.S. Army (retired)
Arch Madsen, President, KSL, Inc.
John McShain, President, John McShain, Inc.
John D. J. Moore, Vice President, W. R. Grace
   and Company
William E. Moran, Jr., Dean of the School of
   Foreign Service, Georgetown University
Robert D. Murphy, President, Corning Glass
   International
John T. O'Rourke, Editor, The Washington
   Daily News
Henry Sargent, President, American and Foreign
   Power Corporation
Edward L. Steiniger, President, Sinclair Oil
   Corporation
John L. Sullivan, Sullivan, Shea and Kenney
Robert L. Walsh, Maj. Gen., USAF (retired)
William B. Walsh, M.D., President, Project HOPE
Victor D. Ziminsky, President, Victor D.
   Ziminsky, Inc.

John E. Shea of Sullivan, Shea, and Kenney was to
provide legal counsel for the proposed institute.
Dewey R. Heising was to be executive director with
offices in Washington.

Primary contacts in Latin America were to be
Gustavo Perez at ICODES, Jaime Otero at IBEAS,
Afonso Gregory at CERIS, Ramon Venegas at DESAL.
Although all of these organizations except IBEAS
were headed by priests and closely linked to the
Catholic Church, the proposal ignored these link-
ages, describing the organizations as "nonprofit,
private entities."

This proposal to AID requested $1,030,112, to be allocated over the four-year period 1966-69. The money was to be spent on the "pilot projects."

However, the proposal was rejected. Had it been accepted, the relations between Perez and Vekemans probably would have been much closer organizationally, the Brazilian Father Afonso Gregory would have been quite visibly linked to the U.S. AID mission (which would have affected his position as chief advisor to Brazilian Bishop Helder de Camara), and the other Catholic research groups in Latin America would have been faced with the necessity of submitting all their proposals for U.S. aid through Perez, Vekemans, Gregory, Otero, and company. This probably would have quickly polarized the Latin American staff sectors into two groups: the "haves" (or decision-makers) and the "have-nots" (or suppliants). But since the proposal was rejected, what resulted was not polarization but a continuing shifting of feeble alliances with a concomitant fragmentation of Catholic forces.

Within FERES, however, relations and fused linkages were growing stronger. This was due to the flow of new capital from ADVENIAT to finance a study of the "image of the Church" in Latin American society as well as from the expectation that the proposal to AID for a study on "fertility" would be approved.

FERES CONSULTANTS' MEETINGS
IN CHICAGO AND SANTIAGO

On January 21, 1965, the first consultants' meeting for the AID fertility study was held at the Edgewater Beach Hotel in Chicago, on the occasion of the annual Catholic Inter-American Cooperation Program (CICOP), an assembly of Catholic interests sponsored by the North American and Latin American Bishops' Conferences.

The closed FERES meeting was attended by
Fathers Renato Poblete, Afonso Gregory, Gustavo
Perez, Isaac Wust (also of ICODES), and Francois
Houtart. They discussed the following topics, as
listed in the memoranda of the meeting:

1.   The Bogota center (ICODES) had saved $1,000
from the original Ford Foundation grant that had
funded a study of official Church documents on the
subject of birth control. This money would be divided between the centers in Chile and Brazil,
which would examine documents in their respective
countries. Gregory and Poblete were to clear this
use of monies with Ford administrator Spencer.

2.   A study of the effects of changes in Catholic ritual (liturgy) was to be done for CELAM.
Father Emile Pin of the Gregorian University in
Rome would devise the theoretical foundations of
the study.

3.   Publication of the FERES Latin American
series would continue with a pamphlet by Gregory
and Perez analyzing pastoral problems of the Church.
This would supplement the statistical studies already published.

4.   The study of the "image" of the Church in
Latin America was to be supervised by Father Antonio
Donini, a collaborator with Father Poblete in Chile.

5.   Gustavo Perez would retain his post as regional secretary for FERES in Latin America.

6.   A study of the "roots of anti-Yankee preju-
dice" was discussed. The majority of the members
present were opposed to the study, which AID was requesting, and it was decided to drop the idea. (One
of the principals present at the meeting later told
me that his objections were based on his "certitude"
that the study was to supplement U.S. counterintel-
ligence.)

On February 21 and 23, 1965, the second consultants' reunion for the FERES group was held.
This time the site was Santiago de Chile, and the
occasion was the meeting of the "triangle." Present were Fathers Poblete, Donini, and Perez. Financial arrangements and roles were agreed upon for
the forthcoming study of Catholic liturgy. Father
Hubert Schwan, a Jesuit exiled from East Germany,
was hired by Perez to design questionnaires for the
Colombian phase of the study. (Schwan later became
upset with the FERES operation and took a position
as head of the Office of Sociological Studies for
the Archbishop of Bogota.)

The proposal to AID was to be drawn up to meet
the specifications AID had set when it brought Gustavo Perez to Washington in early January, 1965.
From Santiago, Perez traveled to Buenos Aires. He
sought to establish a FERES center in Argentina
that would carry out and publish studies. Since
FERES was considered by its founders as a "federation" of independent centers, this required the utmost tact on his part.

In Buenos Aires, Perez spent time with two
priests, Father Justin O'Farrell and Father Enrique
Amato. Although he had good things to say about
both in his report to the other FERES heads (Amato
was "very interested in FERES," and O'Farrell was
"doing ecumenical work among Protestants and Jews"),
Perez was not eager to affiliate with either: Amato
lacked an advanced academic degree, and O'Farrell
was too busy with university teaching and running
the Argentine Jesuit CIAS. Perez eventually settled
on a layman: a lawyer-sociologist named Jose Enrique
Miguens, who had founded the Center for Motivational
and Social Research (CIMS) in Buenos Aires in 1964.

In June, Francois Houtart met with Ford Foundation executives in New York to discuss a proposed
study of "the educational, health, and social activities of religious bodies in the developing countries."

Included in this proposal were projected field studies in Brazil, Cameroun, Colombia, Indonesia, and India. The Brazilian operation was to be done by Father Procopio Camargo of Sao Paulo University. His subject would be "the Natal Movement," organized by Catholic bishops of the Northeast. The Colombian study was to focus on "the impact of Christian secondary schools in Colombia in relation to the socio-economic development of the country." (Andre Benoit eventually undertook this study for ICODES. First published as "Values and Religious Attitudes of the Graduates of 1955 of the High School Graduates of Bogota," it was circulated by Tercer Mundo in 1968 under the title El Bachillerato Colombiano.)

In August, 1965, Poblete wrote to Perez that the study on the image of the Church in Chile was imperiled because Jesuit Father Donini "had found the temptation" of working with Ivan Illich at the Center for Intercultural Formation "too great," and had left Chile for Mexico ("kidnaped," in Poblete's words). Poblete himself had been one of the original co-founders (along with Illich and the North American Jesuit, Joseph Fitzpatrick) of the CIF, but he had found Illich "too demanding" and domineering and so had left.

Throughout the spring and summer of 1965, work went forward on the FERES/AID proposal. Poblete was pleased with the way the proposal was shaping up under Ivan Vallier, and said so in his letter of August 23, 1965, to Perez. On September 8, Gustavo Perez wrote to his affiliated centers, notifying them that AID had approved the study of religious attitudes toward birth control and would allocate $120,000 for the project. The future of the Latin American branch of FERES was assured for several years.

Now that financing for the immediate future was a reality, Perez moved to ensure that prosperity did not slip away with the success of the

moment. He wrote to Father Frederick A. McGuire of
the Latin American Bureau of the North American
Bishops on September 22, 1965, asking for help in
hiring a fund-raiser for FERES. He had in mind
Battle Smith, who worked in a similar position at
St. Louis University. Perez asked McGuire to approach "one of the foundations in the United States"
to secure a salary for Smith:

> What FERES badly needs at the pres-
> ent is the help of an expert in fund
> raising. As you know, the directors
> of the various centers of FERES in
> Latin America are expending much of
> their time in fund raising, without
> training in public relations. This
> means that scarce sociologists are
> spending valuable time in fund raising.

The appeal Perez made was doubly urgent because ADVENIAT, the German Bishops' Fund, was refusing to allocate money to FERES for further studies. They charged that "the directors travel too
much" and that the organization was being left to
"run itself." (Perez told me that he was afraid
that Vekemans had been responsible for adding fuel
to the fire of ICODES/FERES critics since their disagreement in the spring of 1965.)

Gustavo Perez was granted his request directly
by the North American Bishops' Committee, which
agreed to pay a fund-raiser's salary. Unfortunately, Perez then found that Battle Smith was no longer interested in working at ICODES for FERES. And,
as a result, ICODES was unable to find a full-time
fund-raiser.

Other monies found their way to Gustavo Perez
in the fall of 1965. On September 21, he informed
the directors of affiliated centers that the department of education of CELAM was requesting FERES'
help in preparing the Latin American Vocational Congress, whose purpose was to stimulate recruitment
of priests for Latin America. Payment to FERES

would be made either through ADVENIAT, or if they
refused, through the U.S.-based Serra Club, an organization of Catholic businessmen that seeks to
"increase priestly vocations."

On December 29, 1965, the North American bishops released to the press a special declaration an-
nouncing a national collection to be taken up in
all North American churches for the Latin American
Church.[1]   Coming as it did at the end of the Second
Vatican Council, the announcement seemed to some
observers to constitute a "repayment" to the Latin
American Bishops' Conference (CELAM) for support of
North Americans during the Council, especially on
such touchy issues as religious freedom. The North
American bishops' statement recalled that there
were more than 4,000 North American religious functionaries (clerical and lay) serving in Latin
America at the end of 1965, an increase of 50 per
cent in three years.

The North American bishops praised the Latin
American bishops. They pointed with particular approval to the pastoral letters of bishops of Ecuador,
Brazil, Chile, Argentina, Peru, and Guatemala, in
which the bishops committed themselves to solving
the problems of poverty, poor education, low wages,
malnutrition, and unequal distribution of natural
resources and income.

The prospect of millions of American dollars
raised annually for Latin American Catholic projects cheered the hearts of CELAM staff and line
officials and raised their expectations for the
future.

Bishop Eugenio Sales of Brazil, the president
of the department of social action of CELAM, asked
FERES to collaborate in suggesting projects and
proposals to make use of the money that would be
available, without incurring the jealousy or wrath
of competing parties. This initiative revealed
that Bishop Sales expected conflict over resource
allocation to come principally from line sectors,

that is, from the bishops themselves. What actually happened is that the line bishops found themselves surrounded by newly emergent staff organizations that had initially been founded to "solve the
problem of allocation objectively," but that eventually fell to quarreling themselves over the spoils.

Gustavo Perez saw this problem clearly and offered to make of FERES an "integrating organization."
He asked Bishop Sales to invite representatives of
Jesuit CIAS, of Vekemans' DESAL, and of Illich's
CIF to a common meeting in Bogota. It was this
meeting, held in June, 1966, that witnessed the confrontation of conflicting interests, and the accel-
erated fragmentation of Catholic forces; this meeting was the turning point.*

The minutes of the FERES meeting at Berkeley
in March, 1966, reveal that Perez was having problems with Fathers O'Farrell and Amato and with Mr.
Miguens, each of whom was claiming to be the Argentine FERES affiliate. Meanwhile, another, far more
dangerous, issue had emerged.

MISEREOR, the West German Bishops' Fund for
Socio-Economic Development, was being pressured by

---

*Not that what happened in this meeting was un-
predictable. The meeting itself was contingent upon
forces that already had gathered strength and momen-
tum. But after the CELAM meeting of June, 1966,
there was to be no more serious talk of integrating
the Latin American Church. Camilo Torres would be
dead. Ivan Illich would have published his widely
read condemnation of North American bishops (the
"lackeys of U.S. imperialism"), which would be followed quickly by a call for fewer priests within the
Church and an end to Catholic schooling: Ivan Illich,
"The Vanishing Clergyman," Critic, XXV, 6 (June-July,
1967), 18-27. See also Francine du Plessix Gray,
"Profiles: The Rules of the Game," The New Yorker,
April 25, 1970, pp. 40-92.

Latin American bishops such as Chile's Cardinal
Silva to modify the total control it had given to
Roger Vekemans and DESAL over funding to Latin
America.   Two MISEREOR bureaucrats, Koch and Querin,
knowing of the desire Father Perez had expressed of
"collaborating with" MISEREOR, had suggested to
FERES chief Francois Houtart that arrangements be
made for FERES to share the evaluation of projects
with DESAL.   Houtart pointed out the complications
that would inevitably arise with DESAL and emphati-
cally counseled against this: "ICODES in Colombia
was having personnel problems"; not enough qualified researchers would be available for a new influx of projects.

PROBLEMS WITH AID

The FERES/AID study was to have begun in January, 1966, but delays in approving the project
pushed the target date ahead.   Nevertheless, the
plans for beginning research were well advanced.
Gustavo Perez tried to hurry AID along, only to
discover that the delay in making the appropriations was caused by the refusal of the American Ambassador to Argentina to approve that phase of the
study.

On April 14, Perez sent the following letter
to Miss Nadine Saxton of AID:

> I was very disappointed to learn
> from you when you called me at Man-
> hattanville College last week that
> the mission in Argentina did not ap-
> prove our FERES project on popula-
> tion, saying that there is no prob-
> lem in Argentina.
> Let me give you some reasons why
> it is very important for us to in-
> clude Argentina in our study:
> 1.   I would like to stress that
> the FERES study is basically a com-
> parative study; therefore, we need

data not only from countries where
there is a serious population problem, but also from countries where
the growth of population is not so
rapid. This, of course, is speaking
of the problem at the national level,
because at the family level we believe that there are equally dramatic
problems in all the countries in
Latin America, especially in the
slums which, as a matter of fact,
exist in Buenos Aires.

2. Also, we are focusing our
study on the Church in Latin America
as an institution facing the problems of social change. How the
Church adapts its policy to chal-
lenging issues such as population
and family problems.

This kind of information would
help to convince the Church in Latin
America of the need to function as a
catalyst or as a more active participant in the social and institutional
changes occurring in that continent
not only in the field of population
but also in other areas where the
Church, by tradition, plays an important role. Ambassador Oliver [of the
United States] was very specific
about this point in recommending the
project for Colombia.

3. Since the study would be done
on a comparative basis the data obtained could be used by each mission
in the way it wants and therefore
the findings in Argentina could not
jeopardize any policy of the mission
in that country.

Let me add that we are willing
to consider doing the study only in
the countries where you obtain rapid
approval, because as you know, we
were hoping to sign the contract

early this year so as to begin the
study as soon as possible. In January, when I visit you coming from
the CICOP meeting in Chicago, you
mentioned the feasibility of signing
the contract early in March. You
also mentioned this to Father Thomas
McMahon later, and we were very optimistic when you told us that the
project was approved and needed only
the formalities of clearance by the
different missions prior to signing
the contract. For that reason we
went ahead and planned the meeting
at the University of California in
Berkeley with Prof. Ivan Vallier of
the Department of International Studies, who is our chief consultant.

You know also that Prof. Vallier,
the other directors of the study in
the five countries and the other consultants, especially Father Caporale,
have a very heavy schedule and have
to plan ahead.

I would appreciate very much if
you would try to speed up the approval for signature so that we
could receive the first payment as
soon as possible.

I have to define the situation
to all the consultants and directors
by the end of April. . . .

At this time, Perez was experiencing problems
with the trio of Argentines who were competing with
one another to land that phase of the study. Eventually, neither O'Farrell, Amato, nor Miguens was
included full time in the research team. The U.S.
State Department, acting on the advice of the U.S.
Ambassador, rejected the Argentine phase. FERES
then substituted Venezuela, under the supervision
of Father Albert Gruson of the Center for Socio-
Religious Research (CISOR).

The U.S. Embassy in Argentina clearly refused
to risk public identification with the Catholic
Church. In a letter to Miss Saxton on May 26, 1966,
Perez acknowledged this fact, referring to a conversation he had had with Jaime Manzano of AID.
Manzano had informed Perez of his "preoccupation
and that of the AID mission in Argentina" with publicity linking the Embassy to the proposed FERES
study on fertility. Perez had told Manzano that he
felt that all this could be presented under the
name of FERES, without mention of State Department
sponsorship. But the Argentine mission would not
agree.

The AID project was officially approved in
August, 1966. In a letter dated August 2 to all
FERES Latin America directors, Perez wrote that
Father Rocco Caporale had assumed direction of the
preparations for the interviewing in Mexico, where
the first field data was to be collected. He was
working with Luis Lenero, the local FERES director,
and with Rodrigo Olivera.

PROBLEMS WITH ADVENIAT

But before the AID project could be thoroughly
launched, Perez was forced to turn his attention to
a serious problem. In February, 1966, he learned
from Francois Houtart that there had been recurrent
criticism of ICODES at ADVENIAT. This had been instrumental in dissuading ADVENIAT from financing
the study on the image of the Church, as well as
another proposed study of the religious orders.

Perez flew to Germany to meet with ADVENIAT
officials. On February 5, he talked for an hour
and a half with Becher Garcia, Miss Holdegard
Luning, and a Mr. De la Rica. He later issued a
memorandum to all FERES Latin American directors:

Mr. Becher said in effect that
there was preoccupation at ADVENIAT
because much hope had been placed in

ICODES and in the work which it could
realize, but that they saw few results. He commented, "It looks like
ICODES is not functioning well. . . .
There are great expenditures but we
don't know with what efficiency."

The ADVENIAT people made three complaints concerning ICODES: that Gustavo Perez traveled too
much; that he did not have anyone to manage ICODES
while he was gone; and that he did not "generate"
enough publicity. He was told to seek publicity
"so that ICODES may be known not only in Colombia,
but in all of Latin America and in other countries."

Complaints were also made concerning FERES,
but the ADVENIAT representatives seemed less sure
of themselves here. Becher said that "maybe what
they feared was that the same thing was happening
to FERES as had happened to ICODES." Perez reported
in his memorandum that ADVENIAT complained that
FERES "did not publish anything," when in fact they
had published over forty volumes. Complaints were
made that FERES studies did not contain many statis-
tics--"one can't find how many workers are unionized
in Latin America, etc."--when in fact the earlier
FERES publications are statistical in the extreme
and do contain the item in question, the number of
Latin American workers unionized.

One FERES director told me later that he felt
that the criticisms made to ADVENIAT concerning
ICODES/FERES stemmed from two main sources: the
Colombian bishops, who made them through the Colombian Jesuit CIAS, and Roger Vekemans, who feared
FERES expansion and influence with his own European
sources of support.

After 1966, ADVENIAT was "lost" to FERES. In
the following years it provided money to Jesuit
CIAS groups in Chile and Colombia, helping to found
the Institute of Doctrine and Social Studies (IDES)
in Bogota, and the Latin American Institute of Doctrine and Social Studies (ILADES) in Santiago.

These two institutes selected students for training
courses in Catholic social doctrine and in introduc-
tory sociology and economics. Emphasis was placed
upon recruiting potential "leaders" from labor sectors and universities. By the end of 1968, Colombian IDES and Chilean ILADES, although each was
Jesuit-managed, were bickering as each attempted to
dominate common manpower and financial resources.
(This conflict will be discussed in a subsequent
chapter.)

Gustavo Perez made an attempt to recoup some
of his former standing with ADVENIAT by working
through the Catholic University in Lima. The Center for Sociological, Economic, and Political Research (CISEPA) at the university was founded by
and under the direction of Bernard Van Heck. In
1966, the center was involved in four projects: a
study of Peruvian families, funded by the University
of Notre Dame; a study of the "social value of time,"
funded by UNESCO; a pilot study of cooperatives for
the Peruvian government; and consulting work for the
mayor of Lima. Perez persuaded Van Heck to hire a
sociologist specializing in religious questions so
that CISEPA could open a FERES center. Van Heck's
standing with ADVENIAT was good and might provide
renewed access to that source of support. As it
turned out, ADVENIAT remained intransigent with regard to ICODES' financial plight.

Perez also spoke with Father August Beuzeville
who headed the Archdiocesan Office of Investigation
and Parish Planning in Lima. Beuzeville, according
to the ACTA of the October 5 meeting in Lima, was
to try to persuade the Cardinal of Lima, Landazurri
Ricketts, that an "office of religious statistics"
was needed, and to write to ADVENIAT requesting financial support. FERES would then "assist" in the
founding of this office.

1967 was a year of more routine activity for
FERES and ICODES. Work went forward in Mexico,
Colombia, Venezuela, Chile, and Brazil on the AID
fertility project. ICODES had also won contracts

with the Colombian government to coordinate ACCION
COMUNAL programs, and had secured money from the
North American Bishops' Conference to improve the
ICODES audio-visual laboratory.

ICODES had invested about $70,000 of its own
in various Colombian enterprises, for which it was
receiving a steady return.

Gaining 24 per cent a year were investments in--

    ACDAC. . . . . $ 7,561.78
    Alfonso Duarte 58,206.67
    Almacenes Caribe . . .   4,950.00

Gaining 12 per cent a year were investments in
(or loans to)--

    German Bravo $742.75
    Gloria de Alonso . . .   35.53
    FEICO. 150.00

But all was not well at ICODES. The North
American contacts ICODES had enjoyed through its
relationship with the Institute of Human Progress
had, for the most part, atrophied after ICODES
broke with DESAL, and especially after the Camilo
Torres affair. Perez told me that his friendly relationship with W. P. Gullander, president of the
National Association of Manufacturers, had been
irreparably damaged by the "defamations" of the
"Mano Negra," the right-wing organization of Colombian business interests.

THE THREAT OF EPISCOPAL SUPPRESSION

What disturbed Perez more than these problems,
however, was the growing insistence by the Archbishop of Bogota that ICODES place a representative
of the episcopal hierarchy on its governing board.
Archbishop Munoz Duque had been exerting this pressure for some time, but had not yet been able to resort to ecclesiastical punishment. The ICODES board

was made up of the type of businessman acceptable
to archbishops: a former Minister of Agriculture,
the president of the Foundation of Coffee Growers,
and the head of ICETEX, the organization controling
foreign financial assistance to the students of
Colombian universities, including the Jesuit Universidad Javeriana. Moreover, the Junior Chamber
of Commerce of Bogota had named Gustavo Perez its
"man of the year" in 1967, and he enjoyed broad contacts with government officials.

Even so, the Archbishop began to give more and
more attention to the promptings of his chief advisors, Jesuit Fathers Vicente Andrade and Miguel
Angel Gonzalez. They warned that Gustavo Perez had
been a close friend and supporter of Camilo Torres
and that Perez was determined to carry on what
Torres had left unfinished. Although nothing could
have been more unlikely, Perez had given some apparent foundation to this belief by making sporadic
public pronouncements condemning "injustice." Moreover, ADVENIAT's demand that he "make more publicity"
for ICODES prompted him to seek the spotlight at a
most dangerous time.*

In 1968, the city of Bogota began to prepare
for the arrival of Pope Paul VI. Hundreds of thousands of pilgrims were expected, and elaborate arrangements were made to ensure that they would be
well accommodated. As El Tiempo noted on July 15,
the Eucharistic Congress had become "the greatest
business enterprise in Colombia." The tasks of organization fell to the Colombian bishops and their
administrative staffs. They chose as their headquarters the large building that housed ICODES.
Over 200 volunteers worked under the direction of
the Archbishop and his assistant, Ignacio Betancur

---

*On June 6, 1968, the conservative, Church-
oriented daily El Siglo (Bogota) published a letter
that Gustavo Perez had written to its editors advo-
cating that the Pope be housed not in the luxurious
quarters of the Papal Nuncio, but in a neighborhood
of the poor.

Campuzano. They filled the building daily for weeks before the congress. Gustavo Perez closed his own office, removed the files, and took refuge in temporary quarters away from the noise and confusion. He also closed his library to the outsiders. Yet Perez did charge the Archdiocese rent, and instructed his audio-visual lab to produce color slides of Colombian tourist attractions and of the Pope's visit so that these could be marketed while the enthusiasm lasted.

Perez had high hopes for this time of clerical convergence upon Colombia. At the meeting of Latin American bishops at Medellin (discussed in Chapter 6), he hoped to broaden his contacts with prelates who could help him and deepen or renew his influence with the European Church foundations, especially ADVENIAT. Together with Francois Houtart, who had flown in especially for the bishops' meeting, Perez hoped to gain access to the closed meetings where policies would be made and appropriations meted out. His hopes were rudely dashed.

The Jesuit CIAS economist in Colombia, Miguel Angel Gonzalez, had written an article (quoted in Chapter 6) attacking the CELAM working document as the work of European "pseudo-experts." The Jesuits now prevailed upon the Colombian bishops to exclude from the Medellin Conference Francois Houtart and Gustavo Perez. The symbolic significance of this maneuver was not lost upon Gustavo Perez. It served notice that he no longer had a secure base of operations in Colombia, and that ICODES, if it were to survive, would survive without him.

To a great extent, these events had been foreseen. As early as August, 1967, Gustavo Perez had pleaded with Houtart to relieve him of his post as FERES regional secretary for Latin America. The minutes of a FERES general assembly held in Louvain on May 23, 1968, allude to this situation. (They also mention ADVENIAT's continuing refusal to finance studies executed by ICODES centers in Bogota, Brazil, and Chile. Father Gregory of Brazil was to

ask Bishop Eugenio Sales to "intervene" with ADVENIAT
to rectify the situation, but no improvement was in
sight.)

Perez then hired a lay manager for ICODES. In
July, 1968, German Castillo Bernal, another of the
Junior Chamber of Commerce awardees, took over administration. Castillo was made well aware of the problems ICODES faced due to the hostilities of Jesuit
CIAS in Colombia. He preferred to look for solutions
in the "application of marketing principles," hoping
to "corner the market" and drive the Jesuits out.
As they had once held the key to Catholic resources
in Colombia, so now the time had come for ICODES to
assert itself. Castillo told me that he did not
consider the ideological barriers between the bishops
and ICODES to be "insurmountable." He termed "ridic-
ulous" the Jesuit assertion that ICODES was a radical
organization, citing the names of the board of directors.[2]

Perez heard no more from either the Archbishop
or the Jesuits after the Medellin Conference in August, 1968. He was left to wonder about the timing
of the final suppression. By the spring of 1969, he
was ready to relinquish his control of ICODES, having "transformed" it into a "secular" organization.
In a letter to Renato Poblete on March 11, 1969, he
explained his decision.

> PERSONAL AND CONFIDENTIAL
> Dear Renato,
>   As you know, the chancery in
> Bogota and now the Archbishop, Anibal
> Munoz Duque, in his capacity as presi-
> dent of the Colombian Episcopal Con-
> ference, have on repeated occasions
> manifested their reservations with
> regard to ICODES.
>   For reasons which I think are
> very fundamental, I have been op-
> posed to including an official rep-
> resentative of the Episcopate as a
> member of the board of directors of
> ICODES.

Since I have decided to take a sabbatical this year, I have to leave ICODES in full operation while I am gone. Fortunately, there have been some very favorable occurrences for ICODES, thanks to various contracts which the manager has obtained, so that I can leave the Department of Social Research and that of audio-visual systems with plenty of work. I am taking the sabbatical to pay off the current debt (to ADVENIAT for the building: DEM) and am leaving an auditor to control very stringently the internal costs.

The problem is in finding a replacement for me as director--for this I hope to get someone who will stay permanently as a full-time advisor. . . .

But there remains the problem with the chancery and the Episcopate, which may get worse during my absence. The board of directors has studied the problem, and we have decided to cure the evil at its roots. Therefore, we think it necessary that ICODES become a FERES property. This is provided for in the Statutes and there should be no legal problem. . . .

I want to know your opinion in principle, so that we can proceed to work out the practical arrangements. . . .

I trust in your friendship and solidarity.

Cordially,
(signed)
Gustavo Perez Ramirez

Poblete replied on March 17, 1969, agreeing in principle but wanting a say in the selection of the new director. He added that this would be a windfall for FERES, whose total operating capital did not match that of ICODES.

Perez left ICODES at a time when its prestige
and influence with Colombian government decision-
makers was high. The ICODES sub-department of
CODESARROLLO, headed by Pedro Arturo Perez, was
working on the largest ACCION COMUNAL project in
Colombia's history: a "popular integration" project in Upia, Valley of Tenza. Also working with
ICODES were the Secretary of Agriculture, the Federation of Coffee Growers, the Department of Health,
and the Peace Corps. The latter group directed
problems it encountered with ACCION COMUNAL immediately to ICODES, since ICODES expert Arturo Perez
was not only an ICODES department chief but also
the executive secretary for the Colombian government of the Upia project. In a letter dated February 28, 1968, Harold Crow, the regional director of
the Peace Corps in Boyaca, wrote to Arturo Perez requesting reimbursement for an ACCION COMUNAL organizer, Humberto Rodriguez. ICODES was regarded as
liaison between the Peace Corps, which did not want
"to get involved" in a direct redress of what it
felt was an unjust situation, and the Colombian
ACCION COMUNAL authorities. Rodriguez, the wronged
organizer, had written to Arturo Perez earlier (on
February 10) in terms which confirm the impression
that Arturo Perez enjoyed close contacts with ACCION
COMUNAL chief, Emilio Urrea.

Gustavo Perez had also been successful in
securing the financial and technical support of
private enterprise in Colombia. He tried to analyze his success in order to draw up a procedure
whereby the other FERES centers could pattern themselves after the ICODES model. In a confidential
document dated February, 1968, and entitled "Campaign for Fund Raising: Programming and Realization," Perez spoke to the other FERES directors in
Latin America. He first emphasized the necessity
of drawing up lists of private business enterprises
within one's projected sphere of influence and
grouping them according to product (and, thus, according to "interest"). Secondly, he advised "cultivating key individuals" in each group, interesting them in the center's projects and discussing

the center's most intimate problems with them, so
that they would come to regard the center's problems
as their own. The third step would consist in forming a "board of directors" of these key individuals
who were now interested in the center. This board
could then act to promote the center in the private
business community.

This blueprint for linkage formation emphasized
the private business sector as the key to all subsequent linkages. Just as Perez considered FERES to
be a kind of "linchpin" within the Catholic religious system, so he considered private business sectors to constitute the chief channel to influence
in secular society, linking the Church to sources
of political and financial power.

FERES' links to international sources of support were strengthened when Perez brought to a successful conclusion the AID-funded field study of religious attitudes toward birth control. Late in
October, 1968, he made a final oral report to David
Frost of AID in Washington. On December 31, 1968,
a written report was sent to AID, with duplicates
to all FERES Latin America centers. Since this
study represented the chief achievement of FERES
during Gustavo Perez' term as regional secretary,
the final report has a triumphant ring to it. Excerpts follow (translated from the Spanish):

> . . . The results of this study
> will be published in book form. This
> book is to be edited in Mexico City
> in 1969, as part of the series of
> publications of FERES-Latin America.
> A summary of the book is here in-
> cluded in English and in Spanish.
> According to Article IV-C, this
> report is submitted to AID within
> sixty (60) calendar days after De-
> cember 31, 1968, the expiration date
> of this Grant. (Amendment No. 2,
> July 11, 1968.)

Five hundred interviews were conducted in each of the five countries, according to a sample selected in four different urban and rural zones with different levels of demographic pressure and crisis.

Six categories of people were interviewed by professionals: bishops, clergy, lay leaders of apostolic movements, lay members of apostolic movements, practitioners, and non-practitioners.

Besides the interviews, the methodology applied in this study included content analysis of the main documents on birth control in particular and the demographic problem in general issued by the hierarchy and laity. . . .

Both the book and the summary have been prepared by sociologists Luis Lenero and Gustavo Perez Ramirez, who were in constant contact with their colleagues in Brazil, Chile, and Venezuela. The colleagues were consulted and gave their comments and suggestions for the drafts of each chapter. . . .

At the present time, all our efforts are concentrated in a careful revision of the four-hundred-page manuscript to be typed for presentation to the editor.

Preliminary talks have already been established with the editor in Mexico, Mr. Munoz Rivero of "Grafica Panamericana," for the edition in Spanish.

Fr. Afonso Gregory, director of CERIS in Brazil, will be responsible for the edition in Portuguese.

The distribution of the book will be eventually contracted with the Fondo de Cultura Economica in Mexico

and/or with CILA (the Interamerican
Center for Academic Books) for distribution in the United States.
They also have a large net of distribution throughout Latin America.

The various centers of FERES in
Latin America will, of course, handle
the local promotion of the book.

We consider it highly useful and
necessary to organize regional seminars with the clergy and influential
leaders at various levels for an
open discussion of the findings of
the book. These meetings may result in guidelines for action according to national or local conditions. . . .

This report did not of course include description of the many problems that had occurred during
the completion of the project, nor did it attempt
to assess the probable consequences of the published
study. Father Renato Poblete was very much concerned with both of these considerations (as we
shall see in the following chapter) and therefore
attempted to mute some of the language of the published report to make it less offensive to the
Vatican and to the Latin American bishops.

Gustavo Perez had been successful in securing
contracts, in obtaining and in delivering resources
within a highly competitive linkage framework consisting of widely dispersed and heterogeneous organizations. He had cultivated excellent relationships with Colombian government agencies, with
mayors and governors, with private Colombian businessmen, with AID, with private foundations such as
Ford, with the Peace Corps, with administration and
faculty at the National University of Colombia, the
University of the Andes, etc. But in the end he
was threatened with the loss of control over his
prospering organization because he had alienated
the nation's Roman Catholic hierarchy. His close
contacts with bishops in the United States (Cardinal

Cook of New York, for example) and in Latin America
(Dom Eugenio Sales of Brazil, Mendez Arceo of Mexico)
were of little use in the final fight for survival.

Perez' chief differences with the Colombian
hierarchy were not ideological. Ideological rebellion against the hierarchy would come not from
ICODES but from a group of priests supported by the
Bishop of Buenaventura, a coastal city far from the
industrial and cultural centers of Colombia.* The
hierarchy seemed to regard ICODES as a potentially
useful instrument for "coordinating" Catholic activity in the socio-political sphere--a critical link
to much-needed sources of financial support and academic respectability. What they insisted upon was
a decisive control of its resources more than any
"purification" of its ideology or revamping of its
policies. When Gustavo Perez initiated seminars on
such topics as "liberation" of man in the third
world, he was always careful to program discussion
at abstract philosophical and theological levels.
The Colombian hierarchy could accept scholarly debate about the scholastic definition of "liberation"; it was concrete, decisive action that was
feared, whether this took the form of organizing
workers outside of the approved Jesuit organizations, of "strikes," or of guerrilla activity. As
long as ICODES confined its operations to research,
as it did after Camilo's death, it was not feared
by the bishops; on the contrary, it was envied for
its prosperity and sought after for its promise.

In reality, Gustavo Perez was neither a rebel
nor a revolutionary. He was an entrepreneur, as
the Junior Chamber of Commerce proudly attested.

----

*The GOLCONDA movement, formed around Colom-
bian Bishop Valencia Cano, would provide a number
of priest-guerrillas after the manner of Camilo
Torres. The first of these was Domingo Lain. See
NACLA Newsletters, III and IV, North American Congress on Latin America, 1969-70.

His ideology (as can be seen in the early ICODES
and later ICODES studies) was tailored to suit the
tastes of his clientele. His chief tactical mistake came on the one occasion when he ignored his
basic interests and organizational base to support
openly a revolutionary friend who was radically attacking the strongly entrenched interests of the
Colombian Jesuit management system.

Yet to blame Gustavo Perez for his collision
with the Jesuits would be unfair unless part of the
problem were reduced to an inescapable dilemma.
Had Perez accommodated to the Jesuits from the beginning, he might well have ended in even a less
secure position than he did. For it would have
been nearly impossible entirely to satisfy the
Jesuits, who were accustomed to dividing all of
the available Catholic resources but who had late-
ly come upon hard times. Eager to recoup their
former influence, they were in no mood for accommo-
dating to new competition from the priestly ranks
when they had quite enough from their own lay pro-
tégés.

The Church in Colombia is a fragmenting system. It is fragmenting because the traditional internal linkages of solidarity now go unrewarded.
The poverty of Church resources, in terms not only
of operating capital but also of influence and
prestige, has spawned a welter of hungry, quarreling elites. Elite in the sense, above all, of advanced technical training and concurrent needs,
they are underrewarded and therefore not easily
controlled. Their "status disparity" has been made
all the more poignant by the increasing "status
withdrawal" of the priesthood in general. They
are ambitious men, and many of them do not remain
priests. Those who do are frequently at odds.
Those who have the "ear" of the bishops frequently
can determine official Church policy and areas of
operation, for the bishops are ever more fearful
of risking their fragile social status in realis-
tic communication with outsiders.

The staff priest, the priest with special technical training, is a priest seeking a clientele.
When he finds one he is quick to adapt to its interests. This is not only true in Colombia, the
country whose Catholic Church Camilo Torres once
called the "most conservative in the world," it is
also true of Chile, the country whose Church has
been termed by many Latin America's most modern.

NOTES

1. Noticias Aliadas, 29/12/65-M.

2. Conversation with Castillo, September 20,
1968.

III

FRAGMENTATION OF
CATHOLIC FORCES:
CHILE

12

YEARS OF UNITY (1958-64): THE CENTRO BELLARMINO AND THE CHURCH CAMPAIGN AGAINST ALLENDE

The Chilean Church is also fragmenting, due to the conflict of incompatible interests internal to the Church system which compete for scarce resources both within and without. Yet this was not always the case. The years immediately following the Chilean presidential election of 1958 saw a rapid convergence of Catholic forces in Chile, with growing instrumental capacity fed by a network of external linkages to North American and Northern European sources of financial and technical support.

THE CAMPAIGN AGAINST ALLENDE

The reason for this remarkable convergence of Catholic forces lay in the fact that a Marxist, Salvador Allende, had very nearly been elected President of Chile in 1958.* The possibility had been foreseen by Church officials as early as 1956. In that year, the Chilean bishops petitioned the

---

*The official election results, as reported in El Mercurio (Santiago), September 7, 1958, were as follows: Alessandri, 386,192; Allende, 354,300; Frei, 254,324; Bossay, 189,182; Zamorano, 41,224.

Jesuit General in Rome, Belgian Father John Baptist
Janssens, to send Jesuit social scientists to Chile.
Janssens responded by sending a man who would in
the years to come profoundly affect Church opera-
tions in Latin America. He was the Belgian Jesuit
Roger Vekemans.

One of Vekeman's first actions was to enlist
the aid of a Belgian businessman, a former executive of SABENA Airlines, J. M. A. Sierens. Sierens
began in 1957 to compile systematic reports on the
"major Chilean institutions": large business enterprises, universities, branches of government,
political parties, labor unions, etc., with special
reference to the "problem of Communist penetration." Sierens' studies attempted to gauge the
numerical and financial strength of what could be
called "elements in the Chilean power structure."
His findings did not augur well for the anti-
Communists.

In a confidential report entitled "La Poli-
tique Chilienne en 1959," Sierens observed that
the candidacy of Christian Democrat Eduardo Frei
was dangerous because it took votes away from
Arturo Alessandri, the rightist candidate who de-
feated the leftist Allende in 1958 by only 30,000
votes.

Sierens concluded that Frei would either have
to be stopped entirely or assured of victory in
1964:

> Eduardo Frei, the defeated can-
> didate, represents Christian Democracy
> and many independents of the middle
> classes. He has now rallied to
> Alessandri in order to reinforce the
> latter's parliamentary strength in
> all economic questions where there
> is compatibility between Alessandri's
> program and his.

> Undeniably Catholic, Frei's can-
> didacy has once more risked dividing
> the Catholic forces and returning to
> power the socialist and Communist
> left. The present situation is ex-
> tremely dangerous. . . .

Sierens' report continued in a pessimistic
vein, characterizing Alessandri as a "man devoid of
ideas" who had tried hard but "brought no relief"
to the average Chilean. The latter, said Sierens,
was a type "easily discouraged," "impressionable,"
and "inconstant." He would not tolerate economic
sacrifice much longer.

In a second report, "Concerning Communist Activities in Chile," Sierens found that Communists
were "well entrenched and increasing their influence."

> At present there are approxi-
> mately 600 full-time Communist orga-
> nizers in Chile. Of these, half are
> working in the rural areas . . . the
> other 300 are employed as workers or
> as employees in industrial or admin-
> istrative organisms.

Communist financing, according to Sierens,
came not only from the Soviet Union but also from
investments in Chile in "popular restaurants and
soda fountains," and from a string of theaters.

The following sectors were said by Sierens to
have been heavily infiltrated by Communists. Areas
marked with a "P" are "preferred" by the Communists
and rank high in their list of priorities.

> A.   Education
>   Public schools (the teachers)
>   Private high schools
>   Public high schools
>   Night schools
>   Technical schools (P)

Industrial schools and schools
of mining (P)

The University of Chile; the Technical University (P); The University of Santa Maria; University
of Concepcion; University of
Valdivia

B. Unions--especially the mining
unions (P)

C. Working-class neighborhoods
Neighborhood councils
Social centers
Etc.

D. Professional societies
Doctors
Engineers
Dentists
Lawyers
Etc.

E. Enterprises
Chemical
Metallurgical
Maritime
Public Utilities (P)
Telephone
Gas
Water, etc. . . .
especially ENDESA, Empresa
Nacional de Electricidad

Sierens prefaced his second report with the statement that his information derived from "a series
of recent conversations with union leaders,
Christian as well as Marxist, and other persons who
by reason of their occupation have intimate ties
with the Chilean social problem." A typical specific reference is the following:

According to information recently
obtained from a Catholic doctor who
had lived several years in the provinces of Bio-Bio and Arauco, there is
a high level of Communist penetration

in the area, especially in the coal-
mining sector, where there functions
a "School for Marxist Experimentation"
where Marxist agents are trained in
tactics and revolutionary methods to
be sent throughout South America.

Sierens made the following "reflections"
upon concluding his report: the Church should act
in a united fashion to prevent a Marxist electoral
victory in 1964; one that would certainly deprive
the Catholic system of its schools, and possibly
its other installations as well. The bishops
should act, Catholic Action should be alerted and
coordinated, Catholic labor unions (which were then
feuding with each other) should be reconciled.

It is undeniable that the Chilean
Catholic Church is now renovating its
action in all areas. . . . But are
the results sufficient? Undoubtedly,
no. We advance not at all, if the
bishops issue directives and point
out new paths, when we Christians do
not live these directives and do not
follow these paths.
Would it not be possible to achieve
unity (at least the appearance of unity) of all the laymen who work in the
different apostolic movements of the
Church? Would it not be possible in
each diocese or archdiocese for all
the directors of the Catholic Action
movements, male and female: the AUC,
JOC, JAC, JEC, the union movements,
the marian congregations, the Catholic landowners and owners of businesses, the centers of working women,
the associations of professors, etc.,
to convene with the bishop from time
to time to hear from him the concrete
projects in which they are to work,
and for him to hear from them their
problems and complaints?

Sierens made specific reference to the disuni-
ty of two rural unions sponsored by the Catholic
Church in Chile: the Chilean Syndical Action
(ASICH)[1] and the Federation of Chilean Workers
(FEBRECH). He deplored their public quarreling:

> In the countryside, the only
> enemy is Marxism. With giant leaps
> it is penetrating both union leader-
> ship and union bases. Meanwhile, we
> Christians, divided as we are, cannot
> even understand one another, let
> alone deliver a common message in a
> common crisis.

The report closed with a call for a Church-
initiated land reform.

The Sierens reports are significant because
they provided empirical data to support Roger
Vekeman's contention that the Church must unite
around Frei to defeat Allende in 1964.

The Chilean bishops did inaugurate a land-
reform program in Chile, organizing their own institute, INPROA, to distribute five Church-owned
farms,[2] and helped reconcile their feuding rural
unions.

The Jesuit CIAS took special note of Sierens'
analyses and included him in their common projects.
The Belgian Jesuit Roger Vekemans Van Cauwelaert
was the organizer in 1957 of Chilean Jesuit CIAS,
which was housed in the Centro Bellarmino. After
Sierens returned to Europe, Vekemans continued to
develop an organization and an ideology at the
Centro Bellarmino. His success would startle even
his fellow Jesuits.

On September 21, 1961, the Chilean Conference
of Bishops received from their specially constituted

Pastoral Advisory Commission (which included Jesuit
CIAS members Vekemans and Poblete) a unanimous proposal for Church backing of the Frei candidacy
through Catholic Action and all other Catholic organizations.

Church land reform, Church support for the
Frei candidacy, and the formation of the Jesuit
Centro Bellarmino and its subsidiaries were three
initiatives that united Catholic forces in the late
1950's and early 1960's. With Frei's electoral
victory in 1964, the concentration phase ended and
the fragmentation process resumed in earnest. All
three of these initiatives will be discussed below.

THE CENTRO BELLARMINO

The Jesuit Centro Bellarmino played an important part in coordinating the diverse Catholic sectors in the fight against Allende and acted in many
ways as the key linkage, or "linchpin," in coordinating the Chilean land reform and the Frei presidential campaign. Thus when the Centro Bellarmino
began to disintegrate following Frei's victory,
there could be traced in its dissolution almost all
of the conflicts of interest that were fragmenting
the Chilean Catholic system.

The following analysis of the Jesuit Centro
Bellarmino is based on documents that were for the
most part intended exclusively for internal ecclesiastical use, usually by higher participants only.
We begin with excerpts from a confidential report
written in 1966 by Father Hernan Larrain, the
Jesuit director of the center. The report was intended for the Jesuit General in Rome and for
Cardinal Silva of Santiago. Although it did not
describe in detail Jesuit operations in Chile that
might have seemed indiscreet to top management re-
siding in Rome, it is reasonably complete if one is
permitted to read between the lines.

History of Chilean CIAS
Stage of Formulation and Preparation
(1957-59)

Because of the death of Father
Hurtado (1952), the second great pio-
neer of the social apostolate in
Chile--the first was Father Fernando
Vives--our Provincial Superior asked
Father General (John Baptist Janssens)
for a Jesuit specialist in social sciences who could continue the work already begun, above all, the work in
the labor field with the Catholic
Union ASICH. It was in this way that
in 1957 Father Vekemans came to Chile.

Larrain proceeded to describe the "plan" that
Vekemans proposed for CIAS. The organization was
to concentrate not upon scientific investigation
but upon doctrinal elaboration and diffusion.

The social doctrine elaborated
and propounded in papal documents was
not sufficient. What was necessary
was a Christian anthropology and a
social ethics derived from the present
moment, the actual concrete circumstances of Chile.

It was decided that, for lack of time, money, and
qualified personnel, the Jesuits of CIAS would not
launch into research but would rely upon studies
done by CEPAL, CELADE, and UNESCO. Only after a
period of gestation would the CIAS group generate
its own research institute.

The new ideology that was to be devised through
"doctrinal studies" was to be diffused "through
classes, conferences, forums, seminars, articles,
books, etc." It was to "orient the action" of lay
leaders whom the Jesuits would "advise."

In all of this, Father Vekemans
was the one who attained the objectives: through weekly contacts with

> groups of economists, through classes,
> conferences, consultation to business-
> men (USEC), workers (ASICH), etc. . . .

From the beginning, there had been thought of
a joint CIAS: the Jesuits who formed the CIAS
proper, with its emphasis upon developing ideology
and directing it toward the conversion and guidance
of elites, would be joined by the Jesuits who edited
Mensaje. Father Vekemans would be the director of
CIAS and Father Larrain would be the editor of
Mensaje. They would share a common residence with
their collaborators, the Centro Bellarmino, and all
mutually profit from their sustained, total-
institutional interaction.

This arrangement led to problems. The magazine, as we shall see, was oriented primarily to
students, who tended to be radical. The CIAS group,
on the other hand, quickly developed financial ties
to the United States government and to European
foundations. Later, CIAS would be closely linked
to the Christian Democratic Party and, especially,
to the Frei candidacy. The magazine would grow
increasingly critical of Christian Democracy after
Frei's victory, as the Christian Democratic "es-
tablishment" began to alienate sizeable sectors of
its student supporters. After the abortion of
"Project Camelot" (the North American attempt to
improve methods of counterinsurgency through studies
of Chilean discontent), the student readers of
Mensaje made clear their distrust of any Chilean
institution that was dependent upon North American
funding. This came at a time when Roger Vekemans
was deeply committed to the U.S. government and,
most dangerously, to the Central Intelligence Agency for support in union organizing.

Other, more mundane factors contributed to the
breakdown of the Centro Bellarmino. Whereas
Mensaje was losing money by the month, Vekemans'
activities were prospering enormously. He had
fashioned a research and development foundation independent of the Jesuits (DESAL) that exercised

the power of decision over $30 million per year,
which was to be allocated to DESAL-approved "social
development projects" in Latin America. This money
came from the West German government through the
German Catholic Bishops' Fund (MISEREOR). While
Mensaje editors and staffers sat at their typewrit-
ers in the dingy, barren offices of the Centro
Bellarmino, DESAL executives were attending conferences and entertaining potential and actual benefactors in the world's most luxurious hotels.

The Catholic social doctrine emphasizing working for the "poor and underprivileged" was common
currency to both groups. But whereas Mensaje soon
developed solidarity with the underclasses as
against "established interests," Vekemans spoke
more and more of the "marginality" of the poor who
were "without life" and required the "cultural up-
lifting" that only the upper classes ("herodian
sectors," as he called them) could provide.

These divergences will be documented and analyzed at length below. For now, it is expedient to
return to Larrain's short history of Chilean CIAS.

The Stage of Realization (1959-66).

In 1959 a new, larger house was
bought which permitted the fusion of
Mensaje and CIAS in the Centro Bellarmino. Foreign priests were coming in
droves and new projects were undertaken. In 1964 Father Larrain was
named director of CIAS.

The principal new project undertaken was the
Center for the Economic and Social Development of
Latin America (DESAL), founded by Father Vekemans
to provide policies and organization for the presidential campaign of Eduardo Frei. Vekemans was
too busy to direct the other operations of Jesuit
CIAS, so Larrain was given the directorship.

Larrain's "history of CIAS" ends with the
"stage of realization" in 1966. What followed

historically might be called the "stage of fragmentation" or dissolution, but that will be presented
later.

In 1966, CIAS was not "fragmented," but it was
"differentiated." It was housed in four separate
units, which for purposes of analysis are roughly
indicative of four distinct currents of thought and
divergent bases of support.

1. The first of these units was the headquarters, the Centro Bellarmino proper, which in 1966
housed all of the CIAS-Mensaje Jesuits as well as
the editorial offices of the magazine. There were
ten CIAS staff experts. Of these, seven held advanced degrees in social sciences; the remaining
three were theologians. Of the seven social scientists, three were Chilean and the rest were North
American or European. Of the seven Jesuits who
published Mensaje, only two were full time.

The full-time CIAS members were: Vekemans
(sociology); Bigo (social doctrine); Poblete (sociology of religion); Zanartu, Wehner, and Arroyo
(economics); Hurley (mass media, business administration); Larrain (psychology); Gaete (philosophy);
and Ochagavia and Ossa (theology).

Hernan Larrain doubled as a CIAS member and as
head of Mensaje. He was charged with coordinating
the activities of both, often publishing the work
of the CIAS. This linkage between research and
dissemination would soon become problematic.
Larrain's full-time assistant at Mensaje was Hubert
Daubechies, a Belgian Jesuit who was not an intimate of his fellow countryman Roger Vekemans.

2. In 1966, the house adjoining the Centro
Bellarmino was rented by DESAL (according to
Larrain's report, at a cost of $100,000 per year).
DESAL was under the personal control of Roger
Vekemans and was completely independent of the CIAS.
For a time, Arroyo was a close co-worker with
Vekemans at DESAL. DESAL employed upward of eighty

"technicians" (economists, sociologists, demographers, etc.) during the late 1960's and was a far
larger operation than all other Jesuit CIAS groups
in Latin America combined.

3. The house of the Latin American Institute
of Doctrine and Social Studies (ILADES), which was
directed by Bigo, consisted of offices for the
ILADES staff and classrooms for fifty students selected from various Latin American countries and
given scholarships financed by ADVENIAT. Bigo
taught also at IDES in Colombia and was head of
CLACIAS, the coordinating body for all Jesuit CIAS
groups on the continent.

4. The house rented to the Institute of
Christian Humanism stood directly across the street
from that of DESAL, whose founder, Vekemans, had
arranged special financing through channels to be
described below. The Institute of Christian Humanism sought to give ideological training of a decidedly anti-Marxist cast to Chilean union leaders.
University students were brought in to tutor workers in Christian social doctrine.

The "impact" of CIAS upon the Chilean social
system in the 1960's was broad and deep. In a document meant for internal use, Larrain outlined the
following spheres of influence: the Chilean Church,
the Christian Democratic Party, public opinion, the
Catholic University, political pressure groups, the
under classes, Latin America as a whole.

> We have shown the quantitative
> development of our CIAS organization
> --houses, projects, personnel, col-
> laborators--but this development is
> no mere facade. It is a sign of true
> influence.
>   a. Influence in the Chilean
> Church: important collaboration with
> the bishops, helping to write the
> pastoral letters on mass media (1962),
> on education (1966), on the political

responsibilities of Christians (1963),*
the declaration of the episcopal commission concerning divorce legislation
(1964), and the coming one on agrarian
reform. We have also held seminars
of reorientation for the clergy (300
priests at a recent one). Further
influence through the Faculty of Theology at the Catholic University.

This first sphere of influence, the Church
system, was the proper domain of Father Renato
Poblete, who continued throughout the 1960's as a
key advisor to Cardinal Silva Henriquez, even after
Poblete's intimates, Vekemans and Larrain, were out
of favor at the chancery.

Larrain next mentions Jesuit influence in the
Christian Democratic Party. He does so somewhat
cryptically:

b. Influence in the political
sphere: through Mensaje we give doctrinal direction to the "revolution"
which the Christian Democratic Party
is carrying out. We have indirect
influence upon educational reform,
land reform, popular promotion, etc.
There are contacts and informal conversations with high officials.

The specific relationships that Vekemans and Poblete
had cultivated with Eduardo Frei, and the ties

---

*An important document issued first in 1963
and then again during the presidential campaign of
Eduardo Frei in 1964. It explicitly warned of a
Communist "threat" and echoed the exact wording of
Frei's campaign slogan, "toward a new fatherland"
("hacia un patria nuevo"), while calling for a
"revolution in liberty," which both Frei and the
bishops contrasted to what they termed the "totali-
tarian" revolution being prepared by Salvador
Allende.

between Father Zanartu and Christian Democratic
politician, Radimiro Tomic, will be described later.

Larrain then speaks of influence in the Catholic University, not only through ordinary classes
but above all through informal contacts and consultation with "student leaders." He also mentions
that the Jesuits were responsible for the Institute
of Christian Humanism and for the Coordinating Organization for Student Movements (ORMEU). The latter organization was to cause the Jesuits considerable embarrassment when The New York Times revealed in 1967 that it was an outlet for monies
from the United States Central Intelligence Agency.[3]
Only Vekemans seems to have known that the CIA was
the true eminence gris behind the funding of ORMEU.

Larrain wrote that Jesuit influence upon "public opinion" was exercised through Mensaje. There
were also weekly conferences for the public, held
in the Centro Bellarmino. In the early 1960's, and
especially during Frei's presidential campaign,
these had capacity attendance. Larrain also cited
"interviews in magazines of wide distribution," including Look, Life, Time, and Newsweek. Vekemans
at one time hosted a popular television talk show
and frequently was heard on radio panel discussions.

The Jesuits also "advised" businessmen through
the Social Union of Christian Businessmen (USEC),
union leaders through the Chilean Syndical Action
(ASICH), neighborhood organization through the National Association of Pobladores ("Slumdwellers")
(CENAPO), and peasant leaders through the Christian
Peasant Union (UCC). The Jesuits supervised a construction corporation which, with U.S. AID money,
built "more than 10,000 houses for the poor in less
than a year."

Influence on the continental level was exercised through ILADES training and indoctrination
programs and through DESAL, which distributed $30
million of West German MISEREOR funds annually,
while operating on U.S. AID and "foundations" capital.

CHART 2

Chilean Church: Formal Organization of Chilean
Jesuit Centro Bellarmino

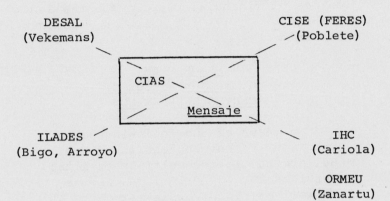

DESAL
(Vekemans)

CISE (FERES)
(Poblete)

CIAS

Mensaje

ILADES
(Bigo, Arroyo)

IHC
(Cariola)

ORMEU
(Zanartu)

CIAS   (Center for Research and Social Action): shifting
            membership
Mensaje   (monthly review: doctrinal, political): Larrain,
            Daubechies, Gaete, Ossa
DESAL   (Center for the Economic and Social Development of
            Latin America).: Vekemans, (Arroyo)
CISE   (Center for Socio-Religious Research): Poblete
            affiliated with FERES (International Federation
            of Institutes for Socio-Religious and Social
            Research): Gustavo Perez
IHC   (Institute of Christian Humanism): Cariola,
            Zanartu, Arroyo
IPT   (Institute for Promotion of Labor): Poblete,
            Zanartu, Vekemans
ICS   (Institute for Social Communications): Hurley
ILADES   (Latin American Institute of Doctrine and Social
            Studies): Bigo, Arroyo, and others
HOGAR DE
CRISTO   ("Christ's Hearth": home construction): Poblete,
            Vekemans
ORMEU   (Coordinating Office for University Student Move-
            ments)

The informal ties to the Christian Democratic Party, to organizations of businessmen, labor unions, etc. are not here
traced out. See the main body of text. In most cases, these
informal contacts were "built into" the ordinary operation of
the formal units.

In 1966, Renato Poblete published a report for
U.S. AID, the Ford and Rockefeller Foundations, and
other sources of financial support for the Centro
Bellarmino proper. A revised version, issued in
1968, is printed below:

<u>MEMORANDUM</u>
<u>On the Activities of</u>
<u>CENTRO BELLARMINO</u>

By means of the following seven
programs, seventeen Jesuits of Centro
Bellarmino provide multi-operational
services to underprivileged people,
as well as to university students and
business, civic, political, and labor
leaders of Chile and to the serious
religious research for the Pastoral
work of the Church in Chile.
          1. A $3 million emergency low-
cost housing program. Last year the
Centro constructed and sold 25,000
prefabricated low-cost homes. The
homes range from one-room shelters at
$60 to four-room houses at $300. Help
from the private sector, assistance
from government, and organizational
labor and skill donated by the Jesuits
of Centro Bellarmino makes these low
prices possible. Earthquake and flood
victims of Santiago, Valparaiso, and
Concepcion seeking to replace homes
destroyed by recent natural disasters
are beneficiaries.
          2. Production cooperatives. With
an annual government subsidy of $80,000
and a U.S. AID grant of $460,000, Cen-
tro Bellarmino organized 65 production
centers in slum areas employing 2,000
persons doing piecework for factories,
as well as manufacturing whole items
for sale, such as overalls, shirts,
furniture, etc. The Centro advises
the cooperative leaders on production

and other management problems, as
well as continues to organize addi-
tional production centers.

3. Central library facilities
for university students. With a
modern cardex and professional li-
brarians, the Centro obtains maximum
use of 20,000 volumes and 120 periodicals, mostly in the fields of
business, labor, and socio-economics.
The Centro Bellarmino Library serves
Santiago students attending the University of Chile and Catholic University and is shared by the Latin American Institute for Doctrinal Formation
(ILADES) and by DESAL.

4. The Socio-Religious Research
Center is one of the four centers of
this kind that operate in Latin America. It has been doing research in
the area of religious vocations, use
of apostolic manpower, religious practices, coordination of seminaries, and
public opinion studies on the Church,
etc. Has done the basic research for
the Bishops' meetings in Chile and
also has been of service to Latin
American Bishops, providing the
speakers and the basic documentation
needed for the meetings of CELAM
(Bishops Council of Latin America).
In this Center work three sociologists
and two assistants. The operational
budget is $15,000 that the Center has
to finance out of its main budget.

5. Institute for Humanities and
Theology. Centro Bellarmino acts as
a Newman Center for university students. Special courses are offered
the students and seminars and conferences are organized on their behalf. Business, labor, political,
and civic leaders also avail themselves
of these services. In addition, Centro

Bellarmino is in charge of pastoral
needs for the university population.

6.   The monthly Mensaje. Organized and directed by four Centro
Bellarmino prists, this monthly supports itself on subscriptions and
advertising, publishing 8,000 copies
at the low cost of $25,000 per year.
Its readership consists principally
of the university population and
leaders in business and government
communities. More than 1,500 subscriptions are sent to different
Latin American countries.

7.   Study Center for public high-
school students. In a pilot program,
library material, a place to study,
and vocational guidance are given at
a central location to students attending five public high schools.

8.   Specialized Service Center.
The following activities employ eight
Centro Bellarmino Jesuits:

a.   Communication media techniques. Centro Bellarmino is organizing a program for the use of television
for secondary and adult education.

b.   The School of Psychology
at Catholic University is directed by
one of the Jesuits from Centro Bellarmino.

c.   Institute to teach Latin
American University students and worker leaders and priests the social
doctrine of the Church. ILADES has
been financed by the German bishops
since the official institute of CELAM
for social training. Almost all the
priests from the Centro Bellarmino
teach there and three priests are
full-time committed to this Institute.

d.   Centro Bellarmino supplies
two Jesuits as teachers on the Faculty
of Theology at Catholic University

and at the Center for Pastoral Formation.
      e. Center for Latin Ameri-
can Economic and Social Development.
Jesuits direct operations of this
organization which prepares projects
on behalf of private, non-profit
agencies for presentation to resource
groups such as the German Bishops'
Fund, MISEREOR.
    The annual budget for the seven-
teen Centro Bellarmino Jesuits who
execute the above programs is $35,000,
of which $15,000 is for room and
board, $10,000 for librarians, and
$10,000 for secretaries. Over one-
half of this total is obtained from
Mass stipends, professorial salaries,
and professional fees earned by the
priests. To continue the above
multi-million dollar program, the remaining amount, $15,000, is sought
through donations.
February 15th, 1968

    The only changes Poblete made in this revised
version were to add a section on newly formed ILADES
and to expand the section dealing with the Socio-
Religious Research Center (Section 4). The latter,
which was composed of Poblete and varying numbers
of university undergraduates and graduates, absorbed $15,000 of the $35,000 Poblete said comprised
the annual budget of the Centro Bellarmino. Since
DESAL cannot really be included in the budget of
the Centro Bellarmino, due to its exclusive sources
of massive financial support, and since ILADES was
run on money from ADVENIAT, the $35,000 that Poblete
mentions could only have covered the upkeep of the
main house, as well as room and board for its Jesuit
lodgers.

    The entire Centro Bellarmino complex, a con-
glomerate of a dozen different enterprises, had a
1966 budget that ran actually, although unreportedly,

into many millions of dollars. Still, one fact
should be made clear: the actual budget for which
the Jesuit order was responsible was miniscule.
Each of the Jesuit operations was self-sufficient.
Nor did financial help derive from the Chilean
bishops. At no time in the 1960's did the bishops
contribute more than $1,000, even for studies or
consultations of which they were the prime beneficiaries.[4] It is not surprising, therefore, that
strains soon developed between the Jesuits and the
bishops. Only Father Poblete remained identified
with episcopal interests. The functions of this
special linkage which Poblete provided will be suggested below.

An organization chart of the Centro Bellarmino,
if drawn to scale, would trace all of the important
linkages that were both intended and unintended by
the CIAS/Mensaje directorate. It would certainly
involve a list of such "conscious targets" of Jesuit activity as Larrain compiled. But there were
other reference groups that modified the behavior
of individual CIAS members without the explicit approval or specific knowledge of CIAS directors.
Some of these informal linkages of CIAS Jesuits to
salient actors and institutions will be described
now. A more precise and comprehensive "linkage
framework" will be provided in Chapter 17.

The CIAS directors were aware that inputs deriving from a welter of conflicting interest groups
might well disrupt the CIAS team. They therefore
monitored the activities of their members. Each
member was to write an annual report of his activities, supplying a list of his "clientele." What
follows are the reports of some CIAS members for
the year 1967 (translated from the Spanish):

REPORT OF THE ACTIVITIES OF
FATHER GONZALO ARROYO
They are the following:
ILADES: undertook the responsi-
bility of chief of studies; also
teaching in two courses: "Theory of

Marginality" and "Land Reform and
Development." Taught a seminar on
"Socialism and Agrarian Reform."
As chief of studies (for the Jesuit
order in Chile: DEM), undertook a
reform of the high school program for
Jesuit high schools, and recruited
teachers (Eugenio Maffei in Chile,
Carlos Armelin from Argentina). As
executive secretary of the ILADES
directorate am in charge of organizing reunions and of working out arrangements between ILADES and the
University of Louvain which will
recognize the ILADES degree.

CIAS: formed commission of
studies for reform of Jesuit high
schools in Chile (members of commission: Carlos Hurtado, Sergio
Cifuentes, Patricio Cariola of the
schools, and Pierre Bigo, Jose
Antonio Vieragallo and Paulo Freire
of ILADES). Finished a report on
previous studies of the indoctrination
of high school students. Represented
Father Poblete in the meeting of CLAR
(Latin American Conference of Superiors of Religious Orders) in Lima
(November).

CLACIAS: represented Hernan
Larrain at the meeting of CLACIAS
(Coordinating Committee of Latin
American CIAS groups) in Paris. Par-
ticipated in conference at Heinrich
Pesch Haus, Mannheim, at request of
Father Zwiefelhoffer.

Catholic University: resigned
position in the Center of Studies for
Agricultural Enterprises and only
kept one course: "Theory of Production," in the Department of Agricultural Economics. Participated in
weekly seminars of the professors of
Economics (Las Condes) and directed

some theses. Also took active part
in strike within the department of
Agronomy in solidarity with the professors there. Starting in 1968 will
give course in School of Economics
entitled "Agrarian Reform and Development."

Institute of Christian Humanism:
Advisor to the University division,
talks, informal consulting. Organized seminars on "Populorum Progres-
sio" (a papal encyclical: DEM), and
on "Introduction to Marxism."

Contacts and informal consulting:
visits to the south of Chile (to land
reform projects, INDAP (government
agency--Institute for Agricultural
and Livestock Development), talks to
peasants (National Peasant Confederation), contacts with CORA (Agrarian
Reform Corporation of Chilean government: DEM), and with university students.

Arroyo also reported "pastoral activity," or
priestly work. He said mass for university students, heard confessions in the university parish,
and directed a group of students who met once a
month to discuss spirituality.

But Arroyo's chief interest lay in his work as
an agronomist. He held a doctorate in agronomy
from the University of Iowa and had worked since
1966 with government planners in Chilean land-reform
agencies. His identification with INDAP (which was
headed by Christian Democratic "terceristas") involved him in a bitter dispute with fellow Jesuit
Roger Vekemans, whose DESAL organization was supporting the United States-backed National Peasant
Confederation (CNC). The CNC regarded INDAP as
"Marxist-infiltrated" and "socialistic."[5]

A more extended report of activities was
rendered to CIAS by Father Mario Zanartu, a Ph.D.

in economics from Columbia University who spent a
semester each year at Notre Dame teaching courses
in developmental economics. Zanartu divided his
report into six parts: theology and spiritual life,
doctrinal elaboration, scientific preparation, consulting, and "pastimes." Of particular importance
to this study were the following:

Zanartu had worked with ORMEU organizers to
develop a definition of "ideology" that would be
compatible with but would not include the "social
doctrine of the Church." He was also working, together with Christian Democratic ideologues such as
Senator Rafael Gumucio and Minister of Justice
Jaime Castillo Velasco, to develop Catholic doctrinal support for a "noncapitalist way to development." The latter would involve the substitution
of a "communitarian system" of property-holding and
decision-making in place of capitalist structures.
Workers and owners would share in decision-making,
but the two classes would remain distinct. A more
specific formulation was not readily forthcoming.
Senator Gumucio tried to resolve the ambiguities
inherent in this type of model: "Our detractors
say that our position is vague and impracticable;
nevertheless, in Chile we have seen put into practice different forms of communitarian property,
without mentioning the Yugoslavian experience in
this respect."[6]

Zanartu also participated in conferences and
meetings dealing with reform at the Catholic University; he was especially interested in American-
izing the Department of Economics at the university.
With regard to scientific formation, Zanartu mentioned contacts at Notre Dame University and the
University of Chicago.*

------

*Zanartu edited a book on Christian Democratic
ideology for Notre Dame which is interesting in
that it contains articles by the officialista wing
of the Party, including 1970 presidential candidate
Radimiro Tomic.

Consulting took up a great deal of Father
Zanartu's time in 1967. His work with ORMEU consisted in

> a lot of activity in the heart of the
> executive committee (with the presi-
> dent of the group and the executive
> secretary of the Institute of Chris-
> tian Humanism) whose purpose is the
> location of complaints or necessities
> of the professional sectors, formula-
> tion of plans for starting new groups,
> obtaining support, evaluation, etc. . . .

Working in other areas with the Institute for
Christian Humanism, Zanartu had contacts with a
group of Chilean and foreign economists (Eduardo
Garcia, Alejandro Foxley, Franz Hinkelammert, Oscar
Munoz), a group of businessmen led by Patricio
Dominguez, and with a group called OMEGA. The latter, informally connected with the Institute for
Christian Humanism, was comprised of "young government officials of all tendencies" who were eager to
"explore the idea of community enterprise" as an
alternative to either orthodox Marxism or capitalism.

Zanartu was also an advisor to the Social Union
of Christian Businessmen (USEC). The USEC found
Zanartu's "communitarian" views distasteful, however, and they eventually forced his resignation as
"official Church advisor." As Zanartu's 1967 report states, his position was untenable.

> I am at an impasse with this or-
> ganization. They want me to submit
> my resignation, but I want them to
> throw me out. From my point of view,
> under the presidency of Sergio Silva,
> the USEC expanded its representation
> but lost all of its "punch." It no
> longer is the kind of organization to
> which those businessmen can turn who
> want to make private enterprise in
> Chile more Christian.

The main problem with the USEC, continued
Zanartu, was that it had become anti-Christian Democracy.

> USEC has become a tool of the Na-
> tional Confederation of Industry and
> Commerce whose president is Sergio
> Silva, the former president of USEC.
> . . . The NCIC is a political pres-
> sure group that opposes the present
> (Frei) government, as is evident from
> the December 5th issue of its new
> magazine, Desfile. The only function
> of USEC at present, a very useful one
> really, is that of distributing travel
> grants for visits to European coun-
> tries. . . .

Zanartu's expulsion from Medellin, Colombia,
where he had been assisting the labor organizers of
CLASC, was recounted in Chapter 8. He continued to
advise CLASC periodically, but by 1967 the organization had transferred its headquarters to Venezuela to try to build a Christian Democratic base for
Rafael Caldera. Zanartu retained his CLASC contacts informally, "through the mails," and stopped
in Venezuela yearly en route to Notre Dame.

As has been noted, Zanartu was included on the
executive council of social studies of ORMEU. He
was, in fact, one of its most important members:

> My task is above all that of ori-
> entation of teaching programs, selec-
> tion of professors, control of the
> direction of the institute insofar as
> it relates to established goals. . . .
> At this level I am the only one who
> assures the general doctrinal orienta-
> tion, to which all of the leaders of
> ORMEU are very firmly committed.

Zanartu taught at the University of Notre Dame,
the Catholic University of Chile, and at ILADES
each year. He also said mass in the homes of

friends and cultivated personal contacts both within the Christian Democratic government and party
and without.

The principal role of forming contacts of an
informal sociable nature with party officials fell
to Renato Poblete, who had known Eduardo Frei and
his wife for many years. Poblete was an intimate of
many of the original founders of the FALANGE, which
later became the Christian Democratic Party.
Poblete baptized their children, confessed their
wives, and attended their parties. However, he
made it a rule not to make financial demands of
these people and looked for financial support elsewhere, directing himself to North American benefactors. Poblete had earned a masters degree in sociology from Fordham University in the late 1950's
and maintained his North American contacts even
after returning to Chile to found a center for
"pastoral research" for the Chilean Cardinal.

Poblete's links to Gustavo Perez of ICODES in
Colombia were described in the preceding chapter.
Poblete shared with Perez an aversion to the Co-
lombian Jesuit Vicente Andrade Valderrama. When
Andrade published an article in the North American
Jesuit weekly, _America_, attacking the slain priest-
guerrilla, Camilo Torres, Poblete wrote a dissent-
ing letter to the editors of the magazine:

> I was in Berkeley with Father
> Gustavo Perez, who studied sociology
> in Louvain with Camilo, and who was
> his intimate friend. Father Perez
> says that the article by Father Andrade
> is full of prejudice. Several priests
> whom I met at the Conference of Theol-
> ogy at Notre Dame reacted very strong-
> ly against the article by Father
> Andrade. Our opinion here in Chile,
> where many of us knew Camilo very
> well, is that _America_ should not have
> published the article.

Poblete was quick to add that he did not imply
that he or any of the Chilean Jesuits were of the
same ideological or political persuasion as Camilo
Torres.

> We do not justify the acts of
> Camilo, as can be seen from the last
> issue of Mensaje, but no Christian
> can say that "he did not have a voca-
> tion" or that he was exploited by
> Marxist extremists in Louvain, or
> that Camilo was immediately overcome
> by such from the moment he entered
> the city, or that "his temperament
> and family history hardly recommended
> him for the life of a priest." I
> think that the last assertion is com-
> pletely false and very uncharitable.[7]

As we shall see, Chilean-Colombian Jesuit antipathy extended to relations between Jesuits at
CLACIAS meetings, where Andrade represented Colombian CIAS and Hernan Larrain, the Chilean CIAS.

Poblete had been active in Chilean CIAS since
the early 1960's. At this point it would be well
to return to that early "stage of realization," as
Larrain termed it, in order to locate the driving
force behind the development of the Centro Bellarmino.

The fear of Marxism in general and of Salvador
Allende's candidacy in particular had driven the
Chilean bishops to call upon the Vatican, the Jesuit General, North American and Northern European
bishops, and the international religious orders to
bolster the efforts of Chilean Catholics in a united front of opposition. Catholic forces gradually
linked up during the first few years after the 1958
presidential elections in Chile; by the beginning
of the 1960's the Catholic bishops and their official staff organizations were integrated enough to
rely upon the Jesuit Centro Bellarmino for detailed
campaign strategies, and the assignment of specific

roles. The Jesuits of CIAS began to blanket the
North American Catholic system with appeals for
help. Aid was sought from North American bishops,
religious orders, and Catholic foundations with the
plea that only they could "save Chile." Documents
such as the following proposal for free education
at the Colegio San Ignacio, sent by Jesuit CIAS to
North American Catholic support groups, were common. This one implies that the victory of Allende,
or of any other FRAP candidate, would automatically
mean the expropriation of Catholic schools. Although Jesuit schools were oriented to the upper
middle class and upper class in Chile, and charged
considerable tuition, the Chilean Jesuits recognized that it was time for a change.

> FREE EDUCATION IN COLEGIO SAN IGNACIO
> 1. Postulant: Rev. Fr. Carlos
>   Aldunate, S.J. Rector of Colegio
>   San Ignacio. General Prefect of
>   Studies for the Society of Jesus
>   in Chile.
>   (Address: Alonso Ovalle 1452,
>   Santiago, Chile)
> 2. Country: Chile
> 3. Archdiocese: Santiago de Chile.
>   Archbishop: Raul Silva Henriquez.
> 4. Project: To collect enough bourses
>   to be able to give free education
>   in Colegio San Ignacio
> 5. Motives: Great danger of Commu-
>   nism in the country
>   Need of strengthening the Church
>   Impossibility of many families to
>   pay for a Catholic education
>   Spiritual need of many excellent
>   boys
>   Danger of such boys strengthening
>   the Freemasons and Communists
> 6. Economic Problem: We need bourses
>   of $U.S. 1,000 each to complement
>   the state subsidy and make the
>   whole school free. As it is im-
>   possible to collect all the money

at once, we would only make half
the school free; i.e., we need
480 bourses now.

7. Collaboration: The produce of
   180 bourses will be supplied by
   one of our schools during the
   first few years until we get more
   funds.
   - The parents of present pupils,
     ex alumni, and friends will do-
     nate from 150 to 200 bourses.
   - Caritas Catholica of Belgium
     will be asked by Msgr. Cauwe
     to donate 20 bourses and to
     lend 30 during 3 years.
   - Therefore we hope to have about
     430 bourses to begin with.

8. Petition: A contribution of 50
   bourses to complete the 480 that
   we need.

9. Administration: The reception
   and administration of the bourses
   is done by Fundacion Educacional
   Santiago, legally founded for
   this object. Its directory includes two Jesuits and five responsible Catholic businessmen.
   President (with full faculties):
   Rev. Fr. Carlos Aldunate, S.J.

10. References: Can be obtained from
    Mr. Guillermo Correa Fuenzalida,
    President of the Banco de Chile.
    (Address: Santiago de Chile.)
    Mr. Fernando Llena, President,
    Bolsa de Commercio, Santiago de
    Chile.

While appeals such as this one were sent to
North American foundations (such as the Peter Grace
Foundation and the Lewis Foundation), the Jesuit
provincial superior of Chile, Father Alvaro Lavin,
was appealing for manpower to North American Jesuit
superiors. In the hope, first, of intervening
through them with the U.S. State Department, he

asked North American Jesuit Francisco Lyon to write
the American Embassy requesting "earthquake relief,"
although his main motive was to bolster up the
southern provinces of Chile against the Marxist
"tides" of which Sierens had warned. Lyon wrote to
the Assistant Secretary of State for Inter-American
Affairs, Robert F. Woodward, in June, 1961, a year
after the earthquakes. The reply he received was
not encouraging. "It is not possible to assure
you," wrote Woodward, "that part of the $100 mil-
lion dollars which the Congress of the United
States has allotted for reconstruction measures in
the South of Chile will be destined for capital improvements of private schools."

However, Secretary Woodward promised that "due
consideration would be given the Jesuit schools,"
adding that the Government of Chile collaborated
with the Embassy in the distribution of said funds.
Lavin could not wait for this kind of solution
through lobbying, and was busy throughout the fall
of 1961 writing letters to North American Jesuit
provincial superiors asking them to send some of
their men to Chile to take over Jesuit schools so
that Chilean Jesuits would be freed to assist CIAS
fight Communism.

This response to crisis--the shifting of emphases from "line" to "staff" sectors--is instructive. Once the crisis fades, or is somehow resolved, attention shifts back to the line, leaving
expanded staff facilities "over-expanded" and heavy
investments in staff upkeep suddenly without long-
range support. This is what occurred in Chile.
The result was staff discontent, complaint, and finally, withdrawal. Today the religious system in
Chile is faced with massive fragmentation, as staff
sectors that were once frantically assembled with
external financing and showered with ad hoc policy-
making powers found themselves on their own to redress accumulated debts.

NOTES

1. For an interesting case study of ASICH (one done with official Church support), see Henry Landsberger and Fernando Canitrot, <u>Iglesia, Intelectuales y Campesinos</u> (INSORA, University of Chile, 1967)

2. For case studies of INPROA, see William C. Thiesenhusen, <u>Reforma agraria en Chile: experimento en cuatro fundos de la iglesia</u> (Instituto de Economica y Planificacion, Universidad de Chile, 1968).

3. <u>The New York Times</u>, February 18, 1967.

4. Informal conversations with Renato Poblete throughout November and December, 1968.

5. For a comprehensive contemporary history of such developments, see Terry Luther McCoy's doctoral dissertation, <u>Agrarian Reform in Chile, 1962-68, A Study of Politics and the Development Process</u>, published by the University of Wisconsin Land Tenure Center, 1969.

6. <u>El Mercurio</u> (Santiago), December 15, 1968.

7. Letter cited in German Guzman Campos, <u>Camilo: El Cura Guerrillero</u> (Bogota: Servicios Especiales de Prensa, 1967), p. 12.

Lavin requested some promise of manpower from
his Jesuit colleagues in the United States. He was
met with polite refusal. When he insisted, he was
again refused. (This lesson would have its effect.
When Jesuits from all over the world sent delegates
to Rome in 1966 to elect a new General and to re-
write Jesuit regulations, the Chilean representative, Larrain, sent back letters reminding his CIAS
associates in Chile of past "Yankee intransigence"
and happily reporting that in Rome that year the
North Americans were not "getting their own way.")

Jesuit provincial superior Lavin sent the
first of his letters to U.S. provincials to Father
John Daley, S.J., the superior of the Maryland
province. In a letter dated September 5, 1961 (in
which Father Daley's name is misspelled as "Daily"),
Lavin wrote:

> We have asked permission from
> Father General to give up the whole
> South of Chile, in order to concen-
> trate our work in the schools and es-
> pecially to dedicate more men to the
> social action. Father General has
> sent us a letter commanding us to put
> more men in the social field due to

the increase of Communism and to the
great social changes that we are experiencing. The Cuban situation is
not a local phenomenon but could be
repeated in many other countries. We
know that we have to do this work but,
again, we see that if we remain with
the same number of schools and works,
we will never be able to face this
problem.

Father Lavin then asked Father Daley for men
to take over the Chilean Jesuit high school in
Puerto Montt. He emphasized the urgency of the request, saying that in three years (election year
1964) all might be lost.

We consider the situation here in
South America so serious that we think
that we have only three years to work
and if we don't do it now, it will
probably be too late in the future.
We have been very lucky to receive
some help from the United States,
which is sending forty-five laymen to
work here in Chile with the Peace
Corps.

Father Daley replied on September 12, 1961,
with regrets that he could not send more men to
Chile. The Maryland Province had already taken
over a school in Osorno, Chile, some years before
"when visas were not obtainable for India," where
the Maryland Jesuits had their regular "mission."

Now we are able to send into India
selected men if the Indian government
approves of them. You can only begin
to imagine the great clamor for more
men in India, since their ranks were
thinned because of no replacements
for five years or more. Now they are
in dire need, and they are struggling
earnestly to provide sufficient men,

and talented men, to take up the work
there. Every second year we are
obliged to send a man to Japan, and
in the past two years three men have
gone on the "International Missions"
of Father General. . . .
        I do assure you sincerely of my
continued prayers for the Church in
South America, and in a very special
way in Chile.

Father Daley added in a postscript that "all
the North American Provinces have recently been
asked to take care of Cuban Province in Exile--with
men and money."

The other North American provincials had their
own style of refusal, some florid, some abrupt, but
all were unequivocal in their negative response.
The provincial of the Chicago Province of the Society of Jesus, John R. Connery, S.J., sent the
following crisp note:

        This is to acknowledge your let-
ter of September 11, requesting that
men be sent from the Chicago Province
to assist the Province of Chile in
its ministries.
        As you no doubt have heard, in
addition to our mission in Patna,
India, Father General has recently
assigned to the Chicago Province the
southern part of Peru, and seven
priests and two scholastics are already in Peru.
        I appreciate your problems and
your need for assistance, but in view
of the mission work to which we are
already committed, I am sure that you
will understand that we are not in a
position to send anyone to Chile.
        With prayers and kindest personal
regards. . . .

In the meantime, Lavin had decided that the
North American provincials might be more willing to
send men to Chile if they themselves had been to
Chile to survey the political situation. He wrote
to the remaining United States Jesuit provincial
superiors proposing that their forthcoming joint
meeting in Boston be transferred to Santiago. He
could not, of course, finance their travel, but he
was sure that they would find such a visit worth-
while.

John J. McGinty, the provincial of the New
York Province of the Society of Jesus, the largest
Jesuit manpower reserve in the United States, was
interested. On September 22, 1961, he wrote:

> The proposition made in your let-
> ter of September 12th is more involved
> and requires more consideration and
> consultation than that I could give
> you any definite answer immediately.
> But I do want to assure you that I
> am very much interested in your pro-
> posal and that it has many possibili-
> ties.
> I was very much taken by your sug-
> gestion that our annual Provincials
> Meeting be held in Chile next year.
> The meeting is scheduled for Boston,
> under the Chairmanship of Father
> Coleran. But it will be interesting
> to see what will be the reaction of
> the American Provincials to holding
> the sessions in Santiago. . . .

The reactions of the other provincials turned
out to be less than enthusiastic. Father John J.
Foley, the provincial of the Wisconsin Province
wrote that,

> The next meeting of the Fathers
> Provincial has already been scheduled
> to take place in Boston, in May, 1962.
> I am afraid that Your Reverence's

> suggestion might create serious prob-
> lems for the New England Provincial,
> who, as Chairman of the meeting, will
> have the task of preparing for the
> meeting and supervising the secretar-
> ial work that must precede and follow
> the meeting. I certainly would not
> wish to express any approval of the
> proposal without knowing what he and
> the other Provincials think about
> it. . . .

Father Foley also mentioned that the Wisconsin Province had "already been given two very important mission assignments by the Holy See, which will tax our manpower capacity for some years to come." (Both were in South Korea.)

Father Andrew Smith, the vice provincial of the New Orleans Province, had manpower problems of his own, but offered to send Jesuit sociologist Joseph Fichter to give lectures at Santiago's Catholic University.

The provincials of the other provinces deferred to Father Coleran on the question of meeting in Santiago.

Lavin was disheartened by these responses. On October 17, 1961, he sent a letter to "All Jesuit Superiors" of the Chilean Province, in which he emphasized the predominant role that the Centro Bellarmino was to play in "saving Chile." The other houses of the Society of Jesus in Chile were to cooperate in any and every way, giving up men and money to finance CIAS operations:

> This is to inform you that Father
> Gerardo Claps has been assigned to
> the Residence St. Robert Bellarmine
> (Centro Bellarmino) so that he may
> coordinate the work of the CIAS with
> the work of the other houses of the
> province. This Center has been

>created by the express concern of
>Very Reverend Father General because
>of the social situation in our coun-
>try.

Lavin related that the priority given to the
Centro Bellarmino reflected the "critical situation
of the entire Church in Latin America in 1961." He
pointed to the "past events in Cuba," where Spanish
Jesuits had been expelled by an "avowed Communist,"
and to the coming elections in Chile, which might
terminate in the election of Salvador Allende. The
creation of the Chilean Centro Bellarmino as the
linchpin of Catholic forces in the fight against
Communism was linked to the preoccupation of the
Jesuit General himself:

>Very Reverend Father General has
>kept insisting that we intensify our
>work in the social field because such
>is the seriousness of the moment in
>Chile and Latin America that the con-
>tinent is ripe for an explosion which
>would annihilate our works whether
>they are parishes, schools, colleges,
>universities, retreat houses, volun-
>tary associations, or whatever. The
>social apostolate is, then, the duty
>to fight for justice and also a de-
>fense of the Church and all her works.

The Vatican was also preoccupied with Latin
America in 1961 and had appealed to the North American and European bishops and heads of religious
orders to send 10 per cent of their men to the continent within ten years. Taking advantage of the
Vatican directive, Lavin made one last attempt to
pry help from the North American Jesuits. Typical
of the North American response is this letter from
Father Alexander F. McDonald, S.J., provincial of
the Oregon Province.

>Your letter of January 15 arrived
>safely, and I can assure you of my

interest and sympathy in your plea
for help.

It is true that religious in the
United States received a request to
send 10 per cent of their men to
South America, but for us the situation is more complicated, since we
have just been given a mission in
Africa by Father General, and we are
unable to close down our high schools
and universities at this time--a move
we would have to make to free any 10
per cent of our men.

I suggest that you appeal directly to Father General, who is in a
better position to direct us in the
most effective disposition of our personnel in our various ministries. . . .

Lavin took Father McDonald at his word and instructed Renato Poblete to write to the Jesuit General, John Baptist Janssens, asking him to order a
joint meeting of Latin American and North American
provincial superiors. Excerpts from his letter
follow:

Some months ago in the United
States there was a reunion of the
major superiors of all religious
orders in which the envoy from the
Holy See, His Excellency Cardinal
Valerio Valeri, communicated the desire of the Holy Father that all of
the religious orders of the United
States and Canada send 10 per cent
of their personnel to Latin America
within ten years.

In January of this year I was in-
vited together with the Auxiliary
Archbishop of Rio de Janeiro, Dom
Helder de Camara, Right Reverend
Monsignor Marcos McGrath, and Mon-
signor Ivan Illich, who directs the
Center for Intercultural Formation

for priests in Cuernavaca (Mexico),
to participate in a week of discussions concerning the Latin American
religious problems in the presence of
forty provincial superiors of the
United States and Canada who were interested in sending men to Latin
America.

The purpose of this preamble was threefold:
first, to remind the General that the Pope had
called for a definite quota of men from North American Jesuits; second, to show that the other North
American religious orders were complying with the
same order; and third, to suggest that the North
American Jesuits would also respond to the Pope's
directive if they were given: (a) a comprehensive
plan agreed upon by all Latin American provincials
as to the allocation of North American personnel,
and (b) a push from the General, in the form of
specific instructions and timetables.

Poblete would undertake the preparation of the
"plan" in conjunction with Roger Vekemans. He in-
timated that both he and Vekemans had already done
such a plan for the Chilean bishops.

Your Paternity will remember a
letter from the Holy Father to the
Latin American Bishops, asking them,
given the urgency of our social and
religious problems, to present a plan
of immediate action to solve the
grave crisis of the Latin American
Church in the present moment. It
seems necessary for us, too, in order
to advance this planning, to prepare
and coordinate our works.
Father Roger Vekemans and I were
commissioned in Chile to elaborate a
plan for the Chilean bishops.

Poblete further suggested a joint meeting of
the North American and Latin American Jesuit

provincials. He confided that he had talked with
some of the North Americans and found that they
were not adverse to meeting in Chile. "It seems to
me," he wrote, "that they would agree with the idea,
but do not want to decide anything definite unless
Your Reverence suggests it."

The General did not attempt to push the North
Americans into a meeting in Latin America, but he
did suggest that the Latin American provincial superiors meet together to coordinate their appeals
to the North American decision-makers. (This "coordination" of what were actually conflicting interests competing for scarce resources had its
parallels in the Latin American Bishops Conference,
as discussed in a previous chapter. Staff sectors,
especially those of CELAM, played a vital role in
containing contact there, too.)

The Latin American provincials met in Medellin
in June, 1962, to set priorities for the assistance
they might realistically expect from the North
American Jesuits. They settled upon the following
order of importance:

1. Training of Latin Americans in the United
States with fellowships granted by the North Americans;

2. Grants from the North Americans for the
training of lay "catechists" in Latin America;

3. North American Jesuits to teach in Latin
American Jesuit high schools;

4. North American aid, financial and otherwise, to Latin American Catholic Universities;

5. Help in improving Jesuit use of mass media.

It is clear from the Medellin meeting that
this set of priorities was dictated not so much by
the felt needs of the Latin American provincials as
by their conception of what the North Americans

would actually give. They had been guided in the
choice of priorities by written communications,
such as those Father Lavin had exchanged with North
American provincial superiors, and by the results
of the meeting of those provincials which took
place in Boston, in May, 1962.

The minutes of that May meeting include a long
section on "South American problems." They also
include suggestions formulated by the North Americans for the Latin American provincial superiors.
The latter largely consist in the proposal that an
"information center for Latin American Jesuits" be
set up in the United States to help make them aware
of existing non-Catholic sources of support that
might be tapped. These would include the United
States government, especially the newly created
Alliance for Progress, the private foundations, the
universities, and so on.

It listed several examples of ongoing projects:

> The Inter-American Board of De-
> velopment is giving the Catholic Uni-
> versity of Rio de Janeiro a grant of
> $200,000 for research in physics.
> The University of Chicago is co-
> operating with the Catholic University
> of Santiago on the teaching and admin-
> istration of a New School of Business.

The North American provincials' report concludes that "examples like the above should be
known, the procedure which was followed to achieve
these loans or grants should be studied for future
application in similar circumstances."

Eventually, the North American Jesuits set up
such an information center and coordinated, through
Fordham University sociologist Joseph Fitzpatrick,
S.J., a program at Ivan Illich's center in Cuernavaca. There, in close collaboration with Illich,
Fitzpatrick sought to accumulate information for
the Latin Americans while Chilean Jesuit Renato

Poblete undertook the editing of <u>Decision</u>, a list
of Latin American developments and needs sent each
month to the heads of North American religious
orders.

The important thing to remember, in terms of
the present analysis, is that the North American
Jesuit line officials sent little aid to Chile at a
time when their Chilean counterparts felt the Church
system to be in great danger. The North Americans,
instead, encouraged the Chileans to look for secular sources of support. When the Chileans did so,
they were drawn into a complex set of linkages
among such highly bureaucratized entities as the
United States Agency for International Development,
the Ford and Rockefeller Foundations, and European
front organizations for the Christian Democratic
Party of West Germany. This, in turn, deepened the
influence of Chilean staff sectors that were already operating in nonecclesiastical environments
with minimal attention to traditional religious
norms and statuses. Eventually, in Chile, the
Cardinal would have far less influence both within
and without the religious system than would be exercised by a staff priest-sociologist, the Jesuit
Roger Vekemans.

Much of the analysis that follows depends upon
the situation here described: staff sectors within
the Chilean Catholic system acquired increased importance as the threat of Communist electoral victory loomed large. Great autonomy was granted Jesuit CIAS, and especially to DESAL, by Church line
officials, from local bishops to the Pope. These
staff sectors were encouraged to form linkages with
any available anti-Communist or neutral entity, at
any ideological price. As a result, definite commitments were made, and staff sectors grew in importance, in resources, and in their own estima-
tion. They not only formed and maintained the
linkages to external secular sources of support,
they themselves became the linkages. Without them
or their compliance, the entire Chilean religious
system would have been thrown into turmoil. After

the immediate crisis of Allende had passed, with
the election of Eduardo Frei in 1964, the bishops
and Jesuit line officials attempted to pull back
from the political arena and the secular environment of U.S. and European financial capital. But
this was no longer quite so easy. The staff organizations now had definite interests in maintaining
their expanded operations; and in safeguarding those
linkages to external powers--which linkages were in
fact themselves.

This situation began to aggravate still more
in the late 1960's when the bishops, seeing the
strong possibility that former President Alessandri
would return to power at the head of the National
Party, became eager to wipe away any overt signs of
Church affiliation with the Christian Democratic
Party. The Frei victory in 1964 had been a "god-
send," as one bishop told me, but with the disap-
pearance of the Marxist threat, the Frei government
began to look like a liability.

(There is a strong feeling within the Catholic
episcopates in Latin America, as well as elsewhere,
that the Catholic Church can tolerate any government "except a Communist one." It is felt, as
Jesuit provincial Lavin wrote, that a Marxist electoral victory would "annihilate" all the works of
the Church. But any government that permitted the
Church "freedom to educate" the young was acceptable, no matter what its structure or ideology, as
witness Paraguay. In a five-year study of all the
pastoral letters written by bishops in Latin America, I have yet to find any condemnation of a specific group in Latin American society, with the exception of the Communist Party or some other Marxist
sector.)

At any rate, there was a convergence of Catholic forces in Chile in the early 1960's due to the
threat of Allende and the reaction to Cuba. With
this convergence came the heavy commitment of Catholic staff sectors to foreign interests and to the
Christian Democratic Party. Once the Marxist

threat had subsided in Chile, the official line authorities of the Church found many of these commitments embarrassing; they also found that the increased functional autonomy of the staff sectors gave promise of long-lasting trouble. When they attempted to reassert episcopal control, they were simply ignored.

At the same time, quarreling broke out within the staff organizations, as the distribution of resources became more unequal and as the external threat and need for common cause subsided. There developed a search on the part of many of the disaffected for new "target groups" of their own, new linkages, new sources of at least normative approbation and esteem if not economic aid. Soon the Jesuit Centro Bellarmino was split into many factions, each with its own reference or target groups, which later were often themselves in conflict. The ensuing fragmentation was inevitable.

The hierarchical line authorities possessed few rewards or effective sanctions. The specialized staff personnel were impossible to replace and accustomed to making policy recommendations that had theretofore been followed. Staff officials had constructed their own organizations, which had become financially self-sufficient.

The staff-line split happened first. When it was well established, the normative restraints the line had always functioned to maintain were no longer in operation. Bitter internal strife then broke out among the staff. In Chile, this strife resulted in the fragmentation of what had once been a powerfully united planning and advisory staff-- the Centro Bellarmino.

14

EVOLUTION OF DESAL
WITHIN
THE
CENTRO BELLARMINO

The following pages will draw the lines of divergent interests that eventually split the Centro Bellarmino. First to be considered are two complementary styles of influence that have bound the organization together since its inception and that, even now, serve to maintain it as a formal facade.

POBLETE AND VEKEMANS

These modes of operation are personified in Jesuit specialists Renato Poblete and Roger Vekemans. Renato Poblete operated officially and formally within the international Catholic system, acting as advisor to CELAM, to the North American bishops, to the Jesuit Curia at Rome, and to the Cardinal of Santiago. Informally, he was very much at home with President Eduardo Frei and his family. He attended the parties, christenings, and weddings of a score of the great and lesser lights within the Frei government. Most of these figures had been members of the original FALANGE founded by older Jesuits. Poblete had gone to high school with the early FALANGE organizers at the exclusive Jesuit school in Santiago, San Ignacio. As an engineering student at the Catholic University, he had remained close to them, but as a priest he confined his dealings with them to purely "social" outings.

Roger Vekemans, a Belgian Jesuit, was sent to
Santiago in 1957 by the Jesuit General to counter
the "Marxist threat" in Chile by organizing Chilean
CIAS. Vekemans soon came to operate formally and
officially with the Catholic labor union, ASICH,
and the Social Union of Christian Businessmen (USEC).
He also was an early advisor of Frei and of the
Christian Democratic Party in Chile. In founding
the Center for the Economic and Social Development
of Latin America (DESAL), Vekemans entered the world
of the international Christian Democratic movement,
the world of U.S. aid agencies and foundations, the
world of Chilean government bureaucracy.

In short, Roger Vekemans' ties were with the
"profane," or secular, environments of the Chilean
Church while Renato Poblete's linkages were chiefly
within the Church system itself. Each had contacts
in the other's home ground, but each respected the
other's special area of expertise. Throughout the
1960's these two men worked as a team. They were,
each in his own way, very successful entrepreneurs.
Even as the last of the Centro Bellarmino's crum-
ling facade fell away in late 1968 and early 1969,
Vekemans and Poblete remained loyal to one another
and firmly entrenched in positions they had so
skillfully constructed for themselves.

They had both started out very much together.
As Poblete wrote in his 1962 letter to the Jesuit
General, the year before both Vekemans and he had
been entrusted by the Chilean bishops to devise a
"pastoral plan" for the hierarchy that would lead
to the election of Eduardo Frei and the defeat of
Salvador Allende. The two Jesuits were successful
in persuading the Chilean bishops that the "risk"
that Frei's candidacy had represented in the eyes
of Belgian sociologist Sierens was one worth taking.
It was true that Frei was taking votes away from
the Chilean right, but the right was bankrupt anyway and could not defeat Allende in 1964. Eventually their counsel would prevail. In 1964, immediately before the election, the bishops reissued
their 1962 pastoral letter, written by the Jesuits,

which defined the "political duty" of Christians in
Chile. In this pastoral letter, the very words of
the Christian Democratic campaign slogan were echoed:
the "revolution in liberty" was the duty of all
Christians. "Marxism" in any form, and therefore
Allende, was unreservedly condemned.[1]

THE PASTORAL ADVISORY COMMISSION

In 1961, however, the Chilean bishops were not
yet convinced that Frei and the Christian Democrats
were the only salvation from the "left." Part of
their hesitancy derived from the fact that their
Pastoral Advisory Commission contained other view-
points than that of Vekemans and Poblete. It took
a year of constant lobbying for Vekemans and Poblete
to convince the commission that Frei, and only Frei,
could defeat Allende in 1964.

The other members of the commission, which met
in secret, were Monsignor Marc McGrath of Panama
(who represented the link between the Latin Ameri-
can bishops and the North American counterparts),
Monsignor Vicente Ahumada, Monsignor Wenceslao
Barra, Monsignor Rafael Larrain, Monsignor Gabriel
Larrain, Father Manuel Edwards, Father Fernando
Jara, Father Carlos Gonzalez, and Santiago Bruren.

The commission met throughout the summer of
1961 and issued a report in September to the Chilean
bishops conference. The confidential report was entitled "Study of Pastoral Theology and Pastoral Planning." It began by analyzing the "actual situation"
of the Church in Chile, outlining "hostile forces"
and the "actual influence" of the Church:

Forces hostile to the Church.
Laicism, Protestantism, Marxism, in
different forms and each in its own
way constitute a serious obstacle to
the action of the Church.

Without going into detail concerning the nature of
these threats, the report proceeded to an analysis
of the Church's influence and concluded that what
was lacking was a mass base. Recruitment to the
priesthood was also problematic.

> It is very difficult to obtain an
> exact idea of the real influence the
> Church exercises in Chile in these
> times. Nevertheless, it is of funda-
> mental importance that we find out.
> Otherwise we can delude ourselves
> and fail to realize the true situa-
> tion we are in.
> There are some indices of "re-
> ligiosity" that can give us an ap-
> proximate idea. These are the re-
> sult of serious surveys and studies
> based on reliable statistics.
> Religious practice is one index:
> 85 per cent of Chileans declare them-
> selves Catholic; only 4 - 10 per cent
> go to mass on Sunday. And we well
> know that mass attendance does not
> represent much effective Church in-
> fluence.

The report also considered the size of parishes. The mean size was 12,500 people. Frequently, there was only one priest per parish, whose
"real influence," concluded the report, "was probably very weak." The number of native priests in
Chile was decreasing. "Between the years 1850 and
1900 there were 590 priests ordained in Santiago;
between 1900 and 1950, only 284."

The Church also enjoyed a "bad image" in the
press and popular mind, according to the report,
and was "out of contact with the problems that are
of concern to most people." The balance of the report painted a picture of depleted resources, lack
of planning and coordination, discouragement among
priests (many of whom would soon leave the priesthood), and little hope for the future. It was

noted that Catholic education, in many ways the
last hope of Christian influence, was imperiled by
government indifference.

> The economic, social, and politi-
> cal evaluation of the country (under
> the Alessandri government) makes it
> evident that the Church will be taken
> less and less into account and her
> rights will be ever more attacked,
> with fewer possibilities of defense.
> The latest tax exemption laws delib-
> erately exclude the Catholic uni-
> versities.

In warning that the Alessandri "rightist coalition"
was taking the Church for granted, the report opened
the way for justification of a new alliance of the
Church with the Christian Democrats.

The report concluded with a plan for developing
grass-roots support in the form of "community development projects," advocated strengthening lay Catholic Action movements, especially among workers, and
called for more attention to the organization of
"professionals" into Catholic Action. "Assistance
to politicians" was also urged:

> See to it at once that Christian
> politicians have clear and precise
> norms concerning what the Church
> asks of them. That they know that
> the Church respects the field of ac-
> tion proper to them, but that at the
> same time it has norms they must re-
> spect. Advise them at once so that
> they can have an effective Christian
> influence upon secular legislation.

The report also targeted as a prime group for
influence the teachers of public-school students
and the professors at the National University.
What was needed was a "policy for penetrating public education, instead of one for expanding Catholic private education."

Under the heading of "tactics," a section
added at the prompting of Father Vekemans, the following suggestions were included:

> In political matters.
>   A.   Demand of the political par-
> ties of Christian inspiration that
> they support slum communities when
> these latter make their necessities
> known to politicians; but be sure to
> advise the parties not to take advan-
> tage of the situation to make overt
> propaganda.   Also, let the slum com-
> munities know that they can depend
> upon the parties of Christian inspi-
> ration to help them with their needs.
> This suggestion is made for the sole
> purpose of seeking to avoid having
> these communities fall into the
> hands of the Marxist parties.
>   B.   Demand of all the Catholics
> of the country that they enroll in
> parties of Christian inspiration,
> since the present danger is very
> serious.
>   C.   Ask the Theological Commis-
> sion to study immediately the atti-
> tude the Church should take with re-
> spect to the elections of 1964.
> This is to provide clear norms im-
> mediately and avoid doctrinal con-
> fusions and passionate outbursts
> during the presidential campaign.
>   D.   Ask the parties of Christian
> inspiration to emphasize, through
> their official organs, the common
> Christian inspiration which unites
> them, more than the differences
> which divide them.

In this way, the commission provided for a counter
to Marxist organization without explicitly endorsing the Christian Democrats.   "Parties of Christian
inspiration" is a term that included not only the

Christian Democratic Party but also the right-wing
Conservative Party.

The Church would eventually back whichever party could defeat Allende, if that party were of
"Christian inspiration," which meant, if it would
not threaten Catholic institutions. The Advisory
Commission had received complaints that Church interests were being ignored by Alessandri's government (which should have known better). But in the
light of the Marxist threat, the majority of members of the Pastoral Advisory Commission would have
willingly accepted a right-wing victory in 1964.
By this time, however, Vekemans and Poblete were
squarely behind Frei.

VEKEMANS AND DESAL

Roger Edward Vekemans van Cauwelaert was born
in Brussels in 1921. His father was a non-Catholic,
and his mother had given up the practice of her religion. Nevertheless, he studied in Catholic
schools and entered the Jesuits when he was seventeen. He was ordained a priest in 1949 at Louvain
after studying theology and political and social
sciences. He studied sociology for three years at
the University of Numigen, Holland, spent a year
writing his doctoral dissertation in Paris, and received his doctorate in 1954. After teaching Latin
and Greek in Brussels, he was assigned to the Gregorian University in Rome, where he taught for one
semester before his assignment to Chile. Once in
Santiago, he undertook the creation of Jesuit CIAS
and founded the department of sociology at the
Catholic University. He became an advisor to both
USEC and ASICH, and also was a consultant to CLASC.
As a member of the Pastoral Advisory Commission, he
advised the Chilean bishops.[2]   In his work with
ASICH and with USEC, Vekemans came to know many of
the men who would later become cabinet ministers
under Frei.*   In 1960, together with the president

_____

*Frei had been a professor of law at the Catho-
lic University for several years and was accepted in

of ASICH, Ramon Venegas, he founded the Center for
the Economic and Social Development of Latin America
(DESAL).

In an undated memorandum written sometime before 1962, Vekemans set forth the objectives, structure, policies, and financial base of DESAL.   The
substance of the memorandum is as follows:

The basic policy of DESAL was manifestly to
"organize the recipients of aid" so that they would
be "active subjects and not mere passive objects"
of the development plans sponsored by the United
States and other governments in the 1960's.

The latent purpose of DESAL was consonant with
that of Vekemans' mission to Chile. He had been
sent by the Jesuit General on request by the Chilean
bishops to oppose Communism in Chile. That meant,
concretely, that he was to help stop Allende.

The major part of the money would come from
MISEREOR, the "German institution for cobating hunger and sickness, which has entrusted to DESAL the
evaluation and administration of projects presented
to the institution in Latin America."

In addition to the money that DESAL supervised,
distributed, and administered for MISEREOR, financial support was forthcoming from the Foundation
Osstpriestterhulp (Aid to Foreign Priests) of Belgium, from Zentralstelle fur Entwicklungshilfe (Center for Development Aid) of the West German government, and from "some North American foundations."
The latter included the International Development
Foundation, which was wholly subsidized by the Central Intelligence Agency. (Although both Ramparts
magazine and The New York Times revealed the finances of the International Development Foundation

---

the inner councils of the Jesuits there; he had
been an intimate of the Jesuit founder of CIAS in
Chile, Father Hurtado.

in 1967, no one was able to prove that DESAL received money from them. Conclusive evidence will be presented below.)

In an interview published by La Voz, a Chilean Catholic newspaper, in 1963, Vekemans maintained that "DESAL has grown by leaps and bounds. From the $1 million which MISEREOR assigned for Latin America in the beginning, the fund has increased to $25 million in 1963 and will be even greater next year."[3]

The ideological pinions that linked MISEREOR to DESAL are clearly exposed in a confidential document Vekemans sent to MISEREOR in 1961. Entitled "General Opinions on a National Inquest Related to MISEREOR Aims," it called for the construction of a "new order" in Latin America and specified what that order must be:

> As this is a revolutionary struggle to restore a New Order, these organizations (of aid recipients, workers, peasants) require an ideology, which in Latin America, must either be Christian or Marxist. There is no alternative. . . .
> For the revolutionary struggle to be successful and for a just and democratic order to be restored, the formation of elites on all levels is required: our universities, our schools for the education of professionals, our technical schools, are indispensable instruments for this task. They should teach our Christian doctrine, the structure of a Christian society, the history of the social-Christian labor movements, the model of basic organization, etc.
> Without this teaching these institutions will not be effective in the face of the change of structures. Furthermore, in many cases, they

> will only serve to swell the Marxist
> ranks, or continue technicians who,
> because of their lack of philosophi-
> cal and social formation, will con-
> tinue to eulogize state solutions or
> collaborate selfishly with the strong
> economic groups. The Communists have
> understood this problem well: when
> they send a technician, he must be
> well versed in Marxist propaganda.

Vekemans demonstrated a lively concern for
those who advocated "state solutions," whether the
states proposed were of a Marxist, military, or
even Christian Democratic mold.

> At the present time in Latin
> America all the solutions offered are
> statutory. Dictatorships, either
> rightist or leftist, obviously uphold
> the power of the state; the liberal
> groups generally turn over to the
> state all the social and educational
> problems; specialists in economic de-
> velopment, either national or inter-
> national, because of their ignorance
> of sociology, always propose statu-
> tory solutions and, naturally,
> Marxism.

The Christian Democrats came in for harsh appraisal
in Vekemans' essay as being also prone to seek
"state solutions":

> As for the Christian Democratic
> groups, in the majority of cases,
> through ignorance and, sometimes,
> because of being demagogues, they
> also favor statutory reforms.

The consequences of all this, said Vekemans in
his report to MISEREOR, is that social and economic
problems are always solved through state institutions and bring in their train the following serious problems:

1. A state paternalism is given
to people who are already passive,
apathetic, and irresponsible.

2. The organizations are lacking
in efficiency (a) because of the
passivity or nonparticipation of
their administration and (b) because
of an irresponsible bureaucracy without any interest in helping, generally recruited in payment of political
party services and the introduction
of inefficient personnel into the institutions, thereby unnecessarily increasing the number of employees.
Therefore, their functioning is very
costly to the detriment of the service which should be given to its
members. This brings about a total
dehumanization of its services. . . .

Vekemans maintained that the "present structures" in Latin America were incapable of solving
the problem of "misery" in which the masses were
living. Communism, "although practically giving no
immediate help, nor any great technical contribution, nor social aid, nor financial help to countries," was making "rapid strides everywhere" because it offered a vision of a better world.

Established governments, "excepting very few,"
were "completely ineffectual" when faced with the
problem of misery.

They are always on the defensive
to maintain the existing order; they
lack all social sensitivity, and are
committed with either leftist or
rightist party groups and, at times,
with Communism, and very often, are
made up of thieves with no morals,
always leaning towards dictatorships
without respect for groups or persons.

Vekemans labeled the strong economic groups
as "usually reactionary."

> They avoid their social responsi-
> bilities and are not ready to make
> the basic sacrifices. . . . They do
> not understand the problem of misery,
> and neither do they foresee the revo-
> lution that is coming either with
> Communism or without. . . . These
> groups are always well organized to
> gain their own ends. They are gen-
> erally wealthy and therefore influ-
> ential, and by maintaining their
> wealth in highly developed countries,
> they are irresponsible towards the
> problems of their own country. From
> the social viewpoint, the agricul-
> tural groups are generally merciless
> exploiters and their farmhands live
> under inhumane conditions.

The working class in Latin America had, according to Vekemans, no "real participation in
problems of general benefit," was not organized,
and was ignored by the governing elites. "Even
the intellectual progressive groups do not believe
in the capacity of the working class nor the efficiency it might yield to solve its own problems."*

The political groups were also in no position
to combat misery.

> In countries that are free to
> form political parties, the demo-
> cratic groups generally lack a solid
> doctrine, and what is still more im-
> portant, a clear concept of the
> structure of a democratic society in
> their own country. Therefore, when
> they come to power or participate in
> it, all their social reforms are

---

*Vekemans here passes over without comment the
extensive Communist-organizing activities in Chile,
including the highly organized CUT.

statutory, drawn up in ignorance of
basic organization, intermediary institutions, and the functional structure of society, especially with regard to the economy.

The Alliance for Progress also contained a fundamental flaw, which prevented it from effectively
contributing to the development of Latin America.

A fundamental error is to be
found in the present plans for the
development of Latin America, and
this refers especially to the Alliance for Progress: the tendency to
believe that those affected by problems of underdevelopment are passive
objects and not active subjects,
not protagonists of these plans.
This generally results in paternal
help, either international, statutory, or private.

For the Catholic Church, however, Vekemans had
a more positive evaluation. The Church still needed
help in retooling its system, but it was basically
sound in its approach to social problems.

The Catholic Church, especially
through the action of its Popes, is
the only international power that
during the last hundred years has
been seriously interested in presenting an ideology and the reformation
of structures for contemporary society. However, many Catholics in
Latin America have not reached the
level needed for the solution of its
social problems. Therefore, although
being able to resort to educational
and cultural institutions (although
these are very good and have been
organized by great Apostolic generosity), they have not been able to

change them into modern institutions
from the scientific and technical
viewpoint. Their programs do not
meet economic and social development and the change of structures.

Vekemans closes this section of the report to
MISEREOR with another blast at Communism," the best
ally of misery":

If this system based on the de-
nial of God and the total destruction
of the people should be successful,
Latin America would be plunged into
a moral and spiritual misery even
worse than now, and what is still
worse, because of its extreme dictatorship, there would be no chance of
escaping from it.

He then addressed the "highly developed countries." These were to be advised that the problem
of misery in Latin America was not principally and
fundamentally one of technical improvements and
the need for capital: "it is primarily a problem
of ideology and structures."

Vekemans' DESAL organization was to supply
both. The ideology was to be constructed to complement the "social doctrine" of the Catholic
Church. The structures would consist in "base
organizations" of "Christian inspiration" that
would gather workers, slumdwellers, peasants, and
other depressed sectors into conscious participation in society.

These "intermediary structures" (the base organizations) were fundamental to Vekemans' program.
He had no great faith in the Christian Democratic
Party as a ruling elite. If the party, and later
the government, would permit the formation of independent, "nonpoliticized" social movements "coordinated" by DESAL, and avowedly anti-Communist,
Vekemans would tolerate Christian Democracy.

(After Frei's election, it soon became clear
that the Christian Democrats would no longer tolerate Vekemans. They had achieved supreme power in
Chile, and were not about to be deprived of their
organizational base--the slumdwellers, to whom they
were furnishing home sites, and the peasants, to
whom they furnished land or organization.)

Vekemans submitted a trimmed-down edition of
the MISEREOR report to the West German government
in 1963. Entitled "Proposed Investment Plan for
German and Government Funds," the document omitted
the sections from the report to MISEREOR that condemned governments, political parties, economic
groups, etc., as ineffective in combatting misery.
It also dispensed with the lavish praise of the
Catholic Church. But it again proposed to create
and coordinate "base organizations" to fight Communism and to provide intermediary institutions to
prevent the concentration of power in the hands of
the state.

Vekemans suggested that the West German government funds be concentrated upon a "few problems" in
the form of "pilot projects." All of these pilot
projects would be tested first in Chile, where DESAL
was headquartered:

> In accordance with the amount to
> be invested and with the time avail-
> able to do it in, only some problems
> of Latin America can be taken into
> account. . . .

Vekemans emphasized that the West German government funds should not be allocated through Chilean or Latin American government agencies, since
this "fostered paternalism" and encouraged the tendency to dictatorship. Instead, DESAL should have
total responsibility and autonomy to allocate and
administer the German monies.

The West German government approved the proposal, and Vekemans received the money that enabled

him to say in the La Voz interview of 1963 that the
$1 million granted by MISEREOR in 1961 "had grown"
to $25 million per year. It had "grown" because
the West German government in 1963 had agreed to
pump $75 million into Latin America before the 1964
Chilean presidential elections.

By the end of 1963, Vekemans had access to the
following sources of massive financial support:
MISEREOR, Zentralstelle fur Entwicklungshilfe,
the Bureau for International Social Aid of the
West German Ministry for Economic Cooperation
(BISH),[4] and the Institute of International Solidarity (ISI) of the Konrad Adenauer Foundation of the
Christian Democratic Union. The Chilean representative of BISH and of ISI was Franz Hinkelammert, a
close associate of Vekemans' until they had a fall-
ing out in 1966. Hinkelammert was a professor at
the Catholic University in Santiago and at the
Jesuits' Latin American Institute of Doctrine and
Social Studies (ILADES).

All of these sources--MISEREOR, Zentralstelle, BISH, and ISI--were coordinated by
Vekemans, together with Christian Democratic deputy
Heinrich Gewandt, in the years immediately preceding and during the Frei presidential campaign of
1964. The organism created to institutionalize
this coordination was planned at DESAL and titled
Coordinating Commission for Popular Development
(CONCORDE). CONCORDE was responsible for coordinating, supporting financially, and helping to organize the following pro-Christian Democratic (and
pro-Frei) base organizations:[5]

    A. Popular organizations
        1. ASICH-CCT: Chilean Union
            Action-Confederation of
            Christian Workers
        2. ANOC: National Association
            of Farm Laborers
        3. UCC: Union of Christian Farm
            Laborers

      4. MCI: Independent Peasant
          Movement
      5. CENAPO: National Association
          of (slum) Neighborhoods
  B. Educational organizations
      1. INCASIS: Institute for Union
          and Social Training
      2. IER: Institute for Rural
          Education
      3. CIEP: Institute for Popular
          Education
      4. IPC: Institute for Civic
          Promotion
  C. Service organizations
      1. CEDEP: Center for Popular
          Development (the Chilean
          branch of DESAL)
      2. INPROA: Institute for Agrar-
          ian Promotion (land reform
          program of Chilean bishops)
      3. CARITAS: Catholic Relief and
          Welfare organization which
          distributed food, money,
          materiel from North American
          and Northern European bishops
      4. IPT: Institute for Work Pro-
          motion (cooperatives)

Later in the chapter, I will take one organization from each of the above categories to show how tensions arose in it and around it, producing conflicts that eventually spread through the Catholic religious system until it was effectively fragmented.

THE BISHOPS' PASTORAL LETTER

In 1964, Eduardo Frei was elected President of Chile, defeating the FRAP leftist candidate Salvador Allende by 400,000 votes. It is instructive that this landslide was provided by the women voters of Chile, to whom the Chilean bishops had issued their strongest warnings of Communism; almost twice as many women voted for Frei as for Allende: 844,423,

as compared with 375,766.   (Among the men, there
were 673,678 votes for Frei, 606,356 for Allende.)

At least partly responsible were the Chilean
bishops, whose pastoral letter "The Social and Political Duty," published in 1962 and recirculated
in the heat of the presidential campaign, had
echoed precisely the recommendations of the Pastoral Advisory Commission of 1961 (see above).
(This was no mere coincidence. As Father Hernan
Larrain asserted in his short history of the Jesuit
CIAS, the bishops' letter was written by the Jesuits
of the Centro Bellarmino, especially by Fathers
Larrain, Vekemans, and Poblete.)

The Pastoral Advisory Commission report had
spoken of the need for a convergence of Catholic
political forces and an organization of the masses.
The Bishops' pastoral letter was consistent with
these concerns. It spoke of the "duty which the
Church feels of orienting Catholic Chileans in this
decisive political moment." In several thousand
words, it recounted the "errors of Marxism."

> In the most serious present situa-
> tion of our country (and of the entire
> world), many citizens are asked to
> give their support to international
> Communism, which promises to solve
> the problems of present society. We
> cannot let this opportunity pass
> without giving clear orientation in
> this respect. We do not do this
> with a negative or polemical vision,
> but because we are profoundly con-
> vinced that this system does not pro-
> vide a remedy for the evils we seek
> to uproot.
> Errors of Marxist Materialism.
> Communism is diametrically opposed
> to Christianity.

Drawing heavily upon citations from Pius XI's
encyclicals and allocutions of the 1930's, the letter proceeds:

> (Communism) . . . holds that
> there is only one reality: matter,
> which in blind evolution becomes
> plant, animal, man. In this doctrine
> there is absolutely no place for the
> idea of God. There is no difference,
> according to Communism, between spir-
> it and matter, nor between body and
> soul; there is no life after death,
> nor any hope for a future life. The
> process of social evolution, accord-
> ing to the Communists, can be accel-
> erated by man. To this end, they
> sow hate, exacerbate the differences
> of social classes, and endeavor to
> make the class struggle violent and
> destructive of the entire present
> order. All the institutions, par-
> ties, or persons who oppose this
> crusade of destruction, which ac-
> cording to the Communists is neces-
> sary for the acceleration of the
> arrival of the new order, must be
> annihilated without any distinction
> as enemies of the human race.

The letter goes on to describe the dangers
that Communism poses for religion, the family, the
individual, private property, the working class.

> From these premises, it is easy
> to deduce clearly the conception that
> Communism has of religion: it is a
> purely human institution, bourgeois
> and retrograde, an opiate of the
> people, which must be persecuted and
> annihilated for opposing the Com-
> munist plans.
> Communism, besides, deprives man
> of his liberty, suppresses all dig-
> nity and morality of the human per-
> son; it denies to the individual all
> natural rights that are proper to
> the human person and attributes them
> to the collectivity.

Individuals have no right whatever of ownership of natural resources or of the means of production; all types of private property,
according to the Communists, should
be destroyed at the root. . . .

For the Communist, the family
has no reason for being; it is a
bourgeois creation upon which bourgeois society is founded. It must
be weakened and destroyed. Communism
destroys any bond between mother and
child; it denies to parents the right
to educate their children; and it
places in the hands of the collectiv-
ity the care of home and children;
woman is thrown into public life and
into work, no matter how heavy, just
the same as man. . . .

In a Communist regime the workers have no rights except those given
them by the state; there is no room
for impartial information nor for
legitimate strikes, nor for free
unionization.

Although these statements were meant primarily
for the edification of the voting public, faced
with the choice of Frei or Allende, the two candidates were never mentioned by name. The attack on
"Communism" was so intense that the writers felt
that their accusations might not be associated with
the intended target, Allende, who was a middle-
class politician who took pains to emphasize his
strong family ties and "business sense." Therefore,
the Jesuit CIAS wrote another section on "Communism" to explain why it did not always _seem_ to be
as horrible as it actually was.

Causes of the Communist Advance.
To what is due the fact that such a
system has spread so rapidly all
over the world? Here are some of
the reasons for its success.

A.   Communism in democratic countries hides its true face; it does
not present itself immediately with
all its demands.   It does not clearly
manifest its opposition to God and to
His Church, to the Fatherland, to
human liberty, the right of property,
the family, parental authority.   It
only proclaims itself as the redeem-
er of the working classes, something
that a great part of the people be-
lieves. . . .

D.   A propaganda that is truly
diabolical, the like of which the
world has probably never seen; propaganda directed from one center and
skillfully adapted to the particular
conditions of each people; propaganda
that uses great economic resources,
numerous organizations, international
congresses, innumerable forces excel-
lently prepared; propaganda that is
made by means of the press, of posters,
in the cinema, in the theater, by
radio, in the schools, and even in
the universities, and which penetrates
little by little all social surround-
ings, even the most healthy ones,
without anyone noticing the poison
that is daily poisoning minds and
hearts.

The bishops' letter concluded that "collaboration with Communism is not possible," although it
left the way open for collaboration with individuals
who happened to be Communists.   "In a matter as
delicate as this . . . one must use prudence and
obey the directives of the Church."

This pastoral letter was printed by the General Secretariat of the Chilean Bishops in 1962,
1963, and 1964.   It was in great demand, and the
Christian Democratic Party distributed it by the
thousands.

The early 1960's were for the Chilean Church a time of unity, cohesion, and increasing instrumental capacity. Roger Vekemans' CONCORDE network of base organizations developed rapidly with the infusion of millions of dollars from European and North American governments and foundations. The imminence of the "Marxist threat" drove together many otherwise disparate interests. Within the Jesuit CIAS group, tensions that were latent in 1960-64 would finally break out into the open after the Christian Democratic election victory and the subsequent withering away of the common threat. (Although, for a short while after Frei's election, Jesuit Father Patricio Cariola, the diocesan superintendent of Catholic schools, was still fearful of hostile action by Frei's "leftist" minister of education.)[6]

POBLETE'S MISSION TO EUROPE
AND NORTH AMERICA

Frei's election in 1964 freed Vekemans to a certain extent from his preoccupation with Chile (although he was to quarrel and break with Frei over control of grass-roots CONCORDE and promocion popular, which had proved so effective during the campaign). DESAL began to function as a Latin American rather than Chilean entity. In late 1964, Vekemans was strengthening his linkages with sources of support and establishing new ones with "affiliates" throughout Central America and the Eastern Cordillera.

To fund the expansion of his operations, Vekemans made new proposals to the European and North American foundations that had granted him the "seed money" to establish DESAL. When they were not immediately responsive (Frei had eliminated Allende, and Castro had not proved quite as frightening as he had been billed), Vekemans sent a personal emissary to remind them of their responsibilities. The man he sent was Renato Poblete.

A private memorandum was given to Poblete because he had not treated extensively with these

sources before. This highly confidential set of instructions is important because it clearly outlines
DESAL's financial base, its linkages with sources
as diverse as the King of Belgium and the U.S. Central Intelligence Agency.

The key people with whom Poblete had to deal
were August Vanistandael, the head of the Vatican's
$100 million aid fund and president of the Inter-
national Confederation of Christian Trade Unions of
which CLASC was the Latin American branch; Belgian
Dominican Werenfried Van Straaten, head of the International Association of Volunteer Builders; North
American Jesuit James Meehan, fund-raiser for the
Jesuit Missions Fund; Edgar Berman of the Department
of Institutional Development of AID in Washington;
and Edward Cohen and George Truitt of the International Development Foundation.

Vekemans' instructions to Poblete indicate
that DESAL was feeling the squeeze of reduced appropriations after the Frei victory. Excerpts from the
memorandum follow (as translated from the Spanish):

> Note: Here is written only the
> information that Father Poblete needs
> to know to fulfill the principal
> charges entrusted him by DESAL.
>
> VANISTANDAEL:
>   1. U.S. $10,000 promised by
> Vanistandael. He promised Father
> Vekemans that he would donate $10,000
> to cover part of the current deficit
> of DESAL. He explained that this
> money is actually destined for fel-
> lowships. If MISEREOR puts Vanistan-
> dael in charge of fellowships, he
> will donate this amount to DESAL.
> Ramon Venegas recently wrote him re-
> minding him of his offer.
>   2. Projects presented to Buro
> for Sozialhilfe (BISH). Vanistan-
> dael, Molt, and Osner (of the German

government) form the Buro to aid
unionization in Latin America by
creating projects that render permanent services to union sectors. At
the beginning of the year DESAL presented thirty projects out of which
the Buro only selected four to be
presented by Osner to the German government. These projects are:
   Mutual social aid
   Legal assistance to the United
      Movement of Chilean Workers
      (MUTCH)
   Rural housing - Cochabamba
   Rural housing - in zones of
      migration
Vanistandael must commit himself to
securing through Osner the financing
of these four projects, at the
least.

(Poblete jotted down on the memorandum after this
meeting that Vanistandael would meet with Osner in
October in Brussels. As it turned out, the MUTCH
project was scrapped. The organization later died
a quiet death.)

      3. Projects for community devel-
opment submitted to Wellecamp.
Wellecamp is the chief advisor to
the Belgian Minister of Finance.
During his last visit, Wellecamp
asked Vanistandael and Father Vekemans to send him good projects for
community development. With these
projects we can make use of a fund
of U.S. $400,000 which is at the dis-
posal of the government. DESAL sent
to Wellecamp, with a copy to Vanistandael, a group of seven projects; soon
we will send him another three. . . .

(Poblete noted that Wellecamp was no longer chief
of advisors, and that there would be some trouble
with his successor.)

　　　　4. <u>Tax exemptions for Belgian
foundations that invest in Latin
America</u>. In his last visit, Father
Vekemans, together with Vanistandael,
proposed to the Belgian Minister of
Finance--a Christian Democrat and,
of course, a Frei supporter--the ex-
emption for a foundation that Cool
and Vanistandael would organize to
transmit funds to Latin America.
You have to push Vanistandael to
get this foundation started and
take advantage of the offer of the
finance minister.
　　　　5. <u>University Triangle</u> (Notre
Dame-Louvain-Catholic University of
Santiago). The initial reunion of
the Triangle should be organized by
Chaumont, in accord with Vanistandael
and Van der Pere. The latter should
propose the date and place. Malan-
greau, the initial organizer, failed,
and during his last visit to Louvain,
Father Vekemans relieved him of his
responsibilities. Now you will have
to talk to Vanistandael and Chaumont
to see if the reunion can be organized, what are the difficulties they
have encountered, and if the latter
are solvable. Also, if all are in
agreement that DESAL organize the
Triangle here in Santiago.

(Poblete scribbled in the margin that the people at
Louvain were in agreement. He himself would see
Father Hesburgh, the President of Notre Dame University, during his trip to the United States a few
weeks later.)

　　　The meeting of the "triangle" did in fact take
place in Santiago in late February, 1965. The
three universities were represented. Also present
were Irving Tragen and Edgar Berman of the U.S.
State Department; Stacey H. Widdicombe, then head

of the Ford Foundation's Latin American desk;
Joseph A. Rupert, representing the Rockefeller Foundation; and John Plank of the Brookings Institution,
among others. Notre Dame University was represented
by Father Hesburgh. The head of Jesuit CLACIAS,
Father Pierre Bigo, attended, as did representatives
of MISEREOR and Franz Hinkelammert of the Institute
of International Solidarity (a subsidiary of the
Konrad Adenauer Foundation).

The purpose of the "triangle" meeting was to
organize a joint program supporting DESAL's "popular promotion" of grass-roots anti-Communist organizations throughout Latin America. The North American foundation heads and State Department representatives present agreed to form a North American advisory committee, and declared that the venture was
supported by the Vice President of the United States,
Hubert Humphrey. John Reilly, Humphrey's special
assistant, made several trips to Chile in that year
to underline the Johnson administration's strong
support.

The research and development proposals to be
channeled through TRIANGLE to North American and
West European governments and foundations would deal,
the first year, with eighteen countries in Latin
America. The project of greatest scope was to involve a social survey of attitudes among social
classes in Brazil. Father Afonso Gregory, FERES
director and Dom Helder de Camara's chief advisor,
was to supervise the survey, which was to cost
$100,000. All in all, the work of the TRIANGLE was
budgeted at over $1 million the first year, of which
DESAL would distribute $821,437,000. The uproar
over Project Camelot would cancel all of these plans,
and, with them, the TRIANGLE.

In addition to speaking to Vanistandael about
the organization of the TRIANGLE, Poblete had to
smooth over relations with Louvain administrator
Chaumont, whom DESAL had promised to contract as
a consultant, but now could not for lack of funds.
This situation reveals the severe shortage of

operating capital that plagued DESAL in 1965. Although DESAL had handled funds of over $30 million
the year before, these had gone into emergency organizing for Frei's election campaign. Vekemans
now needed Chaumont to organize the Belgian side of
TRIANGLE, and told Poblete to assure him that he
would be taken care of:

> Chaumont was offered a contract
> to work three or four months a year
> in DESAL. You have to explain to
> him that DESAL cannot contract him
> until it obtains more financing.
> Nevertheless, DESAL is greatly inter-
> ested in having him here in Chile.
> His name will be given to the King
> (of Belgium: DEM) with the purpose
> of obtaining alternate financing
> from a Belgian source. Since he is
> going to the Congress of UNIAPAC in
> Mexico, DESAL can offer to pay for
> transportation for his wife from
> Mexico to Santiago. All this you
> should discuss with Vanistandael so
> that he will talk to the King and
> with Chaumont.

Vekemans next instructed Poblete to show Vanistandael the costs of the Frei presidential campaign
and of initiating a Christian Democratic legisla-
tive program--what Vekemans called "making Chile a
democratic Cuba."*

----

*The plan to make Chile a "showcase" for the
Alliance for Progress, as Cuba was a "showcase" for
Communism, was referred to by Fidel Castro in a
speech in Havana on September 10, 1964: "Apparently the imperialists want to present the example of
Chile as a counter-example to us. Apparently they
want to use the Chilean experience as an imitation
of the Cuban experience. Well, fine! We are delighted by this emulation." Cited in Eduardo La
Barca, Chile invadido: reportaje a la intromision
extranjera (Santiago: Editores Austral, 1968).

> Give Vanistandael a copy of the
> Social Reforms in Chile. Emphasize
> that (this program) is very expen-
> sive and that it represents the major
> part of the DESAL deficit. It is an
> effort that has had to be made in or-
> der to organize a Democratic Cuba in
> Chile. The doment is without prece-
> dent and has been accepted as a
> package by Frei.

Vanistandael was to be informed of the precise
amount of operating capital that DESAL required in
order to continue functioning.

> The expenses DESAL must meet in
> order to continue functioning in
> 1965 is U.S. $352,000. The total
> income of DESAL in 1965 will be U.S.
> $198,000. This leaves a deficit of
> U.S. $154,000. This does not include
> the financing of INDEP (later, CEDEP,
> the Chilean branch of DESAL which
> was to be financially independent of
> the other DESAL operations: DEM).
> You have to tell him to make some
> effort to help us. The U.S. $10,000
> he has promised is not sufficient;
> we need permanent financing.
> Have him prepare the "soul" of
> ENTRAIDE ET FRATERNITE, because we
> are going to have to run to them
> the same as to MISEREOR. He is the
> director of ENTRAIDE ET FRATERNITE.

Manpower aid was sought from the Belgian government.

> 9. Report to the King. His trip.
> When the King asked Vekemans to help
> organize his trip to Latin America,
> he offered to send experts for the
> organizations which DESAL promotes.
> Tell Vanistandael that Demeure will
> send a report concerning the experts

> that we need and that it is indis-
> pensable that he (Vanistandael) in-
> tervene to make sure that the experts
> are really sent and that they are
> carefully selected. Leave a copy of
> the report with him. Also, Vekemans
> told the King that for the prepara-
> tion of the King's visit there should
> be set up a commission in Belgium
> formed by Cool, Vanistandael, Baekert,
> and other notables, so that they can
> collaborate, interpreting the sugges-
> tions that we will make from Latin
> America.

Poblete was also told to secure Vanistandael's cooperation in obtaining a permanent seat for CLASC
in Santiago. The Latin American Institute for Cooperation and Development (ILALD) was to be the
title of a CLASC fund-raising operation. (This
project failed.)

Another interesting project that Vekemans was
trying hard to finance was the Institute for the
Development of Cuba (IDESC). Vanistandael was in
charge of the original project along with Peter
Molt, chief of the Institute of International
Solidarity. IDESC was to function as a planning
house for a Cuban government-in-exile, preparing
for the day of Castro's "overthrow." Poblete was
to explore the possibilities of increasing support
for this venture.

Finally, Poblete was to tell Vanistandael that
Monsignor Cauwe, the executive secretary of ENTRAIDE
ET FRATERNITE, was "ripe" for a commitment to DESAL.

> He is the equivalent to Dossing
> at MISEREOR. Tell Vanistandael that
> Cauwe was in Santiago and put us in
> charge of a preliminary report of a
> project in Mexico. Tell him that
> Monsignor Cauwe is very well dis-
> posed to start to work with DESAL

just as Dossing was when we started
our consulting with MISEREOR.

The second key contact with whom Poblete was
instructed to deal was Father Werenfried Van
Straaten, O.P., the head of the International Federation of Volunteer Builders, a Louvain-centered
foundation of financing and volunteers that built
houses and churches for the poor. Poblete was able
to secure funds from Van Straaten to finance 10,000
housing units in Chile, which were to be put up
under the auspices of the Centro Bellarmino, in
close cooperation with DESAL's affiliate, the Chilean Association of Slumdwellers (CENAPO). This
last organization functions as a competitor with
the Marxist Central Union of Workers (CUT) for the
control of slum organizations and neighborhood
councils.

MISEREOR was also to come within Poblete's ambit. Vekemans needed more funding from MISEREOR.
To get it, he confessed the ideological "inefficiency" of DESAL and urged MISEREOR to finance a
Latin American Institute (ILAP) to remedy this de-
fect.

The proposed creation of ILAP was an important
step, one that revealed the serious preoccupation
of many priests with DESAL's "Catholic" character.
Vekemans was frequently criticized by fellow Jesuits,
and especially by the French head of CLACIAS, Pierre
Bigo, for failing to create a truly religious image
of the Church and for failing to spread "Catholic
social doctrine." It was partially in order to
neutralize Bigo's criticisms that Vekemans proposed
ILAP, although the added funds that such an agency
would bring with it must also have been attractive
in the period immediately following the elections
of 1964.

The proposal made to MISEREOR can be seen,
then, as a tactic that Vekemans used to stabilize
his own organizational base at a time when financial reserves were dwindling. With the scarcity of

capital a sudden reality, he turned to the world of
moral values and ideological precepts. As the production of expensive socio-economic development
projects became problematic, he tried to retool his
organization for ideological outputs--the creation
of "models."

The following excerpts are from the ILAP proposal to MISEREOR.

> During the two years in which
> DESAL has been in existence, we have
> seen that its action to eliminate
> misery, and especially hunger and
> disease, has not achieved the goals
> set for it. This inefficiency de-
> rives principally from the fact that
> the promoters and administrators of
> projects lack models to inspire and
> orient them so that they will achieve
> a radical and rapid reform of exist-
> ing structures, structures that are
> one of the principal causes of misery.

It soon becomes clear that "radical reform" is
not the sole preoccupation of ILAP. Vekemans reveals that he is very worried that DESAL's "popular
promotion" concept may lead to class-consciousness
in the under-class groups that DESAL is organizing.
Ideological "models" are needed to orient DESAL's
operations.

> It is thus that we have located
> serious faults or errors in the ex-
> isting projects which render them
> not only inefficient in the struggle
> against hunger, but which also make
> certain of these projects the best
> instruments of the Communists.
> We will point out the most flag-
> rant examples of this lack of
> "models."

The report first scores DESAL's "lack of systematic and profound knowledge" of the social doctrine of the Church and its applications.

> In reality there are a large num-
> ber of Christian institutions without
> Christian ideology or orientation
> that form an elite of the working
> class. This refers to agricultural
> schools, professional schools, basic
> education, etc. In none of these
> schools is the social doctrine of
> the Church taught nor its applica-
> tions. The result, which is well
> known in Latin America, is that the
> best Marxist organizers take advan-
> tage of these centers of formation.
> The same problem is posed for
> social and economic organizations,
> such as cooperatives, unions, com-
> munity organizations, which do not
> disseminate adequate material for
> doctrinal formation. Consequently,
> their propositions of solution are
> either vague, without any practical
> value, or they are of a "statist"
> type: in any case, they are always
> inferior to Communist proposals,
> which offer a clear doctrine and
> model of society.

The proposal mentions a non-DESAL radio sta-
tion run by a diocesan priest in Colombia. Radio
Sutatenza, the proposal states, is an example of
"an important project in basic education." It has
achieved very good results "in promoting Man and
especially the peasants."

> But all of this enormous work is
> a failure for two reasons: these
> educational movements do not give
> any doctrinal formation, and second,
> they do not promote, in parallel
> fashion, concrete organizations of

peasants. The result is that the
peasants, having acquired a human
consciousness and an awareness of
their unjust situation--if they do
not find concrete action organizations to respond to their problems--
necessarily join revolutionary movements.

(This fear of class consciousness brought about
by DESAL's organizing activities was not restricted
to Vekemans. The American Embassy in Chile had long
feared "popular promotion" and DESAL's efforts in
the countryside, for exactly this reason. Both
Aurelius Fernandez, U.S. official in charge of political affairs at the Santiago Embassy, and Ambassador Richard Korry regarded Vekemans as "well
intentioned" but "dangerous"[7]--a fear that was ob-
viously not shared by Edgar Berman of AID and the
people who evaluated DESAL's use of U.S. funds.)

The ILAP proposal also decried the "absence in
international organizations such as the Alliance
for Progress, CEPAL, the Inter-American Development
Bank (on whose Board Vekemans sat), etc., of preoccupation with models inspired by doctrine." Of
course, Vekemans' problem was that he was a Catholic priest and that international agencies such as
CEPAL, let alone AID, are not always run by Catholics. Suspicion of Church aims by the U.S. Ambassador to Argentina had led to the cancellation of
Gustavo Perez' FERES survey in that country. Vekemans was well aware of these suspicions and chose
to run DESAL as officially "nonaffiliated" with the
Church. But DESAL's chief source of support came
under the auspices of the West German bishops, who
were concerned with Church membership and vitally
worried about the "spread of Marxism" in Latin
America. So was Vekemans, but he had to keep his
non-Catholic benefactors in mind also. At any rate,
ILAP was a mechanism for satisfying both religious
and profane expectations. It was a way of meeting
the same criticism from Church officials who had
long advocated strong doses of Catholic theology as

an antidote to Marxist "infiltration." From Vekemans' point of view, ILAP was all the more desir-
able since it involved increased capital inputs
which would be unabsorbed by the minimal overhead
required and which could be applied to his budget
deficit.

For this reason, Poblete was instructed in the
memorandum which he received before undertaking his
European mission to pressure MISEREOR about ILAP.

> MISEREOR
> 1. Project ILAP (Department of
> Models DESAL). ILAP was approved in
> principle during the last stay of
> Matte at MISEREOR. It was to be dis-
> cussed in the last meeting of the
> German bishops. You have to empha-
> size to Krock the necessity of its
> immediate approbation for the sum
> agreed to and the immediate trans-
> feral of the funds.

MISEREOR was also to finance a Fund for Latin
American Solidarity that DESAL would administer.
Again Vekemans insisted upon the urgent need for
capital.

The meeting of the TRIANGLE that was forthcoming at the time of Poblete's trip was to center
around a project for studying Brazilian attitudes
following the military golpe of 1964. Afonso
Gregory (Bishop Helder de Camara's chief advisor)
was to direct the survey. MISEREOR was very much
interested in it, but had not yet approved it.

> 3. Brazil survey. Ask Krock
> what MISEREOR has decided, since his
> trip to Brazil. Tell him that Father
> Gregory was in Chile and left a very
> good impression and that with him
> were formed the first accords for
> starting the study, depending on
> what MISEREOR decides.

The final matter to be discussed between
Poblete and MISEREOR involved the creation of a
Jesuit CIAS in Uruguay, to be financed with MISEREOR
funds. Vekemans had not been able to acquire a
DESAL affiliate in Montevideo, and he wanted one
badly.

> 4. CIAS Uruguayo. Tell Steber
> that it is absolutely necessary to
> have CIAS approved. Insist that he
> consider the report that Matte sent.
> CIAS will make up for, in a certain
> sense, the lack of a Uruguayan DESAL.

Uruguayan CIAS was finally approved and set up by
Jesuit Fathers Juan Segundo and Ricardo Cetrullo.
But these men were more interested in working along-
side of Marxist sectors than in opposing them, and
they did not enjoy cordial relations with Vekemans.

The European phase of Poblete's trip ended
with his visit to MISEREOR. He then left for New
York. His first meeting there was of great importance. It involved discussions with George Truitt
and Edward Cohen, the vice presidents of the International Development Foundation, which The New York
Times later listed as receiving all its money from
the Central Intelligence Agency.[8] Truitt and Cohen
had been very active in the CONCORDE-coordinated
Foundation of Popular Education (CIEP) before and
during Frei's presidential campaign. CIEP's formal
stated goals (from a pamphlet published in 1965)
were the "stimulation and support of the slumdwellers of Chile, helping them to increase the number
and capacity of their leaders."

From the Vekemans-Poblete memorandum, it is
clear that DESAL's Chilean affiliate INDEP (later
to be renamed CEDEP) received all of its financing
from the International Development Foundation. IDF
was the sole support of the Institute of Christian
Humanism, one of the Centro Bellarmino's "apostolic
projects." The part of the memorandum instructing
Poblete concerning the IDF follows:

TRWITT (sic) and COHEN

    1. <u>Projects that have been given to them to finance</u>:

    The International Development Foundation is dedicated to the support of base movements that have ideological content.

    Truitt and Cohen definitely support Christian Democracy and Frei. They have in their power the following projects which they finance:

- INDEP (Chilean DESAL) as it is called in English (CEDEP in Spanish).
- Formation of University students of the Institute of Christian Humanism so that these students can advise base movements.

    Vekemans gave them these two projects the last time he was in the United States.

- Peasant settlements of ARADO, Bolivia.
- Peasant settlements of MOSICP, in Cuzco and Puno, Peru.
- Peasant leagues in Panama.

    These three projects were requested recently by Trwitt (sic) and Cohen and given to them.

    You should emphasize these projects, especially Chilean DESAL, explaining that it is already functioning and showing them a copy of <u>Social Reform in Chile</u> (you can leave one with them if necessary).

    DESAL's association with IDF was to be very costly in terms of the internal cohesion of the Jesuit CIAS. IDF was also involved in rural organization in Chile, supporting with money and technical expertise the Christian Peasant Union (UCC) and the National Association of Farm Laborers (ANOC), both of which were militantly opposed to the Marxist Federation of Peasants and Indians (FCI).

The UCC and ANOC later merged in the National Confederation of Farm Laborers (CNC) and continued to receive massive support from the International Development Foundation and assistance from DESAL. When the CNC opposed the government land-reform agency (INDAP) and alienated its Christian Democratic chief, Jacques Chonchol, repercussions were felt in the heart of Jesuit CIAS.

(Jesuit agronomist Gonzalo Arroyo, long a supporter of Vekemans, was also a close friend of Chonchol. Arroyo was enraged by CNC attacks on Chonchol's alleged "statism" and came out publicly in favor of INDAP and against the CNC. The medium he chose was the Jesuit monthly Mensaje, whose editors, for reasons which will be made clear below, were only too happy to condemn a DESAL-sponsored organization. Vekemans "banished" Arroyo from DESAL, and Poblete then began a series of letters to Jesuit superiors in Rome, questioning Arroyo's "doctrinal orthodoxy." These letters will be reproduced later.)

Poblete had three other contacts to meet on his trip to the United States in January, 1965.

The first of these was North American Jesuit James Meehan, who was in charge of raising money for Jesuit foreign missions. Based in St. Louis, Meehan had acquired a reputation among his Jesuit companions for intense, unrelenting "anti-Communism." He had helped DESAL in the past and was now to be asked to finance the purchase of a new DESAL building.

MEEHAN
1. Project House for DESAL.
Father Vekemans left with Meehan a
project for financing the purchase
of a house for DESAL. Emphasize
that this project is very important
because it will permit us to save
$1,000 a month and this will help
reduce the DESAL deficit. Besides
this, thank him for everything which
he has done for DESAL.

Poblete reported that Meehan would come up with the
money.

Dr. Edgar Berman, the personal physician of
Vice President Humphrey and chief of the Department
of Institutional Development of AID, was the next
person with whom Poblete was to discuss the financing
of DESAL projects. Prime among these was an official
AID grant to DESAL's Department of Population Studies
(CELAP) to undertake a study of religious factors influencing attitudes on birth control. (This was the
project that had alarmed Gustavo Perez in Colombia,
who was preparing a similar study for FERES, also
with AID monies.)

In addition to this official AID grant to
DESAL/CELAP, Vekemans had been told that Berman
would "privately" finance various "smaller" projects. As it turned out, at least one of these
smaller projects (ORMEU) was later financed with
CIA money.

> BERMAN
> 1. Project CELAP: . . . .
> 2. Various small projects:
> During the last visit of R. Vekemans,
> Berman asked for small projects to
> be financed privately. These should
> be base organizations and University
> student movements. Matte sent him:
> - Project ANOC (National Associa-
>   tion of Farm Laborers)
> - Project FECETRAG in Guatemala,
>   a project to aid base organi-
>   zations. Ask him how he's do-
>   ing with his search for pri-
>   vate financing. We have many
>   more projects prepared to
>   send him.
> With regard to university-student
> projects, we sent him a project for
> the formation of students as advisors
> to popular movements in Chile: the
> Institute of Christian Humanism.

>Next week we will send him a
>project for ORMEU (Coordinating Or-
>ganization for University Students)
>and another one for organizing a
>training center in Cochabamba,
>Bolivia.

Poblete's last stop on his long journey was
the University of Notre Dame. He was to meet with
Notre Dame president Hesburgh to discuss a possible
linkage leading to a Ford Foundation project for
DESAL.

>FATHER HESBURG (sic)
>   1. Ford projects of urban and
>rural investigations. Father Hesburg
>as a Ford consultant and as Rector of
>Notre Dame was asked to provide two
>sociologists or economists as the
>consultants which Ford had demanded
>for this project. It is important
>that he make a decision on this. If
>he cannot assign the consultants, we
>will ask Louvain.

Vekemans had also left with Hesburgh the year before the Spanish edition of a DESAL publication,
Latin America and Social Development, in the hope
that the book might be published in English by
Notre Dame University Press; this proved incon-
venient for Notre Dame.

To sum up the analysis so far; Poblete's in-
struction sheet and his scribbled observations show
that:

1. DESAL was in serious financial difficulties due to its expenditures of 1962-64.

2. Reliable financial support was forthcoming from U.S. government and private front organizations such as the International Development
Foundation.

3. Support was becoming more and more problematic from various Catholic groups such as Notre Dame University, Jesuit missions, MISEREOR, ENTRAIDE ET FRATERNITE, Van Straaten's group, etc.

4. The result was that DESAL was being forced to turn its attention increasingly toward the U.S. government and to accept what Vekemans must have realized would be a questionable and perhaps dangerous identification with U.S. foreign-policy interests.

NOTES

1. El Deber social y politico en la hora presente (Episcopado de Chile, 1962).

2. The bulk of this data is taken from the Diccionario biografico de Chile, 1962-1964 (12th ed.; Santiago: Empresa Periodistica). The rest of the material is from confidential sources.

3. La Voz (Santiago), December, 1963.

4. In 1968, a book was published by the Communist journalist of El Siglo, Eduardo Labarca Goddard, entitled Chile invadido: reportaje a la intromision extranjera (Santiago: Editores Austral, 1968). It includes a chapter on DESAL's operations which draws upon the private files of CIEP (Center for Popular Education). None of my own data is dependent upon these sources, but neither does my data contradict any of Labarca's findings. The present study focuses almost exclusively upon the Church system, whereas Labarca was interested in the Church as only one means whereby the U.S. government achieved policy goals in Chile.

5. A Proposal to US AID to Provide Planning and Training Assistance for Grassroots Organizations and Voluntary Agencies in Latin America (Washington, D.C.: Institute for Human Progress, n.d.).

6. Conversation with Father Patricio Cariola, August 14, 1966, Colegio San Ignacio, Santiago.

7. Conversation with Aurelius Fernandez at his residence, April 24, 1969, Santiago de Chile.

8. The New York Times, February 18, 1967.

15

DESAL'S OPERATIONS
AND
THE FRAGMENTATION
OF JESUIT STAFF

DESAL's gradual but visible movement toward
North American interests brought it into opposition
with the left wing of the Christian Democratic Party,
the sectors of the party that were to be known after
1967 as the rebeldes and the terceristas. These two
groups, which sought to create a "noncapitalist" way
to development, held strong positions in the Chilean
Government's Agricultural Development Institute
(INDAP), the Young Christian Democratic university
movements, and the leftist labor federation, the
Sole United Headquarters for Workers (CUT).

With DESAL's move into the ambit of the U.S.
State Department and its sister agencies, there
also emerged a polarization of Jesuit CIAS between
those whose interests precluded close identification
with United States foreign policy and those whose
interests profited from such identification. The
polarized forces soon fragmented into many cross-
cutting conflicts. The main lines of division within Jesuit CIAS and the Centro Bellarmino in 1967-69
were as follows:

1. Vekemans (DESAL)   vs. Larrain (Mensaje)
   Poblete (CISE)   also, Gaete, Ossa,
                           Daubechies

   2. Vekemans (DESAL)   vs. Arroyo (ILADES)
       Poblete (CISE)   also De Meneses

   3. Bigo (ILADES)   vs. Arroyo (ILADES)

   4. Vekemans (DESAL)   vs. Bigo (ILADES,
       Poblete (CISE)   CLACIAS)

   5. Zanartu (isolated)

   6. Cariola (isolated)

   7. Ochagavia (isolated)

   8. Wehner (isolated)

Behind this fragmentation pattern lay a series of
"disintegrative" linkages, each providing friction
of its own to the general pattern of internal conflict.

   1. DESAL was operating on a yearly budget of
over $30 million, in terms of the international
projects it was financing. It employed nearly 100
non-Jesuit technicians. DESAL was, then, operating
in grand style.

   2. DESAL was not "sharing" the wealth with
CIAS, not employing other Jesuits nor hiring them
as consultants. DESAL was to be considered (as
Larrain mentioned in his history of CIAS) as a "work
of Fr. Vekemans, independent of CIAS."

   3. The other CIAS Jesuits were forced to
forage for their own sources of financial support
and secular legitimation, their own projects and
"target groups." At the same time they could not
escape being identified with DESAL in the minds of
the people whom they sought to influence. Vekemans
was a Jesuit, DESAL was therefore considered by outsiders as Jesuit, and all Jesuits were identified
with DESAL.

   4. CIAS Jesuits attempting to influence sectors that were anti-Frei found these sectors to be
anti-DESAL and therefore anti-Jesuit.

5. Since wealthy Frei supporters were effectively monopolized by Vekemans (through his ties to foreign governments, foundations, the International Christian Democratic Movement, etc.), the other CIAS Jesuits began to work with dissident Christian Democrats, leftist student groups, university professors, Marxist organizations, etc.

6. To prove their good faith to these groups, and also to relieve their own resentments, many CIAS Jesuits, Arroyo especially, openly assumed "leftist" or at least anti-Frei postures.

7. Vekemans became alarmed at this. Bigo (the CLACIAS doctrinal expert and coordinator) became upset. The Chilean bishops were aroused. Accusations of "lack of orthodoxy" were leveled against offenders. The accused withdrew from the CIAS system, sought to establish their own organizational bases. Counter-accusations of "paternalism," "Yanquism," and even of "corruption" were privately leveled against DESAL by alienated former CIAS Jesuits.

8. Although this was the main line of conflict, there were various sub-plots. Vekemans and Bigo were not very diverse ideologically. But, as CLACIAS coordinator for all CIAS centers, Bigo was theoretically empowered to regulate Vekemans' activities. Vekemans was not about to surrender any of his autonomy to the former French director of Popular Action, and relations between the two men became abrasive.

9. Poblete acted as a counterpart to Vekemans, while remaining firmly allied with him. Poblete operated "inside" the Church system as advisor to the Cardinal of Santiago, to CELAM (The Latin American Bishops' Conference), to the North American Bishops, etc. Vekemans, for the most part, operated "outside" the Church system: even in dealing with MISEREOR, he dealt for the most part with laymen on matters of political and socio-economic concern. His dealings with the United States government,

foundations such as Ford, the Christian Democratic
Party, etc., gave DESAL a decidedly nonecclesiastical atmosphere.

10. But Poblete, working within the Church
system for financial support and for influence, found
that these were spread so thin among so many different sources that he had to overextend his own fund-
raising and consulting efforts, leaving too little
time to meet the expectations of other CIAS members.
In this way, by forgetting to answer letters, by
failing to follow up initiatives, he alienated
Zanartu, Larrain, Arroyo, and others.

These conflicts broke out after the common
threat of Marxist victory had passed. They first
became acute in 1966, the year in which Vekemans
alienated Frei, or was discarded by him. The point
at issue was control of CONCORDE, the prototype of
Vekemans' idea of "popular promotion" of "base
organizations" among the masses. Vekemans demanded
that DESAL continue to administer the program (which
included organizations of peasants as well as of
slumdwellers) as a private agency, nonaffiliated
with the Christian Democratic government. Frei refused, but was unable to get his own "popular promotion" program through the legislature.[1]

At this juncture, Hernan Larrain, the Jesuit
editor of Mensaje, began to act. He was, at this
time, an official delegate to the Jesuit General
Congregation meeting in Rome to elect a new General
(Janssens had died) and to reform the constitution
of the Society of Jesus. Larrain felt that, by
antagonizing Frei, Vekemans was putting himself and
the Jesuits in a perilous position. It was not so
much that Vekemans might lose his U.S. and European
contacts (a prospect that did not seem to worry
Larrain) as that he might invite the united opposition of all of Frei's Chilean supporters, which in
1966 included large sectors of university youth.
In 1966, the Mensaje Jesuits were striving to project a progressive image of the Society of Jesus
and of the Church. As long as Frei was respected

by _Mensaje_ target groups, and especially as long as
Christian Democratic students held control of the
National and the Catholic University senates, Larrain
was anxious to maintain good relations between Frei
and the Jesuits. (Later, as students became disen-
chanted with the Frei-led _officialista_ wing of the
Christian Democratic Party, and as _rebelde_ and
tercerista wings emerged, Larrain and _Mensaje_ would
drop their support of Frei and seek common ideology
with the new PDC "left.")

At any rate, Larrain saw the present situation
as one fraught with opportunity as well as peril.
It afforded an occasion to appeal to Jesuit line
officials in an attempt to bind Vekemans and DESAL
to the internal decision-making processes of the
Jesuit order.

Poblete was also upset by Vekemans' break with
Frei, although for entirely different reasons. It
was he who had informed Larrain of the crisis, in a
long letter written in October, 1966. Poblete's
fear was that Frei, who had always supported the
Centro Bellarmino, would now ignore them because of
Vekemans and DESAL. Poblete realized that his own
status as consultant to the Cardinal and as international expert would be threatened if his close
personal ties to Chile's President were cut.

Larrain responded to Poblete's letter on October 26, 1966. He revealed that he was petitioning
newly elected Jesuit General Arrupe to "do something" about Vekemans.

> Vekemans affair. I have talked
> at length with Gavin and Schonen-
> berger (Jesuit "assistants" to the
> General for Belgium and Germany:
> DEM). They both see very clearly
> the dangers. Even Schonenberger.
> Even the General is worried. I
> wrote a memorandum of five pages
> (officially) concerning Vekemans
> and DESAL. Gavin and Schonenberger

> have read it carefully, so has the
> General. One of these days we will
> have a meeting: Father General,
> Gavin, Schonenberger, Aldunate (the
> Chilean Provincial Superior: DEM)
> and I. I will copy part of your
> letter and add it as an appendix to
> my memorandum.

Larrain's attempt to sever Vekemans from his Belgian
and German sources of support (by appealing to
Jesuit staff sectors in Rome) and from his ecclesiastical legitimation (by appealing directly to the
highest Jesuit line superior, the General) was unsuccessful. It did have repercussions, however,
and forced a change in DESAL's planning and operations.

By this time (October, 1966), there was a
strong possibility of organizational ties that would
have bound together, in ILADES, Larrain, Poblete,
and Bigo. The latter was being considered by Larrain and by Poblete as an effective counterweight to
Vekemans. Bigo had close contacts with ADVENIAT,
which might have provided large-scale financing on
a level approaching that of MISEREOR. Bigo, however, was very much aware of how much he was valued,
and therefore demanded a corresponding measure of
power and autonomy. As ILADES began to move from
the planning stage to full operationalization, Bigo
was making decisions that Poblete and Larrain felt
belonged properly to them. Nevertheless, Bigo remained the object of pursuit. This ambivalence is
reflected in Larrain's letter to Poblete:

> Bigo. I am completely on your side.
> I have talked to Laurent and Calvez
> (Jesuit theologians overseeing the
> creation of doctrinal institutes
> such as ILADES: DEM) on this point
> (Bigo's scope of authority: DEM),
> but I had to do it prudently, be-
> cause if they suspect that we are
> unhappy they will take him away.

The main point on which Bigo differed with the
two Chileans was the extent to which ILADES should
support the ideology of the Frei Christian Democratic government. Bigo was already wary of becoming overly identified with a political party that
might fail to survive the next election. But
Poblete had excellent rapport with Frei and with
most of his ministers, and had been able to secure
for the Centro Bellarmino important subsidies for
its operations. Larrain therefore suggested that
Poblete arrange a meeting between Frei and Bigo,
with the others also present. In the days before
his election, Frei had sometimes come to seminars
at the Centro Bellarmino, where the philosophies of
Maritain and Mounier and the "social doctrine of
the Church" were avidly discussed. Larrain suggested that Poblete might be able to arrange another
of those meetings. Bigo would be able to discuss
theology with the Christian Democratic President and
would be impressed by the latter's orientation.

Frei had talked to both Poblete and Larrain
about collaboration between ILADES and youth sectors
of the Christian Democratic Party. Bigo was opposed to any such collaboration. The two Chilean
Jesuits were wholeheartedly in favor of it.

Larrain wrote to Poblete after the latter had
met with Frei.

>It would be good if you talked to
>Bigo and gave him Frei's opinions. . . .
>Why don't you arrange a meeting be-
>tween Frei and Bigo so that Frei can
>explain all this? It would be easy
>to invite Frei to a seminar with
>only those people attending who are
>really significant.

As it turned out, Bigo was not willing to compromise himself. Although Frei had told Poblete how
upset he was with Vekemans and DESAL, and although
Poblete had assured him that there were Jesuits at
ILADES, Mensaje, etc., who wholeheartedly supported

Frei, no new coalitions could be made between Jesuits and Christian Democrats to replace the one
Vekemans had enjoyed in former years.[2]

The opportunity was lost, and another one was
not to come. Eventually the subsidies from the
government to the Centro Bellarmino stopped, and
Mensaje fell into debt and sought to increase its
readership with student sectors who were disen-
chanted with the Frei government. The result was a
break between Larrain and Poblete.

Vekemans turned from open antagonism to the
Frei government (a posture that was discouraged by
the Jesuit General) to the quiet planning of DESAL
centers throughout Latin America. He had never
been told by Poblete of the latter's discontent,
and their symbiotic relationship survived.

But in October, 1966, Hernan Larrain was still
trying to promote the idea of a "truly Jesuit
DESAL"--one that would foster some of the same projects as did Vekemans but in support of Frei. He
finished his letter to Poblete in those terms and
added that the German Jesuit Assistant Schonenberger
was very interested. Schonenberger was deemed
especially important because he had access to both
MISEREOR and ADVENIAT.

Larrain well understood that Bigo was not interested in the kinds of projects that DESAL had
been carrying out and which Larrain longed to direct.
Rather than creating and promoting grass-roots
organizations of workers, peasants, slumdwellers,
etc., Bigo preferred his own specialty, "elaboration
of Catholic social doctrine"; ideology would trans-
form structures. Bigo made his own position quite
clear in a speech to a closed session of CIAS directors in Lima, on July 25, 1966.

> CONSTITUTION AND OBJECTIVES
> OF A CIAS
> . . . 1. The necessity of a pre-
> cise conception and firm direction
> of the objectives of CIAS.

> Very often CIAS is spoken of as
> if it were dedicated to the founda-
> tion of labor unions, cooperatives,
> or training courses.
> The documents of the Society of
> Jesus propose a much broader per-
> spective: to elaborate, teach, and
> disseminate a global doctrine of
> development and of social change in
> all its aspects, so as to help in the
> preparation of models, to function
> according to the reality of each
> country, with the object of trans-
> forming mental and social structures
> to a Christian perspective.

As is evident from even this short excerpt, the
ideas of Bigo were identical with those mentioned by
Vekemans when he suggested to MISEREOR the creation
of an ILAP department of model-building to correct
the "deficiencies" of DESAL.

Vekemans and DESAL had been alerted to those
"deficiencies" by none other than Pierre Bigo, who,
as head of CLACIAS and as a consultant to MISEREOR/
ADVENIAT, had definite leverage which Vekemans chose
not to ignore. But Vekemans capitalized on Bigo's
criticisms by asking for large sums of money (which
he received) to comply with them. Vekemans was able
to create his own "doctrinal monitoring agency"
within DESAL. ILAP operated under Vekemans', and
not under Bigo's, control.

Bigo's linkages to MISEREOR/ADVENIAT and other
sources of funding made him the object of attention
and pursuit by Larrain and Poblete in Chile, and
also by the Colombian Jesuits of CIAS, Bogota. The
year 1966 was to see this contest turn into open
conflict. Throughout 1966 there had been bitterness
between Chilean and Colombian Jesuit CIAS groups.
Poblete had written a letter condemning Andrade's
America article on Camilo Torres (cited above), and
there was bad feeling in Santiago over Zanartu's
treatment at the hands of Colombian Jesuit officials
when he had tried to give a seminar to a CLASC affiliate in Medellin (see Chapter 14).

At the meeting in Lima, all of these currents
were brought into play. The results were predictable. At a closed session on July 26, Andrade delivered a paper on the "Formation and Orientation of
Leaders; Consulting to Movements; and the Direction
and Promotion of Social Works." It was roundly attacked by Chilean Jesuits Arroyo, Larrain, and
others, as well as by Pierre Bigo. Andrade was
forced to resign as director of Colombian CIAS.

Arroyo pointed out that a Jesuit who advised
one political pressure group (as Andrade did with
the UTC labor unions) could not have access to important elites because they would identify him with
one interest. The following comments are taken from
the minutes of the closed session of July 26 (translated from the Spanish):

> P. Andrade: . . . I have noticed
> in this meeting an underevaluation
> of men of action. Men of action are
> an integral part of the work of CIAS.
>
> P. Arroyo: There should be men
> of CIAS present in temporal move-
> ments . . . but . . . there is also
> a necessity for influencing impor-
> tant decision-makers: politicians,
> CEPAL officials, etc. The assump-
> tion of a public position to an
> agrarian-reform program is incom-
> patible with CIAS because it com-
> promises CIAS, binding it to deter-
> mined policies and pressure groups.
>
> P. Larrain: It is not fitting
> to have an advisor to a pressure
> group as the director of a CIAS,
> because to commit oneself to one
> group's policies is to commit the
> whole CIAS to them. . . .
>
> P. Bigo: There is danger in
> having a CIAS director as the
> director or advisor of a pressure
> group. He tries to concentrate

all of the CIAS personnel into the
movement. The director of CIAS
must have: (1) freedom of action
so that he can dedicate himself to
the most important work of elabo-
rating doctrine, and (2) freedom
of decision. These two requisites
are not found in a CIAS director
or advisor to pressure groups. A
CIAS director cannot commit himself
to just one movement, because he
has to be open to all Christian
movements.

Faced with Andrade, the Chilean Jesuits and Bigo
were united. Later, in Santiago, they would find
plenty to quarrel about among themselves.

In July, 1967, the Chilean CIAS met at the
Centro Bellarmino to undertake a "survey" of the
Chilean situation, similar to the surveys being
taken by CIAS groups throughout the world. The objective was an analysis of potential areas of
Jesuit influence. Two months were set aside for a
preliminary study, divided among the following members of Jesuit CIAS (translated from an official
memorandum for internal use only):

Socio-economic: Demographic situa-
(Arroyo)   tion, economic dis-
(Zanartu)   tributions, social
                 classes, employment,
                 unions, living con-
                 ditions, etc.

Political: No political analyst
                 available. Larrain
                 will talk to a lay-
                 man, Abraham Santi-
                 banez, who would do
                 the study with the
                 help of Brazilian
                 Jesuit Pablo de Mene-
                 ses. Possible col-
                 laborators: Federico
                 Gil and Mario Artaza.

Cultural: Larrain will talk to
                   Guillermo Blanco who
                   may do it.

Educational: There is no existing
                   analysis of education.
                   The analysis will have
                   to combine educational
                   data with socio-economic
                   and cultural data.
                   There is nothing avail-
                   able on rural education
                   either. Father Larrain
                   will talk to Patricio
                   Cariola and put him into
                   contact with Pablo de
                   Tarses and others.

Religious: Complete what has been
(Poblete)   done concerning the
                   Synod of the Archdio-
                   cese, and other studies.

The Church: A study is proposed on
                   the historical role of
                   the Church in Chilean
                   society.
                   1. Poblete is in
                       charge of asking
                       the Cardinal to
                       entrust this
                       study to Julio
                       Jimenez, S.J.
                   2. The actual role
                       of the Church is
                       to be studied by
                       Manuel Ossa and
                       Juan Ochagavia.

Roger Vekemans was conspicuous by his absence from
these proceedings. He had, on several previous
occasions, severely criticized the kinds of "research" done by Chilean CIAS Jesuits and preferred
to entrust his own research to non-Jesuit specialists.[3]

The low state of CIAS internal resources is
well reflected by the fact that this proposed
"Jesuit" survey was delegated for the most part to
laymen who would be working with secondary data. Jesuits Ossa and Ochagavia were to analyze the needs of
the Church, but in a doctrinal theological frame of
reference. Julio Jimenez was the official historian
of the Society of Jesus in Chile. Poblete had done
some "surveys" without systematic samples and had
compiled some public documents on the synod the
Cardinal had called the year before.

The results of the survey were disheartening
to most of the Jesuit participants, who began to
see very clearly the limited extent of their resources.[4] All that could be produced was a series
of short essays devoid of factual information.

The year 1967 continued to be a critical one
for CIAS. On September 28, 1967, CIAS director
Hernan Larrain petitioned the Christian Democratic
Minister of Housing, Sergio Molina, for the annual
subsidy the Centro Bellarmino had become accustomed
to receiving under governments "of Christian inspiration." The sum for 1967 had been 30,000 escudos, but Mensaje alone was now losing 40,000 escudos
per year. The CIAS Jesuits therefore asked the
Christian Democratic government for 100,000 escudos
in 1968. The request was refused.

The document framing the CIAS petition is interesting because it provides some financial information concerning CIAS not otherwise available and
gives some indication of the linkages that had
bound CIAS to the Christian Democrats in previous
years.

REF.: Petition for Subsidy
Santiago, September 28, 1967
Hernan Larrain Acuna, S.J.
President of the Educational Foundation Robert Bellarmine Institution
of Private Right of juridical person,
conceded by Decree No. 2169, May 23,
1961, with location in Santiago,

Avenue Bernardo O'Higgins 1801, to
the Minister of Interior, Don Sergio
Molina, with all respect explains
and requests:

1. That the Educational Foundation Robert Bellarmine has obtained
for some years annual subsidies from
the State to compensate for expenses
of the Foundation incurred in the
course of its rendering gratuitous
services to the public interest. In
1967, the amount of the subsidy was
30,000 escudos. . . .

4. That the Educational Foundation Robert Bellarmine finances in
part the Latin American Institute of
Doctrine and Social Studies (ILADES)
with seat in Santiago, Almirante
Barroso 17, an organism of studies
at university level, whose objective
is to prepare professionals, university students, union leaders, etc.,
from all of Latin America so that
these can integrate their thought
and action into a global conception
based on Christian social principles. . . .

5. That the Educational Foundation Robert Bellarmine collaborates
actively in the social betterment of
the country, lending aid, technical
assistance, and professional help to
diverse organizations, such as those
of slumdwellers, unionized workers,
peasants, etc.

6. That the Educational Foundation Robert Bellarmine edits a monthly magazine, Mensaje, through which
it disseminates culture in all its
facets, general information, and social orientation.

This magazine is received by
more than 2,000 students and its
monthly circulation is approximately

7,000 copies. Its monthly circulation leaves an annual deficit of
40,000 escudos. . . .

    For all of the reasons expressed
above, a renewal of the subsidy that
has been given in past years is requested. In view of our considerable
expenses, due to the increased demand
of the public for our free services,
we petition that for the year 1968 we
be given a subsidy of 100,000 escudos.

    The financial and circulation statistics pre-
sented in the petition were not, of course, necessarily reliable. In fact, grave doubt is cast upon
their reliability when they are compared with the
figures given in a report to Jesuit line superiors
six months later. Entitled "Campaign for Subscriptions to _Mensaje_," the report was meant for internal
use only, especially for Chilean Jesuit comptroller
Father Raul Montes. The subscription figures given
in this document were much lower than the 7,000 mentioned by Larrain. It is true that six months had
passed since Larrain had written the petition to the
Minister of the Interior. But in March, 1968, the
"subscription campaign" document reported that "this
month, _Mensaje_ reached a new low in subscribers,
2,569." The report then outlined a campaign aimed
at present subscribers who would act as promoters.
It is clear that student readership was a hope
rather than a reality: "The clergy represents the
largest group of subscribers."

    Yet Larrain and the other _Mensaje_ Jesuits
realized that the prime target group should be university students, particularly since powerful or
wealthy sectors considered the former to be centers
of subversion and Marxist agitation. Money for
Mensaje might be forthcoming from North American
private Catholic sources that were agitated by the
fear of a Communist takeover in Chile. Larrain sent
the following letter to Catholic foundations and
universities in the United States in 1968:

    This is to present for your con-
sideration the following project:

in Chile, as well as in most of the
other Latin American countries, there
is a great and rapid growth of student
political movements. In the case of
Chile, for example, the Christian
Democrats have gained full control of
the University Student Federation.

The great problem confronting the
students is a lack of doctrinal orientation and spiritual formation that
would guide them in accordance with
the Christian social teachings.

We in Chile have hit upon the
publication of a magazine, Mensaje,
as an immediate means to partially
remedy this lack of proper student
orientation at this critical time in
Latin America's political development.
The magazine has enjoyed a good reception not only among the students
in Chile but even among students in
other Latin American countries.

The circulation of the magazine
could be greatly increased, and con-
sequently its influence, if we could
afford to sell it to the students
for a lower "student" price. At
present the cost of subscription is
U.S. $3, or 9 Chilean escudos (mini-
mum wage for a laboring man is 1 1/2
escudos per day, for a white-collar
worker, about 5 escudos per day),
and hence it is extremely expensive
for them. We would like to give
students 2,500 subscriptions at one-
third the price, that is to say, at
U.S. $1 or 3 escudos for each yearly
subscription. For that we ask your
help in the amount of $5,000--for a
period of one year to carry on and
expand this project.

We consider this project of
great importance at this moment for
the students of Latin America, which
we hope will meet with your approval
and kind consideration and help.

With weak financial linkages to the Christian
Democratic government that had denied them their
usual subsidy, with no financial resources forthcoming from DESAL, and with the desire to forge new
linkages to student sectors, the Mensaje Jesuit
staff set out in 1968 to carve a path for Mensaje
that would be clearly independent both of the Frei
government and of the official Church hierarchy.

In a series of articles written during the student strikes at the Catholic Universities of Santiago and Valparaiso, Mensaje clearly sided with the
students,[5] candidly assessing the students as a "new
power" in Chile and Latin America. Then, in August,
1968, Hernan Larrain published an editorial on the
"Diary of Che Guevara" that praised the Communist
revolutionary for his "great love" and "revolutionary conviction."[6]

> The life and death of Che: an
> example and a lesson on which we
> must meditate at length. . . . He
> could have saved himself but he
> preferred to keep fighting so that
> the doctor (Moro) could escape
> along with a Peruvian guerrillero.
> They shot him in the little school-
> house of Higuera, but the bullets
> could not close his eyes nor blot
> his smile; a smile which, as
> Ricardo Rojo, his friend, said so
> well, "signified disdain for the
> murderers and for the rest of the
> world, simply, love."

Eduardo Frei was "profoundly disturbed" and
communicated his reaction through Poblete to Larrain.[7] The Chilean bishops published an open letter
condemning the editorial and reprimanding Mensaje.
The Cardinal told Poblete that Mensaje was "neither
Christian nor much of anything else."[8]

The open letter of the bishops was published
on October 4, 1968. It did not refer to the Che
editorial by name, saying only that the bishops

"disapprove of certain articles published in <u>Men-saje</u>. They are extremist and we do not sense in them the breath of love, of Christian love for men which is made up of respect and humble service."

Larrain could not afford to alienate the bishops permanently. He was forced to reconcile his operations with Cardinal Silva and the rest of the Chilean hierarchy, who otherwise could have forced their priests to cancel their subscriptions to <u>Mensaje</u>, thus effectively closing the magazine.

Larrain met with the bishops in October. He said that he would not attack the hierarchy or advocate violent revolution, but that <u>Mensaje</u> was seeking to influence "advanced" sectors in the Church and needed to speak their language. The explanation was accepted, and the President of the Episcopal Conference, Bishop Jose Manuel Santos Ascarza, sent <u>Mensaje</u> a letter of support, which the magazine published in its November, 1968, edition.

> We the bishops know that <u>Mensaje</u>
> confronts the problems of today, that
> it moves many times on the frontiers
> of the Church, and that it has a cir-
> culation in very diverse sectors.
> This is a commendable quality that we
> are happy to recognize.
> Therefore . . . our word has not
> been one of condemnation for the mag-
> azine itself, nor of the articles to
> which we alluded, because it wasn't
> the intent of the bishops to make a
> definitive statement in this area.
> Nevertheless, that doesn't simply mean
> that we disagree with the articles. It
> means that articles such as "The Diary
> of Che Guevara" cannot be approved by us
> because in our judgment the mission
> of every Christian, in time of change,
> of worry, of insecurity, is not to
> awaken anxieties, <u>guerrilla</u>, hate,
> but to be positive, visionary, orien-
> tating, with a clear message of
> love. . . .

> We know that this task of con-
> struction is difficult and requires
> much imagination, but we also judge
> that Mensaje has the required re-
> sources to meet the challenge that
> is offered by our times.

The letter was published in an issue dedicated
to a study of "violence in Latin America." The
lead article was by Gonzalo Arroyo, who drew heavily
upon the "Document on Peace" of the Latin American
bishops assembled in Medellin, to treat the concept
of "institutionalized violence" which the Pope himself had implied was the "constant inevitable seed
of rebellions and wars."[9]

In Chile, the official Communist Party had long
held to the Soviet line that "armed insurgency" was
only "one of the roads" the revolution might take.
Mensaje quoted Chilean Communist student leader
Sergio Ramos to that effect, and also Catholic labor
leader Victor Arroyo,[10] who stated that although
violence was being exercised in Chile by the ruling
classes to suppress the under class, he did not believe in armed revolution--yet. "The worker class
is divided into many sub-classes. Popular violence
in this case would be revisionist, because the time
is not ripe." Moreover, the neighboring military
dictatorships of Peru, Argentina, and Bolivia would
stifle a Chilean popular revolution, according to
Arroyo.

On this occasion, Mensaje was able to side with
the "left" without explicitly rejecting the warnings of the hierarchy. The bishops had also been
worried about Mensaje's previous opposition to the
Pope's encyclical against artificial birth control,
but this issue was simply not raised any more as
Mensaje editors came to respect the position of many
leftists that "population control" was simply another "imperialist" strategy for suppressing third
world peoples.

There was, therefore, on the surface, a kind of
modus vivendi between Mensaje and the bishops. In

actuality, however, the tensions remained. The
Chilean bishops continued to express privately their
lack of confidence in the Centro Bellarmino and instituted their own "department of sociological research" to supplant it. Mensaje was careful not to
criticize the hierarchy in print, and when it received letters to the editor that did, it published
them with accompanying refutations.[11] When speaking
with student leaders and other "leftists," however,
Mensaje editor Larrain was careful to oppose himself to the Cardinal's views and operations and even
to the activities and policies of the Jesuit order
in general.[12]

In 1968, tensions rose not only between Mensaje
editor Larrain and the Chilean bishops, but also between Larrain and other Jesuits of the Centro Bellarmino. In the course of that year he would break
off relations with them. Larrain was frequently advised by Vekemans and Poblete in 1968 that Mensaje
articles criticizing the Frei regime were not prudent;[13] when the articles continued to be published,
a definite coolness came over the daily relations
of the men.

Every Friday from 11 A.M. to 12 P.M., CIAS members were accustomed to meeting at the Centro Bellarmino. The minutes of these meetings reveal a
steady deterioration of contact between Larrain and
the others who did not work on Mensaje. In 1968,
Larrain asked to be relieved as director of CIAS.
By July, he had stopped attending meetings. On
August 2, he was effectively "read out" of CIAS when
the majority present decided that he was no longer
to be a member "in the strict sense." (Members in
the strict sense were Vekemans, Poblete, Zanartu,
Arroyo, Wehner, and Vander Rest. Bigo, as head of
CLACIAS, was also included.)

At the August 2 meeting, Father Arroyo made
clear that the prestige of the Chilean CIAS was so
low that the Jesuit General had named no CIAS members to the official staff positions of "consultors"
to the Chilean provincial superior. The General

indicated that Father Ochagavia, a Jesuit theologian
who lived at the Centro Bellarmino, could make the
views of CIAS known at consultors' meetings. The
minutes of the meeting reveal the "crisis" of the
Centro Bellarmino as it was perceived and conceptu-
alized by its different members.

> Father Arroyo also reported that
> he had not been appointed a consultor
> to the provincial even though he was
> an official Counselor for Social Af-
> fairs. He observed that the ambiguity
> of an "expanded" CIAS (one including
> Larrain and others who had offended
> Jesuit superiors) was responsible for
> this type of situation.
> Father Poblete proposed that the
> internal differences of CIAS members
> be aired. Father Bigo said that he
> felt that there was general agree-
> ment concerning objectives, but that
> there might be discussion of methods.
> Vekemans replied that the "agreement
> concerning objectives" was only
> agreement concerning abstract objec-
> tives, not concrete ones.

Vekemans said further that there was at CIAS
no bond between doctrinal investigation and action,
and maintained that a "problem" such as this seems
to have "deep roots." He added that the situation
of the old ACTION POPULAIRE (which Bigo had headed
in France) had been much the same.

Zanartu proposed that the main problem was one
of conflicting personalities rather than one caused
by philosophical/organizational variables.

Hurley, a North American Jesuit interested in
mass communications, suggested that the problem was
one of role conflict: the same person fulfilled
many different roles.

But it was Vekemans who provided most of the
material for the minutes. He spoke at length on a

three-sided conflict within CIAS among doctrinal ex-
perts--experts in direct action--and social scientists.

> Father Vekemans believes that, re-
> garding doctrine, Chilean CIAS resents
> the displacement of doctrinal studies
> outside of the Centro Bellarmino at
> ILADES.

He added that there was little scientific research
and few action projects based in the Centro Bellarmino.

The group then began to discuss the possibilities of "common projects" that would involve the entire CIAS, including Roger Vekemans and DESAL.
Vekemans resolutely opposed this, and the minutes
conclude with the observation that the meeting ended
in "personal antagonism," when Vekemans suggested
that the "common project" be ILADES or Mensaje.

It is clear that what was happening in CIAS was
due to the reaction of "displaced" sectors to the
functional autonomy of those who had been more successful, or at least to those who controlled access
to scarce resources. Vekemans with DESAL, Larrain
with Mensaje, Bigo and Arroyo with ILADES--each had
constructed a privileged "enclave" and kept it free
from the "interference" or "incompetence" of fellow
CIAS Jesuits.

Vekemans refused to hire Jesuit researchers and
organizers for DESAL. Larrain refused to print any
more articles by Vekemans, Zanartu, Poblete, and
others unless they met his specifications. Bigo and
Arroyo refused either to share ILADES professors
with Poblete or to permit him to teach at ILADES unless he would either (a) pay half the contract of
the professor borrowed, or (b) give evidence that
his own teaching would enhance ILADES prestige. The
same held not only for Poblete but for the other
CIAS members as well.

In other words, what was happening was the
breakdown of a religious system as normative

ascriptive bonds were forcibly replaced by instrumental achievement orientations. It no longer sufficed for a man to be a Jesuit, and assigned by Jesuit line superiors to a staff position. He had also to satisfy the technical and political requirements and expectations imposed by those staff members who had achieved secular success.

These tensions have long lain dormant within the Jesuit model of formal organization. The emphasis upon rationality, upon fitting individuals as means to "higher ends," of training specialists to operate as staff sectors to the highest line authorities within and outside of the Jesuit order and the Church: all of these postulates of the Jesuit system, once designed to give it flexibility and maneuverability, now tended in the Chilean aftermath of political victory to create a fragmentation of Jesuit interests. The reason for this lay in the fact that the Jesuit system possessed few instrumental resources and non-normative rewards at a time when competition for outside resources was very keen.

DESAL could not compete for secular funding if it had to limit its manpower inputs to the Jesuit order, or if it had to accept the inputs that Jesuit line superiors might wish to make. Therefore, Vekemans recruited lay experts, promoting them according to his evaluation of their achievement. The same was true for Larrain, the editor, and Bigo-Arroyo, the directors of ILADES.

But apart from the dilemma posed by the need for specialized experts who could render practical services to research organizations, magazines, or indoctrination programs, the Jesuits also faced the conflicts of interests that confronted each of those entities in the secular marketplace. The Chilean political system in 1967-68 was itself fragmenting. At the party convention in 1968, three groups emerged within the Christian Democratic Party. The officialistas, under Frei and his Minister of the Interior, Perez-Zuchovich, were, for the most part, close friends of Poblete and had been Vekemans'

clients in the early 1960's. The terceristas and the
rebeldes broke from the "official wing" of the party
in 1969, although their discontent had been evident
for a year or more. Eventually the rebeldes would
leave the party entirely to ally themselves with the
"leftist" coalition FRAP. Long before this, however,
the Jesuits of CIAS had taken sides.

In an interview, Arroyo bristled when he said
that Poblete was "a friend of Frei and Perez-
Zuchovich."[14] This statement was meant as a condemnation, since only days before Minister of Interior
Perez-Zuchovich had issued orders leading to a mas-
sacre of land-invading peasants in Puerto Montt.
This incident triggered a wave of protests throughout Chile, as student and worker groups took to the
streets. Larrain ran articles in Mensaje condemning
the Frei administration.[15] Arroyo wrote one of the
articles attacking the officialista detractors of
INDAP, the CUT, and other rebelde and tercerista
strongholds.[16]

Articles by Arroyo defending INDAP against the
Vekemans-supported National Peasant Confederation
(CNC) began to alarm the International Development
Foundation and eventually led to Arroyo's break with
Vekemans, who relied upon the CIA front organization
for critical financial support.

The International Development Foundation also
was under contract to AID, for whom it issued periodic reports of the Chilean political scene. One
such report, written in 1966 and meant for AID use
only, marks the beginning of the break between Gonzalo Arroyo and Roger Vekemans. DESAL had been
responsible for a government plan on agrarian reform, which Arroyo and a colleague had bitterly attacked. Quoting from the IDF field report:

A Chilean government report that
had been highly touted by government
officials as the definitive work on
"Chile, land tenancy and socio-
economic development of the agrarian

sector" was unexpectedly attacked by
A. Valdes and Gonzalo Arroyo, S.J.

With Arroyo firmly opposed to those groups that
Vekemans supported in the rural sector, and with
Larrain firmly opposed to what he considered to be
"repressive" policies of the Frei government against
students and workers, the stage was set for the
eventual denouement.

On October 16, 1968, Hernan Larrain and his
Mensaje associates Manuel Ossa, Arturo Gaete, and
Hubert Daubechies officially announced their intention of withdrawing from the Centro Bellarmino, although remaining Jesuits. Official permission from
Rome was finally obtained for this move, after a
flurry of letters between interested parties and the
Latin American "assistants" to the Jesuit General.
Mensaje offices would have to remain in the Centro
Bellarmino, but Mensaje editors would be permitted
to "take up residence with the poor" in a barrio to
the west. This would be an explicit reminder to the
directors of DESAL that their life style was not
shared by other Jesuits in Chile.

In August, 1968, Manuel Ossa had written a letter to the "official" CIAS members, expressing his
personal anguish at the thought of separation, but
explaining the major factors in his decision:

> 1. I think that the national
> situation and that of the Church re-
> quires that our manner of life coin-
> cide with what we proclaim in Mensaje
> and in our courses. We have been
> playing with words: change in re-
> ligious life, commitment to the poor,
> support for the young people, re-
> structuring of society. We have
> played with words in Mensaje, in our
> courses and conferences, in the re-
> flection groups in which we take
> part, in our collaboration with the
> Synod. It is necessary, and it

seems to me urgent, that our deeds
correspond to our words--that our
deeds precede our words! I think
that our manner of life must show
more poverty; we must separate more
effectively the money we have for
our works (CIAS, Mensaje) from what
we have to live on--which should be
our salaries; we have to share (all
of us) in the janitorial duties of
the house--so that we can dispense
with servants and stop living like
patrones.

2. I think that in our times,
an official journal, one which pretends to represent either the Church
or the Society of Jesus . . . would
have to condemn itself to such a
level of abstraction or generality
that it could no longer represent
the search or the answer that our most
active Christians are in need of. I
think that Mensaje has to be something
else: a magazine that takes one of
the "lines" possible within Christianity, some of the options responsible Jesuits can take. This doesn't
mean that it should become a protest
magazine, protesting for the sake of
protest. But it means clear language,
unambiguous, decided. . . .

Such is the importance which I
give to the study and realization of
these two objectives that, if one of
them cannot be attained within a
reasonable length of time, I will feel
obligated to seek, with those who feel
the same necessity, a new orientation
and style of community life and a new
type of teamwork. I would hope that
this letter would serve to begin a
dialogue which will be immensely constructive and indispensable.

The events that followed show that the objectives
Ossa (and with him, Larrain, Gaete, and Daubechies)
had hoped to reach could not be accepted by the other
CIAS Jesuits. The reasons for this are not hard to
find.

Vekemans could not really be expected to operate
his multimillion dollar enterprise while living the
poverty of a Jesuit novice, much less that of a very
unusual Jesuit who washed his own dishes, cleaned
floors, etc. He could not easily forego his chauf-
feured car, around-the-world travels, banquets, and
cocktail parties. These were the indispensable ac-
couterments of his style of campaigning for strate-
gic resources. They were just as indispensable to
the maintenance of his image vis-à-vis his clients
as was the cultivation of a visible poverty to the
image of Mensaje editors. A common life style was
not really feasible for men who courted antagonistic
social classes. Collaboration in tactical matters
was difficult enough. Total identification of life
style was impossible.

A similar difficulty beset the "dialogue" on
problems of the magazine. Whether Larrain and Ossa
wished it or not, Mensaje was considered to be the
"voice" of the Centro Bellarmino and of the Jesuit
order in Chile. Until such time as the Jesuits became willing to advertise their differences with
the same prominence as they gave their subscription
ads, the articles in Mensaje by Jesuits and the
editorials would be taken as representative of a
united Jesuit front.

This clearly would not do for Vekemans and
Poblete, each of whom represented and courted interests clearly antagonistic to the interests of Larrain and to the general orientation of Mensaje.
Poblete counseled the Chilean Cardinal, who was not
edified by articles and editorials openly rejecting
papal encyclicals or siding with students against
Catholic University deans. Vekemans received all
of the money for his Chilean operation, CEDEP, from
the International Development Foundation, a CIA

front, and many of his other organizational operations were funded in some form or other by the U.S.
State Department. He could not afford further alienation of the United States Embassy in Santiago, whose
Ambassador already considered Vekemans as "dangerous" and Larrain as "psychotic."[17] The field representative of the International Development Foundation, Steven Smith, was an admirer of Vekemans, but
he was not happy with the articles of Gonzalo Arroyo
in Mensaje, nor, for that matter, with Arroyo's
lectures in ILADES, "which some people say are
Marxist."[18]

As a result, the Mensaje dissidents were not
encouraged by the reactions of the CIAS Jesuits to
their requests for change. On October 16, 1968,
they finally announced that they were breaking with
the Centro Bellarmino to form a community in a lower
class barrio. They would continue to edit the magazine in the basement of the Centro, but their main
contacts and orientation would be directed outside.
The announcement, marked "private," promised continued "brotherly cooperation" with those who remained,
but made it clear that they had not found in the
Centro Bellarmino the "minimum conditions for true
community." No one wanted to terminate all contacts
between the dissident groups. The Mensaje people
still needed a library, and DESAL's was the largest
and most modern available. They needed a place to
work, and the Centro Bellarmino had ample space.
The directors of Mensaje would still accept articles
for publication by CIAS members if the editors found
them of "high quality."

These overtures were met by a complete lack of
enthusiasm by the official CIAS members, who, on
October 20, wrote a letter to Larrain, Gaete,
Daubechies, and Ossa terming their departure "pre-
mature" and due to a lack of understanding of the
difference between "a community of work" and a "community of living." The breaking up of the former,
said the letter, would affect CIAS "in ways which
we cannot yet precisely describe." It was clear
that the departure of the Mensaje Jesuits would call

attention to divisions within the order that the
Cardinal, the Jesuit General, and others might find
alarming.

These fears were compounded a few months later
when Gonzalo Arroyo and Paulo Meneses of ILADES also
withdrew from the Centro Bellarmino to found what
Arroyo had called a "rebel community" that would give
witness to their solidarity with the under classes
against the ruling powers of Chile.

> These communities, insofar as
> they provide a place for critical
> reflection of history, made in con-
> tact with the people, could have
> indirectly a certain political ef-
> ficacy because they would contribute
> toward the creation of a revolution-
> ary consciousness among popular
> leaders and also among politicians,
> intellectuals, artists, university
> students, and Catholic Action move-
> ments.[19]

These groups were the ones with which Arroyo
was most involved. They also were the ones most
likely to be critical of Frei and the official wing
of the Christian Democratic Party in 1968. They
were in general suspicious of the Cardinal, who was
regarded as a "clever diplomat,"[20] and were hostile
to his CARITAS operation, which distributed North
American aid to the poor while importing cars,
trucks, and office equipment for the Chilean Church.*

Arroyo's activities as a CIAS member in 1967
were cited along with his report at the beginning
of this chapter. His involvement in a strike at the
Catholic University had put him in close contact
with the dissident professors and students and
strengthened his opposition to the Chilean hierarchy,

---

*See below for reactions of local Chilean
bishops to CARITAS.

who only belatedly resolved the crisis by removing
their subordinate line officers.

Arroyo, as an agronomist, was closely involved
with Christian Democratic radicals in the government land-reform agencies (INDAP and CORA), who opposed the DESAL and U.S. government-backed National
Confederation of Farm Laborers. The latter was
funded and organized by the International Development Foundation. After the linkages of IDF to the
Central Intelligence Agency had been established,
Arroyo moved out of DESAL, where he had been working,
and into ILADES. Arroyo then published articles
defending INDAP and began to alarm not only Vekemans
and Poblete but also Pierre Bigo, the CLACIAS coordinator who ran ILADES. Arroyo's courses on
agrarian reform and Marxism began to arouse suspicion.

Vekemans could not afford to see DESAL's
relationship with the National Peasant Confederation imperiled, because the CNC was the main
project in Chile of the International Development
Foundation, one of Vekemans' chief sources of support. According to the confidential reports of the
International Development Foundation, DESAL contributed manpower, contacts, and advice to help shore
up the Frei government in moments of political
crisis. DESAL's Chilean affiliate, CEDEP, was the
main channel of influence.

According to Project Achievement Report of
January 25, 1968 (Amendment No. 1 to Grant No. AID/
1a-409), written by the Chilean field officer of
the International Development Foundation,

> The responsible national role
> which the CNC can play was well
> indicated by its support for the
> salary readjustments and forced-
> savings proposal of President Frei's
> government. After reviewing the
> proposal in the light of technical
> studies prepared by economists with

the Center of Popular Development,
CEDEP, cooperating with the Technical Service Department (available
on request), the CNC leadership indicated to President Frei in a private interview as well as to the
Minister of Finance and of Labor
their basic support of the proposal.
In addition, they suggested that
workers earning less than one
"vital" (308 escudos per month) be
exempted from the forced savings
plan.

Miguel Cartagena of CEDEP, "a cooperatives expert," acted as an instructor in syndical and cooperative training courses and helped CNC head Mario
Alarcon formulate "a plan of action" with regard to
Frei's salary adjustment and forced savings plan.

Continuing with "Attachment A" of the International Development Foundation's Project Report of
January 25, 1968:

The immediate reaction (to Frei's
plan: DEM) of a large number of labor
organizations, especially the Marxist-
oriented ones--was to call a general
strike for Tuesday, November 23. Even
though the strike was, according to
some estimates, only 50-60 per cent
effective, serious clashes between
citizens and law enforcement agencies
produced a number of deaths. Reliable reports indicate that peasant
participation in the general strike
was practically non-existent.

The credit for limiting "peasant participation"
was claimed, of course, by the International Development Foundation, which had been effectively organizing the peasants into the CNC so that they would
not oppose Frei's policies.

Arroyo's reaction to these operations was one of bitter opposition after he realized what was happening. He began to side more and more with the Marxist groups and Catholic radicals who opposed Frei, the CNC, and DESAL. As Arroyo became more out-spoken, Vekemans and Poblete took decisive action against him.

On January 4, 1969, Father Renato Poblete wrote to Rome, suggesting that something be done to silence fellow Jesuit Arroyo, because he was "alarming the Cardinal" and other dignitaries with his "extremist" views. Poblete addressed the letter to a friend of his, Father Francisco Ivern, S.J., who was in charge of Jesuit research in Latin America. Ivern replied on January 29:

> I received your letter of January 4 very late and after Gonzalo Arroyo had left Rome.
> It is difficult to get an exact idea of the situation in ILADES from here, since we are getting contra-dictory reports. After Gonzalo left, Father Bigo was here for a couple of days, almost a week. According to Bigo, you and Vekemans agree with him that there are definite extremist tendencies in the teaching at ILADES. Bigo assures us that the majority of the personnel teaching at ILADES agree with Bigo's point of view and that only a small minority there hold points of view which are irreconcil-able, according to Bigo, with the doctrine of the Church.
> I have asked Father Bigo to pre-pare a dossier with the necessary material so that we can form here an opinion of all this. I also would be grateful if you and Vekemans would send us the necessary reports. It would be a shame if this affair were resolved in a conflict of

> personalities and each should try
> to prove his own point of view. I
> think that ILADES must come closer
> to CIAS and that these problems
> should be discussed within the group,
> in common with all the Fathers of
> CIAS. Nevertheless, I don't know if
> Gonzalo Arroyo and Father Bigo are
> disposed to lose a little of their
> independence and subject themselves
> to . . . CIAS. . . .

The financing of ILADES was dependent upon
ADVENIAT, the German Bishops' Fund, for religious
projects. All projects underwent continual review
according to the recommendations of the local (in
this case, Chilean) bishops. Since Poblete had
said that the Cardinal was unhappy with ILADES, he
could also express his doubts as to whether ADVENIAT
would fund the institute for 1969. Ivern's letter
resumes:

> Concerning the problem of the
> financing of ILADES, it looks like
> this is all taken care of for 1969.
> Nevertheless, there is confusion
> about this, too. Gonzalo assured me
> that the Cardinal has nothing against
> ILADES, but given the fact that other
> bishops had expressed doubts concern-
> ing the orthodoxy of the Center, this
> was causing him some problems. Ac-
> cording to Father Bigo, the Cardinal,
> in the interview which Bigo had with
> him, was more explicit. It seems that
> several bishops, during their last
> meeting, expressed their fears con-
> cerning the instruction which was
> being given in ILADES. These declara-
> tions do not appear in the minutes of
> their meeting.
> Another thing which complicates
> this affair is the fact that Father
> Bigo does not seem to have any dif-
> ficulty with the other Fathers of

> the other Latin American CIAS groups.
> According to him, difficulties are
> confined to some of the countries of
> the southern cone. I tell you all
> this so that you can see that it is
> not easy to form an exact idea about
> what is happening.
>
> I hope that when everybody is
> here for the February meeting,
> Vekemans, Gonzalo, and Bigo can have
> a frank discussion with us together
> with Father Gavina (the assistant
> to Latin America) and Father Gen-
> eral. . . .
>
> I will write you later when there
> is something more definite.

Ivern wrote again to Poblete on March 11, 1969,
informing him that he had talked to Vekemans. He
agreed that Poblete, as the appointed director of
the Centro Bellarmino, should "be the one to keep
Father General informed of what was happening."
This was to prove particularly unfortunate for Arroyo.

Ivern had also by this time talked to the
Cardinal of Santiago, who had passed through Rome.
Ivern found that, as Poblete had insisted, the
Cardinal also was worried about "extremists" at
ILADES.

> I also had a long conversation
> with your Cardinal of Santiago. He
> told me of the fears not only of
> the other bishops but also of his own
> personal fears concerning the somewhat
> extremist tendencies which had become
> manifest in the teaching at ILADES.
> I tell you this, confidentially, not
> that I think you don't already know
> it, but because I wouldn't want you
> to divulge what the Cardinal told me
> in this private conversation. . . .

Poblete was to be in Rome at the end of March,
at which time he would be able to pursue the Arroyo
affair at close range.

NOTES

1. A confidential source close to Vekemans.

2. Ibid.

3. Conversations with Vekemans in his office,
August 12, 1966, and validation from sources close
to him.

4. Conversations with the principals.

5. See, especially, "Los Jovenes: poder
nuevo?," Mensaje, XVII, 170 (July, 1968).

6. "El Diario del Che Guevara," Mensaje,
XVII, 171 (August, 1968).

7. Conversations with Hernan Larrain at the
Centro Bellarmino and at his residence after he
moved, April-June, 1969.

8. Conversations with Renato Poblete, April,
1969.

9. Gonzalo Arroyo, "La Violencia institu-
cionalizada en America Latina," Mensaje, XVII, 174
(November, 1968).

10. Ibid., pp. 553 and 541.

11. See, especially, the criticism of the
Cardinal contained in a letter to Mensaje, "'Iglesia
Joven' y la eleccion de obispos," XVII, 179 (June,
1969), 194ff., which blames Cardinal Silva for not
permitting young people to dissent at the investiture of a Chilean bishop and for not stopping the
violent repression of the dissenters that ensued
in the church vestibule.

12. Conversation of Hernan Larrain with student leaders during intermission at the Pena de la
Parra, Santiago, March 21, 1969.

13. Conversation with Hernan Larrain at his residence, March 19, 1969.

14. Conversation with Gonzalo Arroyo, April 1, 1969, at ILADES.

15. See, especially, the article by Javier Cid, S.J., in Mensaje, XVIII, 177 (April, 1969).

16. Articles by Arroyo defending INDAP against the CNC began to alarm the International Development Foundation and eventually led to Arroyo's break with IDF-supportee and -supported Vekemans. IDF Field Report for November 9, 1966, stated that a Chilean government report "which had been highly touted by government officials as the definitive work on 'Chile, land tenancy and socio-economic development of the agrarian sector' was unexpectedly attacked by A. Valdes and Gonzalo Arroyo, S.J." The article referred to appeared in Mensaje, XV, 149 (August, 1966). It was followed by "Dos posiciones divergentes en torno a la reforma agraria chilena," Mensaje, XV, 151 (October, 1966), again by Arroyo, and by numerous articles throughout 1967 and 1968 which dealt with the Frei government in a critical manner.

17. Conversation with Ambassador Richard Korry at home of Aurelius Fernandez, on April 24, 1969.

18. Conversation with Steven Smith, October 25, 1968, at his office.

19. Gonzalo Arroyo, "Las Comunidades rebeldes," Mensaje, XVII, 170 (July, 1968).

20. Convergent testimony from a variety of Catholic and non-Catholic sources.

16

Poblete at this time had other problems with which to cope. As the principal advisor on socio-economic affairs to Cardinal Silva Henriquez, he was in charge of handling the mounting number of complaints from Chilean priests concerning the Cardinal's administration of CARITAS--the international Catholic relief agency. CARITAS had become a big business in Chile, handling the importation (tax free) of cars, trucks, office equipment, and food. Critics of the Cardinal accused him of using this apparatus to further Christian Democratic campaigning in 1963 and 1964 by rewarding well organized juntas de vecinos (neighborhood political organizations) with choice CARITAS supplies. By 1968, bishops from all over Chile were receiving complaints from parish priests who said that CARITAS operations made the Church appear to be a powerful and wealthy institution, that the people who stood in the "bread lines" despised those who parceled out the food and medical supplies, and that the Church should quickly get out of the aid distribution business even if it meant that local priests would have to give up their newly imported automobiles. These criticisms were transmitted to Poblete, who was in charge of compiling a report to the Cardinal.

Poblete wrote to all the Chilean bishops asking what to do about CARITAS. The following replies are excerpted from Poblete's report to Cardinal Silva:

Bishop of
ARICA : Counseled more austerity in the main office of CARITAS, but advised continuing the program.

Bishop of
IQUIQUE : Advised continuing program. These programs inspire confidence of the people in CARITAS and predispose them to receive civic, artistic, religious culture. . . .

Bishop of
ANTAFAGASTA : Was in favor of continuing it, but asked for more autonomy for his diocesan operation.

Bishop of
COPIAPO : No response.

Bishop of
LA SERENA : No response.

Bishop of
ILLAPEL : No response.

Bishop of
SAN FELIPE : No response.

Bishop of
VALPARAISO : No response.

Cardinal of
SANTIAGO   : He has no complaint
                     about the institu-
                     tion: he suggests
                     that those aspects
                     which have been
                     criticized be re-
                     formed. . . .

Bishop of
RONCAGUA   : No response.

Bishop of
TALCA   : No response.

Bishop of
LINARES   : No response.

Bishop of
CHILLAN   : Against stopping
                     the program of giv-
                     ing food to aban-
                     doned mothers,
                     widows, old people,
                     and the helpless (a
                     decision taken in
                     August, 1968, to
                     stop complaints by
                     priests that they
                     were blamed for
                     shortages by the
                     people: DEM).

                     Re complaints con-
                     cerning:
                     VEHICLES. The sepa-
                     rated brethren (Prot-
                     estants: DEM) bring
                     in vehicles freely
                     for their propaganda
                     work. No one says
                     anything about it.
                     PAID SERVICES. There
                     are some objections

concerning services
paid to CARITAS:
the office of tour-
ism, sale of furni-
ture, bus service,
etc. No one objects
to the funeral ser-
vice of HOGAR DE
CRISTO and it is
the most important
in the country.
CARITAS OFFICE BUILD-
ING. Some people
call it an anti-
testimonial. It
can't be considered
such. A modern,
simple, economical
building. It is not
in a luxurious neigh-
borhood.

Bishop of
CONCEPCION   : Since he is on the
                   commission which
                   will decide, he
                   doesn't want to
                   commit himself.

Bishop of
LOS ANGELES   : Same as that of
                   CONCEPCION.

Bishop of
TEMUCO   : Gives a bad image
                   in the minds of
                   those who consider
                   the Church to be
                   rich. Should import
                   jeeps instead of new
                   cars. Criticisms are
                   heard concerning the
                   office building in
                   Santiago, concerning

the manner in which
CARITAS officials
behave, concern-
ing the effect of
donations on a
people who might
otherwise fight for
justice. Many
people say that some
of the CARITAS-Chile
distributions have
been used by candi-
dates for congress
to help their elec-
toral position, mak-
ing it seem that
they obtained the re-
sources to be dis-
tributed. . . .
The Bishop of Temuco
said that he had not
been able to verify
the above accusation.

Bishop of
ARAUCANIA   : Cited the bad impression that the dole-
lines give. Sug-
gested giving aid
only to (a) school
children, (b) work-
ers on highways and
other community
projects as pay, and
(c) medicine to the
sick, . . . (f) par-
ish priests in the
form of cars, (g)
clothing for the
parish priest to
distribute as he
saw fit.

Bishop of
VALDIVIA   :   It is an undeniable
                        fact that there is a
                        great resistance not
                        only on the part of
                        priests, but also on
                        the part of laymen
                        to the aid received
                        and the pastoral ef-
                        fects which the same
                        entails. . . .

Bishop of
OSORNO   :   Criticized the "busi-
                        ness" emphasis of
                        CARITAS, which he
                        saw as suppressing
                        the "religious"
                        quality of the aid.

Bishop of
PTO. MONTT   :   No response.

Bishop of
ANCUD   :   Suggested CARITAS
                        be discontinued.
                        It was not properly
                        the work of the
                        Church but of a
                        temporal agency.
                        It had contributed
                        notably in Chile to
                        extend the slogan,
                        "the Church is rich."
                        It gave to priests a
                        power which is not
                        compatible with their
                        role as preachers of
                        the gospel. There
                        are "irregularities,"
                        i.e., corruption. It
                        is especially impres-
                        sive to see what

interest the politi-
cians have in the
action of CARITAS.
Suggests a plan of
from 3 to 5 years
within which to
phase out CARITAS
as a church agency.

Bishop of
AISEN   : Wants CARITAS to
continue, but wants
the dole-lines to
be replaced by other
methods.

Bishop of
PUNTO ARENAS   : Wants CARITAS to
continue with more
autonomy for local
bishops, less con-
trol by U.S. bishops.

Priests, as is evident, were complaining about
having to make difficult allocation decisions.
Bishops wished to enhance the image of the Church.
Poblete was to act as liaison with the representatives of the North American bishops to secure more
autonomy for the Chilean bishops, so that the latter could adapt the CARITAS program to their own
interests. Poblete was an ideal man to work out
these difficulties with North American sources,
since he had studied in the States, was a regular
consultant to the U.S. Bishops' Conference, and
could reciprocate favors on a global scale through
Jesuit CIAS and, indirectly, through Vekemans' DESAL.

But the Chilean bishops had many other problems
besides CARITAS. One of the more important was the
defection of Chilean priests. In 1968, more than
200 priests, 10 per cent of the priesthood in Chile,
left the priesthood, some waiting for dispensation,
most not.[1] At the same time, recruitment to the
priesthood was very poor: only two new priests were

ordained in 1968. When defections were computed together with loss of priests through death or illness,
the organizational problems of the Church appeared
serious indeed.

The same figures (diminution of native clergy
by more than 10 per cent annually) held true for
1967 and 1968. Poblete was commissioned to find
out why priests were leaving and what could be done.
(For obvious reasons, the bishops feared to "dilute"
their own authority by ordaining married men or al-
lowing priests to marry.)

Most of the Chilean priests who left during
the years 1966-69 had occupied "staff" positions:
advisors to Catholic Action movements, writers,
chancery bureaucrats, etc. They were not, for the
most part, parish priests or other line officials.[2]
The degree to which episcopal authority in Santiago
had broken down can be partially gauged by an item
taken from the minutes of a Pastoral Advisory Commission closed meeting on April 16, 1969, when Cardinal Silva told one of his advisors that he wished
to speak with a priest in one of the staff positions
of a Catholic Action movement. (The following is a
translation from the transcript of the session.)

> CARDINAL: As far as the list of
> names goes, we decided in the bishops'
> meeting that it would be best for each
> zone (Santiago is divided into five
> pastoral zones by the Church: DEM) to
> select its own Pastoral Committee,
> and for these to elect representatives
> to talk with us. . . . In respect to
> Apostolic Movements, we still have to
> talk to "X."
> A. BAEZA: I talked with him and
> he has no interest in coming. "Y"
> might be able to come.
> FCO. MASSAD: "Y" doesn't have
> the time, he is very busy. "Z" is
> on the other commission. What are
> the norms according to which the

vicars (five bishops who head the
five zones: DEM) are going to staff
the commissions?
        CARDINAL: We will have to in-
form the vicars of the norms.
        FARMIN: If "X" doesn't come, we
can always call "Q."
        CARDINAL: First, I have to con-
sult "X"; if he won't come, I will
go to his house.

Late in 1968, it became apparent to all the
higher line officials in the Chilean Church that
the influence they had exercised over Chilean society in the early 1960's had gradually diminished
after Frei's election victory. What was particularly troubling was that another presidential election was scheduled for 1970, and Frei would not be
eligible to succeed himself.

The bishops again commissioned a study of
their linkages to Chilean power groups, but this
time they did not entrust the task to the Society
of Jesus. By 1968 the Jesuit Centro Bellarmino was
so badly divided that it could not have responded
with one voice as it had ten years before. This
time the bishops called on a non-Jesuit priest, an
enemy of Poblete and Vekemans, the head of the Institute for Rural Education, Father Rafael Larrain.
Larrain prepared a confidential report on the "image" of the Church in Chilean society and sent it
to the Cardinal, who approved it for confidential
distribution to the other bishops in March, 1968.

The first chapter of the report dealt with the
image of the Church in public opinion.

A.   The Political Forces
        The political parties, channel-
ing ideologies toward concrete objectives, make them tangible and percep-
tible for the mass of the population,
at one and the same time simplifying
and distorting them. All this can

serve as a point of reference for
discovering the mentalities, the
attitudes, the opinions of Chileans
with respect to the Church, her
message, her men, and her works.

1. The Marxists see the Church
more than anything as the carrier of
a false and prejudiced message. The
Church and all it signifies should
disappear. Whether to achieve this
through bloody persecution or slow
asphyxiation is merely a matter of
tactics. In any case, they have the
greatest interest in discrediting
the Church little by little in the
eyes of the people, without appear-
ing officially as antireligious to
the believing masses.

2. The Radicals, inspired in
great part by masonic ideology, see
the Catholic Church as their old
irreconcilable and dogmatic enemy,
obscurantist and fanatic. Their
attitude shifts between sectarian-
ism and tolerance, according to individual temperaments and circumstances. The fact that a political
party of Christian inspiration now
has power exacerbates their anti-
Catholicism.

3. The Conservative Party
(Conservative-Liberal coalition)
is made up to a large extent of
Chileans educated in Catholic high
schools, who belong to traditionally Catholic families, and who are
many times practicing Catholics themselves. Nevertheless, the fact that
the Church has assimilated in large
part Christian Democracy and has
made itself responsible, at least in
part, for the line followed by the
party and by the present government,
contributes to maintain among the

Nationals an anticlericalism that is
often violent, directed toward certain Church figures and toward concrete doctrines and positions, without affecting their traditional
faith.

4.   The Christian Democrats. One
must distinguish between two forces:
the _officialista_ wing, which is comprised by and large of those party
militants over forty years of age,
and the _rebelde_ wing, the youth.

Among the first, there is a
friendly attitude toward the Church,
with traces of anticlericalism
directed toward the traditionalist
elements within the Church or toward
those who appear too much involved
in politics.

Among the second wing, there is
great independence with respect to
the Church, a desire to make decisions entirely by themselves, a desire to see the Church as far removed as possible from politics and
to consult her only on personal matters. Many of these people are antireligious or absolutely areligious.

Besides these "political currents," the report
describes "ideological tendencies": the Protestants
("suspicious"), the modernists (viewing the Church
as "out of date"), the yough ("expecting nothing"
of the Church), the popular classes (maintaining
their "simple faith" in the Church and its priests,
but "disturbed by changes"), the agnostics (who believe in "nothing and no one").

The report concluded that the Chilean Church
had made "great efforts in the last few years" to
"gain ground" with all of the groups mentioned above.

Enormous amounts of money have
been spent. Enterprises of great

scope have been mounted. Hundreds of
automobiles have been imported. Technicians have been consulted: economists, sociologists, psychologists,
pedagogues, public relations men.
Foreign intellectuals have been
brought in. There has been planning,
organizing, integration, through
thousands of commissions, study days,
workshops, and there have been pastoral plans and synods. Thousands
of surveys, statistical studies, reports and organization charts have
been made. (Emphasis in original:
DEM.)

All this has contributed to the
creation of an image of an open
Church, one that is active, present
everywhere, and at the same time
sophisticated, blessed with great
resources, influential in the centers of power. In the same measure
there has gone up in smoke the image of a simple Church, of the
people, humble, poor, rooted in tradition and historical continuity,
which was valued more for its holi-
ness and the loyalty of its priests
and people than for its resources
and talent.

The institutions of the Church
and their financing contribute powerfully to the creation of this image.
Because of this we will examine them
in a chapter apart.

The next chapter opens with the statement that
"the Catholic Church in Chile must fight over the
long run, in union with other Churches and groups
with similar ends, for the principle of subsidiar-
ity," which meant for the right to the monies of
the state while maintaining schools, hospitals,
etc., not under state control.

After noting that the Chilean Church "has many institutions: educational, promotional, welfare, etc.," and that all these "are producing good things," the report mentions several "difficulties."

1. Will it be possible to maintain these institutions, which are so costly, in a secularized and socialized society like ours? Private fortunes are on the decline and are even disappearing; they are less and less at the service of the Church. Fiscal subsidies from the state to the Church are unpopular with most of the political parties and even with public opinion. Foreign aid is unreliable and precarious and is the occasion of much criticism.

2. How many people do we reach in our institutions? Only a small percentage of the population, and one which is decreasing. And the major part of our personnel and financial resources are consumed by our institutions. Are we not committing an injustice in giving much to a few and little to so many?

3. To maintain these institutions means compromising contacts either with the rich, the government, political parties, foreign countries: those who deprive us of our independence and moral authority in the eyes of public opinion. It means obtaining and administering great sums of money, which creates among us a climate of suspicions. It means constantly relying on technology, which makes us lose sight of the spiritual. It also means failures, errors, discontent, envy, protest . . . for things which are not our direct responsibility. (Emphasis in original: DEM.)

All of these difficulties were seen as having
a "double repercussion": on public opinion, which
regarded the Church as rich and powerful, and on
the internal structures of the Church, which became
highly diversified and increasingly bureaucratized--
the old ascriptive norms yielding to new instrumental imperatives, the staff-line division becoming a
major source of conflict.

> The Church does not project an
> attractive image to public opinion.
> Those who have or want power look at
> her with jealousy and try to take ad-
> vantage of her. The rich refuse to
> help her because they think she
> doesn't need it. The poor, thinking
> her rich, spend more time trying to
> extract some material benefit from
> her than on clinging to her in faith
> and love. The clergy, the members
> of the religious orders, have become
> privileged figures, living in solid
> buildings which from the outside
> look like palaces and using trucks
> and big cars (literally, "boxcars":
> DEM) which we buy at half price and
> which cause envy in many people.
> The repercussions within the
> Church itself are even more serious.
> The well paid religious functionary
> has replaced the militant who sacri-
> ficed himself without pay for the
> cause. The technician has replaced
> the full time worker who brought only
> his good will and apostolic zeal.
> Professional degrees count more than
> do hard work and abnegation. . . .
> The influx of foreign intellectuals,
> of seminars and international con-
> gresses, of study trips, of European
> or American journals--all have satu-
> rated us with half-assimilated ideas
> which are ill-adapted to our needs,
> producing an inflation of concepts,

constructing the image of a Church
for vanguard intellectuals which con-
fuses the great mass of the faithful.
(Emphasis in original: DEM.)

The final section of the report proposes solutions to these difficulties: emphasis upon anti-
bureaucratic norms, penetration of existing public
institutions in place of constructing parallel
Catholic schools, welfare agencies, land reform
projects, etc., and an attempt to recruit unskilled
but highly motivated (and "loyal") volunteers in
place of "technicians."

This report is significant for many reasons.
In terms of the present analysis, it shows that the
Chilean bishops had come full circle, for with the
rejection of technical expertise and the cultiva-
tion of elites would come the rejection of the
Jesuit staff sectors.

The report, as mentioned above, was written by
Rafael Larrain, himself the head of a staff-
institution, albeit a "deprived" one, the Institute of Rural Education. His organization was one
which had once depended upon Vekemans' CONCORDE
network, but it had been squeezed out of the competition for German and North American monies when
Larrain's co-worker, Father Oscar Dominguez, had
struggled to wrest control of IER from Vekemans and
lost.

The Institute of Rural Education was effectively discredited by Vekemans in the eyes of MISEREOR
when he sent to the German Bishops' Fund a damning
evaluation of the program. Excerpts from the report follow, in my translation.

Development of the Institute
     A. Initially this institute had
little of an organizational character. It was formed by small group
of persons gathered together by the
founder. It was naturally a personalistic venture. This was no problem

given the simplicity of the project and the accessibility of the
people who formed it.

Yet, according to the report to MISEREOR, the personalistic emphasis in IER remained even after IER had
become a large complex organization with a sizable
administrative staff. In reality, Vekemans had been
the inspiration of the Institute. As it grew in
size he could no longer oversee all of its operations and arranged for the election of Rafael Larrain
as its director. When Larrain attempted to imitate
Vekemans' personalistic style of decision-making in
the daily operation of what was now a large, hier-
archically organized operation, Vekemans became
alarmed and found that tensions within the IER between lower levels of personnel and Larrain would
permit him to make an intervention.

The report to MISEREOR outlined the problem as
one in which Larrain was concentrating too much
power in his own person, ignoring his "base" in the
countryside, and depreciating his co-workers.

We can show the basic problems
as they occurred sequentially.
1. Change of president and the
new election of a directorate.
2. A majority clique formed
within the directorate. The founder
of IER (Larrain: DEM) formed the
clique.
3. An executive committee was
formed. It was chosen by the "majority" clique of the directorate.
4. The directorate no longer
met regularly. It was called merely
to approve decisions of the executive committee.
5. In the new administrative
structure . . . various posts re-
sided with one person: the founder
of IER. These posts were:
--Director of Education and
  Community Development

--Coordinator
--Member of the Directorate
--Member of the Executive Council
6. The constitution of the Institute was changed on two fundamental
points:
> a. an absolute majority was
>   necessary to change the
>   constitution until the
>   directorate arbitrarily
>   dispensed with this pro-
>   vision.
> b. salaried personnel were
>   forbidden posts on the
>   directorate.

In cases where the assembly voted on
such changes as the above, there was
no secret vote, and only "qualified
persons" were permitted to vote at
all. . . .
7. The heads of the peasant
delegations . . . were no longer
elected democratically by the assembly. Instead, they were named by
the executive council. . . .

The Vekemans report not only accused the IER
of "personalism," it also maintained that the institute "lacked planning," "lacked organized contact with its peasant bases," gave "false orientation in its courses," "was superficial in its solving of peasant problems," was "inefficient," and
"acted as if the IER were the only means of peasant
liberation."

The report also included a damning indictment
of the National Association of Peasant Organizations
(ANOC), which the IER had founded. ANOC later
merged with the Christian Peasant Union (UCC) to
form the National Peasant Confederation (CNC), which
Vekemans would fund together with the International
Development Foundation (IDF).

Vekemans forced this merger by denying Rafael
Larrain the funding from MISEREOR that would have

ensured autonomy. Larrain's Institute for Rural
Education therefore became a service group to the
large peasant-union federation which Vekemans and
the CIA-funded IDF were forming to combat Marxism
in the countryside.

Despite this loss of autonomy in the peasant
sector, Rafael Larrain won important points with
Chile's Cardinal, Raul Silva, who was disturbed by
DESAL's powerful hold on MISEREOR monies. (See
Chapter 4.) The Cardinal took note of Larrain's
disaffection with Vekemans and began to encourage
the former to take over the planning and advisory
role in the chancery that the Jesuits had hitherto
enjoyed. The Chilean Cardinal knew that DESAL
could not be dismantled. Its links to powerful interests inside and outside Chile were much too
strong for the isolated Chilean bishops to counter.
But the Jesuits could be displaced from their positions as the privileged counselors of the episcopal
hierarchy.

Other conflicts broke out within the Jesuits,
and between them and other sectors, in the late
1960's. It would be needless to recount them all.
But, as the once ample and rewarding area of episcopal consultation was closed off the Centro Bellarmino; as Mensaje and DESAL staffers condemned one
anothers' operation; as ILADES came more and more
to resemble a "last bastion" for Jesuit dissidents
unwilling to compromise with Vekemans and Poblete,
the American Embassy, on the Frei government; as the
threat of a Communist election victory and the destruction of Catholic institutions gave way to the
realization that the latter were counterproductive
anyway; as all of these old alliances broke down,
the Chilean Catholic system, which had long moved
in tandem with its Jesuit designers, now spun slow-
ly off that center, leaving it to its own peculiar
afterlife.

The great crusade that had culminated in 1964
with the defeat of Salvador Allende had long since
been forgotten by Chile's bishops. The government
that had been planned by Church staff sectors to be

"compatible" with Catholic social doctrine had itself fallen to pieces upon its accession to power
and had seen its young rebelde wing leave the Christian Democratic Party en masse.   The party elders
had resisted Roger Vekemans' attempts to control
their mass political base and were scarcely more receptive to lesser clerical or episcopal interference.

The Jesuit staff of the Centro Bellarmino was
so divided within itself (for reasons previously
discussed) that it could no longer be relied upon
by Chile's bishops for coherent policy proposals.
Jesuits were replaced by other advisors who did not
share the fears outlined by Sierens in 1958. They
did not see the wisdom of abandoning the Chilean
right.

The opening of the 1970 presidential campaign
was to bring forth no new episcopal declarations
on the duty to vote.   There was really very little
apprehension in the Arzobispado.*   The reckoning
there was that Jorge Alessandri would win easily in
September.   Allende did not appear to be much of a
threat, since he had run three times previously
without success and seemed to be having trouble during the late months of 1969 and the early months of
1970 in putting together a united FRAP coalition.
The Christian Democrats were thought too divided to
win and, by 1970, too far "left" to siphon off votes
from the Catholic "right."   If Christian Democracy
was to be a spoiler, the threat would be to Allende.
The argument continued that the Church hierarchy had
become much too closely associated "in the public
mind" with the Christian Democratic Party and that
1970 was the time to give evidence of episcopal
"neutrality."   Alessandri was "muy catolico" and
highly acceptable.

But Jorge Alessandri did not win in 1970. Although he was judged the front runner during the

_____

*From conversations with high Church officials.

early months of that year, his most effective strategy had been hibernation. The decision to risk
television appearances proved catastrophic. His advanced age and flawed reactions were transmitted
all too clearly and his ratings tumbled.

In the meantime, Allende did put together a
united FRAP coalition. He won a plurality of the
votes cast, bettering his 1958 showing by six percentage points.* In October, Congress duly designated him the President of Chile for the next six
years. The panic that then gripped the Chilean upper classes (and the Chilean Cardinal Silva Henriquez) for a few months knew no bounds. Wealthy
churchmen and laymen alike scrambled to liquidate
their Chilean financial holdings and to deposit
them in North American or European banks. Roger
Vekemans swept up his DESAL operations and flew off
to Venezuela, only to be denied entry there. (He
has since relocated in Bogota, to the obvious confusion of Gustavo Perez.)

---

*A comparative table of percentage vote re-
ceived by presidential candidates in Chile during
the last three elections shows, among other things,
that Allende was elected president in 1970 with a
smaller percentage of the vote than he received in
1964. One of the chief differences was that in
1964 he was faced by a united Church front in the
person of Frei. In 1970 he found the Church split
between Tomic and Alessandri and picked up considerable Catholic votes himself with the addition of
the Christian Democratic rebelde sector to his own
FRAP coalition.

	1958	1964	1970
Allende	28.9	38.3	36.3
Alessandri	31.6	----	34.9
Christian Dem. Party	20.7	56.6	27.8
Radical Party	15.6	4.9	----

Source: Election returns as reported in El Mercurio,
          Santiago de Chile.

The churchmen who remained might well have pondered thoughts similar to those Jesuit Father Lavin penned in 1961, as part of a passage quoted earlier: "such is the seriousness of the moment in Chile and Latin America that the continent is ripe for an explosion which would annihilate our works whether they are parishes, schools, colleges, universities, retreat houses, voluntary associations, or whatever. . . ."

But there were other clerics who had actively campaigned for Allende and were delighted by his election. One of these was Jesuit Father Gonzalo Arroyo, whose precarious position within the Jesuit Centro Bellarmino had been steadily undermined by Vekemans and others in the last years of the Christian Democratic government. Arroyo had been denounced in Rome for his "lack of orthodoxy" in supporting Marxist movements, in general, and Jacques Chonchol, the Christian Democratic rebel, in particular. Now Jacques Chonchol was Minister of Agriculture to Salvador Allende, and Arroyo suddenly became an object of some special deference in Jesuit circles. Overlooked were his earlier "lapses" from true doctrine. More and more he was hailed by Renato Poblete and his other former detractors as "a prophetic figure." And, truly, what happens next within the Church, and especially among the Jesuits, in Chile will depend in no small measure upon Gonzalo Arroyo and the other priests who have long supported the non-Catholic left and who are now in a position to represent the hierarchy to the Allende government and the government to the Church.

This chapter closes with my translation of the complete text of a letter sent in desperation by Jesuit agronomist Gonzalo Arroyo to Jesuit sociologist Renato Poblete a year before the election of Allende, at a time when the future usefulness of Arroyo had not yet been divined. The letter gives some indication of the kinds of wounds that will have to heal if the Church in Chile is to reknit its wasted fabric and recover a measure of its political influence. For the bishops and the line superiors of religious

orders will have to hope for generosity from those
staff sectors, exemplified by Arroyo, that were excluded from decision-making throughout the 1960's.
These latter will have to forget the bitter harass-
ment they are wont to receive whenever Church policy-
makers have alternative sources of support and ties
to other, more conservative, governments.

     In the letter to Poblete, Arroyo shows himself
unaware of the forces that have contributed to his
state of distress. He is writing to Poblete for
help against Bigo, without realizing that it was
the temporary alliance of those two men that formed
the accusations that discredited him in Rome.
Poblete's letters to the Jesuit Curial official
Ivern (see pp. 355-56), written because of his and
Vekemans' indignation, gave Bigo the pretext he
needed to take control of ILADES. Arroyo's defiance
of the DESAL-backed CNC peasant organization and his
passionate defense of the rebelde sector of the
Christian Democratic Party have earned for him the
ultimate sanction of ostracism from the Jesuit power
club. Although he will be permitted to remain a
member of the Society of Jesus, he will take no part
in the inner councils of what remains of the Centro
Bellarmino.

          Father Bigo, the General Director
     of ILADES, has just informed me that
     I have been relieved of my posts as
     Assistant Director and as Chief of
     Studies. He has also decided that I
     give up the seminar which I was teach-
     ing.
          In an open letter to all full-
     time professors at ILADES, Father
     Bigo explained this decision which
     leaves me without a position other
     than that of teaching "courses in
     which I am competent." He says that
     since I have a research project pend-
     ing with the University of Louvain I
     cannot "take on new responsibilities."
     In other words, he is relieving me of

my functions at ILADES so that I can
perform other functions that as yet
do not exist since the research
project is being delayed.

Please note the strange procedure
he has followed. Father Bigo refers
in the open letter to the "recent
constitution of an Academic Council
with definitive powers" and the "permanent presence of the Director" at
ILADES to justify the elimination of
my post as Assistant Director. Nevertheless, the professors were not
consulted about this reorganization,
which has repercussions on the academic level and which contradicts
previous statutes. This decision
was made autocratically by the Director and then communicated to us. He
should have consulted professors and
students if the differences between
him and me--which are for the most
part just a difference of emphasis--
seemed to him so serious as to lead
him to take these measures. It is
true that in the last course evaluations, the students made a unanimous
complaint concerning his course,
Social Doctrine of the Church, and
passed the complaint to the Academic
Council.

Perhaps Father Bigo has the
strange idea that it was I who fo-
mented the rejection of his course.
Actually, the rejection was sponta-
neous and had been building up since
the beginning of the year, even more
strongly than in previous years.
Father Bigo accused me during the
first weeks of the semester of having created a course to contradict
the one which he was teaching.
This is pure fantasy, probably the

result of psychological rationalization for the failure of a course
based on obsolete theology and a
European mentality foreign to the
fine students which we have this
year. But what is going to happen
in the future? Will the Director
feel he has the right to eliminate
whomever does not agree with him?

ILADES is an institution that is
becoming more and more oriented to
interdisciplinary research at a high
scientific level within a humanistic
conception of society. The present
monarchical structure within the administrative and academic spheres,
as these events demonstrate, will undoubtedly lead to the death of ILADES
as it has been conceived and promoted
these many years by the Centro Bellarmino. We have to be consistent. We
cannot support the doctrine of participation of masses, disseminate
documents in Mensaje such as the conclusions reached on university participation at Buga, and now maintain
these attitudes against academic freedom in ILADES. The people expect actions and not words from Christians
and from the Church.

But this irregular way of pro-
ceeding is not limited to ILADES.
I am more disturbed by the fact that
Father Bigo did not consult the members of CIAS. I am sure that there
is some misunderstanding in his af-
firmation which he made to me personally, that he was supported fully by
the Director of CIAS in taking this
step which amounts to the open repu-
diation of the Assistant Director of
ILADES who was approved and nominated
by the previous Director of CIAS,
Father Hernan Larrain, in September
of 1966 with the approval of CIAS.

I think that a step of this kind
should be discussed in CIAS and
should be communicated before the
fact to the person affected so that
he is aware that CIAS no longer has
confidence in him. When I accepted
the position as Assistant Director
of ILADES, giving up the direction
of a Research Center at the Catholic
University, I was in a certain
sense meant to be a counter-weight
to the position of Director which
was occupied by a French Jesuit
whose prestige derived from his
books on doctrine, but who possessed
little experience in Latin American
affairs and who was ignorant of empirical studies made on our continent. For this reason I thought
that my assignment was not only personal but that it also implied a certain representation of Chilean CIAS
within the Institute.

I told Father Bigo that he does
not have the power to depose me and
since CIAS has not been consulted I
still consider myself to be Assistant
Director, especially since I presented
to CIAS in December of last year the
differences between Father Bigo and
myself and I received, after ample
discussion, a full vote of confidence. Later, against my own judg-
ment, but at the request of yourself
and of Father Vekemans, I went to
Rome to personally discuss these conflicts with Father General and his
Assistants. At that very time in
Rome I told Father Bigo that my collaboration with him in 1969 would
not include my not speaking my ideas
to my students, even though I would
respect his ideas and his position
as Director. I think that in

conscience this is what I have done.
I imagine, Renato, that you gave
your approval to Father Bigo without
knowing this lack of legitimate
cause for removing me from the post
of Assistant Director.

Finally, Father Bigo has not put
this matter on the agenda of the next
meeting of the Directorate. This
also seems to me to be out of order.
I believe that these actions will
cause unforeseen repercussions both
among the professors and among the
students of ILADES.

I greet you in Christ. . . .

With the castigation of Arroyo in June of
1969, Father Poblete took over the directorship of
the doctrinal institute ILADES. After the election
of Allende the next year and the subsequent flight
from Chile of Father Vekemans, Poblete was all that
remained of the earlier Centro Bellarmino. Without
the return of Arroyo and without the return of
scores of other priests and ex-priests to the formal organizational structures of the Chilean Church,
the Church in Chile will cease to be of significant
political importance.

NOTES

1. Statistics compiled by the Chancery of the
Cardinal Archbishop. (Confidential.)

2. Eduardo La Barca, Chile invadido: reportaje
a la intromision extranjera (Santiago: Editores
Austral, 1968), p. 244.

17

A MODEL
OF
CHURCH
DISINTEGRATION

The model of Church disintegration that emerges
from the preceding considerations is premised upon
definite assumptions about the exercise of power in
modern societies. The chief assumptions are the
following:

The exercise of power requires the development
of formal organization, which in turn implies functional differentiation and task specification (division of labor). This complex division of labor
results, however, in consequences dysfunctional for
the original power holders. The specialized sub-
units acquire a measure of functional autonomy and
of solidarity among themselves that permits them to
challenge the leadership. They also have ample opportunity to develop informal alliances and sources
of support unsuspected by formal line officials.
If these challengers are not absorbed in some type
of "circulations process" or expelled, they will
mobilize sufficient support to destroy the original
organization. If they are co-opted, or absorbed,
all is well, at least temporarily. The problem is
that they may be too many to be accommodated. In
the event that the internal resources of the power
system are insufficient to permit absorption of all
of the challengers, the partial co-optation only
intensifies the disintegrative process. The chal-
lenging elites that are "left out" of policy-making

or the division of spoils are enraged by the sight
of their former allies now securely ensconced in the
seat of power. Fragmentation proceeds with a vengeance.

It is my contention that the Roman Catholic
Church in Latin America is undergoing just such a
fragmentation because it constitutes this type of
organization: old elites (whose authority rests
upon ascriptive normative bases) have become newly
dependent upon specialized sub-units for the capability to compete in the secular marketplace for
resources that are contingent upon instrumental performance. But the old elites are unable to reward
their specialized sub-units financially and unwilling to accept all of them into formalized positions
of policy making. The old rewards of episcopal approval, of normative legitimation, are no longer
valued. The former sanctions of excommunication or
deprivation of ecclesiastical "faculties" are no
longer feared. The bishops are learning the lesson
that Tawney spoke of some time ago:

> (Power) is thus both awful and
> fragile, and can dominate a continent,
> only in the end to be blown down by a
> whisper. To destroy it, nothing more
> is required than to be indifferent
> to its threats, and to prefer other
> goods to those which it promises.
> Nothing less, however, is required
> also.[1]

It is clear from the examination of the organizational conflict in Colombia and Chile that significant sectors of the Church are quite prepared
to construct bases of power that include only tan-
gential linkages to traditional hierarchies.

THE DALTON MODEL

Once the vertical power linkages have been
broken, and bishops are effectively neutralized,

the linkages among staff units become increasingly problematic. Many of the conflicts that break out among staff units are responses to the broken linkages of the earlier line-staff conflicts. The Dalton model (see Chapter 1) of line-staff conflict also gives premonition of ensuing staff-staff conflict once the line sectors are overcome. According to Dalton, tensions derive, in the first place, from functional differences between line and staff officials. In relating this to the Church structure of Latin American Catholicism, it is instructive to contrast the bishops' meetings analyzed in Chapter 1 with staff activities in Chapters 2 and 3. Thomas Sanders has observed that the role of the bishop is to symbolize the unity of frequently diverse factions of his diocese.[2] Line officials (bishops, rectors, parish priests) usually perform functions of normative coordination. They heed the counsel voiced by Detroit's Archbishop Dearden (in Chapter 1): the official Church must not "overcommit itself" to any single interest group; it must spread its risks.

Staff officers are much more likely to be engaged in instrumental activities. The functional autonomy of the latter increases with increased functional differentiation and frequently finds expression in the construction of a quasi-independent organizational base. The staff experts of ICODES, Jesuit CIAS, and CELAM in Colombia all found it necessary to seek financial and technical resources outside the Colombian Church and even outside the international Church system. They competed for scarce resources both within and without the Church system: the Jesuits winning within the Colombian Catholic system, the CELAM appointees within the continental system, and the ICODES group forced to turn outside the Church, where they discovered the richest resources of all. In turn, ICODES became the most hated group and was eventually forced out of the Catholic system altogether.

The problem with the instrumental sphere is that resources there consist of money and technology

as well as highly trained manpower. These resources
tend to be scarce. In the purely normative sphere,
the resources consist of values, which are always
plentiful. Competition within a normative context
may simply result in a reinforcement of the commitment of the competitors to common norms. But when
conflict occurs in a context that is a mixture of
both normative and instrumental emphases, the at-
tendant strife can well be internecine. As Coser
states, after Simmel:

> Conflicts in which the partici-
> pants feel that they are merely the
> representatives of collectivities and
> groups, fighting not for self but
> only for the ideals of the group they
> represent, are likely to be more radi-
> cal and merciless than those that are
> fought for personal reasons.[3]

The "personal" element in the present case
would include questions of personal/organizational
interest. The sub-units that staff members created
for their own personal contribution to Latin American Catholicism during the 1960's were clearly perceived by them as "serving the Church and mankind,"
and not merely "self." (See, for example, the letters exchanged by Father Gustavo Perez and Roger
Vekemans, in Chapter 2.) But, nonetheless, these
organizations carried with them strong instrumental
emphases that reflected the urgency of appropriat-
ing whatever material resources were at hand. The
operation of Jesuit CIAS, ICODES, and even of more
secular DESAL was clearly consistent with the admonition of St. Ignatius of Loyola, who counseled
"pray as if everything depended on God" (normative),
but "work as if everything depended on you" (instrumental). With this in mind, it is not difficult to understand how Fathers Poblete, Vekemans,
and Bigo could coldly decide to "silence" fellow
Jesuit Gonzalo Arroyo by sending reports of his
"radicalism" to Rome. They were not acting out of
"personal hostility" but only out of a regard for
the common cause. Similar in many respects was the

action taken by Jesuit Father Andrade in Colombia
to have the actions of ICODES and of Father Gustavo
Perez "suppressed."

Dalton's second variable in accounting for
line-staff tensions is the differentials in the
ages, formal education, potential occupational
ceilings, and status group affiliations of members
of the two groups. (The staff officers are younger, have more education but lower occupational potential, and form a prestige-oriented group with
distinctive consumption patterns and recreational
tastes.) Again, the pattern here describes relationships between bishops and their specialized
staffs as well as differentials among staff members
that may also account for intra-staff conflicts.

The Catholic bishops in both Colombia and Chile
who were at odds with staff sectors were at least
ten and often thirty years older than the oldest
staff member. They held ecclesiastical degrees in
Thomistic theology, while the staff positions were
being increasingly occupied by younger men with degrees from American or European universities:
economists, sociologists, statisticians, psychologists, etc. For the most part, the advanced degrees of staff specialists had been financed by
sources other than the national episcopal hierarchies: through OAS fellowships, grants from European or American Catholic groups, or under exchange
programs negotiated within the international religious orders. Staff members were often members of
professional organizations, wrote for learned jour-
nals or specialized publications, attended conven-
tions and international symposia. They often enjoyed life styles that even the Latin American
archbishops could not afford, yet they had little
of the direct influence of the bishop or cardinal
and none of the authority.

Within the network of staff organizations
there were clear divisions along the same lines.
It is no coincidence that the Jesuits of CIAS Colombia came into conflict with the diocesan priests

who headed ICODES.   They belonged to different status groups (religious order vs. diocesan), the Jesuits were older, the ICODES people held advanced
degrees from European universities while Jesuit
Father Andrade had been educated exclusively inside
Colombia in Jesuit seminaries.   Only one Colombian
CIAS Jesuit had a Ph.D. from a North American University (University of Wisconsin), and he was careful to maintain a neutral stance during Andrade's
war upon ICODES.

In Chile, Jesuit Fathers Bigo, Vekemans, and
Poblete were at least ten years older than Gonzalo
Arroyo.   The latter was the only one of the four to
have a Ph.D. (from the University of Iowa).   Arroyo
made a point (as did the Jesuits of Mensaje) of
maintaining a life style apart from and more humble
than that of the older staff Jesuits.   Arroyo,
Larrain, de Meneses, and the other younger Jesuits
moved out of the Centro Bellarmino to be closer to
their own reference groups, the students and polit-
icized workers.

Dalton's third variable is the need of the
staff groups to justify their existence.   There is
often little basis for differentiating the work
done by clerics in Catholic staff organizations
from that done by lay specialists or technicians.
The staff member frequently must explain, to himself at least, how he considers his work to be
"priestly," since most of it is regulated by secular (scientific, professional, business) norms.   At
the same time, he must be able to defend the pro-
priety of applying profane knowledge to sacred
preoccupations.

The conflict is basically between the ascriptive status of line personnel and the achieved status of staff.   This tension carries over into relationships among staff members themselves insofar as
the latter are grouped into a staff sub-unit with
an appointed, or at least nonelective, chief.   Arguments between Arroyo, the professional agronomist,
and Vekemans, the head of DESAL, over correct policy

regarding agrarian reform in Chile led to the oust-
er of Arroyo and the beginnings of a conflict that
eventually helped dissolve the Jesuit Centro Bellarmino.

At the same time, Jesuit staff specialists in
Chile had given offense to the bishops when they
had made what they considered to be scientific
analyses of a socio-political situation the bishops
deemed fraught with theology. In encouraging confrontation politics in the countryside while eulo-
gizing the memory of Che Guevara, the editors of
Mensaje ran up against a sacred taboo. It was a
matter of grave concern not only to the bishops but
also to their fellow Jesuits, Vekemans and Poblete,
who relegated the prescriptive force of sociology
to the mandates of the "social doctrine of the
Church." This is clear from many sources, among
them the document Vekemans addressed to MISEREOR
recounting the aims of DESAL in Chile and in Latin
America. There were only two choices available for
the continent: Christianity or Communism. Science
as well as technology would be bent to serve the
Church lest it be co-opted by the enemy.

Dalton's fourth variable is the fear in the
line that staff bodies, by their expansion and
well-financed research activities, will undermine
line authority; a fear that seems to be well founded. The Pope took special pains to reprimand staff
groups during his visit to Bogota, addressing himself sarcastically to the "new theologians" who
"arrogate to themselves the permission to proclaim
their own personal opinions." The Pope was especially concerned that Thomism, which has formed the
basis of seminary study for centuries, be retained
as the official and guiding orientation of Catholic
staff theologians. The staff experts who assisted
at the Latin American Bishops' Conference in Medellin, which convened soon after Pope Paul's Bogota speech, startled many bishops by requesting that
they receive the same voting powers the bishops
themselves enjoyed. The present storm of dissent
over the Pope's encyclical condemning artificial

birth control is another indicator of the clear
tendency of the staff theologians, demographers,
sociologists, etc., to articulate and mobilize dis-
satisfaction with line performance.

A final variable is the fact that aspirants to
higher staff offices can gain promotion only through
approval of influential line executives. The bishop
(or provincial superior) always holds at least the
veto power and thus is capable of preventing promotion. This reinforces the fact that line mobility
seems to be largely contingent upon conformity with
ascriptive norms (Italian nuncios "nominating" for
the bishopric men who have been "prudent" priests)
while staff mobility hinges upon effective instrumental performance.

Besides divisions between staff and line,
there is a tendency for tensions to mount among
staff positions, as we have seen, once the competition increases for relatively scarce resources.
Vallier's differentiation between "pluralists" and
"papists" blurs the distinction between successful
and unsuccessful ecclesiastical entrepreneurs.
Those who have been unable to find good pickings in
the secular marketplace must turn to the less lucrative (and frequently less demanding) Church operations. Some of the papists are really frustrated pluralists. Witness the Jesuits of Colombian
CIAS, who turned to their Colombian episcopacy as
to an exclusive private preserve once they had been
decisively rejected by U.S. AID and given only to-
ken assistance by the West German Bishops' Fund,
ADVENIAT.

Yet there are ways to prime the pump, to stimulate secular demand for clerical expertise. In
the short run, these methods proved profitable in
the 1960's and slowed down Church fragmentation
among staff bodies by increasing the distance of
staff from line. The birth-control controversy is
a case in point. The more unyielding the hierarchy
(line) is shown to be on the matter of artificial
regulation of births, the more in demand are

"progressive" churchmen who can work for a change
in attitudes and policies within the Church, or act
as "cover" for secular family-planning programs that
take place "under the very nose" of the bishop.
The "Trojan horse" function of the progressives implies a walled and implacable Troy. However, recent studies have shown that Latin American Catholics are most unlikely to be dissuaded from contraceptive use by religious considerations.[4] Interviews with twenty-three of the twenty-nine Chilean
bishops in April, 1968, revealed that the majority
of Chile's bishops had no objection to the use of
the pill.[5] Yet the image of a powerful and opposed
hierarchy remains, and the myth is useful for those
who are paid to fight the last bastions of "conservatism."

Although an increase in the demand for clerical expertise could lessen the tensions among competing staff sectors, it would at the same time
lead to greater problems. The very success of
staff officials in meeting secular demands leads to
an alienation of those Catholic groups that are
properly neither staff nor line but marginal to the
official Church: the priest-workers, the lay Catholic radical groups, the nationalistic student
movements. These groups are acutely sensitive to
the relative autonomy-dependence of the Church system and are particularly wary of foreign, especially North American, "imperialism." Unfortunately,
foreign organizations are among the more popular
staff target groups. It is difficult to conceive
of any solvent entity (from the Methodist Church to
AID) which has interests in Latin America and which
requires legitimation in the society, that is not
being serviced at present by some Catholic staff
sector.

Paying Protestant groups are as welcome at
Catholic training centers as are the missionaries
sent by the North American and Western European
episcopal hierarchies. AID makes contracts with
clerical consulting agencies for help in programming family planning, strengthening "moderate"

labor unions, training Peace Corps volunteers.
United States business interests, such as the
United States Steel Corporation, and their European
counterparts support Pro Deo University in Rome,
which attempts ("in a favorable climate") to in-
still in select Latin American clerics a respect
for capitalist development. The Institute for Human Progress--whose board of directors includes
J. Peter Grace, executives of Sears, Roebuck, and
the presidents of ITT, Standard Oil Corporation,
and Corning Glass International--recently proposed,
in conjunction with ICODES, DESAL, and their Brazilian and Bolivian counterparts, a project that
would place large numbers of United States and
Latin American nonprofit organizations under the
tutelage of those Catholic pluralist agencies.

The result is a growing proliferation of Catholic service organizations that are oriented to the
power structure of secular society, looking to
groups outside the Church for support, protection,
and legitimation. Their tactics are remarkably
similar to those once employed by traditional Catholic line sectors operating under the aegis of the
powerful national oligarchies who inherited the
continent in the years following Spanish rule.

Perhaps the truest distinction between the
traditional Catholic (line) elites and the new
staff sectors is akin to that suggested by Stinchcombe:

> . . . the political activity of
> different sections of the elite of
> modern societies is oriented primarily
> toward the system of stratification
> among organizations rather than the
> class system of individuals and fami-
> lies.[6]

Viewed in this light, the traditional Roman
Catholic hierarchical system loses its preeminence,
yielding to a scramble of newly created interest
groups that are geared not to the production of

normative support for any national social class but
to the instrumental needs of organized publics.
The priest-worker no less than the priest-executive
usually risks open conflict with his bishop or with
his fellows only when the group he is servicing has
become sufficiently organized and articulate to demand his full commitment. In Latin America today,
as student groups, workers, and campesinos are
awakening to their interests and as governments and
international agencies, businesses, and armies are
developing organizationally sophisticated responses
and concurrent needs, ecclesiastical expertise and
instrumental capacity is inevitably drawn in. The
old ascriptive distinction between higher and lower
clergy is no longer of paramount importance.

To gauge the instrumental capacity of the
Catholic system in Latin America, it is no longer
sufficient to examine its status system nor its
formal hierarchies. Much more salient are the direct and indirect linkages that bind Catholic "sub-
units" to international sources of logistic and financial support and to local political parties,
armies, student movements, or other elementary
power systems.

Following the Rosenau "agenda" for research
into national-international linkages, one can sum-
marize much of the data in preceding chapters in a
simple input-output model. The model is conceptu-
alized under two aspects: the integrative linkages,
which staff services provide the Catholic system,
and the disintegrative linkages, which result from
staff operations. In Rosenau's terminology, the
integrative links can be termed "direct" since they
were formally intended, from the outset, by the
staff officers in question. The bulk of the disintegrative linkages were not programmed but occurred as the unanticipated latent consequences of
this phase of bureaucratization.

INTEGRATIVE LINKAGES

Catholic staff structures in Latin America, as we have seen in Chapter 1 of this study, were formed and given authorization to seek monies and technical assistance from external (U.S. and West European) sources in order to increase Catholic influence among Latin American elites and masses. During the 1960's, two staff organizations proved outstanding in their ability to win support from abroad in dollar terms: ICODES, under Father Gustavo Perez in Colombia, and DESAL, under Jesuit Father Roger Vekemans in Chile. By the end of the 1960's, these two organizations, although grossly unequal, dominated the supply of money available from foreign sources. DESAL's operating budget of upwards of $30 million a year dwarfed that of ICODES, but the latter held a near monopoly upon Church-directed research monies in Colombia and was the center of an extensive network of research affiliates (FERES) throughout Latin America.

The "integrating function" of Catholic staff operations in the 1960's was clearly to connect United States and West European policy interests with Latin American target groups: students, workers, slumdwellers, peasants, public opinion. The effect upon the internal cohesion of the Catholic system was devastating. ICODES and DESAL quickly became alienated from the upper line positions (local bishops and cardinals) whom they had been enlisted to "advise."

DISINTEGRATIVE LINKAGES

In addition to the fissures that developed between successful staff entrepreneurs and their line superiors, the bishops, other conflicts emerged among their peers. ICODES was itself from the outset opposed by the Colombian Jesuits of CIAS, who were finding grantsmanship a zero-sum game. With every new ICODES contract there was less left for the Jesuits--or so it seemed to them. ICODES, in

its international operations, ran head-on into
DESAL, which was also bidding for and winning U.S.
AID grants for population study. (The resulting
confusion is documented in Part II of this study
with the analysis of correspondence that passed
back and forth between the two organizations.)

Other deep-seated antagonisms linked the following groups:

1. Jesuit Colombian CIAS to Jesuit Chilean
CIAS. Both groups competed for ADVENIAT funds and
for French doctrinal expert Pierre Bigo. Chilean
Jesuit Renato Poblete was linked through FERES to
the Colombian Jesuits' enemy, ICODES head Gustavo
Perez. Chilean Jesuits, in attempting to spread
Christian Democracy in its labor front, CLASC, to
Colombia had collided with the Colombian Jesuit la-
bor network in Medellin. Chilean Jesuit Zanartu
was expelled by the Colombian Jesuits.

2. CELAM, the Conference of Latin American
Bishops, had been by-passed by the West German
Bishops when they appointed DESAL as the administrator of their annual funds to Latin American
projects. There were, therefore, tensions, between
CELAM and the West German Bishops and between CELAM
and DESAL. One of the more influential bishops in
CELAM was Chilean Cardinal Silva, who was especially unhappy over Vekemans' control of MISEREOR
monies in Chile. (See Chapter 1.)

3. DESAL itself was locked in conflict with
its sister agency, ILADES; both of them belonged to
the original Centro Bellarmino which the Jesuits
had constructed in the late 1950's in Santiago.
ILADES was closely aligned with the "rebel" wing of
the Christian Democratic Party (the youth sectors),
while DESAL maintained many of its ties to the
founders of Christian Democracy in Chile. While
ILADES followed the doctrinal and analytic line of
the Chilean Institute of Economics (under Claudio
Veliz and Osvaldo Sunkel), which stressed the "dependent" character of Chilean economic relations

with the United States, Vekemans was actively lobbying for U.S. funds and boasted of his friendship
with United States senators, ambassadors, and presidential assistants.* Vekemans scoffed at charges
that his acceptance of U.S. monies tied him to U.S.
policy interests; one of his stock phrases was,
"Money does not stink."[7] The editors of Mensaje
disagreed, claiming that DESAL "reeked" of "Yanqui"
iniquity.

4. Mensaje had changed during the 1960's from
the Centro Bellarmino's house organ promoting
Frei's government to an exponent of antigovernmen-
tal initiatives. This transformation was gradual,
almost imperceptible at first, but when the youth
sectors abandoned the official wing of the party in
1968, Mensaje became clearly identified with Catholic radicalism. The editorial on the death of Che
Guevara was a case in point. Mensaje began publishing fewer and finally no articles by Vekemans and
Poblete, while devoting more of its space to ILADES
programs and analyses.

5. The Cardinal of Santiago employed CIAS director Poblete as an advisor on social problems.
Poblete was especially helpful in carrying out

---

*DESAL publishes an annual report of some of
its activities in which it includes a visitors list
of foreign dignitaries who were received at DESAL
headquarters in Santiago. The 1968 edition listed,
among many others, Joseph Tydings (U.S. Senator
from Maryland), Sidney Weintraub (Director of AID
in Chile), Felipe Herrera (President of the International Development Bank, on whose board Vekemans
sits), Edward Korry (U.S. Ambassador to Chile),
Raul Prebisch, John Reilly (Special Assistant to
then Vice President Humphrey), Lincoln Gordon
(President of Johns Hopkins University), and Sol
Linowitz (Ambassador of the United States to the
OAS). The report also includes a list of publications throughout the world that carried stories on
DESAL in 1968.

opinion polls and in briefing the Cardinal on developments within the Christian Democratic Party's
"official wing." Poblete was a close friend of
Frei, Interior Minister Perez-Zuchovich, presidential hopeful Radimiro Tomic, and other PDC stal-
warts. The Cardinal did not trust the Jesuits of
Mensaje, however, and was worried about the radicalism evidenced by ILADES seminars. He was overtly hostile to Vekemans, who controlled the purse
strings of monies which the Cardinal felt should
come under his jurisdiction.

6. Chilean Jesuit CIAS became, by the end of
the 1960's, a closed directorate comprised of
Vekemans and Poblete, with occasional inputs from
French Jesuit Pierre Bigo. For the most part,
Vekemans operated outside of the Chilean Catholic
system. Poblete operated very much inside of it.
Officially, DESAL was a "secular" institution,
under neither Jesuit, episcopal, nor papal control.
Unofficially, of course, Vekemans reported directly
to the Jesuit General in Rome, who served as intermediary between Vekemans and the Papal Commission
for Latin America. In spite of the conflicts that
Vekemans' operations generated inside the Jesuit
order in Chile, the Jesuit General was never able
to affect DESAL's policies, since they held the
explicit sanction of the papacy.

Vekemans and Poblete supported one another
closely. Poblete had access to Frei and to the
Cardinal: access in both cases denied to Vekemans.
Vekemans held access to North American, Western
European, and Vatican decision-makers who could
prove useful to Poblete. The two men shared an
aversion to the ideologies of the younger Jesuits
and an unwillingness to abandon their own linkages
to elites in order to concentrate solely upon a
mass base.

LINKAGE PROCESSES

Penetrative process. It is clear that Catholic staff sectors in Latin America have at least

provided North American decision-makers with access
to areas beyond their immediate control. DESAL was
instrumental in providing the International Development Foundation, a front organization for the
Central Intelligence Agency, with legitimation in
its efforts to build peasant organizations in Latin
America parallel to Marxist or leftist movements.
The Colombian Jesuits, with monies and technical
assistance from ORIT, the international labor organization of the AFL-CIO, did the same thing in
Colombia, although they did it themselves, whereas
Vekemans only serviced anti-Marxist movements.

     In the urban sector, DESAL helped CLASC unions
form and compete with the non-Catholic left in
Venezuela as well as Chile. The election of a
Christian Democratic president in Caracas to complement the base in Chile was a long-term project
which Chilean Jesuits helped plan. Chilean Jesuit
Zanartu was active not only in Colombia, where his
efforts failed, but also in Venezuela.

     ICODES in Colombia as well as DESAL in Chile
provided legitimation for studies by AID of Catholic attitudes toward birth control and of Catholic
decision-making processes. This "Trojan horse
function" was discussed earlier, together with the
concomitant exaggeration of episcopal resistance to
artificial means of contraception.

     United States business interests found ready
assistance all through the 1960's from such staff
sectors as ICODES, DESAL, and Jesuit CIAS. The
reciprocity involved was less specific and more
diffuse than other contractual arrangements and was
rooted in the belief of many U.S. businessmen based
in Latin America that Catholic universities were
"responsible" while the national universities were
"whorehouses" and seedbeds of Communism.[8]

     The Vatican, of course, had its own interests
to defend as well as those of the international
hierarchical system. The Jesuit Centro Bellarmino,
CELAM, ICODES/FERES, Jesuit CIAS were all means of

influencing local political activity indirectly and
"safely" rather than through Catholic bishops who
were supposedly committed to remain politically
neutral.

Reactive process. The construction of the
Catholic staff system in Latin America came as a
clear response, or reaction, to Marxist and Protestant organizing activities. With the near election
of Marxist candidate Allende in Chile in 1958, and
with the expulsion of Spanish clergy from Cuba in
1959-60, the Vatican alerted North American and all
other "free world" bishops to send men to Latin
America. Since the bishops of the United States
preferred to send money rather than diocesan priests,
the Pope requested that each religious order in the
United States send 10 per cent of their men over a
ten-year period. Staff specialists, such as the
Belgian Roger Vekemans, were sent to Latin America,
training centers for North American clergy were
opened by Father Ivan Illich at Petropolis, Brazil,
and at Cuernavaca, Mexico, and a host of other foreign experts followed.

The problem was that each group of experts attached itself to a different base: some to the
bishops, some to student movements, some to middle-
class intellectuals, some to urban workers, some to
peasant unions. A complete disregard for central-
ized planning within Latin American Catholicism
permitted the functional autonomy of these staff
sectors to burgeon beyond control. The subsequent
crystallization of power centers left decision-
making, for the most part, in staff areas, beyond
the reach of the traditional power holders, the
bishops.

Emulative process. The influx of North American and West European monies and technical assistance to Latin American Catholicism became quickly
contingent upon the ability of the latter to develop bureaucratic procedures for distributing it.
Latin American staff sectors, which had been created in an earlier era (e.g., after World War II)

for the purpose of combating Marxist penetration,
had not been required to go beyond the phase of
ideology formation and indoctrination. In the early
1960's, such groups as Colombian Jesuit CIAS attempted to maintain their traditional style of operations only to find that if they were to compete
for secular sources of support (especially U.S. AID
funds), they would have to develop a more sophisticated, or at least more "modern," set of responses. They, too, began to send their younger
men to the United States for degrees in sociology
and economics. But they were too late.

The groups that adapted quickest to North
American styles of grantsmanship and programming
were those that came to form ICODES in Colombia,
DESAL in Chile, and CERIS in Brazil. They quickly
mopped up most of the money and prestige, built
their organizations around these early winnings,
and achieved a kind of "take-off" into sustained,
long-term growth.

Other sectors turned away from the U.S.-Western
European model to a more direct identification with
the masses: worker priests abandoned the French
strategies of Action Populaire (embodied in Pierre
Bigo) and began to live not only with the workers,
but as workers. Many stopped saying mass and hear-
ing confessions, preferring to "listen" and to "remain open" to what the masses had to say. This
type of emulative process produced linkages between
priest and urban worker that were very different,
of course, from the linkages formed by such groups
as DESAL with working-class groups they chose to
"indoctrinate."

Only ICODES and DESAL, for the most part, have
been represented as linking up the cold war environment with local target groups. The other staff
sectors, cut off from foreign funding, were forced
to forge fused linkages with their local target
areas, living from whatever these same groups chose
to give them. In this way, Mensaje and ILADES became dependent upon local Chilean resources;

Colombian Jesuit CIAS, apart from its dependence
upon ORIT funds, required legitimation from the
Colombian bishops whose interests they defended.

In contrast, ICODES opposed the Colombian
bishops, DESAL ignored the Chilean Cardinal, and
CELAM found itself tied to the Latin American Bishops Committee of the North American Bishops until
the latter cut the umbilical cord. When that happened, Brazilian bishops emerged as CELAM's spokes-
men, assailed U.S. policies, and began to steer
CELAM toward a rendezvous with students and Catholic radical movements.

THE PROSPECTS

By the end of the 1960's, it had become increasingly clear to Church decision-makers that
their chief problem lay not with the threat of
Marxist revolution or of Protestant conversions but
with the internal hemorrhaging of the Catholic system. Priests were leaving the Church in record
numbers, recruitment was practically nonexistent,
Catholic Action movements were moribund, the masses
were awakening to new aspirations of a nonreligious
quality, and urbanization and industrialization
were transforming the peasant societies that had,
since the Spanish conquest, provided the bishops
with a mass base.

Only scattered staff sectors had managed to
emerge from the frenzy of the anti-Communist crusade of the 1960's with any increased degree of external influence or internal cohesion. And even
these groups had undergone such traumatic divisions
and alienation of former friends as to cast doubt
upon their future within Catholicism.

As the attention of the United States turned
increasingly toward Southeast Asia rather than
Latin America, staff sectors in that area of the
Church's operations began to recreate the Latin
American experience of the 1960's. The 1970's

brought an intensification of Jesuit operations in
the Philippines, as North American priests at the
Ateneo in Manila channeled resources from the U.S.
government, business sectors, and even the military
into a struggle for the hearts and minds of that
country's future elites. Philippine and Spanish
Jesuits turned their attentions to the organization
of peasant unions and workers' cooperative.

As perceived by its top line and staff officers, the future of Catholicism is as an instrumental system: one that will provide trained technicians in community development, education, mass
media, etc., to aid "development" along non-Marxist
lines. "Organization" and "resources" are the by-
words.

As perceived by many of its lower line and
staff officers, the future of Catholicism lies not
in its instrumental capacities, its political power,
its size or "impact" upon national policies or international relations. These lower participants
would jettison the major institutional structures
of the Church: not only the old line structures of
parish, Church, and school, but also the recent
bureaucratic embellishments of systems-programming
and international relief service. For these groups,
Catholicism remains an ideological entity, one
whose norms are in need of reformulation, but nevertheless a force whose power should derive not
from alliances with the wealthy of this world but
from the simple strengths of the poor.

In Latin America, the staff system of Church
modernization aimed at increased instrumental capacity has been tried. It has, in the long run,
failed. It is true that it was able to thwart a
Marxist victory in Chile and to place a Christian
Democrat in the presidency in Venezuela. But in
the process, it splintered the Catholic system. As
long as line bishops were able to command the allegiance of their staff sectors, they could have it
both ways: they could pose as being interested in
transcendental values and "above" politics, while

at the same time making sure that their organizational mass base and alliances with elites remained intact. But once staff sectors had tested episcopal power and found how weak it really was, the staff could no longer be controlled. The result was fragmentation and internecine competition among staff sectors for dwindling resources.

Indications are many that in the 1970's the Church in Latin America will turn more and more to a policy of real poverty and political abstention. To the extent that this policy is implemented, there is a good chance that Catholicism may reknit its wasted fabric, little by little. However, in the face of increasing urbanization and concomitant secularization, it is highly unlikely that it will ever achieve a truly mass base.

NOTES

1. R. H. Tawney, Equality (London: Allen and Unwin, 1931), p. 229.

2. Thomas G. Sanders, in private conversation.

3. Lewis Coser, The Functions of Social Conflict (New York: Free Press), p. 118.

4. A study by the DESAL sub-unit, CELAP, is one of the more recent confirmations of this phenomenon. See DESAL/CELAP, Encuesta sobre la familia y la fecundidad en poblaciones marginales del gran Santiago, 1966/67, Part III: "Resultados globales de la muestra de mujeres" (Santiago de Chile: CELAP, 1968).

5. Thomas G. Sanders, "Chile's Bishops," Newsletter, Institute of Current World Affairs, May, 1968.

6. Arthur L Stinchcombe, "Social Structure and Organizations," in James G. March (ed.), Handbook of Organizations (Chicago: Rand McNally, 1965), p. 144.

7. Conversations with Vekemans on two occasions: in August, 1966, and February, 1968.

8. Interviews in April, 1968, with officials of Anaconda, Ford Motor Company, Kennecott, and with the president of the Chilean telephone company, a subsidiary of ITT.

A recent attempt by the RAND Corporation to use quantitative data for a study of the Latin American Catholic Church resulted in findings that support the thesis of Church fragmentation which I have been defending.* Three tables from the RAND study are reproduced on pp. 425-27. The first two tables list the figures for total "religious personnel" operating in Latin America and in three European countries in 1968. Table 3 details the numbers of "newly ordained priests" from the ranks of native clergy in Latin America during one year, July 1, 1966, to June 31, 1967.

When one compares the total religious work force of 1968 with that of 1960 and before, the immediate impression is that of steady development of Church strength. Turning to statistics compiled by FERES, for example, one could chart the following increase in numbers of priests working in Latin America:

	Diocesan Priests	Order Priests	Total
1912	11,776	4,578	16,364
1945	12,992	11,389	24,381
1950	14,270	13,282	27,552
1955	16,145	16,010	32,155
1960	18,451	19,185	37,636
1968	21,702	21,255	42,957

Several factors combine to cloud this superficially hopeful picture. First, of all priests now in Latin America, approximately 35 per cent are

---

*Luigi Einaudi, Richard Maullin, Alfred Stepan, and Michael Fleet, Latin American Institutional Development: The Changing Catholic Church. Prepared for the Office of External Research, Department of State, by The RAND Corporation, Santa Monica, California, October, 1969.

foreigners.* Werner Promper, in 1965, broke down
the foreign inputs this way:

Foreign Priest Total	17,045
Spain	8,000
Italy	2,000
United States	1,850
Germany	1,500
Holland	1,400
France	600
Canada	465
Belgium	300
Poland	150
Ireland	130
Austria	100
Portugal	100
Switzerland	100
Others	350

The foreign Catholic presence in Latin America
is not, of course, limited to priests. Religious
orders of women and of lay brothers account for far
greater numbers than those of priests. If there
are 40,000 priests operating in Latin America (as
Table 1 indicates), there are 140,000 "brothers"
and "sisters." Lay workers are also active.

The Spanish input has, of course, been contin-
uous since the Spanish conquest. The North American and West European inputs are concurrent with
more recent polity interests, especially with the
Alliance for Progress era of the 1960's. The number of Catholic personnel from the United States
operative in Latin America went from 2,405 in 1960
to 5,116 in 1967.** But as I have tried to show in
the main body of text, it is not the sheer quantity
but the peculiar nature of foreign inputs that has

---

*Noticias Catolicas, 4/22/67-S.

**Noticias Aliadas, 1/28/67-S.

triggered the most telling transformation of Latin American Catholicism.

The fragmentation thesis is further strengthened by the results of an attitude survey which I designed in 1968 for the Chilean Centro de Estudios Socio-Religiosos. This study garnered the response of 700 of Chile's 1,000 diocesan priests. When asked to assess the impact of foreign priests in Chile, 43 per cent responded that "those who have adapted to Chile have been of help, but there are many who have not adapted."

As Table 3 shows, the level of native recruitment to the priesthood in Latin America is, on the whole, disastrous. Even in Mexico and Colombia, where new ordinations amount to more than 100 per cent of that required to maintain 1968 numbers of priests, this figure is meaningful only if one is willing to assume, as do the RAND authors, that the priests ordained will have fifty-year careers, with no attrition. Attrition rates in these two countries now, as in Latin America as a whole, are fluctuating between 10 and 15 per cent of all clergy per year, counting only attrition due to priestly defections. This figure was supplied to me by a Brazilian Jesuit sociologist charged with surveying clerical resources worldwide for the Vatican. In Chile I was able to secure a list of 124 priests, including a bishop, who had left the diocesan priesthood with the consent of Church authorities in 1967. The number who did not bother with ecclesiastical permission is not available, but is estimated to be considerable.

Moreover, there is no evidence that the priests who remain within the institutional structures are willing to submit to episcopal authority on what they consider to be vital issues. In my survey of diocesan priests in Chile, I asked the question: "If you were openly in favor of a workers' strike or some social conflict, and ecclesiastical authority forbade your support, in the event that all dialogue was exhausted, what would you do?"

Thirty-five per cent of the respondents said they
would support the strike. When the same situation
was applied to the voicing of "advanced theological
ideas," only 51 per cent of the diocesan priests
said that they would obey the ecclesiastical authority.

Other items of the questionnaire drew out a
welter of opposing views on such questions as the
competence of the Church hierarchy, the value of
Catholic schools, the possibility of working together with Communists, the inevitability of violent revolution, the role of the priest in politics.
One of the few questions that drew forth widespread
consensus was the suggestion that the Church in
Chile ordain married men: 43 per cent thought that
it "was a possibility to be seriously studied."
Another 43 per cent thought it "one of the changes
most necessary for the future of the Chilean
Church."

TABLE 1

Religious Personnel in Latin America, 1968

	Diocesan Priests	Religious Order Priests	Total Priests	Brothers	Sisters	Grand Total
Brazil	4,844	6,766	11,610	7,602	33,354	52,566
Mexico	5,734	2,111	7,845	3,419	22,384	33,648
Colombia	3,150	1,694	4,844	4,070	16,926	25,840
Argentina	2,541	2,880	5,421	3,045	11,833	20,299
Chile	999	1,544	2,543	1,966	5,631	10,140
Venezuela	830	1,071	1,901	1,352	5,026	8,279
Peru	919	1,417	2,336	1,700	4,079	8,115
Ecuador	728	836	1,564	1,351	3,469	6,384
Uruguay	256	437	693	628	1,902	3,223
Bolivia	208	505	713	670	1,507	2,890
Dominican Republic	121	322	443	499	1,133	2,075
El Salvador	192	233	425	363	946	1,734
Guatemala	178	316	494	288	707	1,489
Costa Rica	220	175	395	173	914	1,482
Haiti	223	180	403	203	736	1,342
Paraguay	213	235	448	243	474	1,165
Nicaragua	111	141	252	199	508	959
Panama	63	143	206	155	361	722
Cuba	93	127	220	126	204	550
Honduras	79	122	201	86	106	393
Totals	21,702	21,255	42,957	28,138	112,200	183,295

Source: Luigi Einaudi, Richard Maullin, Alfred Stepan, and Michael Fleet, Latin American Institutional Development: The Changing Catholic Church. Prepared for the Office of External Research, Department of State, by the RAND Corporation, Santa Monica, California, October, 1969. See the note on statistical sources on p. 12 of the report.

TABLE 2

Religious Personnel in France, Poland, and Ireland, 1968

	Diocesan Priests	Religious Order Priests	Total Priests	Brothers	Sisters	Grand Total
France	40,531	7,387	47,918	13,481	102,631	164,030
Poland	13,524	2,982	16,506	3,650	18,641	38,797
Ireland	3,923	1,991	5,914	5,078	14,557	25,549

Source: Luigi Einaudi, Richard Maullin, Alfred Stepan, and Michael Fleet, Latin American Institutional Development: The Changing Catholic Church. Prepared for the Office of External Research, Department of State, by The RAND Corporation, Santa Monica, California, October, 1969. See the note on statistical sources on p. 12 of the report.

TABLE 3

Newly Ordained Priests, 1966-67

	New Ordinations, 1966-67[a]	New Ordinations as Percentage of Ordinations Required to Maintain 1968 Numbers of Priests on the Basis of National Vocations Alone[b]
Costa Rica	15	190%
Cuba	8	182
Panama	6	150
Mexico	211	134
Colombia	128	132
Paraguay	7	78
Haiti	6	74
Uruguay	10	72
Brazil	151	65
Guatemala	6	61
El Salvador	5	59
Ecuador	18	58
Peru	25	54
Honduras	2	50
Argentina	48	44
Bolivia	6	42
Nicaragua	2	40
Chile	18	35
Venezuela	12	32
Dominican Republic	2	22
Totals	686	80

[a]July 1, 1966 to June 31, 1967. Though for one year only, these figures are on the whole representative, despite possible fluctuations by country.

[b]Assuming fifty-year careers with no attrition. Since most priests die or leave the priesthood for other reasons before serving fifty years, the potential shortage of new Latin American priests is actually considerably greater than even these figures imply. Should the actual average length of service after ordination (an interesting topic for future research in itself) in fact approximate twenty-five years, for instance, the percentages given in the second column would have to be halved.

Source: Luigi Einaudi, Richard Maullin, Alfred Stepan, and Michael Fleet, Latin American Institutional Development. The Changing Catholic Church. Prepared for the Office of External Research, Department of State, by The RAND Corporation, Santa Monica, California, October, 1969. See the note on statistical sources on p. 12 of the report.

BIBLIOGRAPHY

The items below are not intended as an exhaustive list of the sources on which I have drawn; they consist primarily of works that, in one or another way, have shaped the thinking that has gone into this study.

Adams, Richard N. The Second Sowing: Power and Social Development in Latin America. San Francisco: Chandler Publishing Co., 1967.

Agor, Weston. "Senate vs. CORA: An Attempt to Evaluate Chile's Agrarian Reform to Date," Inter-American Economic Affairs, XXII, 2 (Autumn, 1968), 47-54.

Aizcorbe, Roberto. "La nueva iglesia de los pobres," Primera Plana. Buenos Aires, IV, 198 (October 11-17, 1966).

Alexander, Robert J. Labor Relations in Argentina, Brazil, and Chile. New York: McGraw-Hill Book Co., 1962.

Alfaro, Carlos. Guia apostolica latinoamericana (Guide to Apostolic Organizations and Movements in Latin America). Barcelona: Editorial Herder, 1965.

Allen, Louis. "Identifying Line and Staff," in Joseph A. Litterer (ed.), Organizations: Structure and Behavior. New York: John Wiley and Sons, 1963.

Alonso, Isidoro. "Estadisticas religiosas de America Latina" (Religious Statistics for Latin America). September, 1966. Mimeographed.

_____. La Iglesia en America Latina. Fribourg: Oficina Internacional de Investigaciones Sociales de FERES, 1964.

Anderson, Charles W. "Toward a Theory of Latin American Politics," Occasional Paper No. 2. Nashville: Vanderbilt University, 1964.

D'Antonio, William V., and Frederick B. Pike (eds.). Religion, Revolution, and Reform. New York: Frederick A. Praeger, 1964.

Batista, Antonio Fragoso. "Evangelico y justicia social," Cuadernos de Marcha (Montevideo), XVII (1968).

Beatty, Donald W. "The Chilean Dilemma," Current History, XLIX (December, 1965).

Becker, Howard S. "Problems of Inference and Proof in Participant-Observation," American Sociological Review, XXIII, 6 (December, 1958), 652-60.

Bernal, Alejandro Escobar. La Educacion en Colombia. Louvain and Bogota: Oficina Internacional de Investigaciones Sociales de FERES, 1965.

Blau, Peter M. Exchange and Power in Social Life. New York: John Wiley and Sons, 1964.

Bosworth, William. Catholicism and Crisis in Modern France. Princeton, N.J.: Princeton University Press, 1962.

"El 'Caso' del Padre Camilo Torres," Inquietudes, No. 5, Numero Especial. Bogota: Ediciones Tercer Mundo, July 30, 1965.

Castillo, Gonzalo Cardenas. "Christians and the Struggle for a New Social Order in Latin America," in Donald R. Cutler (ed.), The Religious Situation: 1968. Boston: Beacon Press, 1968.

Castro, Bernardo Villagrana, et al. (eds.). La Iglesia, el subdesarrollo y la revolucion. Mexico: Editorial Nuestro Tiempo, 1968.

"The Church Embattled," The Economist, August 24,
     1968, p. 228.

Coleman, William J.   Latin American Catholicism:
     A Self-Evaluation. Maryknoll, N.Y. Maryknoll
     Publications, 1958.

Comblin, Joseph.   "Notas sobre el Documento Basico
     para la II Conferencia General del CELAM,"
     Cuadernos de Marcha (Montevideo), XVII (1968).

_____. "Uma politica a favor da revoluca na America
     Latina." Recife, 1968. Mimeographed.

_____. "Problemes sacerdotaux d'Amerique Latine,"
     CIDOC Document 68. Cuernavaca, 1968.

Consejo Episcopal Latinoamericano. Presencia ac-
     tiva de la iglesia en el desarrollo y en la
     America Latina. Salvador: Departamento de
     Accion Social, 1967.

Considine, John J. (ed.). The Church in the New
     Latin America. Notre Dame, Ind.: Fides Pub-
     lishers, 1964.

Cope, Orville G. "The 1964 Presidential Election
     in Chile: The Politics of Change and Access,"
     Inter-American Economic Affairs, XIX (Spring,
     1966).

_____. "The 1965 Congressional Election in Chile:
     An Analysis," Journal of Inter-American
     Studies, X, 2 (August, 1968).

Coser, Lewis. The Functions of Social Conflict.
     New York: Free Press, 1957.

Dalton, Melville. "Conflict Between Staff and Line
     Managerial Officers," American Sociological
     Review, XV (1950), 342-45.

_____. "Preconceptions and Methods in Men Who Man-
     age," in Phillip E. Hammond (ed.), Sociologists
     at Work. Garden City, N.Y.: Doubleday, 1964.

Damboriena, Prudencio. "The Pentacostals in Chile," Catholic Mind, LX (1962), 27-32.

El deber social y politico en la hora presente. Episcopado de Chile, 1962.

Demerath, N. J. "Initiating and Maintaining Research Relations in a Military Organization," Journal of Social Issues, VIII, 3 (1952).

_____. "Rationalization and Instrumental Capacity: A Theory of Economic Growth and Social Differentiation." Paper presented to the Midwest Sociological Society Meeting, April 17, 1970.

DESAL (Centro Para El Desarrollo Economico y Social de America Latina). Informe de actividades ano 1968. Santiago de Chile: DESAL, 1968.

Dewart, Leslie. Christianity and Revolution. New York: Herder and Herder, 1963.

Diccionario biografico de Chile, 1962-1964. 12th ed. Santiago: Empresa Periodistica, 1965.

Dix, Robert. Colombia: The Political Dimensions of Change. Chapter 11: "Traditional Institutions: The Church." New Haven, Conn.: Yale University Press, 1967.

Dominguez, Oscar. El Campesino chileno y la accion catolica rural. Fribourg: FERES, 1961.

Egana, Antonio de. Historia de la Iglesia en la America Espanola, desde le descubrimiento hasta comienzos del siglo XIX, hemisferio sur. Madrid: Biblioteca de Autores Cristianos, 1966.

"Enter the Catholic Left" Atlas, X (December, 1965), 374-76.

L'Etat de l'opinion en Amerique Latine a l'heure de Medellin," Informations Catholiques Internationales, No. 319 (September 1, 1968), 5-6.

Fichter, Joseph. "Catholic Church Professionals,"
     The Annals, CCCLXXXVII (January, 1970).

Fisch, G. "Line-Staff Is Obsolete," Harvard Busi-
     ness Review, XXXIX (1961).

Francis, E. K. "Toward a Typology of Religious Or-
     ders," American Journal of Sociology, LV
     (March, 1950), 437-49.

Gannon, Francis X. "Catholicism, Revolution and
     Violence in Latin America," Orbis, XII (Winter,
     1969).

Garcia, John Alvarez. Camilo Torres: His Life and
     His Message. London: Templegate, 1969.

Gil, Federico, and Charles Parrish. The Chilean
     Presidential Election of September 4, 1964.
     Washington, D.C.: Institute for Comparative
     Development of Political Systems, 1965.

Golembiewski, Robert. Organizing Men and Power:
     Patterns of Behavior and Line-Staff Models.
     New York: Rand McNally, 1967.

Gouldner, Alvin. Enter Plato. New York: Free
     Press, 1965.

_____. "Reciprocity and Autonomy in Functional
     Theory," in Llewellyn Gross (ed.), Symposium
     on Sociological Theory. Evanston, Ill.: Row,
     Peterson, and Co., 1959.

Guzman, German Campos. Camilo, El Cura Guerillero.
     Servicios Especiales de Prensa, 1967.

Haddox, Benjamin. Sociedad y religion en Colombia.
     Bogota: Tercer Mundo, 1965.

Halperin, Ernest. Nationalism and Communism in
     Chile. Cambridge, Mass.: M.I.T. Press, 1957.

Hicks, Frederick. "Politics, Power and the Role of the Village Priest in Paraguay," Journal of Inter-American Studies, IX, 2 (April, 1967), 273-82.

Horowitz, Irving Louis. "The City as a Crucible for Political Action," in Glen H. Beyer (ed.) The Urban Explosion in Latin America. Ithaca, N.Y.: Cornell University Press, 1967.

_____ (ed.). Latin American Radicalism. New York: Random House, 1970.

_____ (ed.). Masses in Latin America. New York: Oxford University Press, 1970.

_____. The Rise and Fall of Project Camelot; Studies in the Relationship Between Social Science and Practical Politics. Cambridge, Mass.: M.I.T. Press, 1967.

_____. Three Worlds of Development: The Theory and Practice of International Stratification. New York: Oxford University Press, 1966.

Housley, John B. "The Role of the Churches in United States-Latin American Relations," in David S. Smith (ed.), Prospects for Latin America. New York: Columbia University Press, 1970.

Houtart, Francois, and Emile Pin. The Church and the Latin American Revolution. New York: Sheed and Ward, 1965.

_____. La iglesia latinoamericana en la hora del concilio. Fribourg: FERES, 1963.

_____, and A. Delobelle. "The Roman Catholic Church and Economic Planning--at the National and International Level," in Harvey Cox (ed.), The Church Amid Revolution. New York: Association Press, 1967.

Huff, Russell J., C.S.C. "Is the Church Losing
    Latin America?" Interview with Roger Vekemans,
    Ave Maria, January 9, 1960.

Huntington, Samuel. "Political Development and
    Political Decay," _World Politics_, XVII (April,
    1965).

Illich, Ivan. "The Seamy Side of Charity," _America_,
    January 21, 1967.

_____. "The Vanishing Clergyman," _Critic_, XXV, 6
    (June-July, 1967).

Jimenez, Gustavo Cadena. _Sacerdote y cambio social_.
    Bogota: Ediciones Tercer Mundo, 1967.

Jimenez, Jesus Maria Suarez. _La asociacion sindi-
    cal en la doctrina pontificia y en la legisla-
    cion colombiana_. Editorial Universitaria de
    Antioquia, 1964.

Kadt, Emanuel de. "The Latin American Church and
    Pope Paul's Visit," _World Today_, XXIV (Septem-
    ber, 1968).

_____. "Paternalism and Populism: Catholicism in
    Latin America," _Journal of Contemporary His-
    tory_, II, 4 (October, 1967).

Katz, Daniel, and Robert L. Kahn. _Social Psychology
    of Organization_. New York: John Wiley and
    Sons, 1966.

Kaufman, H. "Organizational Theory and Political
    Theory," _American Political Science Review_,
    LVIII, 1 (March, 1964).

Kennedy, John J. _Catholicism, Nationalism, and
    Democracy in Argentina_. Notre Dame, Ind.:
    University of Notre Dame Press, 1958.

_____. "Dichotomies in the Church," _The Annals_,
    CCCXXXIV (March, 1961).

Kling, Merle. "Toward a Theory of Power and Political Instability in Latin America," The Western Political Quarterly, IX, 1 (March, 1956).

Kolb, Harry D. "The Headquarters Staff Man in the Role of a Consultant," in David R. Hampton, et al. (eds.), Organizational Behavior and the Practice of Management. Glenview, Ill.: Scott, Foresman & Co., 1968.

Kuriloff, A. "Management by Integration and Self-Control," Proceedings of the Industrial Engineering Institute, February, 1963.

Labarca, Eduardo Goddard. Chile invadido: reportaje a la intromision extranjera. Santiago: Editores Austral, 1968.

Lalive, Christian d'Epinay. El Refugio de las masas: estudio sociologico de protestantismo chileno. Santiago: Editorial del Pacifico, 1968.

Landsberger, Henry, and Fernando Canitrot. Iglesia, intelectuales y campesinos. University of Chile-INSORA, 1967.

Larrain, Manuel Errazuriz. Desarrollo: exito o fracaso? en America Latina. Santiago: Editorial Universitaria Catolica, 1965.

Latin American Episcopal Council. Bogota, General Secretariat of CELAM, Apartado Aereo 5278, C. 1967.

Von Lazar, Arpad, and Quiros Videla. "Christian Democracy: Lessons in the Politics of Reform Management," Inter-American Economic Affairs, XXI, 4 (Spring, 1968), 51-72.

Lopez, Francisco. Proceso al poder religioso en Colombia. Bogota: Ediciones Hispana, 1968.

Lozano, Gustavo Gutierrez. "El Sindicalismo colombiano ante la doctrina social de la iglesia." Bogota, 1960. Mimeographed.

McCoy, Terry Luther. <u>Agrarian Reform in Chile,</u>
    <u>1962-68, A Study of Politics and the Develop-</u>
    <u>ment Process</u>. Madison: University of Wiscon-
    sin Land Tenure Center, 1962.

Mackay, John A. "Latin America and Revolution--II,
    The New Mood in the Churches," <u>The Christian</u>
    <u>Century,</u> LXXXII, 47 (November 24, 1965).

Magnet, Alejandro. <u>El Padre Hurtado</u>. 3rd ed.
    Santiago: Editorial del Pacifico, 1957.

Maldonado, Oscar. "Colombia, la jerarquia catolica
    y los Problemas de control de la Natalidad,"
    <u>CIDOC Dossier</u>, No. 24, 1968.

March, James G., and Herbert A. Simon. <u>Organiza-</u>
    <u>tions</u>. New York: John Wiley and Sons, 1958.

Mecham, J. Lloyd. <u>Church and State in Latin America</u>.
    Rev. ed. Chapel Hill: University of North
    Carolina Press, 1966.

Miller, George. "Professionals in Bureaucracy:
    Alienation Among Industrial Scientists and En-
    gineers," <u>American Sociological Review</u>, XXXII,
    5 (October, 1967), 755ff.

Mutchler, David E. "Adaptations of the Roman Catho-
    lic Church to Latin American Development: The
    Meaning of Internal Church Conflict," <u>Social</u>
    <u>Research</u>, XXXVI, 2 (Summer, 1969).

_____. "Roman Catholicism in Brazil," <u>Studies in</u>
    <u>Comparative International Development</u>, I, 8
    (1965).

Parkinson, C. N. <u>Parkinson's Law</u>. New York:
    Houghton-Mifflin, 1957.

Parrish, Charles, Arpad von Lazar, and Jorge Tapia
    Videla. <u>The Chilean Congressional Elections</u>
    <u>of March 7, 1965: An Analysis</u>. Washington,
    D.C.: Institute for Comparative Development
    of Political Systems, 1965.

Pattee, Richard (ed.). El Catolicismo contemporaneo en Hispano-America. Buenos Aires: Edicion Fides, 1951.

Perez, Gustavo, and Isaac Wust. La Iglesia en Colombia. Estructuras eclesiasticas. Bogota: FERES, 1962.

Perez, Gustavo Ramirez. El problema sacerdotal en Colombia. Fribourg and Bogota: Oficina Internacional de Investigaciones Sociales de FERES, 1962.

Petras, James. Chilean Christian Democracy: Politics and Social Forces. Berkeley: University of California, Institute of International Studies, 1967.

_____. "Chile's Christian Peasant Union: Notes and Comments on an Interview with Hector Alarcon," Newsletter No. 23. Land Tenure Center, University of Wisconsin, March-July, 1966.

Pike, Frederick B. (ed.). "Catholic Church and Modernization in Peru and Chile," Journal of Inter-American Affairs, XX, 2 (March, 1966).

_____. The Conflict Between Church and State in Latin America. New York: Alfred A. Knopf, 1964.

Pin, Emile. Elementos para una sociologia del catolicismo latino-americano. Fribourg: Oficina Internacional de Investigaciones Sociales de FERES, 1963.

Platt, William J., et al. Training and Educational Needs in Chile's Agricultural Development. Stanford, Calif.: Stanford Research Institute, 1965.

Poblete, Moises Troncoso, and Ben G. Burnett. The Rise of the Latin American Labor Movement. New Haven, Conn.: Yale University Press, 1960.

Poblete, Renato Barth. _Crisis sacerdotal_. Santiago:
    Editorial del Pacifico, 1965.

_____. _La Iglesia en Chile_. Fribourg and Bogota:
    Oficina Internacional de Investigaciones So-
    ciales de FERES, 1962.

The Priesthood in Latin America. Pro Mundi Vita
    Monographs No. 22. Brussels, 1968.

Promper, Werner. _Priesternot in Latin America_.
    Brussels: University of Louzain, 1965.

Rosenau, James (ed.). "Of Boundaries and Bridges:
    A Report on a Conference on the Interdependen-
    cies of National and International Political
    Systems." Center of International Studies,
    Woodrow Wilson School of Public and Inter-
    national Affairs, Princeton University, 1967.

_____. (ed.). _Linkage Politics; Essays on the Con-
    vergence of National and International Political
    Systems_. New York: Free Press, 1969.

_____. "Pre-theories and Theories of Foreign Policy,"
    in R. Barry Farrell (ed.), _Approaches to Com-
    parative and International Politics_. Evanston,
    Ill.: Northwestern University Press, 1968.

Rourke, Francis (ed.). _Bureaucratic Power in Na-
    tional Politics_. Boston: Little, Brown, 1968.

Salazar, Maria Cristina. _El caso del Padre Camilo
    Torres_. Bogota: Taller Grafico de Ediciones
    Tercer Mundo, 1965.

Sanders, Thomas G. "Catholicism and Development:
    The Catholic Left in Brazil," in Kalman H.
    Silvert (ed.), _Churches and States: The Re-
    ligious Institution and Modernization_. New
    York: American Universities Field Staff, 1967.

_____. "The Priests of the People." Field Letter
    (TGS-11) to Richard C. Nolte, Institute of
    Current World Affairs, New York, March 24,
    1968.

_____. "Religion and Modernization: Some Reflections." Field Letter (TGS-14) to Richard C. Nolte, Institute of Current World Affairs, New York, August 4, 1968.

Santis, Sergio de. "Chile," _International Socialist Journal_, II (August, 1965).

Scott, W. Richard. "Field Methods in the Study of Organizations," in James March (ed.), _Handbook of Organizations_. New York: Rand McNally, 1967.

Selznick, Philip. "Institutional Integrity, Precarious Values, and Elite Autonomy," in Alan Altshuler (ed.), _The Politics of the Federal Bureaucracy_. New York: Dodd, Mead & Co., 1968.

O'Shaughnessy, Hugh. "The Chilean Experiment," _Encounter_, XXV (September, 1965).

Schwartz, Morris and Charlotte. "Problems in Participant Observation," _American Journal of Sociology_, LX, 243-53.

Stinchcombe, Arthur L. "Social Structure and Organizations," in James G. March (ed.), _Handbook of Organizations_. Chicago: Rand McNally, 1965.

Strauss, G., and L. Sayles. _Personnel_. New York: Prentice-Hall, 1960.

Stycos, J. M. "Contraception and Catholicism in Latin America," _Journal of Social Issues_, XXIII (October, 1967), 115-33.

Sunkel, Osvaldo. "National Development Policy and External Dependence in Latin America," _Journal of Development Studies_, VI, 1 (October, 1969).

Las tareas de la iglesia en America Latina. Fribourg: FERES, 1964.

Tawney, R. H. Equality. London: Allen and Unwin,
     1931.

Thiesenhusen, William C. Chile's Experiments in
     Agrarian Reform. Land Economics Monograph
     No. 1. Madison: University of Wisconsin
     Press, 1966.

_____. "Grassroots Economic Pressures in Chile:
     An Enigma for Development Planning," Economic
     Development and Cultural Change, XVI, 3
     (April, 1968), 412-30.

Thompson, Victor. Modern Organization. New York:
     Alfred A. Knopf, 1961.

Tibesar, A. "Shortage of Priests in Latin America:
     A Historical Evaluation of Werner Promper's
     Priesternot in Latin Amerika," America, XXII
     (April, 1966), 413-20.

Camilo Torres, por el Padre Camilo Torres Restrepo.
     Sondeos No. 5, Centro Intercultural de Docu-
     mentacion (CIDOC), Mexico. Cuernavaca, 1966.

Torres, Camilo Restrepo. "Social Change and Rural
     Violence in Colombia," in Irving Horowitz (ed.),
     Masses in Latin America. New York: Oxford
     University Press, 1970.

Vallier, Ivan. Catholicism, Social Control, and
     Modernization in Latin America. Englewood
     Cliffs, N.J.: Prentice-Hall, 1970.

_____. "Church 'Development' in Latin America:
     A Five Country Comparison," Journal of Devel-
     oping Areas, I, 4 (July, 1967).

_____. "Religious Elites: Differentiations and
     Developments in Roman Catholicism," in Seymour
     M. Lipset and Aldo Solari (eds.), Elites in
     Latin America. New York: Oxford University
     Press, 1967.

_____. "Roman Catholicism and Social Change in Latin America: From Church to 'Sect,'" CIF Reports, III (May 3, 1964).

_____, and Rocco Caporale. "The Roman Catholic Laity in France, Chile, and the United States: Cleavages and Developments," Information Documentation on the Conciliar Church, Nos. 68-7 and 68-8 (February 18 and February 25, 1968).

_____, and Vivian Vallier. "South American Society," International Encyclopedia of the Social Sciences, ed. David Sills. XV. New York: The Macmillan Co. and The Free Press, 1968.

Vidich, Arthur J. "Participant Observation and Collection and Interpretation of Data," American Journal of Sociology, LX, 354-60.

Vroom, Victor (ed.). Methods of Organization Research. Pittsburgh: University of Pittsburgh Press, 1967.

Wakin, Edward, and Joseph Scheuer. The deRomanization of the American Catholic Church. New York: Macmillan, 1966.

Willems, Emilio. Followers of the New Faith: Culture Change and the Rise of Protestantism in Brazil and Chile. Nashville, Tenn: Vanderbilt University Press, 1967.

Williams, Edward J. Latin American Christian Democratic Parties. Knoxville: University of Tennessee Press, 1967.

Wolpin, Miles. "Chile's Left: Structural Factors Inhibiting an Electoral Victory in 1970," Journal of Developing Areas, III (January, 1969), 207-30.

Womack, John. "Priest of Revolution," The New York Review of Books, XIII, 7 (October 23, 1969).

Zaffaroni, Juan Carlos. *Sacerdocio y revolucion en
     America Latina*. Buenos Aires: Editora America
     Latina, 1968.

Zeldich, Morris. "Methodological Problems of Field
     Studies," *American Journal of Sociology*, LXVII,
     5 (March, 1962), 566-76.

The following periodicals were of constant help
throughout the study:

CIF Reports, *CIDOC Informe* (Cuernavaca, Mexico)

Frente Unido (Bogota)

Informations Catholiques Internationales (Paris)

Mensaje (Santiago de Chile)

NACLA Newsletters (Berkeley, California)

Primera Plana (Buenos Aires)

Vispera (Montevideo)

INDEX

ABOUT THE AUTHOR

David E. Mutchler has spent the past six years researching the role of the Roman Catholic Church in Latin American development. He was a member of the Jesuit order from 1959 until 1967 and has lived in houses of the Society of Jesus in Mexico, Colombia, Chile, Argentina, Uruguay, Brazil, and Venezuela. He has published articles concerning Church political influence in Studies in Comparative International Development and in Social Research.

Professor Mutchler was formerly on the staff of the Facultad Latinoamericana de Ciencias Sociales (FLACSO) in Santiago de Chile. He is the author of a forthcoming study of "role ambiguity" and "role conflict" among Chilean priests, which utilizes data from a survey of diocesan priests in Santiago that he designed and conducted in 1969.

Dr. Mutchler studied philosophy at St. Louis University and obtained his doctorate in sociology from Washington University in St. Louis.